Images of Music

Bilder der Musik   Images de Musique

ERICH AUERBACH

Images of Music
Bilder der Musik   Images de Musique

Text by Michael Rose
Picture research by Leon Meyer

KÖNEMANN

Front cover: The hands of Mstislav Rostropovich, 24 July 1961.
Umschlagvorderseite: Die Hände von Mstislaw Rostropowitsch, 24. Juli 1961.
Couverture : Les mains de Mstislav Rostropovitch, le 24 juillet 1961.

Back cover: Igor Stravinsky, 8 December 1958.
Umschlagrückseite: Igor Strawinsky, 8. Dezember 1958.
Dos de couverture : Igor Stravinski, le 8 décembre 1958.

Half title   Schmutztitel   Faux-titre :
Erich Auerbach (1911-1977)

Frontispiece: One of Erich Aucherbach's early photographs of a musician: a Slovak gypsy boy,
about 1936.
Frontispitz: Diese frühe Fotografie eines Musikers von Erich Auerbach zeigt einen slowaki-
schen Zigeunerjungen um 1936.
Frontispice : Une des premières photographies de musicien réalisées par Erich Auerbach:
un jeune bohémien slovaque, vers 1936.

*Note to the reader: the dating of most of Auerbach's pictures is meticulous and detailed. For some of the
later ones, however, particularly those in colour, accurate details are lacking. In such cases we have
given whatever information could be obtained by our own researches, or otherwise limited ourselves to
approximate datings based on circumstantial evidence.*

*An den Leser: Auerbachs Fotos sind meistens sorgfältig und genau datiert. Bei einigen späteren
Aufnahmen, besonders bei den Farbfotos, fehlen jedoch die genauen Angaben. In diesen Fällen haben
wir alle Informationen zusammengetragen, die wir recherchieren konnten, oder haben uns auf eine
angenäherte Datierung anhand beweiskräftiger äußerer Umstände beschränkt.*

*Note au lecteur : la plupart des photographies d'Auerbach sont precisément datées et annotées. Toutefois,
pour certaines d'entre elles (généralement les plus récentes et les photos couleurs), les détails manquent.
Pour ces clichés, nous avons choisi soit de fournir les informations que nous avons pu recueillir d'après
nos recherches, soit d'indiquer une simple date approximative, déterminée en fonction des éléments
connus et visibles.*

First published in 1996 by Könemann Verlagsgesellschaft mbH
Bonner Str. 126, D-50968 Köln

© Könemann Verlagsgesellschaft mbH
Photographs © 1996 The Hulton Getty Picture Collection, London
with grateful acknowledgement to Mrs. Lizzie Auerbach

This book was produced by The Hulton Getty Picture Collection Limited
Unique House, 21-31 Woodfield Road, London W9 2BA

Art direction and design: Peter Feierabend
Layout and production: Bärbel Messmann
Project editor: Elisabeth Ingles
Editing and typesetting: Peter Delius and Ulrike Sommer
Contributing editors: Sally Bald and Kristina Meier
German translation: Barbara Delius, Marianne Kurda, Ulrike Sommer
French translation: Accord, Christine Berthier and Magali Guenette
Production manager: Detlev Schaper
Darkroom printing: Brian Doherty and Steve Eason
Colour separation: Imago Publishing Ltd.
Printing and binding: Partenaires Fabrication
Printed in France

ISBN 3-89508-216-3

CONTENTS
INHALT
SOMMAIRE

1

Erich Auerbach was born at Falkenau (now Sokolov) in the Sudetenland in 1911. His father, a doctor, loved music, and encouraged his son to learn both piano and violin. Auerbach went to school in the nearby town of Karlsbad, where he played regularly in the school orchestra, and after matriculation continued his musical studies at university in Prague. He began going to concerts and after a while, in order to supplement his student's allowance, became a part-time music critic on the *Prager Tagblatt*. It was during this period that he started to take photographs, partly for his own satisfaction, partly for publication, and this became a more and more important part of his life – rather against the wishes of his father, who was more concerned that his son should get a degree. And it is true that Auerbach had no formal training in photography. But he had a model, 'the incomparable Dr Erich Salomon, the photographer who has not to this day been surpassed (he perished in Auschwitz) who taught me though we never met', and the inspiration of Salomon's example won the day. In the end Auerbach never did get a degree, and remained an enthusiastic amateur musician for the rest of his life. But his first professional camera was a present from his father.

Music in Prague in the 1930s centred round the Czech Philharmonic Orchestra, then under the leadership of the great Czech conductor Václav Talich, and the two opera houses: the National Theatre, which Talich took over in 1935, and the German Theatre under the young Hungarian conductor George Szell (see page 206/207). But Auerbach's photography was not necessarily confined to locals. There were rich opportunities to catch visiting musicians as well – Ravel on his last tour of Europe, Casals after his exile from Spain (see page 224/225), Bruno Walter a month before the *Anschluss*, composers, conductors and instrumentalists from all over Europe. Sadly, not all the photographs from these days have survived, for in the summer of 1939 Auerbach himself had to leave Czechoslovakia and before doing so burnt the vast majority of

his pictures. Taking with him the negatives of the few that he most treasured, he crossed the border to Poland on foot and used journalistic channels to get to England, arriving in London in July.

Weeks later Britain was at war with Germany, and Auerbach's position became difficult. He was not allowed to take a job, and found accommodation at a student hostel, where he managed to make himself a small space for developing and printing and from there continue his work as a photographer. But before long he was approached by the Czech government in exile and asked to undertake publicity work, so that until the end of the war his basic employment was assured. In 1942 he married and moved into a small apartment in St John's Wood, in the same block that his widow lives in to this day.

Opportunities for musical photography in wartime London were limited. With many of their members called to the armed forces, the London orchestras were badly reduced in numbers. The BBC Symphony Orchestra was evacuated to Bristol at the beginning of the war, so that broadcast music at least was assured, but the London Symphony Orchestra and the London Philharmonic had a hard struggle to keep going, particularly after the traditional home of London orchestral concerts, the Queen's Hall, was destroyed by bombing in 1941. The Royal Opera House at Covent Garden was taken over by Mecca Cafés and turned into a dance hall, and the only alternative opera stage in London closed when Sadler's Wells Theatre became a rest centre for local people bombed out of their homes.

Appropriately enough, the subject of Auerbach's first musical photograph in London was that grand old British institution Sir Henry Wood. The founder of the Promenade Concerts was now in his 72nd year (the Proms were in their 46th), after a lifetime spent in forming and developing British musical taste, fostering new talent and tirelessly working to

raise orchestral standards. He had always been a dogged promoter of new music: 'Stick to it, gentlemen,' he called out to the orchestra at a rehearsal of Schoenberg's *Five Orchestral Pieces* in 1912, 'this is nothing to what you'll be doing in 25 years' time.' And he was not easily beaten. When the Proms were bombed out of the Queen's Hall he moved with them to the Royal Albert Hall where he directed three more seasons, until the 50th, in 1944, had to be curtailed in deference to Hitler's flying bombs. A few weeks later Sir Henry died; with his first photograph Auerbach had caught the end of an era.

On a smaller scale, the most remarkable of London's wartime musical activities was the series of chamber music concerts given in the National Gallery from the second week of the war onwards. These were thought up by the pianist Myra Hess, to make use of the empty gallery after its pictures had been banished for safety to the Welsh mountains. For six and a half years daily lunchtime recitals were presented to audiences that varied between 250 and 1,750 – depending on the weather, the programme and the air-raid sirens. For sheer range and unbroken continuity they have probably never been equalled since. But with the end of hostilities pictorial masterpieces began to reappear from Wales, and in April 1946 the concert series came to a reluctant close.

As musicians returned from their military activities the London orchestras began to revive and institutions to sort themselves out. Within a month of the ceasefire Sadler's Wells Theatre re-opened its doors and set the British musical world alight with the première of Britten's opera *Peter Grimes*. Not long afterwards Covent Garden emerged from its dance hall interregnum and launched a new opera company of its own under the direction of Karl Rankl. A senior executive of the Gramophone Company named Walter Legge seized the opportunity provided by the changing times to form the Philharmonia Orchestra, an ensemble of star players intended above all for the recording of top-quality opera and concert

2

3

performances, and installed Herbert von Karajan as its principal conductor. Only a year later, not to be outdone, Sir Thomas Beecham formed the Royal Philharmonic Orchestra, thus adding the final component to what Auerbach described as 'that five-orchestra metropolis', and in 1950 Sir Malcolm Sargent took over the Proms, of which he was to remain the indefatigable figurehead until his death in 1967.

With so much performing capacity available, London looked set for a period of abundant musical activity, and in 1951 a new centre for this was created to replace the sadly missed Queen's Hall. The Royal Festival Hall, built as part of the Festival of Britain in that year, rapidly became the hub of London concert life, and leading conductors and soloists from all over the world flooded into the capital during the 1950s, providing a feast of music and offering an endless succession of fascinating material for Auerbach's inquisitive lens.

Auerbach's wartime work had come to an end when the Czech government in exile returned to Prague in 1945, but by that time he was able to get a job as a staff cameraman with the weekly magazine *Illustrated*, where he was to remain for the next 12 years. His work for *Illustrated* covered all fields of photo-journalism; naturally, given his specialist experience, the best musical opportunities tended to be pushed his way, but inevitably some chances were missed. He was always disappointed not to have captured Toscanini, for example, on his one post war visit to conduct at the Festival Hall in 1952. On the other hand, he was fortunate to live not far from the BBC main studios at Maida Vale where many distinguished musicians came to make recordings or broadcasts, and just round the corner from the famous Abbey Road Studios of EMI.

His friendship with Walter Legge was one of the factors that ensured him personal access to so many of the great artists who visited London in the years following the war. This was a great period for the recording industry and Legge, at EMI, was at the centre of it. In the early 1950s the long-playing

record was at last beginning to replace the venerable 78 r.p.m. discs that had served the recording industry since its earliest days, and an altogether new recording market opened up with immensely increased possibilities for serious music. London, with its wealth of orchestras, studio space and professional expertise, became a magnet for the international musical world, even more so when stereo recording began to be introduced from 1958 onwards. The studio, the control unit and the cutting room became as important as the concert hall to the musicians of the post-war era.

From 1957, when *Illustrated* closed down, until his death 20 years later Auerbach worked entirely as a freelance photographer. But thanks to Legge he was still able to be present at sessions where an ordinary photo-journalist would not have been allowed access. He would often be invited to parties and other occasions at the house in Hampstead where Legge lived with his wife, the soprano Elisabeth Schwarzkopf, and in many cases he made friends with the artists themselves, so that Oistrakh or Menuhin would invite him to private rehearsals in their hotel rooms or homes. Essentially a discreet cameraman, informal in his approach and utterly without self-importance, he was liked by his subjects not least because he was himself a musician and could appreciate the music they were playing. His widow remembers him sitting with tears running down his face as he listened to the performers he had come to photograph.

It was of course this innate understanding of music and the role of the interpretative artist that was the secret of Auerbach's art. The inspiration of Salomon, 'the photographer who has not to this day been surpassed', may have provided the model and the impetus, but in the pictures that follow in this book it is the musician's ear as much as the photographer's eye that produces such intimately expressive results. It is the personal, psychological and musical observation that gives Auerbach's record of the post-war decades its uniquely revealing quality.

The Years in Prague: (1) The celebrated Austro-German conductor Bruno Walter had a long and harmonious relationship with the Czech Philharmonic Orchestra, which he conducted at the Luzerna in February 1938 in one of his last European concerts before the outbreak of the war. (2) Maurice Ravel in 1932, leaving the stage door of the German Theatre after hearing his own piano concerto in a concert conducted by George Szell (right) with the dedicatee Marguerite Long (left) as solist. (3) The German conductor Fritz Busch in action at the German Theatre.

Die Prager Jahre: (1) Den gefeierten deutsch-österreichischen Dirigent Bruno Walter verband eine lange und harmonische Beziehung mit dem Tschechischen Phiharmonieorchester, das er im Februar 1938 in Luzern, in einem seiner letzte Konzerte in Europa vor Ausbruch des Krieges, dirigierte. (2) Maurice Ravel verläßt das Deutsche Theater durch den Künstlereingang, nachdem er der Aufführung seines eigenen Klavierkonzertes unter der Leitung von Georg Szell (rechts) mit Marguerite Long als Solistin beigewohnt hat. (3) Der deutsche Dirigent Fritz Busch im Deutschen Theater.

Les années à Prague: (1) Bruno Walter, le célèbre chef d'orchestre austro-allemand, eut une relation longue et harmonieuse avec le Czech Philharmonic Orchestra, qu'il dirigea au canton de Lucerne en février 1938 dans un de ses derniers concerts européens avant la guerre. (2) Maurice Ravel quitte le Théâtre Allemand par l'entrée des artistes après avoir écouté son propre concerto pour piano dirigé par Georg Szell (à droite) avec Marguerite Long (à gauche) comme soliste, 1932. (3) Le chef d'orchestre Fritz Busch en concert au Théatre Allemand.

The Dutch conductor Willem Mengelberg, here seen rehearsing with the Czech Philharmonic Orchestra, about 1934, had been a friend and champion of Mahler and Strauss and, by the time of this photograph, conductor of the Amsterdam Concertgebouw for some 40 years.

Der holländische Dirigent Willem Mengelberg – hier abgebildet bei einer Probe mit dem Tschechischen Phiharmonie Orchester um 1934 – war befreundet mit Mahler und Strauss; zur Zeit dieser Aufnahmen war er ungefähr 40 Jahren Dirigent am Amsterdam Concertgebouw.

Le chef d'orchestre néederlandais Willem Mengelberg répétant ici avec le Czech Philharmonic Orchestra vers 1934, avait été un ami et le champion de Mahler et Strauss et, à l'époque où cette photographie fut prise, il dirigeait le Amsterdam Concertgebouw depuis a peu près 40 ans.

Erich Auerbach wurde 1911 in Falkenau, dem heutigen Sokolov, im Sudetenland geboren. Sein Vater, ein Arzt und Musikliebhaber, ermunterte ihn, Klavier und Geige spielen zu lernen. Auerbach, der im benachbarten Karlsbad zur Schule ging, musizierte schon dort regelmäßig im Schulorchester, intensivierte seine Musikstudien aber vor allem später an der Prager Universität. Er begann außerdem, Konzerte zu besuchen, und um seine Studentenbezüge aufzubessern, schrieb er Musikkritiken für das *Prager Tageblatt*. In dieser Zeit machte er auch seine ersten Fotos. Er fotografierte zu seinem Vergnügen, aber auch professionell für die Zeitung. Diese Tätigkeit faszinierte ihn immer mehr – sein Vater war davon jedoch weit weniger begeistert, denn er wünschte sich vielmehr, daß sein Sohn einen ordentlichen Studienabschluß machte. Auerbach hatte in der Tat keine fotografische Ausbildung; er hatte aber ein Vorbild, und zwar den „unvergleichlichen Dr. Erich Salomon, einen bis zum heutigen Tage unübertroffenen, in Auschwitz ums Leben gekommenen Fotografen, der mich das Fotografieren lehrte, obwohl wir uns nie begegnet sind." Das Vorbild inspirierte ihn so sehr, daß er auf einen Studienabschluß verzichtete und stattdessen ein begeisterter Amateurmusiker blieb. Trotz des abgebrochenen Studiums schenkte ihm sein Vater seine erste professionelle Kamera.

In den 30er Jahren waren das Tschechische Philharmonieorchester (damals unter der Leitung des großen tschechischen Dirigenten Václav Talich) und die beiden Opernhäuser – das Nationaltheater, das 1935 von Talich übernommen wurde, und das Deutsche Theater unter der Leitung des jungen ungarischen Dirigenten George Szell (siehe S. 206/207) – die Zentren des musikalischen Lebens in Prag. Auerbach portraitierte jedoch nicht nur die lokalen Größen, sondern nahm auch häufig gastierende Musiker auf – wie zum Beispiel Ravel auf seiner letzten Europatournee, Casals im Exil (siehe ab S. 224/225), Bruno Walter einen Monat vor dem Anschluß Österreichs sowie Komponisten, Dirigenten und Interpreten

aus ganz Europa. Leider blieben nicht alle Fotos aus diesen Tagen erhalten, denn im Sommer 1939 mußte Auerbach die Tschechoslowakei verlassen und verbrannte zuvor den größten Teil seiner Bilder. Er überquerte zu Fuß die Grenze nach Polen und nahm dabei nur seine besten Negative mit. Über journalistische Kontakte gelangte er nach England und traf im Juli in London ein.

Bereits wenige Wochen später befand sich England mit Deutschland im Krieg, und Auerbachs Situation wurde schwierig, da er keine Arbeitserlaubnis bekam. In einem Studentenwohnheim, in dem er Unterkunft fand, konnte er sich eine kleine Dunkelkammer einrichten, so daß er wenigstens seine Arbeit als Fotograf fortsetzen konnte. Als bald darauf die tschechische Exilregierung Kontakt zu ihm aufnahm und ihn bat, die Öffentlichkeitsarbeit für sie zu übernehmen, war seine Beschäftigung bis zum Kriegsende gesichert. 1942 heiratete er und zog mit seiner Frau in ein kleines Appartement in St. John's Wood, wo sie auch heute noch lebt.

Während des Krieges gab es in London selten die Gelegenheit, Musiker zu fotografieren. Viele Londoner Orchestermusiker waren eingezogen und die Orchesterbesetzungen entsprechend dezimiert. Das BBC Symphony Orchestra war nach Bristol evakuiert worden, um wenigstens die Rundfunkmusik zu sichern. Das London Symphony Orchestra und das London Philharmonic Orchestra kämpften in London ums Überleben, insbesondere nachdem der traditionelle Veranstaltungsort der Londoner Orchesterkonzerte, die Queen's Hall, 1941 durch Bombenangriffe zerstört wurde. Mecca Cafés hatte das Royal Opera House in Covent Garden übernommen und zu einem Tanzsaal umfunktioniert, und als ausgebombte Anwohner im Sadler's Wells Theatre Zuflucht suchten, schloß damit auch die letzte Opernbühne in London.

Es war eine glückliche Fügung, daß Auerbach sein erstes Londoner Musikerportrait ausgerechnet von der „Institution" Sir Henry Wood machen durfte. Der damals 71jährige hatte

46 Jahre zuvor die bis heute berühmten Promenadenkonzerte (die sogenannten „Proms") ins Leben gerufen, die jährlich in den Sommermonaten einem breiten Publikum zu niedrigen Eintrittspreisen den Zugang zur klassischen Musik ermöglichen. Zudem hatte er sein Leben lang an der Bildung und Entwicklung des britischen Musikgeschmacks gearbeitet, neue Talente gefördert und sich unermüdlich dafür eingesetzt, das Niveau der Orchester anzuheben. Er war immer ein begeisterter Anhänger der Neuen Musik gewesen: „Bleiben Sie dran, meine Herren", rief er dem Orchester 1912 bei der Probe von Schönbergs *Fünf Orchesterstücken* zu, „gemessen an dem, was Sie in 25 Jahren spielen werden, ist das noch gar nichts." Und er gab auch nicht so leicht auf. Als der Veranstaltungsort der „Proms" durch Bomben zerstört wurde, verlagerte er sie in die Royal Albert Hall, wo er sie für drei weitere Jahre dirigierte. Die 50. Saison 1944 mußte jedoch mit Rücksicht auf Hitlers Fliegerbomben verkürzt werden. Wenige Wochen später starb ihr Initiator Sir Henry Wood – so hatte Auerbach mit seinen ersten Londoner Fotos das Ende einer Ära eingefangen.

Zu den bemerkenswertesten musikalischen Ereignissen kleineren Rahmens während des Krieges gehörte eine Reihe von Kammermusikkonzerten in der National Gallery, die von der zweiten Kriegswoche an dort stattfanden. Die Pianistin Myra Hess hatte sie initiiert, um die leeren Ausstellungsflächen zu nutzen, nachdem die Bilder aus Sicherheitsgründen in die Waliser Berge geschafft worden waren. Sechseinhalb Jahre lang wurde täglich zur Mittagszeit eine Vorstellung für ein Publikum gegeben, das je nach Wetterlage, Programm und Bombenalarm 250-1750 Zuhörer umfaßte. Seither hat wohl keine Veranstaltungsreihe mehr über einen so langen Zeitraum so regelmäßig stattgefunden. Mit dem Ende der Feindseligkeiten kehrten die Gemälde jedoch aus Wales zurück, und im April 1946 wurden die Konzerte eingestellt.

Early Years in London: Sir Henry Wood, founder of the Promenade Concerts, rehearsing the London Symphony Orchestra at the Queen's Hall in 1940, the year before it was destroyed.

Die frühen Londoner Jahre: Sir Henry Wood, Gründer der Promenade Concerts, probt 1940 mit dem London Symphony Orchestra in der Queen's Hall, ein Jahr vor ihrer Zerstörung.

Les premières années à Londres: Sir Henry Wood, fondateur des Promenade Concerts, répétant avec le London Symphony Orchestra au Queen's Hall en 1940, un an avant qu'il ne soit détruit.

Mit den heimgekehrten Musikern lebten die Londoner Orchester und Institutionen wieder auf. Innerhalb eines Monats nach Kriegsende öffnete Sadler's Wells Theatre wieder seine Tore und erweckte die britische Musikwelt mit der Premiere von Brittens Oper *Peter Grimes* zu neuem Leben. Nicht lange danach erholte sich Covent Garden von seinem Zwischenspiel als Tanzsaal mit einem neuen eigenen Opernensemble unter der Leitung von Karl Rankl. Ein führender Kopf der Gramophone Company namens Walter Legge nutzte den Wandel der Zeit, um das Philharmonic Orchestra zu gründen, ein Ensemble von Starmusikern, das insbesondere Opern- und Konzertaufnahmen von höchster Qualität einspielen sollte und für das Legge Herbert Karajan als Chefdirigenten gewann. Nur ein Jahr später gründete Sir Thomas Beecham das Royal Philharmonic Orchestra. Damit wurde London, wie Auerbach es nannte, zur „Metropole der fünf Orchester". 1950 übernahm Sir Malcolm Sargent die Promenadenkonzerte und leitete sie bis zu seinem Tod im Jahre 1967.

In dieser Vielfalt fehlte der Londoner Musikszene nur noch ein neues Zentrum, das die schmerzlich vermißte Queen's Hall ersetzen konnte. Die Royal Festival Hall, die in jenem Jahr für das Festival of Britain gebaut wurde, entwickelte sich rasch zum Mittelpunkt des Londoner Konzertlebens, und in den 50er Jahren strömten führende Dirigenten und Solisten aus aller Welt in die Hauptstadt. London feierte musikalische Höhepunkte, und Auerbachs neugierige Linse schwelgte in einer Fülle von faszinierendem Material.

Als die tschechische Exilregierung 1945 nach Prag zurückkehrte, fand Auerbachs Öffentlichkeitsarbeit ein Ende. Er bekam eine Stelle als Fotograf bei der wöchentlich erscheinenden Zeitschrift *Illustrated*, die er für die nächsten 12 Jahre behielt. Seine Arbeit bei *Illustrated* erstreckte sich auf alle Bereiche des Fotojournalismus. Dank seiner besonderen Erfahrung wurden ihm zwar die herausragendsten und wichtigsten musikalischen

Ereignisse anvertraut, jedoch ließ es sich auch nicht vermeiden, daß er einige andere ihm wichtige Gelegenheiten verpaßte. Er hat es zum Beispiel stets bedauert, Toscanini nicht fotografiert zu haben, als dieser 1952 bei seinem einzigen Besuch nach dem Krieg in der Festival Hall dirigierte. Andererseits hatte Auerbach das Glück, sehr günstig in der Nähe der BBC Studios in Maida Vale zu wohnen, wohin viele berühmte Musiker kamen, um Aufnahmen oder Sendungen zu machen; und gleich um die Ecke lagen die berühmten Abbey Road Studios von EMI.

Seine Freundschaft mit Walter Legge half ihm, die vielen bedeutenden Künstler, die in den Nachkriegsjahren nach London kamen, persönlich kennenzulernen. Es war eine große Zeit für die Plattenindustrie, und Legge saß bei EMI direkt im Zentrum der Entwicklung. In den frühen 50er Jahren ersetzte die Langspielplatte allmählich die altehrwürdige Single, die der Musikindustrie seit ihren Anfängen große Dienste geleistet hatte. Außerdem öffnete die erheblich verbesserte Aufnahmetechnik einen ganz neuen Musikmarkt für ernste Musik. So wurde London mit seinem Orchesterreichtum, seinen Studios und Experten ein Magnet für die internationale Musikwelt. Ab 1958 hat die Stereotechnik diesen Trend noch einmal verstärkt, und für die Musiker der Nachkriegszeit wurden das Aufnahmestudio, das Mischpult und der Schneideraum genauso wichtig wie die Konzerthalle.

1957 wurde *Illustrated* eingestellt, und Auerbach arbeitete die nächsten zwanzig Jahre lang bis zu seinem Tod ausschließlich als freiberuflicher Fotograf. Dank seiner Freundschaft mit Legge hatte er auch weiterhin Zugang zu Zusammenkünften, bei denen kein gewöhnlicher Fotojournalist anwesend war: Oft lud ihn Legge zu Parties und anderen Veranstaltungen in sein Haus in Hampstead ein, wo er mit seiner Frau, der Sopranistin Elisabeth Schwarzkopf, lebte. Auerbach hatte aber auch selbst Freunde unter den Künstlern; Oistrach und Menuhin beispielsweise luden ihn persönlich zu privaten Proben in ihren

Hotelzimmern oder bei sich zu Hause ein. Auerbach war ein sehr diskreter Fotograf mit einem unkonventionellen Ansatz, der ganz hinter seine Arbeit zurücktrat. Seine Modelle schätzten ihn nicht zuletzt deshalb, weil er selbst Musiker war und ihre Kunst wirklich würdigen konnte. Seine Frau erinnert sich daran, daß ihm Tränen über das Gesicht liefen, wenn er den Interpreten, die er fotografieren wollte, zuhörte.

Dieses innerste Musikverständnis und die Tatsache, daß er sich selbst als ein interpretativer Künstler verstand, machen das Geheimnis von Auerbachs Kunst aus. Erich Salomon – „der bis zum heutigen Tage unübertroffene Fotograf" – war zwar das Vorbild und der Auslöser, aber die intimen, ausdrucksvollen Fotos in diesem Band entstammen ebensosehr dem Ohr des Musikers wie dem Auge des Fotografen. Es ist diese genaue Beobachtung der Personen, das Einfühlungsvermögen und die musikalische Sensibilität, die Auerbachs Archiv der Nachkriegsjahrzehnte zu einem so einzigartig aufschlußreichen Dokument machen.

Within one week of the outbreak of the war the pianist Myra Hess launched a series of lunchtime concerts in the empty halls of the National Gallery that were to continue unbroken for six and a half years.

In der Woche des Kriegsausbruchs begann die Pianistin Myra Hess mit einer Konzertreihe in den leeren Hallen der National Gallery, die ohne Unterbrechung sechseinhalb Jahre lang fortgesetzt wurde.

Dans la semaine où la guerre éclata, la pianiste Myra Hess lança une série de concerts à l'heure du déjeuner dans les salles vides de la National Gallery, concerts qui se poursuivirent sans interruption pendant six ans et demi.

C'est dans les Sudètes, à Falkenau près de Sokolov, qu'Erich Auerbach vit le jour en 1911. Son père, qui était médecin, adorait la musique et le poussa à apprendre le piano et le violon. À l'école qu'il fréquentait dans la ville voisine de Karlovy Vary (ou Karlsbad en allemand), il jouait régulièrement au sein de l'orchestre et, lorsqu'il entreprit ses études à Prague, il poursuivit naturellement sa formation de musicien. Là, il commença à se rendre plus fréquemment aux concerts et, sa bourse d'étudiant n'étant pas assez élevée, il travaille à mi-temps en tant que critique musical pour la *Prager Tagblatt*. C'est à cette époque qu'il prend ses premières photos à la fois pour se faire plaisir, mais aussi pour les besoins de la publication. Progressivement, la photographie allait prendre une place importante dans sa vie, au grand mécontentement de son père, qui aurait préféré le voir obtenir un diplôme. Il est vrai qu'Auerbach n'avait aucune formation théorique à la photographie, mais il avait « un modèle incomparable, Erich Salomon (mort en concentration à Auschwitz), un photographe dont le travail n'a encore jamais été égalé » et qui lui inspira le talent nécessaire pour convaincre par ses images. Auerbach ne finit jamais ses études, mais il resta toute sa vie durant un excellent musicien amateur et c'est malgré tout son père qui lui offrit son premier appareil photographique professionnel.

Dans les années 30, Prague la musicienne se retrouvait essentiellement autour de la Philharmonie tchèque (alors sous la direction du grand Václav Talich) et de ses deux opéras, national et allemand, ce dernier étant dirigé par le jeune chef d'orchestre hongrois George Szell (voir p. 206/207). Auerbach ne se restreignait toutefois pas à l'activité des musiciens locaux et il eut de nombreuses occasions de fixer sur le papier ceux qui passaient à Prague en visiteurs : Ravel, lors de sa dernière tournée en Europe, Casals exilé d'Espagne (voir p. 224/225) ou Bruno Walter venu jouer à peine un mois avant la signature de l'*Anschluss* et encore bien d'autres, compositeurs, chefs d'or-

chestre et virtuoses venus de toute l'Europe. Malheureusement, nombre de ces épreuves n'ont pu parvenir jusqu'à cette fin de siècle, car Auerbach en brûla lui-même une grande partie lors de l'été 39, avant de devoir quitter la Tchécoslovaquie. Il n'emporta avec lui que les négatifs de celles qu'il chérissait le plus, traversa à pied la frontière avec la Pologne et grâce au réseau de journalistes parvint à gagner Londres en juillet.

Quelques semaines plus tard, la Grande-Bretagne entrait en guerre avec l'Allemagne et la situation du photographe devenait pour le moins incertaine. Interdit de travail, il trouve à se loger dans un foyer d'étudiants où il réussit à aménager un coin pour développer ses photos et poursuivre son travail. Peu de temps après, le gouvernement tchèque en exil lui demande de mettre son art au service du pays, et le voilà assuré d'un emploi jusqu'à la fin de la guerre. En 1942, il se marie et emménage dans un petit appartement à St. John's Wood, dans le quartier qu'habite encore aujourd'hui sa femme.

Pendant la guerre, Londres offrait peu de possibilités de réaliser des reportages sur la musique. De nombreux musiciens étant appelés sous les drapeaux, les orchestres étaient réduits à leur minimum. Si l'Orchestre symphonique de la BBC avait pu trouver refuge à Bristol dès le début des hostilités, d'où l'on pouvait au moins assurer la radiodiffusion d'œuvres musicales, les orchestres symphonique et philharmonique de Londres avaient quant à eux toutes les peines du monde à survivre, notamment après le bombardement en 1941 du Queen's Hall, le bâtiment qui accueillait traditionnellement les grands concerts londoniens. Le Royal Opera House de Covent Garden avait été repris par Mecca Cafés ; on en avait fait un genre de salle des fêtes où l'on organisait des bals, et la seule scène qui restait disponible devait disparaître elle aussi rapidement, lorsque le Sadler's Wells Theatre fut réquisitionné pour abriter les londoniens que les bombardements avaient poussés à la rue.

Pour ses premières photographies de la scène musicale londonienne, Auerbach eut la chance d'avoir comme sujet Sir

Henry Wood, qui représentait alors une véritable institution. On ne pouvait rêver mieux. Le créateur des concerts-promenades était alors dans sa 72e année (les « Proms » dans leur 46e) et avait consacré toute sa vie à développer la musique, à former le goût musical des Britanniques, à encourager les jeunes talents et à travailler sans cesse pour rehausser le niveau des orchestres. Il était depuis toujours un ardent défenseur de la musique contemporaine ; la preuve en est cette remarque qu'il lança à son orchestre lors d'une répétition des *Cinq pièces pour orchestre* de Schoenberg, en 1912 : « Messieurs, rappelez-vous que cela, ce n'est rien en comparaison avec ce que vous ferez dans 25 ans. » Inutile à ce sujet de tenter de le décourager ! Lorsque les bombardements touchèrent le Queen's Hall, les fameuses « Proms », accompagnées de Sir Henry Wood, durent déménager au Royal Albert Hall où le grand chef d'orchestre les dirigea encore trois saisons, jusqu'à la cinquantième qui, en 1944, dut être abrégée en raison des missiles de Hitler. Quelques semaines plus tard, Sir Henry Wood devait décéder ; grâce à ses quelques photographies, Auerbach avait réussi à immortaliser la fin d'une grande époque.

À un autre niveau, on peut considérer les concerts de musique de chambre de la National Gallery comme comptant parmi les plus admirables moments de la vie musicale londonienne durant la période de guerre. Deux semaines à peine après la déclaration de guerre, Myra Hesse eut l'idée d'utiliser les salles désertes du célèbre musée, dont les œuvres avaient été mises à l'abri au Pays de Galle. Pendant plus de six ans et demi, des déjeuners en musique firent chaque jour la joie de 250 à 1 750 personnes, la présence du public variant en fonction du temps, du programme, mais aussi de l'appel des sirènes d'alarme. Ces concerts sont un exemple encore inégalé de continuité et de richesse musicale ; ils ne prirent fin qu'à regret après le retour en 1946 des œuvres de la National Gallery.

À mesure que les musiciens revenaient de la guerre, les orchestres londoniens commencèrent à reprendre vie et les

An opera recording of the stereo age: the line up for the 1962 recording of Mozart's opera *Cosi fan tutte*, under Karl Böhm, for EMI in the Kingsway Hall, London. Elisabeth Schwarzkopf, Christa Ludwig, Walter Berry, Hanny Steffek, Alfredo Krauss, and Giuseppe Taddei, with Prof. Heinrich Schmidt at the harpsicord.

Eine Opernaufzeichnung im Stereo-Zeitalter: Die Phalanx der Künstler für die Aufnahme von Mozarts *Cosi fan tutte* unter der Leitung von Karl Böhm in der Londoner Kingsway Hall, 1962. Elisabeth Schwarzkopf, Christa Ludwig, Walter Berry, Hanny Steffek, Alfredo Krauss und Giuseppe Taddei; Prof. Heinrich Schmidt am Cembalo.

Un enregistrement d'opéra à l'ère de la stéréo: une file pour l'enregistrement en 1962 de l'opéra de Mozart *Cosi fan tutte*, sous la direction de Karl Böhm, pour EMI dans le Kingsway Hall, Londres. Elisabeth Schwarzkopf, Christa Ludwig, Walter Berry, Hanny Steffek, Alfredo Krauss et Giuseppe Taddei, avec le Professeur Heinrich Schmidt au clavecin.

institutions, à se réorganiser. Un mois après le cessez-le-feu, le Sadler's Wells Theatre ouvrait de nouveau ses portes et faisait resplendir la musique britannique en donnant la première de *Peter Grimes*, le célèbre opéra de Benjamin Britten. Peu après, le Covent Garden sortait de son intermède de gala, pour lancer sa propre troupe d'opéra, dirigée par Karl Rankl. Un producteur de la société EMI, Walter Legge, profite alors de cette ère de renouveau pour créer le Philharmonia Orchestra, un ensemble qui allait réunir les plus grands virtuoses afin, surtout, de produire des enregistrements de la plus haute qualité. Comme premier chef d'orchestre, Walter Legge choisit Herbert von Karajan. Un an plus tard, Sir Thomas Beechman forme le Royal Philharmonic Orchestra, ajoutant ainsi la touche finale à ce qu'Auerbach appelait lui-même « la métropole aux cinq orchestres ». En 1950, Sir Malcolm Sargent reprend la direction des « Proms », dont il resterait l'inlassable figure de proue jusqu'à sa mort, en 1967.

Forte de telles ressources, Londres pouvait sembler complètement parée pour connaître l'une de ses périodes d'activité musicale les plus florissantes. En 1951, un nouveau « bijou » vient remplacer le Queen's Hall, cette salle de concert tant regrettée des londoniens. Le Royal Festival Hall, construit pour le Festival of Britain cette même année, devient rapidement le cœur de la musique londonienne et attire dès les années 50 les plus grands noms du monde, qu'ils s'agissent de solistes ou de chefs d'orchestre. La musique était redevenue reine et donnait de nouveau à Auerbach matière à photographier.

Le retour du gouvernement tchèque à Prague en 1945 avait mis un terme à l'emploi du photographe, mais Auerbach retrouva facilement un poste dans l'équipe de l'hebdomadaire *Illustrated*, où il allait rester douze ans. Pour ce magazine, il couvrait tous les domaines habituels du journalisme photographique, mais en raison de son expérience musicale, on lui confiait aussi plus particulièrement la couverture des événements artistiques. Bien entendu, il manqua certaines grandes

occasions et garda, par exemple, toujours une immense déception de n'avoir pu saisir Toscanini lors de sa seule visite d'après-guerre à Londres, pour diriger au Festival Hall en 1952. Mais, Auerbach avait tout de même la chance d'habiter non loin des principaux studios de la BBC, à Maida Vale, qui ont entendu, enregistré et diffusé les musiciens les plus renommés de la planète. Et puis, à quelques rues de là, se trouvaient aussi les fameux studios d'Abbey Road, les studios d'EMI.

L'amitié qui le liait à Walter Legge ne fut sans doute pas étrangère à son succès et elle lui permit d'approcher tant de personnalités de la musique. Ces années d'après-guerre furent une grande période pour les enregistrements ; Walter Legge et EMI y régnaient en maître. Dans le début des années 50, le microsillon longue durée commençait à remplacer les vénérables 78 T qui avaient fait les beaux jours de l'industrie du disque depuis ses débuts. De nouveaux marchés allaient enfin s'ouvrir, offrant de merveilleuses perspectives à la grande musique. Londres, avec tous ses orchestres, ses studios et son professionnalisme, devint une sorte d'aimant vers lequel les musiciens du monde entier étaient attirés, et cette réalité se fit de plus en plus frappante avec l'arrivée des techniques d'enregistrement stéréophonique en 1958. Pour les musiciens de l'après-guerre, studios d'enregistrement et de mixage se révélaient bientôt aussi importants que les salles de concert.

Lorsque l' *Illustrated* mit la clef sous la porte, en 1957, Auerbach s'installa à son propre compte ; il resterait photographe indépendant jusqu'à sa mort, quelque 20 ans plus tard. Grâce à Walter Legge, il eut toujours accès à des séances d'enregistrement et à des concerts auxquels aucun journaliste n'aurait pu normalement assister. Il était également souvent invité à des soirées, voire parfois aussi, à Hampstead, dans la maison que le producteur d'EMI partageait avec sa femme, la célèbre soprano Élisabeth Schwarzkopf. Dans la plupart des cas, il se nouait d'amitié avec les artistes, de sorte qu'Oïstrakh et Menuhin, entre autres, l'invitèrent à des répétitions privées

dans leurs chambres d'hôtel ou à leur domicile. Auerbach était un photographe discret, informel et tellement modeste. Ses « modèles » ne pouvaient que l'apprécier, d'autant qu'il était lui-même musicien et savait apprécier la musique qu'ils jouaient devant son objectif. Sa femme se rappelle encore comment il pouvait rester là, assis, les larmes coulant sans fin sur ses joues alors qu'il écoutait ces musiciens qu'il était pourtant venu photographier.

C'est bien évidemment cette compréhension innée de la musique et du rôle de son interprète qui fut le secret d'Auerbach. Salomon, « le photographe dont le travail n'a encore jamais été égalé », lui a certes montré l'exemple et donné l'envie de photographier, mais l'on peut dire que c'est bien l'oreille du musicien, tout autant que l'œil du photographe, qui a su rendre toute la profondeur de ses admirables moments que nous découvrirons en photo au fil de ce livre. C'est son sens personnel de l'observation, sa psychologie et son côté musical qui ont donné à ses témoignages photographiques de l'après-guerre leur qualité unique.

COMPOSERS
KOMPONISTEN
COMPOSITEURS

The Brazilian composer Heitor Villa-Lobos (1887-1959) talking
about his music outside the Hotel Wilson, Prague, 1936.

Der brasilianische Komponist Heitor Villa-Lobos (1887-1959)
erläutert vor dem Hotel Wilson in Prag seine Musik, 1936.

Le compositeur brésilien Heitor Villa-Lobos (1887-1959) parle de
sa musique devant l'hôtel Wilson à Prague en 1936.

LUCIANO BERIO *1925

Berio's association with the musical avant-garde goes back to the early 1950s, when he met Bruno Maderna, Henri Pousseur, Pierre Boulez and Karlheinz Stockhausen. For five years he was a frequent visitor to the Summer Courses for New Music at Darmstadt, but there has always been an accessibility, almost a lightness of touch, in his work that distinguishes it from the somewhat turgid seriousness of much that emanated from that powerhouse of musical intellect. His interest in electronic music, evident in so many of his compositions, goes back even further, to 1950 and his first visit to the United States which was later to become his second home: many of the works of those early days were written for the remarkable voice of his American first wife, Cathy Berberian, whose amazing versatility could encompass anything from the strange gurgles and vocal gestures of *Visages* to the expressive simplicity of *Folk Songs* – a work in which the relationship between folk music and twentieth-century musical invention has been given an altogether new definition.

Berio has travelled a lot and spent a good deal of his time outside his native Italy, often teaching – at Darmstadt itself, at Tanglewood, Mills College and the Juilliard School in America, and at Dartington in England. In his home country his music did not always meet with approval. But he is a man of spirit: before the first night of *Passaggio* at the Piccolo Scala in Milan, knowing that the audience would interrupt, he warned the chorus that they should pick up and improvise on whatever they heard being shouted. 'And that is precisely what happened. Some people shouted 'Buffoni!' whereupon the chorus took it over, speeded it up, whispered it, lengthened the 'o', and eventually the improvisation became part of the performance. The audience became hysterical because it had lost even the chance of protest.' (One somehow feels that Berio must have had more fun than most composers.) But recognition came in the end, even in that last bastion of nineteenth-century musical culture, and in the early 1970s he bought a farmhouse in the hills near Siena and transferred his activities back to the country he had never really left.

Schon in den frühen 50er Jahren knüpfte der Italiener Luciano Berio enge Kontakte zur musikalischen Avantgarde: Er traf mit Bruno Maderna, Henri Pousseur, Pierre Boulez und Karlheinz Stockhausen zusammen und besuchte fünf Jahre lang regelmäßig die „Ferienkurse für Neue Musik" in Darmstadt. Seine Musik behielt jedoch stets eine gewisse Zugänglichkeit, ja Leichtigkeit, die seine Arbeiten von dem übersteigerten Ernst jener Werke abhob, die sonst aus diesem Kraftzentrum des musikalischen Geistes hervorgingen. Berios Interesse an elektronischer Musik, das in vielen seiner Werke deutlich zum Ausdruck kommt, wurde 1950 während seiner ersten Reise in die Vereinigten Staaten (die später zu seiner zweiten Heimat wurden) geweckt. Viele seiner frühen Werke schrieb Berio für die bemerkenswerte Stimme seiner Frau, der Amerikanerin Cathy Berberian, deren Stimmvolumen vom seltsamen Glucksen und den stimmlichen Figuren von *Visages* bis zu der ausdrucksvollen Schlichtheit seiner *Folk Songs* reichte – ein Werk übrigens, das die Beziehung zwischen der Volksmusik und den musikalischen Innovationen des 20. Jahrhunderts neu definiert hat.

Berio reiste viel, so daß er einen großen Teil seiner Zeit außerhalb seines Heimatlandes Italien verbrachte. Oft lehrte er im Ausland – in Darmstadt selbst, in den USA in Tanglewood, am Mills College und an der Juilliard School und in England in Dartington. In seiner Heimat fand seine Musik häufig keinen Beifall. Daher bewies er Einfallsreichtum und bereitete den Chor am Abend vor der Uraufführung von *Passagio* in der Mailänder Piccolo Scala darauf vor, daß das Publikum das Konzert unterbrechen würde und bat die Sänger, Zwischenrufe aufzugreifen und damit zu improvisieren. „Und genau das geschah. Einige riefen ‚Buffoni!', und der Chor nahm es auf, steigerte das Tempo, flüsterte, zog das ‚o' in die Länge, und allmählich wurde die Improvisation ein Teil der Aufführung. Das Publikum verfiel in Hysterie, weil ihm sogar die Möglichkeit des Protestes genommen war." (Es scheint, als habe sich Berio besser amüsiert als viele andere Komponisten.) Doch schließlich versagte ihm diese letzte Bastion der Musik des 19. Jahrhunderts nicht länger die Anerkennung, und in den frühen 70er Jahren kaufte Berio ein Bauernhaus in den Hügeln bei Siena, um seine Aktivitäten zurück in jenes Land zu verlagern, das er nie ganz verlassen hatte.

L'union entre Berio et la musique avant-gardiste date du début des années 50, lorsqu'il rencontra Bruno Maderna, Henri Pousseur, Pierre Boulez et Karlheinz Stockhausen. Pendant cinq ans, il fréquenta assidûment les universités d'été de Darmstadt sur la musique contemporaine, mais il a toujours gardé dans son travail une certaine ouverture, une légèreté de toucher qui le différencient du sérieux quelque peu grandiloquent qui émanait de cette machine à intellect musical. Son intérêt pour la musique électronique, que l'on ressent avec évidence dans beaucoup de ses compositions, remonte encore un peu plus en arrière, précisément à 1950, année de son premier séjour aux États-Unis, pays qui deviendrait ensuite sa seconde patrie. Dans ces premiers temps, il écrivait alors de nombreuses œuvres pour la voix remarquable de sa première femme, Cathy Berberian, qui était américaine. Son incroyable polyvalence lui permettait de tout exprimer : des étranges gargouillis et mouvements vocaux de *Visages* à l'éloquente simplicité des *Folk Songs*, morceaux qui redéfinirent à neuf les relations entre les musiques traditionnelles et les nouveautés musicales du XXe siècle.

Berio voyageait beaucoup et passait une large partie de son temps hors de son Italie natale, souvent pour enseigner – à Darmstadt, à Tanglewood, au Mills College ou la Juilliard School aux États-Unis, ainsi qu'à Darlington en Angleterre. Sa musique ne trouva pas toujours très bon accueil dans son propre pays. En homme d'esprit lors de la première de *Passaggio* à la Piccolo Scala, il en avertit les choristes, leur conseillant d'improviser sur toutes les interjections que le public risquait de lancer pour interrompre la représentation. Il avait vu juste et, lorsque certains commencèrent à crier « Buffoni ! », le chœur les prit au mot et amplifia l'insulte, lui donnant un rythme plus vif, la murmurant, laissant traîner le « o »... A tel point, que cette improvisation fut ensuite incluse dans le spectacle. Le public en devenait hystérique, car les chanteurs lui enlevaient ainsi toute chance de protester. (Quelque chose nous dit que Berio a dû s'amuser bien plus que la plupart des compositeurs !) La reconnaissance finit par arriver, venue même des plus âpres défenseurs de la culture musicale du XIXe siècle et, dans le début des années 70, Berio acheta une propriété au milieu des collines siennoises et put transférer ses activités sur sa terre natale, qu'il n'avait jamais vraiment quittée.

Luciano Berio at the Queen Elizabeth Hall, about 1971.

Luciano Berio in der Queen Elizabeth Hall, ca. 1971.

Luciano Berio au Queen Elizabeth Hall vers 1971.

LEONARD BERNSTEIN   1900-1989

I Hate Music seems a curious title for the work that first introduced Bernstein to the New York public, because if ever there was a man whose obsessive love for music was manifest in his every action and in every fibre of his being it was Bernstein. And he was good, prodigiously good, at so many aspects of it – as composer, pianist, conductor, teacher, writer. In his Harvard days a friend had already commented 'Lenny is doomed to success', and his doom overtook him early.

It came first through conducting. Taken on at the age of 25 as assistant to Artur Rodzinski at the New York Philharmonic Symphony Orchestra, he was asked to deputize at short notice for Bruno Walter and seized the opportunity with characteristic energy. The American publicity machine went into action and Bernstein leapt to national fame overnight. But the composer in him didn't lag far behind. There are not many musicians who could easily bridge the gulf that separates the Philharmonic from Broadway – but that is where Bernstein's next success followed only six weeks later. It was a full-length musical called *On the Town* and it ran for 463 performances.

On the Town was followed by a succession of theatre pieces including ballets, musicals, a comic operetta based on Voltaire's *Candide* and the ground-breaking musical version of Romeo and Juliet in gangland, *West Side Story*. But side by side with these came more serious preoccupations, often with a strongly religious slant, embodied in huge works like the three symphonies and the *Chichester Psalms*. The style is eclectic and the influences predictable – Mahler, Stravinsky, Copland, jazz, Yiddish, a dash of Gershwin – all bound together in a sophisticated amalgam of 'popular' and 'classical' that blurs the borderline between those two concepts with enthusiasm and conviction.

As a conductor, having stepped firmly into the limelight at the outset of his career he never really left it. He became the first American to conduct at La Scala, Milan (with Callas, in *Medea*) – and ended up in 1958 as musical director and chief conductor of the New York Philharmonic, a post which he held for the next 11 years. They were years in which his name, voice and face became widely known in the United States, because to his other talents he added an extraordinary gift for teaching and presenting music, and his many television appearances as conductor, pianist and speaker made him a well-loved figure, particularly to the young.

For Bernstein was, above all, a communicator – and to see him conducting was to realize how intensely important the act of communication was to him. The works he most enjoyed conducting were those in which there was most emotional content to be put across to the audience – Beethoven, Brahms, Mahler, Shostakovich – and no conductor put more physical effort into getting the result he wanted from his orchestra. Perhaps it all came to him a bit too easily; he was sometimes accused of learning symphonies as he performed them, and his antics in 'wringing the last drop of emotion from the score' were not always approved by the sterner critics. But in the end what emerged was music that pulsated with life, life that communicated itself utterly to the audience. And that is, after all, the first aim of a conductor.

Ich hasse Musik – der Titel des Musikstücks, das Leonhard Bernstein erstmals in der New Yorker Öffentlichkeit bekannt machte – ist eine eigenartige Werkbezeichnung für jemanden, dessen besessene Liebe zur Musik in jedem seiner Werke und in jedem Zug seines Wesens so deutlich zum Ausdruck kommt. Bernstein war in mehr als einer Hinsicht ein Meister – ein hervorragender Komponist, Pianist, Dirigent, Lehrer und Schriftsteller. Bereits während seiner Studienzeit in Harvard bemerkte ein Freund: „Lennys Erfolg ist vorprogrammiert", und tatsächlich folgte Bernstein seiner Berufung schon sehr früh.

Seine ersten Erfolge hatte er als Dirigent. Als er im Alter von 25 Jahren als Assistent von Arthur Rodzinski zum New York Philharmonic Symphony Orchestra kam, sollte er kurzfristig die Vertretung für Bruno Walter übernehmen, und er ergriff diese Gelegenheit mit der ihm eigenen Energie. Die amerikanischen Medien taten das ihrige, und Bernstein wurde sozusagen über Nacht im ganzen Land berühmt. Auch als Komponist machte er bald auf sich aufmerksam. Es ist nicht vielen Musikern gegeben, eine Brücke von der Philharmonie zum Broadway zu schlagen – aber gerade dort hatte Bernstein nur sechs Wochen später seinen nächsten Erfolg mit einem Musical namens *On the Town*, das 463mal aufgeführt wurde.

Es folgten einige Ballettstücke, Musicals, eine komische Oper nach Voltaires *Candide* und seine bahnbrechende Musicalversion von Romeo und Julia im Reich der Streetgangs, die *West Side Story*. Gleichzeitig entstanden auch ernstere, geistlich geprägte Werke wie z. B. die drei großen Symphonien und die *Chichester Psalms*. Der Stil ist eklektisch, und die Vorbilder sind deutlich auszumachen – Mahler, Strawinsky, Copland sowie Elemente aus dem Jazz und der jüdischen Musik und etwas Gershwin, alle zusammengefaßt in einer bemerkenswerten Kombination aus Unterhaltung und ernster Musik, deren neue und unerwartete Harmonie überzeugte und begeisterte.

Seine ersten öffentlichen Erfolge als Dirigent begründeten seinen Ruf, den er zeit seines Lebens festigen sollte. Als erster Amerikaner dirigierte er die Mailänder Scala (die *Medea* mit der Callas); 1958 wurde er schließlich Musikdirektor und Chefdirigent des New York Philharmonic Orchestra, eine Stellung, die er elf Jahre lang innehaben sollte. Im Laufe dieser Jahre lernte ganz Amerika seinen Namen, seine Stimme und sein Gesicht kennen, denn zu all seinen anderen Talenten gesellte sich auch eine außerordentliche Begabung, den Menschen die Musik nahe- und beizubringen, und seine vielen Fernsehauftritte als Dirigent, Pianist und Redner machten ihn besonders bei der Jugend sehr beliebt.

Bernstein war in erster Linie ein Vermittler, und wenn man ihn dirigieren sah, konnte man deutlich spüren, welch eine große Rolle die Vermittlung für ihn spielte. Am liebsten führte er das Publikum in Werke von hoher Emotionalität ein – Beethoven, Brahms, Mahler, Schostakowitsch –, und kein Dirigent zeigte eine größere physische Präsenz als er, wenn es darum ging, dem Orchester den gewünschten Klang zu entlocken. Vielleicht hat er es ein bißchen zu leicht gehabt. Man hat ihm vorgeworfen, er lerne die Symphonien erst bei der Aufführung kennen, und seine Bemühungen „auch noch den letzten Tropfen Gefühl aus der Partitur herauszuwringen" wurde von ernsteren Kritikern nicht immer begrüßt. Gerade daraus resultierte aber jene pulsierende Lebendigkeit seiner Musik, und es ist ihm gelungen, dem Publikum diese Lebendigkeit wirklich zu vermitteln – und das ist doch die wichtigste Aufgabe für einen Dirigenten.

Je déteste la Musique est un titre qui peut paraître bizarre pour une œuvre qui devait présenter pour la première fois son auteur, Bernstein, au public de New York. En effet, s'il y eut jamais un homme dont la grande passion pour la musique était manifeste dans chacun de ses actes et dans chacune des impulsions qui firent vibrer son être, il s'agissait bien de Bernstein. Il était excellent, un maître en bien des aspects : comme compositeur, pianiste, chef d'orchestre, professeur, écrivain. Alors qu'il était encore à Harvard, un ami disait déjà de lui : « Lenny est destiné au succès », et le destin se jeta vite sur lui.

Ce fut d'abord en tant que chef d'orchestre. Engagé à l'âge de 25 ans comme assistant d'Arthur Rodzinski au New York Philharmonic Symphony Orchestra, on lui demanda à la dernière minute de remplacer Bruno Walter. Il sut saisir l'occasion avec une énergie qui lui est caractéristique. La machine américaine de publicité s'étant activée, Bernstein connut la célébrité du jour au lendemain. Cependant le compositeur en lui ne faisait que sommeiller. Peu de musiciens ont pu aisément passer du monde philharmonique à celui de Broadway – pourtant c'était bien là que son prochain succès, *On the Town*, allait naître six semaines plus tard. Il s'agissait alors d'une vraie comédie musicale qui eut 463 représentations.

On the Town fut suivi par une série de compositions parmi lesquelles des ballets, des comédies musicales, une opérette comique basée sur *Candide* de Voltaire, ainsi que l'originale version musicale de Roméo et Juliette au pays des gangs, *West Side Story*. Outre ces genres, d'autres, plus sérieux surgirent, souvent fortement inspirés par la religion qui caractérisent des œuvres énormes, telles que *Chichester Psalms*, et les trois symphonies. Son style est éclectique et ses influences sont évidentes – Mahler, Stravinski, Copland, le jazz, le yiddish, un soupçon de Gershwin – le tout formant un amalgame recherché de styles « populaire » et « classique », qui parvient à brouiller la distinction entre ces deux concepts avec allégresse.

Dès le début de sa carrière, alors qu'il était chef d'orchestre, il fut promu au rang de la célébrité, place qu'il ne devait jamais vraiment quitter. Il fut le premier Américain à diriger l'orchestre de la Scala, à Milan (avec Callas, dans *Medea*). Enfin, il devint en 1958 directeur musical et premier chef d'orchestre du New York Philarmonic, un poste qu'il allait garder pendant onze ans. Ces années firent connaître son nom, sa voix et son visage à travers les États-Unis : en effet, à ces autres talents, il faut ajouter son don extraordinaire pour l'enseignement et l'interprétation de la musique, et sa présence à de nombreuses émissions télévisées comme chef d'orchestre, pianiste ou invité en firent un personnage bien aimé, particulièrement des jeunes.

Par dessus tout, Bernstein savait communiquer – et de le voir diriger un orchestre, on réalisait l'importance monumentale qu'était pour lui l'acte de communication. Les œuvres qu'il dirigeait avec le plus de plaisir étaient celles où il fallait faire passer un message des plus émotionnels à son audience – Beethoven, Brahms, Mahler, Chostakovich – et aucun autre chef d'orchestre ne se donna comme lui, aussi physiquement pour obtenir ce qu'il voulait de son orchestre. Peut-être réussit-il un peu trop facilement ; on l'a quelquefois accusé d'apprendre des symphonies alors qu'il en donnait une représentation, et sa manière d'« extorquer l'ultime goutte d'émotion d'une partition » n'était pas toujours appréciée des critiques plus stricts. En fin de compte, ce qui s'en dégageait, c'était de la musique qui rimait avec la vie, vie qui se communiquait totalement au public. Et ceci est, après tout, le but premier d'un chef d'orchestre.

◄ Leonard Bernstein at the piano, about 1968.

Leonard Bernstein am Klavier, ca. 1968.

Leonard Bernstein au piano, en 1968.

Bernstein in rehearsal: three different ways of coercing an orchestra.

Bernstein beim Proben: drei verschiedene Möglichkeiten der Orchesterarbeit.

Bernstein lors d'une répétition: trois façons différentes de plier un orchestre à sa volonté.

Bernstein in performance.
Bernstein im Konzert.
Bernstein en concert.

Bernstein, spellbinder, 1968 or 1969.
Bernstein, der Zauberer, 1968 oder 1969.
Bernstein, l'enchanteur, 1968 ou 1969.

Bernstein pensive.

Bernstein in Gedanken versunken.

Bernstein pensif.

PIERRE BOULEZ ✶1925

Of all the avant-garde composers who emerged in the period immediately following the Second World War, Boulez is the one who has had most regular contact with the ordinary concert-goer. To be fair, this really has more to do with his conducting than with his activities as a composer. In his early days in Paris he was mainly occupied with Schoenberg, Berg, Webern and his own contemporaries, but as his interpretative skills developed his fame spread through Europe and America, and his interests took some unexpected turns. Carefully selected works of Beethoven, Schubert and Mahler began to appear in his programmes; in 1966 he conducted *Parsifal* at Bayreuth and ten years later the Bayreuth centenary cycle of *The Ring*. But in the end his cool, objective approach was heard at its best in performances of Debussy, Messiaen, Stravinsky and the central European composers of the 20th century, as well as the younger and more adventurous of the musical avant-garde. It was with this repertory that he made such a spectacular impact on the BBC Symphony Orchestra (and the Prom audiences) during his five years as its chief conductor in the early 1970s.

In the 1950s and early 60s, however, he was still a relatively unfamiliar figure in London, and known mainly as a composer of music that the general public found 'difficult'. He had been a pupil of Messiaen, but his association with the intellectual world of the New Music courses at Darmstadt, where he taught for 12 years and formed close relationships with Karlheinz Stockhausen and Bruno Maderna, helped him to develop the essentially logical thinking that underlay his composing activities and to regulate his growing preoccupation with the principle of serialism inherited from Webern.

The work which first brought him international success, as well as the admiration of Stravinsky, was *Le marteau sans maître* of 1954, which has now come to be regarded as one of the key works of 20th-century music, to be set beside *Le sacre du printemps* or *Pierrot Lunaire*. By the time of these photographs he had advanced further into serialism, particularly with *Pli selon pli*, a work for soprano and large orchestra in five movements of which the three movements entitled *Improvisations sur Mallarmé* had been written and performed as individual pieces in 1957 and 1959, and the two remaining movements added in 1959 and 1962 respectively. This concept of what Boulez saw as 'open form' has meant that no composition can ever be regarded as finished: *Pli selon pli* has been subjected to radical revision several times since 1962, and in any case the freedom of choice given to the performers in matters such as tempo, rhythm and note values means that no two performances are ever going to be identical.

Boulez's iconoclastic views, particularly on 20th-century opera, have earned him notoriety as well as some hostility, and his coolly analytical music is not to everyone's taste. Some may still regard him mainly as a theorist and polemicist; more see him as a composer of uncompromising originality and strength; many others admire him as a skilful and perceptive conductor of the works with which he feels in sympathy – but throughout the musical world he has to be recognized as one of the most powerful influences in music since the Second World War. It is an influence based, like his own compositions, on clarity and logic, the natural complement to the charm, wit, and penetrating intelligence of the man himself. Boulez is not a Frenchman for nothing.

Pierre Boulez, 21 February 1964.
Pierre Boulez, 21. Februar 1964.
Pierre Boulez, le 21 février 1964.

Von allen avantgardistischen Komponisten aus der Zeit nach dem Zweiten Weltkrieg stand Pierre Boulez dem Geschmack des traditionellen Konzertpublikums noch am nächsten. Doch um der Wahrheit die Ehre zu geben, muß dies mehr seiner Tätigkeit als Dirigent als seinen Aktivitäten als Komponist zugeschrieben werden. In seinen frühen Pariser Tagen beschäftigte er sich hauptsächlich mit Schönberg, Berg, Webern und seinen eigenen Zeitgenossen. Sein Ruhm in Europa und Amerika gründete sich jedoch auf seine interpretativen Fähigkeiten, die sich auch ganz anderen Themen widmeten. So nahm er sorgfältig ausgewählte Werke von Beethoven, Schubert und Mahler in seine Programme auf. 1966 dirigierte er den *Parsifal* in Bayreuth und zehn Jahre später anläßlich der Hundertjahrfeier von Bayreuth den Zyklus *Der Ring des Nibelungen*. Sein kühler, objektiver Ansatz kam jedoch bei seinen Aufführungen von Debussy, Messiaen, Strawinsky und den wichtigsten europäischen Komponisten des 20. Jahrhunderts oder bei der Interpretation der jüngeren und gewagteren musikalischen Avantgardisten am besten zum Ausdruck. Gerade mit diesem Repertoire beeindruckte er das BBC Symphony Orchestra (und das „Prom"-Publikum), das er in den frühen 70er Jahren fünf Jahre lang als Chefdirigent leitete.

In den 50er und 60er Jahren war er in London noch verhältnismäßig unbekannt und galt hauptsächlich als Komponist einer Musik, die dem breiten Publikum „zu schwierig" war. Er war ein Schüler von Messiaen, aber sein Kontakt zur Szene der Neuen Musik in Darmstadt, wo er zwölf Jahre lang lehrte und enge Beziehungen zu Karlheinz Stockhausen und Bruno Maderna knüpfte, förderte ganz wesentlich die Herausbildung der Logik, die seinen Kompositionen zugrunde liegt. Auch seine zunehmende Vertiefung in die Prinzipien der seriellen Musik, die er von Webern übernommen hatte, muß diesem Einfluß zugerechnet werden.

1954 brachte ihm *Le marteau sans maître* den ersten internationalen Erfolg und die Bewunderung von Strawinsky ein. Das Stück gilt inzwischen neben dessen *Le sacre du printemps* oder Schönbergs *Pierrot Lunaire* als ein Schlüsselwerk der Musik des 20. Jahrhunderts. Als diese Fotos entstanden, war Boulez' serielle Musik bereits weiter entwickelt, wovon insbesondere *Pli selon pli* (etwa: „Zug um Zug") zeugt, ein Stück für Sopran und großes Orchester in fünf Sätzen. Drei der Sätze mit dem Titel *Improvisations sur Mallarmé* waren bereits 1957 und 1959 als Einzelstücke aufgeführt worden, die beiden anderen hatte er 1959 bzw. 1962 dem Zyklus hinzugefügt. Nach dem Boulez'schen Konzept der „offenen Form" kann keine Komposition je als abgeschlossen gelten und so wurde *Pli selon pli* seit 1962 mehrmals radikal überarbeitet, und die Variationsmöglichkeiten von Tempi, Rhythmen und Notenwerten bei verschiedenen Aufführungen sind so groß, daß es niemals zwei gleiche Interpretationen geben wird.

Boulez' radikale Ansichten, insbesondere zur Oper des 20. Jahrhunderts, haben ihm sowohl Ruhm als auch Feindschaft eingetragen, und seine kühle, analytische Musik wird nicht jedermann begeistern. Einige werden in ihm auch weiterhin hauptsächlich den Theoretiker und Polemiker sehen; andere bewundern ihn als einen kunstfertigen und einfühlsamen Dirigenten jener Werke, die ihm persönlich nahe sind – sein maßgeblicher Einfluß auf die Entwicklung der Musik nach dem Zweiten Weltkrieg ist jedoch unumstritten. Er basiert genau wie seine Kompositionen auf Klarheit und Logik, die in dem Charme, dem Witz und der durchdringenden Intelligenz dieser Persönlichkeit ihre natürliche Ergänzung finden – verständlicherweise, denn immerhin ist Boulez ja Franzose.

De tous les compositeurs d'avant-garde qui surgirent dans la période qui suivit immédiatement la Deuxième Guerre mondiale, Pierre Boulez est celui qui est le plus régulièrement en contact avec les habitués ordinaires des concerts. Pour être juste, cela tient plus à sa qualité de chef d'orchestre qu'à celle de compositeur. Au début de son séjour à Paris, il était principalement intéressé par Schoenberg, Berg, Webern et ses propres contemporains. Puis, comme son habileté pour l'interprétation se développa, sa célébrité se répandit en Europe et en Amérique, pourtant alors qu'on ne s'y attendait pas, son attention fut attirée vers d'autres horizons. Des œuvres choisies avec soin de Beethoven, Schubert et Mahler commencèrent à apparaître dans ses programmes ; en 1966 il dirigea *Parsifal* à Bayreuth, et dix ans plus tard pour le centenaire de Bayreuth le cycle *Der Ring*. Son approche posée et objective est le mieux ressentie dans son interprétation de Debussy, Messiaen, Stravinski, des compositeurs d'Europe centrale du XXᵉ siècle, ainsi que des compositeurs plus jeunes, plus audacieux de musique d'avant-garde. C'est grâce à ce répertoire qu'au début des années 1970, il fit une si forte impression sur le BBC Symphony Orchestra qu'il dirigea pendant cinq ans.

Pourtant, dans les années 50 et au début des années 60, on ne le connaissait relativement pas encore très bien à Londres, où il avait une réputation de compositeur d'une musique jugée « difficile » par le grand public. Il fut un élève de Messiaen, mais son association avec le milieu intellectuel des cours de la Nouvelle Musique à Darmstadt, où il enseigna pendant 12 ans et où il se lia d'étroite amitié avec Karlheinz Stockhausen et Bruno Maderna, l'aida à développer l'esprit essentiellement logique qui était à la base de son travail de compositeur, et à se pencher de plus près sur ce qui ne cessait de l'intéresser, c'est à dire, le principe du sérialisme qu'il tenait de Webern.

La première œuvre qui lui apporta un succès international ainsi que l'admiration de Stravinski, fut *Le marteau sans maître* en 1954, maintenant considéré comme l'une des œuvres clés de la musique du XXᵉ siècle, aux côtés du *Sacre du printemps* ou de *Pierrot lunaire*. A l'époque de ces photos, il avait déjà bien avancé dans le sérialisme, en particulier avec *Pli selon pli*, une œuvre en cinq mouvements pour soprano et grand orchestre. Trois de ces cinq mouvements intitulés *Improvisations sur Mallarmé* furent écrits et joués en 1957 et 1959, alors que les deux autres mouvements ont été ajoutés respectivement en 1959 et 1962. A travers ce concept de « formule non restrictive », Boulez voulait montrer qu'une composition musicale ne pouvait jamais être considérée comme finie : *Pli selon pli* fut maintes fois radicalement revue et corrigée depuis 1962, et la liberté de choix dont les exécutants jouissaient quant au tempo, au rythme et à la valeur donnée à chaque note font qu'il n'y aura pas deux représentations identiques.

Les vues iconoclastes que Boulez portait sur l'opéra du XXᵉ siècle lui apportèrent la célébrité aussi bien que de l'hostilité, et sa musique analytique n'était pas du goût de tous. Certains le considèrent encore comme un théoriste ou un polémiste ; plus, cependant, voient en lui un compositeur d'une force et d'une originalité qui n'admettent aucun compromis ; d'autres encore admirent le chef d'orchestre doué et sensible qui dirigea les œuvres qu'il appréciait – mais dans le monde de la musique, on se doit de le considérer comme l'une des grosses influences en musique depuis la Deuxième Guerre mondiale. Cette influence est basée, comme ses propres compositions, sur la clarté et la logique, compléments naturels à ajouter au charme, à l'esprit et à l'intelligence pénétrante de l'homme lui-même. Boulez n'est pas français pour rien.

(1, 2, 3) Pierre Boulez, 21 February 1964. (4) Gallic reaction during a television interview, 4 March 1966.

(1, 2, 3) Pierre Boulez, 21. Februar 1964. (4) Launige Reaktion während eines Fernsehinterviews, 4. März 1966.

(1, 2, 3) Pierre Boulez, le 21 février 1964. (4) Le 4 mars 1966 : exaspération lors d'une interview à la télévision.

1

2

3

4

Boulez at rehearsal, 8 March 1967. It is extraordinary that he produces such analytical clarity without ever using a baton.

Boulez beim Proben, 8. März 1967. Es ist faszinierend, daß er zu einer solchen analytischen Klarheit kommen kann, ohne jemals einen Taktstock zu benutzen.

Boulez, lors d'une représentation, le 8 mars 1967. Qu'il puisse produire une telle clarté sans sa baguette est extraordinaire.

BENJAMIN BRITTEN (LORD BRITTEN OF ALDEBURGH)   1913-1976

When Britten returned from the United States in 1942 he brought back to England the reputation he had taken away with him three years before – that of a prodigiously gifted young composer with a taste for social satire and a technique so brilliant that it almost inevitably drew criticisms of 'too clever by half' from the more conservative English critics. But he also brought back the initial ideas for an opera which, three years later, was to confound.

The first performance of *Peter Grimes* marked the renewal of opera as a native art form in Great Britain. But it also marked the beginning of Britten's acceptance as the outstanding British composer of the post-war years. By the middle of the century Vaughan Williams was 78 years old, Walton had retired to Ischia, and though each still had more to give, the great creative periods of both were over. Only Michael Tippett, a late developer, was nearer to Britten in spirit and musical outlook, but whatever his other qualities he could never compete with the technical assurance, the teeming invention, the abundant output and the constant involvement with every aspect of practical music-making that established Britten as an omnipresent figure on the British musical scene.

From his home in Aldeburgh, Suffolk, Britten guided the destinies of the English Opera Group and the Aldeburgh Festival, involving musicians of international fame in the activities of both. Many of his best works were written for one or other of these organizations, sitting in his music room overlooking the North Sea, or later in the more sheltered haven of the Red House to which he moved when his presence in Aldeburgh had become too popular a public attraction. Of the 14 operas that followed *Grimes*, ten were written for the type of chamber ensemble that Aldeburgh inspired; only two received a full-blown Covent Garden première. And that was absolutely in the Britten spirit. He was not the man for the grand public gesture or the star appearance: even when he was involved in a large public occasion, like the first performance of the *War Requiem* at Coventry, he somehow played down his own part and managed to appear just one musician among others.

In musical technique, the sheer knowledge of how to produce sound, there was nothing that Britten didn't know – right down to which finger to put on which string. Partly this knowledge was a by-product of his own abilities as a performer: as a pianist he could appear on equal terms with Sviatoslav Richter or Clifford Curzon, and as an accompanist he was second to none. His Schubert was meltingly beautiful, particularly when he was playing for Peter Pears, his lifelong friend and partner, for whom he wrote virtually all his tenor roles and whose voice is so indelibly associated with them. It is still difficult to hear the folk-song arrangements, or the many song cycles, or the canticles, or indeed any of the operatic tenor roles, without recalling that curiously unmistakable sound.

'Our Brilliant Ben', Rostropovich called him, and to a truly extraordinary extent Britten was the very type of the all-round artist. At Aldeburgh he was as wonderful with the amateur side of the festival, and the works involving children like *Let's Make an Opera* or *Noye's Fludde*, as he was with the international guests – and often he touchingly brought them together in performance. He could be fun to work with, but above all, whether as composer, conductor, pianist, or simply a musical presence, he was inspiring wherever he appeared.

Als Benjamin Britten 1942 aus den USA zurückkehrte, brachte er den Ruf, den er drei Jahre zuvor dorthin mitgenommen hatte, wieder mit nach England zurück – er galt als ein hochbegabter junger Komponist mit einer Neigung zur gesellschaftlichen Satire und mit einer so brillanten Technik, daß es die konservativeren englischen Kritiker mißtrauisch stimmte. Er brachte jedoch auch die Grundidee für eine Oper mit, die drei Jahre später die Kritiker widerlegen sollte.

Die Uraufführung von *Peter Grimes* gab den Engländern die Oper als einheimische Kunstform zurück. Sie legte auch den Grundstein für die Anerkennung Brittens als herausragender britischer Komponist der Nachkriegsjahre. Mitte des Jahrhunderts war Vaughan Williams 78 Jahre alt, und Walton hatte sich nach Ischia zurückgezogen. Beide arbeiteten zwar weiterhin, aber ihre großen Schaffensperioden waren vorüber. Nur Michael Tippett, ein kompositorischer Spätentwickler, war Britten im musikalischen Sinne und in seiner Kreativität nahe. Er besaß jedoch, bei all seinen anderen Qualitäten, niemals die technische Sicherheit, den sprudelnden Einfallsreichtum und die ständige Präsenz in allen Bereichen der musikalischen Praxis, die Britten zu einer allgegenwärtigen Erscheinung der britischen Musikszene machten.

Von seinem Haus in Aldeburgh (Suffolk) aus lenkte Britten die Geschicke der English Opera Group und der Aldeburgh Festspiele, und engagierte dafür Musiker von internationalem Rang. Viele seiner besten Arbeiten schrieb er für die eine oder andere dieser Organisationen – in seinem Wohnzimmer mit Blick auf die Nordsee und später etwas geschützter im Red House. Er war dorthin umgezogen, als sein Bekanntheitsgrad in Aldeburgh zu groß wurde. Von den vierzehn Opern nach *Peter Grimes* sind zehn für kammermusikalische Besetzungen geschrieben, für die Aldeburgh den idealen Rahmen bot. Lediglich zwei erlebten eine ausverkaufte Premiere in Covent Garden. Und das war ganz in Brittens Sinn. Er war nicht der Mann für publikumswirksame Auftritte. Selbst wenn er in bedeutende öffentliche Veranstaltungen involviert war, wie bei der ersten Aufführung des *War Requiem* in Coventry, spielte er seine eigene Rolle herunter, und es gelang ihm, wie ein Musiker unter vielen zu erscheinen.

Die Technik der Musik, das reine Wissen um die Entstehung der Töne, waren Britten bis ins letzte vertraut – bis hin zur Lage der einzelnen Töne auf den Saiten. Dieses Wissen entstand zum Teil aus seiner eigenen musikalischen Praxis: Als Pianist konnte er sich mit Swjatoslaw Richter und Clifford Curzon messen, und als Begleiter war er unerreicht. Sein Schubert war ein Genuß für den Zuhörer, besonders wenn er Peter Pears begleitete, seinen lebenslangen Freund und Gefährten, für den er all seine Tenorrollen geschrieben hat. Pears Stimme gehört so untrennbar dazu, daß es immer noch schwer fällt, die Folksong-Bearbeitungen, die vielen Liederzyklen, die Lobgesänge oder gar irgendeine Opernrolle zu hören, ohne sich an seinen unverwechselbaren Tenor zu erinnern.

„Unser brillanter Ben" nannte ihn Rostropowitsch, und Britten war auch wirklich ein außergewöhnliches Allround-Talent. Bei den Festspielen in Aldeburgh konnte er genausogut mit Amateuren umgehen wie mit internationalen Gästen und Kindern, die z.B. in *Let's Make an Opera* oder *Noye's Fludde* mitspielten, und oft brachte er sie alle auf rührende Weise in den Aufführungen zusammen. Die Arbeit mit ihm konnte wirklich eine Freude sein. Vor allem aber, sei es als Komponist, Dirigent, Pianist oder einfach als musikalische Präsenz, wirkte seine Anwesenheit immer anregend.

Lorsqu'en 1942, Britten revint des États-Unis, il ramena en Angleterre la réputation qu'il avait emportée avec lui trois ans auparavant – celle d'un jeune compositeur prodigieusement doué avec un penchant pour la satire sociale et une technique tellement remarquable qu'elle s'attira inévitablement des critiques du genre « elle est un peu trop maligne », de la part des critiques anglais plus conservateurs. Il rapporta également les premières idées pour un opéra qui, trois ans plus tard, allait déconcerter les critiques.

La première représentation de *Peter Grimes* marqua une renaissance de l'opéra sous la forme d'un art originaire de Grande-Bretagne. Ce fut aussi le moment où Britten fut accepté comme le compositeur britannique exceptionnel d'après-guerre. Au milieu du siècle, Vaughan Williams était âgé de 78 ans, Walton se retira à Ischia, et bien que tous deux aient encore eu plus à offrir, leur grande époque créatrice s'était éteinte. Seul Michael Tippett, qui réussit plus tard que les autres, était plus proche de Britten par l'esprit et sa conception de la musique, mais quelles que soient ses autres qualités, il ne put jamais rivaliser avec lui quant à la maîtrise technique, les inventions innombrables, la production abondante et son engagement constant dans chaque aspect de la composition musicale qui firent de Britten le personnage omniprésent dans le monde musical britannique.

Depuis sa maison à Aldeburgh, dans le Suffolk, Britten guida les destinées de l'English Opera Group et du festival d'Aldeburgh, faisant venir des musiciens réputés dans le monde entier pour jouer dans ces deux organisations. Il écrivit nombre de ses œuvres pour l'une ou l'autre, depuis son bureau qui s'ouvrait sur la mer du Nord, et plus tard, depuis la Red House, son havre mieux protégé où il avait emménagé lorsque sa popularité à Aldeburgh prit de trop grandes proportions. Parmi les 14 opéras qui suivirent *Peter Grimes*, dix furent écrits pour des ensembles de chambre que lui avait inspiré Aldeburgh ; seuls deux eurent leur première à Covent Garden. Cela ressemblait bien à Britten. Ce n'était pas un homme à l'allure de vedette, ni à vouloir se montrer en public : même lorsqu'il devait avoir affaire au public, comme pour la première représentation à Coventry du *War Requiem*, il s'arrangea toujours pour qu'on ne le voit pas trop, et se mêlait alors aux musiciens.

Quant à la technique musicale, la pure connaissance de savoir comment produire un son, Britten savait tout – jusqu'à quel doigt il fallait mettre sur quelle corde. En partie, c'était la conséquence de ses compétences d'artiste : comme pianiste on pouvait le comparer à Sviatoslav Richter ou Clifford Curzon, et comme accompagnateur, personne ne pouvait rivaliser avec lui. Son interprétation de Schubert était d'une beauté attendrissante, particulièrement lorsqu'il jouait pour Peter Pears, son ami de toujours et partenaire, pour qui il écrivit pratiquement tous ses rôles de ténor, des chants folkloriques, les nombreux cycles de chants.

« Notre brillant Ben » comme l'appelait Rostropovitch, et Britten était réellement un artiste complet. A Aldeburgh, il était aussi merveilleux au festival avec les invités internationaux qu'avec les amateurs, ou bien les œuvres auxquelles des enfants prenaient part, par exemple, *Let's Make an Opera* ou encore *Noye's Fludde* – souvent il rapprochait de façon touchante ces deux catégories lors d'une représentation. Il était agréable de travailler avec lui, mais, ce qui est plus important, qu'il s'agisse du compositeur, du chef d'orchestre, du pianiste, ou simplement d'une présence musicale, il était une source d'inspiration partout où il allait.

Benjamin Britten at the Royal Festival Hall, 23 October 1965, for the rehearsal of his cantata *Voices for Today*. He is holding the score of the work, which was written for the 20th anniversary of the United Nations and performed simultaneously in New York, Paris and London on 26 October.

Benjamin Britten in der Royal Festival Hall bei den Proben zu seiner Kantate *Voices for Today*, 23. Oktober 1965. In den Händen hält er die Partitur, die er zum 20jährigen Bestehen der United Nations schrieb. Am 26. Oktober 1965 wurde das Werk in New York, Paris und London gleichzeitig uraufgeführt.

Benjamin Britten au Royal Festival Hall à Londres le 23 octobre 1965, lors de la répétition de sa cantate *Voices for Today*. Il tient à la main la partition de l'œuvre écrite pour le 20e anniversaire des Nations unies, et jouée simultanément à New York, Paris et Londres le 26 octobre.

Britten's *War Requiem* was written to celebrate the consecration of the new cathedral at Coventry, designed by Sir Basil Spence to replace the Gothic building destroyed by enemy action in 1941. The opportunity was deliberately taken for a grand gesture of reconciliation and the three soloists for whom Britten wrote his work were the Russian soprano Galina Vishnevskaya, the German baritone Dietrich Fischer-Dieskau and the English tenor Peter Pears. In the event Vishnevskaya was discouraged from appearing by the Soviet authorities, and her place was taken by the English soprano Heather Harper (5, seen sitting with the composer). Auerbach was the only photographer admitted to the final rehearsal on 29 May 1962. Here (1) he caught a moment of consultation between the composer (who conducted the Melos Ensemble, on whom he has just turned his back) and the conductor Meredith Davies, who directed the City of Birmingham Symphony Orchestra and the Coventry Festival Chorus (seen beyond him, beneath Graham Sutherland's immense tapestry of Christ in Majesty). For the recording of the *War Requiem* Vishnevskaya was given permission to sing the soprano part. She and the composer are evidently pleased with the result (2, 3, Kingsway Hall, 3 January 1963). (4) It was obviously a typical English summer's day on 29 May. Peter Pears rehearses in his greatcoat, while Fischer-Dieskau, behind him, awaits his turn huddled against the cold.

Britten schrieb sein *War Requiem* für die Einweihungszeremonie der neuen, von Sir Basil Spence entworfenen Kathedrale in Coventry, nachdem der alte gotische Bau 1941 den Luftangriffen zum Opfer gefallen war. Die Gelegenheit wurde entschlossen zu einer großen Geste der Versöhnung genutzt. Britten hatte das Werk für die russische Sopranistin Galina Wischnewskaja, den deutschen Bariton Dietrich Fischer-Dieskau und den englischen Tenor Peter Pears geschrieben. Die sowjetischen Autoritäten untersagten der Wischnewskaja jedoch die Teilnahme an dem Ereignis, und ihr Part wurde von der englischen Sopranistin Heather Harper gesungen, die man hier (5) mit dem Komponisten zusammensitzen sieht. Auerbach war der einzige Fotograf, der zu der Generalprobe am 29. Mai 1962 Zutritt hatte. Hier (1) konnte er einen kurzen Moment der Beratung festhalten zwischen dem Komponisten (der das Melos Ensemble dirigiert, dem er gerade den Rücken zuwendet) und dem Dirigenten Meredith Davies, der das City of Birmingham Orchestra und den Coventry Festival Chorus dirigiert (das im Hintergrund zu sehen ist, unter Graham Sutherlands riesigem Wandteppich, der Christus als Weltenherrscher zeigt). Bei den Platteneinspielungen des *War Requiems* durfte die Wischnewskaja dann ihren Sopranpart singen. (2, 3) Kingsway Hall, 3. Januar 1963: Sie und der Komponist sind mit dem Ergebnis sichtlich zufrieden. (4) Der 29. Mai war offenbar ein typisch englischer Sommertag. Peter Pears probt in seinem Mantel, und Dietrich Fischer-Dieskau wartet fröstelnd auf seinen Einsatz.

Le *War Requiem* de Britten fut écrit pour fêter la consécration de la nouvelle cathédrale de Coventry, conçue par Sir Basil Spence pour remplacer le bâtiment gothique détruit par l'attaque ennemie en 1941. On profita à dessein de cette occasion pour faire un geste de réconciliation, et les trois solistes pour qui Britten écrivit cette œuvre, furent la soprano russe Galina Vishnevskaya, le baryton allemand Dietrich Fischer-Dieskau et le ténor anglais Peter Pears. En l'occurrence, Vishnevskaya se laissa décourager par les autorités soviétiques, et fut remplacée par la soprano anglaise Heather Harper (5, assise avec le compositeur). Auerbach fut le seul photographe à être admis à la répétition générale du 29 mai 1962. Ici (1), il photographia le compositeur (qui dirigeait l'Ensemble Melos, auquel il venait juste de tourner le dos) en consultation avec le chef d'orchestre Meredith Davies qui dirigeait le City of Birmingham Symphony Orchestra et le Coventry Festival Chorus. (Derrière lui, on voit l'immense tapisserie du Christ en Majesté de Graham Sutherland). Pour l'enregistrement du *War Requiem*, Vishnevskaya fut autorisée à chanter le rôle de soprano. Elle est, ainsi que le compositeur, manifestement satisfaite du résultat (2, 3, Kingsway Hall, le 3 janvier 1963). (4) De toute évidence, c'était un typique été anglais, en ce 29 mai. Peter Pears répète avec son pardessus, pendant que derrière lui, Fischer-Dieskau, recroquevillé par le froid, attend son tour.

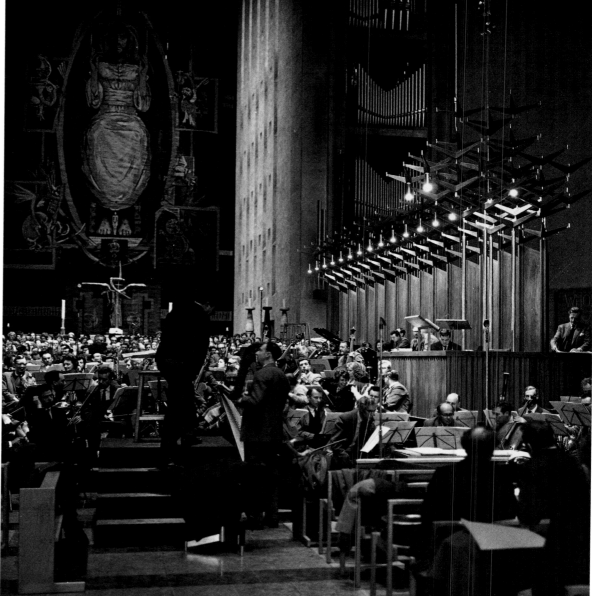

1

2

3

4

5

Britten and Mstislav Rostropovitch rehearsing the *Cello Sonata* in the composer's music room at Aldeburgh, 1 July 1961. Rostropovitch's wife, Galina Vishnevskaya, and the Swiss conductor and musical Maecenas Paul Sacher are among those listening.
'I learnt the sonata at one go,' wrote Rostropovitch. 'On 5 March 1961, on my way to South America, I called on Benjamin Britten in London to play [it] together with him. Our meeting took place in Peter Pears's flat. For some reason I was terribly excited. Fifteen minutes passed after I entered the tiny room with the piano, then twenty, but still I was afraid to begin playing. I took a long time settling down with my cello. I took still longer in preparing my instrument and music. It appeared to me that Britten was also in not too much of a hurry. Drinks were served. 'Let's have a drink, maybe it'll go easier,' the composer said. I was so excited I could not even tell how we played. I only noticed that we came to the end of the first movement at the same time. I jumped up, hopped over the cello, and rushed to the composer to embrace him in a burst of spontaneous gratefulness.'

Britten und Mstislaw Rostropowitsch beim Proben der *Sonate für Cello und Klavier* im Musikraum des Komponisten in seinem Haus in Aldeburgh am 1. Juli 1961. Auch Galina Wischnewskaja, die Gattin von Rostropowitsch, und der Schweizer Dirigent und Mäzen Paul Sacher sind unter den Zuhörern.
„Ich lernte die Sonate in einem Zug", schrieb Rostropowitsch. „Am 5. März 1961, auf meinem Weg nach Südamerika, verabredete ich mich mit Benjamin Britten in London, um sie mit ihm zu spielen. Wir trafen uns in der Wohnung von Peter Pears. Aus irgendeinem Grund war ich furchtbar aufgeregt. Nachdem ich den winzigen Raum mit dem Klavier betreten hatte, vergingen fünfzehn Minuten, zwanzig Minuten, und ich konnte immer noch nicht anfangen zu spielen. Ich ließ mir viel Zeit dabei, mich mit meinem Cello einzurichten und brauchte noch einmal so lange, um es zu stimmen und mich vorzubereiten. Mir schien, Britten hatte es auch nicht allzu eilig. Getränke wurden serviert. ‚Lassen Sie uns etwas trinken, vielleicht geht es dann leichter', sagte der Komponist. Ich war so aufgeregt, ich könnte überhaupt nicht sagen, wie wir gespielt haben. Ich merkte nur, daß wir gleichzeitig das Ende des ersten Satzes erreichten. Da sprang ich auf, hüpfte über mein Cello und umarmte den Komponisten in einer spontanen Aufwallung von Dankbarkeit."

Britten et Mstislav Rostropovitch répétant la *Sonate pour violoncelle et piano* dans la salle de musique du compositeur à Aldeburgh, le 1er juillet 1961. La femme de Rostropovitch, Galina Vishnevskaya, et le chef d'orchestre suisse et mécène de la musique, Paul Sacher, sont parmi ceux qui écoutent. « J'ai appris la sonate en une seule fois, » écrivit Rostropovitch. « Le 5 mars 1961, alors que je me rendais en Amérique du Sud, je suis allé voir Benjamin Britten à Londres afin de [la] jouer avec lui. Nous nous sommes retrouvés dans l'appartement de Peter Pears. Pour une raison ou une autre, j'étais terriblement agité. Quinze minutes ont passé avant que je n'entre dans la petite pièce où se trouvait le piano, puis vingt autres, mais même, j'avais peur de commencer à jouer. J'ai mis beaucoup de temps avant de m'installer avec mon violoncelle. J'ai mis encore plus de temps à préparer mon instrument et la musique. Il me semblait aussi que Britten n'était pas trop pressé. On nous a servi à boire. ‹ Buvons un verre, cela ira peut-être mieux ›, m'a alors dit le compositeur. J'étais tellement agité que je ne pourrais pas dire comment nous avons joué. J'ai seulement remarqué que nous sommes arrivés en même temps à la fin du premier mouvement. Je me suis levé d'un bond, par-delà le violoncelle, et je me suis précipité sur le compositeur pour l'étreindre dans un élan de gratitude spontanée. »

Britten loved fast cars, and the open-topped Alvis was an important ▶
feature of life at Aldeburgh. Here is the composer at the wheel,
outside the front door of the Red House, with Vishnevskaya,
Rostropovitch and the cello as passengers, while Peter Pears looks on.

Britten liebte schnelle Wagen, und sein Alvis-Kabriolet war in
Aldeburgh allen bekannt. Hier sitzt der Komponist am Steuer seines Wagens vor der Eingangstür des Red House mit der
Wischnewskaja, Rostropowitsch und dem Cello. Peter Pears schaut
zu.

Britten adorait les voitures rapides, et son Alvis décapotable fut un
trait important de sa vie à Aldeburgh. Il est ici au volant de cette
voiture devant l'entrée principale de la Red House, avec comme
passagers, Vishnevskaya, Rostropovitch et le violoncelle, sous le
regard de Peter Pears.

JOHN CAGE   1912-1992

'Nothing is accomplished by writing a piece of music', wrote the American John Cage in 1952 – and immediately added 'hearing' and 'playing' as equal alternatives to 'writing'. It was in the same year that he produced his most notorious composition, *4'33"*, for any combination of instruments, in which the players sit in total silence for the duration of the piece and the performance is made up of any sounds that are incidentally produced in or outside the concert hall.

It is difficult to apply the term 'composition' to such activities, and there are many who do not, preferring to write Cage off as a charlatan and a publicist. (They usually add that he was an expert on wild mushrooms – which is actually true, as also was his addiction to games such as bridge, poker and Scrabble.) But the charlatan label does not really cover the facts. As a pupil of Schoenberg and the American experimental composer Henry Cowell, his purely musical credentials were excellent, and the works he produced during the first 40 years of his life, though always avant-garde, were certainly 'compositions'. Many of them were designed for Cowell's invention, the 'prepared piano' (in which bolts, hatpins, elastic bands and various other articles of ironmongery or haberdashery were inserted between the strings to alter the timbre and create new percussive effects), and some included electronic sound: a Guggenheim award in 1949 praised him for 'having thus extended the boundaries of musical art'.

His involvement with Zen Buddhism and other Eastern philosophies, however, brought about a change in his attitude to composition, and during the 1950s he became interested in the element of chance in artistic creation, with the composer relinquishing control over the eventual realization of his work. It was at this point, when the philosopher began to take over from the traditional role of the composer and extramusical concepts more and more determined the resulting performances, that Cage's influence on Stockhausen and much avant-garde musical thinking reached its zenith. But the idea that all distinctions between life and art should be broken down, and that it was the composer's job to use any means at his disposal to make his audience more aware of the world in which they were living, was not an easy one for people in whose experience 'art' was something which happened in a specific place that you went to at a specific time, and which you either enjoyed or didn't according to specific criteria. In most of Cage's 'compositions' it seemed that the real composers were God, the audience and the traffic outside.

Cage himself regarded *4'33"* as his most significant composition and followed it up ten years later with *0' 00" (4'33" No. 2)*, to be performed in any way, by anyone – presumably in no time flat. But not necessarily in silence: in his own performance he cleaned and sliced vegetables, put them in an electric blender and drank the resulting juice – the sounds produced being amplified electronically to the audience. Cage was a man of enormous charm as well as compelling personality: no question that his activities were influential one way or another, but with the best will in the world (and that is not always available to Cage) it is difficult not to wonder whether sometimes he may have felt unable to resist just a tweak at the musical establishment's rather complacent leg?

„Hat man ein Musikstück geschrieben, ist noch nichts getan", schrieb der Amerikaner John Cage 1952 – und stellte das „Hören" und das „Spielen" damit als gleichwertige Komponenten neben das „Schreiben". Im selben Jahr komponierte er sein berühmtestes Stück *4'33"*, ohne dafür eine bestimmte Besetzung vorzuschreiben. Die Musiker verharren während der gesamten Dauer des Stückes in vollkommenem Schweigen, und die Aufführung besteht aus den Geräuschen, die im Konzertsaal oder draußen zufällig entstehen.

Es fällt nicht ganz leicht, das als „Komposition" zu bezeichnen, viele tun es auch nicht und bezeichnen Cage eher als einen Scharlatan und Effekthascher. (Meistens erwähnen sie dabei noch, er sei ein ausgezeichneter Pilzkenner gewesen – was auch zutraf; zudem kannte man ihn als leidenschaftlichen Bridge-, Poker- und Scrabblespieler.) Der Vorwurf der Scharlatanerie trifft ihn jedoch zu Unrecht. Als Schüler Schönbergs und des amerikanischen Komponisten experimenteller Musik Henry Cowell brachte er ausgezeichnetes musikalisches Rüstzeug mit, und alle Werke, die er in 40 Jahren seines Lebens komponierte, waren zwar avantgardistisch, aber gewiß immer „Kompositionen". Er schrieb viele Stücke für Cowells Erfindung, das „präparierte Klavier" (bei dem Klammern, Hutnadeln, Gummibänder und verschiedene andere Artikel aus Eisenwarenhandlungen oder einem Kurzwarengeschäft in das Instrument eingeführt werden, die den Klang und die Wirkung des Anschlags verändern). Manchmal arbeitete er auch mit elektronischen Klängen. 1949 erhielt er dafür einen Guggenheim Preis, weil er „auf diese Weise die Grenzen der Musik erweitert hat."

Seine Beschäftigung mit dem Zen Buddhismus und anderen fernöstlichen Philosophien veränderten jedoch sein kompositorisches Konzept. In den 50er Jahren interessierte ihn das Element des Zufalls im kreativen Prozeß. Der Künstler gab die Kontrolle über die Endform seines Werkes auf. In dieser Phase, als der Philosoph an die Stelle des traditionellen Komponisten getreten war und außermusikalische Konzepte die Aufführungen immer stärker bestimmten, erreichte Cages Einfluß auf Stockhausen und die avantgardistische Musiktheorie seinen Höhepunkt. Die Vorstellung, daß alle Grenzen zwischen Kunst und Leben aufgehoben werden sollten und daß der Komponist alle verfügbaren Mittel nutzen sollte, dem Publikum die Welt, in der er lebte, ins Bewußtsein zu bringen, fand keine positive Resonanz bei jenen, nach deren Erfahrung „Kunst" etwas war, das zu bestimmten Zeiten an besonderen Orten stattfand – und das man dann an Hand bestimmter Kriterien genoß oder eben nicht. In vielen von Cages „Kompositionen" scheinen Gott, das Publikum und der Straßenverkehr die wirklichen Komponisten gewesen zu sein.

Cage betrachtete *4'33"* als seine bedeutendste Komposition, und zehn Jahre später folgte ihr die Komposition *0'00" (4'33" Nr. 2)*, zur Aufführung auf jede Weise, von jedermann und zu keiner bestimmten Zeit – jedoch nicht notwendigerweise schweigend: Bei seiner eigenen Uraufführung putzte und schnitt der Künstler Gemüse, füllte die Stücke in einen elektrischen Mixer und trank den Saft – die entstehenden Geräusche wurden dem Publikum elektronisch verstärkt übermittelt. Cage verfügte über unglaublichen Charme, und er war eine überzeugende Persönlichkeit: Seine Aktivitäten mußten irgendeinen Einfluß haben. Selbst mit dem besten Willen jedoch (und den hatte Cage nicht immer auf seiner Seite) fragt man sich manchmal, ob er sich nicht gelegentlich doch dazu hinreißen ließ, die etablierte Musikszene einfach aufs Glatteis zu führen.

« On n'a encore rien fait quand on a écrit un morceau de musique », note l'Américain John Cage en 1952 – en ajoutant immédiatement qu'« entendre » et « jouer » sont des éléments de même valeur qu'« écrire ». Ce fut cette année-là qu'il produisit sa composition la plus célèbre, *4'33"*, jouée avec n'importe quelle combinaison d'instruments. Pendant toute la durée du morceau, les joueurs restent assis dans un silence total, et tout bruit provoqué accidentellement dans la salle de concert ou à l'extérieur, sera la musique de la représentation.

Il est difficile d'appliquer le terme de « composition » à de telles activités, et beaucoup refusent de le faire, préférant qualifier péjorativement John Cage de charlatan qui aime la publicité. (Ils ajoutent souvent qu'il était expert en champignons – ce qui d'ailleurs est vrai, mentionnant également son grand penchant pour les jeux tels que le bridge, le poker et le Scrabble.) Mais il serait quand même injuste de lui coller cette étiquette de charlatan. Élève de Schoenberg et du compositeur innovateur américain Henry Cowell, ses références purement musicales étaient excellentes, et les œuvres qu'il produisit pendant les quarante premières années de sa vie, malgré leur côté toujours d'avant-garde, étaient à n'en pas douter des compositions. Beaucoup furent créées pour l'invention de Cowell, le « piano préparé » (dans lequel on avait inséré entre les cordes, des boulons, des épingles à chapeau, des élastiques et différents articles de quincaillerie ou de mercerie, afin de créer de nouveaux effets percutants). D'autres œuvres contenaient des sons électroniques : il reçut en 1949 le prix Guggenheim pour « avoir ainsi repoussé les limites de la musique. »

Son engagement dans le boudhisme zen et autres philosophies orientales, changea son attitude envers la composition. Pendant les années 50, il s'intéressa au facteur chance dans le domaine de la création artistique dont le compositeur renoncerait à tout contrôle sur ce qui allait devenir sa composition. Dès le moment où le philosophe prit la relève sur le compositeur traditionnel, et que des concepts extra-musicaux définirent la musique des représentations, l'influence de Cage sur Stockhausen et sur la pensée de la musique d'avant-garde atteignit son apogée. L'idée que toute distinction entre la vie et l'art devait disparaître, et que le travail du compositeur était d'utiliser tous les moyens disponibles pour rendre le public conscient du monde dans lequel il vit, n'était pas chose aisée pour des gens qui voyaient l'art comme un événement qui devait avoir lieu dans un endroit bien spécifique, à une heure donnée, et que l'on aimait ou pas selon des critères, eux aussi, bien définis. Dans la plupart des « œuvres » de Cage, on aurait dit que les vrais compositeurs n'étaient autres que Dieu, le public et ce qui passe dehors.

Cage considérait *4'33"* comme la plus importante de ses œuvres. Une autre allait suivre dix ans plus tard, *0'00" (4'33" n° 2)*, qui devait être exécutée par qui voulait, pas nécessairement en silence, mais doucement quand-même : il lavait alors des légumes qu'il coupait ensuite pour les passer dans un mixer électrique ; puis il buvait le jus obtenu – les bruits étaient amplifiés électroniquement pour l'audience. Cage avait beaucoup de charme et sa personnalité était irrésistible : on ne peut dénier son influence d'une façon ou d'une autre, mais avec la meilleure volonté du monde (et Cage ne l'avait pas forcément de son côté), il est difficile de ne pas se demander , si parfois, il n'a pas tout simplement succombé à la tentation de taquiner l'institution plutôt honorable de la musique.

John Cage charming, 22 May 1972.
John Cage bezaubert, 22. Mai 1972.
John Cage, charmant, le 22 mai 1972.

AARON COPLAND   1900-1990

For most Europeans in the first half of the 20th century American music meant on the one hand ragtime and jazz, on the other the American musical, with Gershwin the only figure laying claim to concert-hall status. No one east of the Atlantic knew much about the rather dreary succession of 'minor' composers turning out pallid reflections of the German Romantic tradition (though it is true that MacDowell's *Woodland Sketches* and *New England Idyls* graced many an English drawing-room in the early years of this century), and the one figure who might have shattered that indifference, Charles Ives, remained virtually unknown in Europe until after the Second World War.

It was out of this background that Aaron Copland emerged, the first 'serious' composer to be accepted by the rest of the world as recognizably American. His parents were Russian Jewish émigrés, and he got away from America as soon as he could to study with the great composition teacher Nadia Boulanger in Paris. When he returned to the States four years later, transformed by contact with all that was new and radical in the European music of the 1920s, the extreme dissonance of his music did not find favour with the old guard: at the first performance of his *First Symphony* (which incorporated a resounding organ part for Boulanger to play at her American début as organist), the conductor, Walter Damrosch, swung round to the audience at the end of the work and said: 'If a young man at the age of 23 can write a symphony like that, in five years he will be ready to commit murder.'

But he wasn't. After the *First Symphony*, feeling that the European influence in his music had become too strong, Copland deliberately set about looking for more American ingredients, particularly jazz – though his use of it did not necessarily make his work any less dissonant and the music from this period remains obstinately austere. In the end what created the real Copland style was his awareness of the gulf that was gradually widening between the contemporary composer and the ordinary musical public, and the need to simplify and clarify his harmonic idiom in order to bridge it. He made brilliant and peculiarly personal use of borrowed tunes as well, and out of this new accessibility sprang the ballets that turned him into a popular composer and a powerful American influence – *Billy the Kid*, *Rodeo* and *Appalachian Spring* – as well as more purely orchestral works like the *Third Symphony*.

That was written in 1946, and the 1940s was the period of Copland's music that most people remember today. The works he wrote in later years are once again austere and have not achieved the popular success of their predecessors. For a composer of Copland's integrity and strength of purpose this was a necessary step in the pursuit of his inner vision, though the lack of success worried many of his American admirers. But his reputation as a teacher, educator and encourager of the young never lessened: he was a tireless promoter of American music, and in later years spent more time touring the world as a conductor and musical ambassador than he did in composition. Yet the immense number of honours and tributes that flooded in as the years continued to pass proved that the beautifully judged simplicity and originality of his best works were not forgotten by the people for whom they were written.

Aaron Copland rehearsing, 9 February 1962.

Aaron Copland beim Proben, 9. Februar 1962.

Aaron Copland en pleine répétition, le 9 février 1962.

In der ersten Hälfte des 20. Jahrhunderts dachten Europäer bei amerikanischer Musik einerseits an Ragtime und Jazz, andererseits an das amerikanische Musical. Gershwin war der einzige, der Eingang in die Konzerthallen fand. Östlich des Atlantiks hatte niemand je etwas von jener Reihe „weniger bedeutender" Komponisten gehört, die als eher schwaches Echo der deutschen Romantik galten (und dies, obwohl MacDowells Waldlandschaften und Neu-England-Idyllen zu Beginn des Jahrhunderts viele englische Wohnzimmer zierten). Charles Ives, der einzige, der diese Mauer der Ignoranz hätte durchbrechen können, blieb bis nach dem Zweiten Weltkrieg in Europa ein Unbekannter.

Vor diesem historischen Hintergrund taucht Aaron Copland in Europa als der erste „ernste" amerikanische Komponist auf. Seine Eltern waren ausgewanderte russische Juden, und sobald er konnte, ging Copland nach Paris, um bei der großen Kompositionslehrerin Nadia Boulanger zu studieren. Als er vier Jahre später in die Staaten zurückkehrte, hatte ihn die Begegnung mit der neuen und radikalen europäischen Musik der 20er Jahre verändert. Die extremen Dissonanzen seiner Musik fanden keinen Beifall: nach der Aufführung seiner *Ersten Symphonie* (mit einer klangvollen Orgelpartie für das amerikanische Debüt der Boulanger) sagte der Dirigent Walter Damrosch am Ende zum Publikum gewandt: „Ein junger Mann, der mit 25 Jahren eine solche Symphonie schreibt, wird in fünf Jahren bereit für einen Mord sein."

Dazu kam es nicht. Nach dieser ersten Symphonie fühlte Copland, daß der europäische Einfluß in seiner Musik zu stark geworden war, und experimentierte mit musikalischen Formen, die eher in Amerika zu Hause waren – besonders mit dem Jazz. Seine Werke verloren dadurch nicht unbedingt ihre Dissonanz, und seine Musik aus dieser Phase behält eine eigenwillige Strenge. Sein eigentlicher Stil entwickelte sich schließlich aus dem Bewußtsein der stetig wachsenden Distanz zwischen den zeitgenössischen Komponisten und dem durchschnittlichen Auditorium. Um diese Distanz zu überbrücken, mußte sein musikalisches Idiom schlichter und harmonischer werden. Auf brillante und eigentümliche Weise verarbeitete er auch fremde Melodien. Aus diesem neuen Ansatz entwickelten sich die Ballettmusiken, mit denen ihm der Durchbruch gelang. Mit *Billy the Kid*, *Rodeo* und *Appalachian Spring* brachte er einen kraftvollen amerikanischen Einfluß in die Musik, aber er schuf auch ausschließlich orchestrale Werke wie die 1946 entstandene *Dritte Symphonie*.

All diese Stücke, die noch heute zu seinen bekanntesten zählen, schrieb Copland in den 40er Jahren. Seine späteren Werke kehrten zu der ursprünglichen Strenge zurück und erreichten nie mehr vergleichbare Erfolge. Für einen Komponisten mit der künstlerischen Integrität und Entschiedenheit Coplands bedeutete dies einen notwendigen Schritt auf dem Weg zur Verwirklichung seiner Vision, obwohl der ausbleibende Erfolg viele seiner amerikanischen Bewunderer beunruhigte. Sein Ruf als Lehrer und Unterstützer der jüngeren Generation wurde davon jedoch niemals beeinträchtigt: Er blieb ein unermüdlicher Förderer der amerikanischen Musik. In seinen späteren Jahren verbrachte er mehr Zeit als Dirigent und musikalischer Botschafter auf seinen Tourneen in aller Welt als mit seinen Kompositionen. Die vielen Ehrungen und Auszeichnungen, die ihm im Laufe der Zeit zuteil wurden, bewiesen, daß die wunderbar maßvolle Schlichtheit und Originalität seiner besten Werke von seinem Publikum niemals vergessen wurden.

Pour la plupart de Européens de la première moitié du XXe siècle, la musique américaine était, d'un côté le ragtime et le jazz, et de l'autre les comédies musicales américaines avec Gershwin, le seul à pouvoir prétendre à un certain prestige dans des salles de concert. Pratiquement tout le monde, de ce côté de l'Atlantique ignorait la série plutôt morne des compositeurs « secondaires » aux œuvres pâles qui suivent la tradition romantique allemande (pourtant on ne peut nier que les paysages forestiers et ceux idylliques de Nouvelle-Angleterre de MacDowells aient embelli de nombreux salons anglais au début de notre siècle), et la seule personne qui aurait pu briser cette indifférence, Charles Ives, resta presque totalement inconnue en Europe jusqu'après la Deuxième Guerre mondiale.

Aaron Copland a réussi à sortir de ce milieu, premier compositeur « sérieux » venu d'Amérique à être accepté par le reste du monde. Ses parents étaient des émigrés juifs russes. Il quitta l'Amérique pour Paris aussi vite que possible afin d'étudier avec le grand professeur de composition musicale Nadia Boulanger. Après quatre ans de contact étroit avec tout ce qui était nouveau et radical dans la musique européenne des années 20, il s'en retournera transformé aux États-Unis : Cependant, l'extrême discordance de sa musique ne fut pas appréciée par un public qui était plus traditionaliste : à la fin de la première représentation de sa *Première Symphonie* (Boulanger, qui se voulait organiste à ses débuts sur les scènes américaines, joua un morceau d'orgue tonitruant), le chef d'orchestre, Walter Damrosch, se tourna vers le public et dit : « Si un homme de 23 ans est capable d'écrire une telle symphonie, dans cinq ans, il sera bon pour commettre un meurtre. »

Mais cela n'arriva pas. Après la *Première Symphonie*, Copland comprit que l'Europe avait trop fortement influencé sa musique. Il se mit alors à la recherche d'éléments plus américains, en particulier le jazz – bien que sa façon de s'en servir n'ait pas adouci sa musique, et ses compositions de cette période restèrent obstinément austères. En fin de compte, son style se précisa, d'une part quand il prit conscience de l'abîme qui allait en s'élargissant, entre le compositeur moderne et le public ordinaire, et d'autre part lorsqu'il réalisa qu'il fallait impérativement, pour combler cet abîme, simplifier et clarifier son idée de l'harmonie. Il emprunta aussi des airs qu'il saura brillamment arranger, et de cette nouvelle idée naquirent des ballets qui le rendirent populaire et firent de lui une figure américaine influente – *Billy the Kid*, *Rodeo*, et *Appalachian Spring* ; il créa également des œuvres purement orchestrales, comme la *Troisième Symphonie*.

Celle-ci fut écrite en 1946, et la musique des années 40 de Copland est celle dont se souviennent aujourd'hui la plupart des gens. Les œuvres qu'il composa plus tard redevinrent austères et n'acquièrent pas le succès des œuvres précédentes. Mais pour un compositeur comme Copland, intègre et résolu, il était important de suivre ses propres idées, quoique le manque de succès ait fini par inquiéter ses admirateurs d'outre-Atlantique. Cependant, sa réputation de professeur, d'éducateur qui savait aiguillonner les jeunes n'en souffrit jamais : infatigable promoteur de la musique américaine, il passa, plus tard dans sa vie, plus de temps à faire des tournées dans le monde comme chef d'orchestre et comme ambassadeur de la musique, qu'à composer. Toutefois, les maints honneurs et hommages qui lui furent rendus au fil des années, montrent bien que la simplicité et l'originalité très appréciées de ses meilleures œuvres ne furent pas oubliées par ceux pour qui elles furent composées.

Aaron Copland rehearsing, 9 February 1962.
Aaron Copland beim Proben, 9. Februar 1962.
Aaron Copland en pleine répétition, le 9 février 1962.

Rehearsing in a television studio, 27 October 1965 –
characteristically warm and friendly studies of Copland.

Probe im Fernsehstudio, 27. Oktober 1965 – die Fotos zeigen
Coplands typisch warmherzige und freundliche Art.

Répétition dans un studio de télévision le 27 octobre 1965 –
comme on peut s'y attendre, une étude chaleureuse et affectueuse
de Copland.

It seems unlikely, somehow, that it should have been a Gilbert and Sullivan operetta at the age of four which first aroused the composer in Peter Maxwell Davies. Certainly he moved on from Sullivan fairly quickly, though until he went to the Manchester College of Music in 1952 he was more or less self-taught – and even then he was slung out of the regular composition classes after a few weeks. Nevertheless it was at Manchester that he was first able to meet and exchange ideas with other young musicians, among them the composers Harrison Birtwistle and Alexander Goehr and the pianist John Ogdon. Together they formed the Manchester New Music Group, to study and perform the then unknown music of the European avant-garde and to produce experimental compositions of their own.

Where Maxwell Davies always differed from his Manchester colleagues was in his interest in early music and plainsong. It was an interest that ran through every area of his work, from the carol sequence *O magnum mysterium*, written for the children of Cirencester Grammar School where he was director of music in the early 1960s, to the choral-orchestral *Veni Sancte Spiritus* of 1964, and the two orchestral *Taverner Fantasias* which preceded the full-scale opera *Taverner*, eventually given at Covent Garden in 1972. But it is in no way a romantic or nostalgic interest: as Davies said, 'I just wanted to learn what I could from those composers and from plainsong. I could see in it so many pointers to large-scale design... there was some kind of instinctive complete sense of the rightness of it.'

If there is any nostalgia in his music it is to be found in the foxtrots and camped-up jazz that recall the 1920s, especially in the many works for music theatre that he wrote for his own performing group, the Fires of London. But certainly neither 1920s dance tunes nor medieval structures preclude ruthlessly progressive, often freakish, musical results in the works of the late 60s, as is made abundantly clear in semi-dramatic pieces like *Revelation and Fall* (where the hard-tried soprano eventually has recourse to a loud-hailer) or *Eight Songs for a Mad King*.

But there are other sides to Maxwell Davies's activities as a composer. Like Britten, he has written a number of pieces for specific, sometimes social, occasions, and he has always enjoyed working with children; this has become more and more the case since he made his home on the remote island of Hoy in the Orkneys, where he founded the St Magnus Festival at Kirkwall in 1977. It can hardly be coincidence that at about this time the more violent gestures of his earlier music begin to soften, and a more reflective, lyrical quality pervades the compositions – now often flaunting the more traditional titles of Symphony or Concerto.

Not that Maxwell Davies's later music can be called by any stretch of the imagination 'easy listening' – but then he wouldn't want that. It may not be as disturbing as it was, or as complex, but it remains commandingly austere, and the vitality and originality of his creative impulse, even in the tranquillity of his Orcadian solitude, are still as piercing and unexpected as ever.

Es klingt nicht sehr glaubhaft, daß es eine Operette von Gilbert und Sullivan gewesen sein soll, die in Peter Maxwell Davies im Alter von vier Jahren den Komponisten erweckte. Sicher ist, daß er sich sehr schnell von Sullivan entfernt hat. 1952 trat er schließlich in das Manchester College of Music ein. Bis dahin war er mehr oder weniger Autodidakt – und selbst am College wurde er nach wenigen Wochen aus der regulären Kompositionsklasse ausgeschlossen. In Manchester lernte er dann aber doch zum ersten Mal andere junge Musiker kennen, mit denen er seine Gedanken austauschen konnte. Zu ihnen gehörten auch die Komponisten Harrison Birtwistle und Alexander Goehr und der Pianist John Ogdon. Gemeinsam gründeten sie die Manchester New Music Group, um die bisher unbekannte Musik der europäischen Avantgarde zu studieren und aufzuführen. Die Gruppe war auch das Forum für ihre eigenen experimentellen Kompositionen.

Maxwell Davies unterschied sich von seinen Kollegen in Manchester von Anfang an durch sein Interesse an alter Musik und am Gregorianischen Gesang. Dieses Interesse begleitet alle Phasen seines Schaffens, angefangen von dem Weihnachtsliederzyklus *O magnum mysterium*, den er für die Kinder der Cirencester Grammar School schrieb, an der er in den frühen 60er Jahren als Musikdirektor tätig war, über das *Veni Sancte Spiritus* für Chor und Orchester von 1964 bis zu den beiden Orchesterwerken *Taverner Phantasien*, gefolgt von der vollständigen Oper *Taverner*, die 1972 in Covent Garden aufgeführt wurde. Davies' Auseinandersetzung mit der alten Musik war weder nostalgisch noch romantisch motiviert. Er selbst sagt: „Ich wollte von den alten Komponisten und vom Gregorianischen Gesang so viel wie möglich lernen. Ich fand darin so viele Ansätze zu großen Kompositionen ... ich fühlte darin etwas zutiefst Richtiges."

Wenn es in seiner Musik nostalgische Elemente gibt, dann sind es die Foxtrots und die Jazzstücke, mit denen er die 20er Jahre wieder aufleben läßt. Das gilt besonders für die vielen Musiktheaterstücke, die er für sein eigenes Ensemble Fires of London schrieb. Weder die Tanzmusik der 20er Jahre noch die mittelalterlichen Musikformen konnten ihn jedoch von seinen rückhaltlos progressiven und oft auch befremdlichen musikalischen Werken der späten 60er Jahre abhalten. Die halb dramatischen Stücke *Revelation and Fall* (wo der strapazierte Sopran schließlich auf das Megaphon zurückgreift) oder *Eight Songs for a Mad King* liefern den überzeugenden Beweis.

Der Komponist Maxwell Davies hat jedoch auch ganz andere Seiten. Ebenso wie Britten schrieb er eine ganze Reihe von Stücken zu bestimmten Anlässen oder sozialen Ereignissen, und er hat immer gerne mit Kindern gearbeitet. Nachdem er sich auf die stille Orkney-Insel Hoy zurückgezogen hatte, wo er 1977 in Kirkwall das St. Magnus Festival ins Leben rief, wurde diese Neigung immer stärker. Es wird kaum ein Zufall sein, daß gerade zu dieser Zeit die heftigeren, provozierenden Gesten in seiner Musik zurücktraten und eine zunehmend reflektiertere, poetische Qualität in den Kompositionen dominierte. Seinen neueren Werken gab er immer öfter traditionelle Bezeichnungen wie Symphonie und Konzert.

Maxwell Davies Spätwerk ist ganz und gar keine „leichte" Musik – das lag auch nicht in seiner Absicht. Es irritiert vielleicht nicht mehr so sehr, ist weniger komplex, aber es bleibt von herausfordernder Strenge. Selbst in der Stille seiner Orkadischen Einsamkeit bleiben die Vitalität und Originalität seines künstlerischen Schaffens so eindringlich und überraschend wie zuvor.

On a peine à croire qu'à l'âge de quatre ans, une opérette de Gilbert et Sullivan ait pu éveiller Peter Maxwell Davies à la musique. Certes, il s'est assez rapidement éloigné de Sullivan, bien qu'il étudiât plus ou moins en autodidacte jusqu'à ce qu'il aille à l'école de Musique de Manchester en 1952, – mais même là, il fut après quelques semaines expulsé des cours de composition. Néanmoins, ce fut à Manchester qu'il eut l'occasion de rencontrer et d'échanger ses idées avec d'autres jeunes musiciens, parmi lesquels les compositeurs Harrison Birtwistle et Alexander Goehr, et le pianiste John Ogdon. Ensemble, ils formèrent le Manchester New Music Group, afin d'étudier et jouer la musique européenne d'avant-garde alors inconnue, et aussi pour présenter leurs propres compositions expérimentales.

Ce qui le différenciait de ses collègues de Manchester était son intérêt particulier pour la musique très ancienne et pour les plains-chants. On retrouvera ces thèmes dans chacune de ses œuvres, depuis la série de chants de Noël *O magnum mysterium*, écrite pour les enfants du lycée Cirencester, dont il fut le directeur au début des années 1960, en passant par le *Veni Sancte Spiritus* pour choeur et orchestre de 1964 jusqu'aux *Taverner Fantasias* orchestraux qui devaient précéder l'opéra, *Taverner*, que l'on put enfin entendre à Covent Garden en 1972. Mais ce n'était pas par pur intérêt romantique ou nostalgique : comme Davies le disait : « Je voulais seulement tirer le plus de choses possible de ces compositeurs et de ces plains-chants. J'y voyais tellement de petits détails qui pouvaient mener à de grandes choses... Quelque part, comme par instinct, je sentais bien qu'il fallait s'en servir. »

Si l'on recherche l'idée de nostalgie, on la trouvera dans les fox-trot et le jazz fou qui rappelle les années 1920, spécialement dans beaucoup de ses œuvres pour la scène qu'il composa pour son propre groupe, Fires of London. Cependant il est certain, que ni les airs dansants, ni les formes médiévales n'excluent des œuvres au résultat musical impitoyablement progressiste, souvent incongru, comme les pièces semi-théâtrales telles que *Revelation and Fall* (dans laquelle le soprano très éprouvé a fini par utliser un porte-voix.), ou comme *Eight Songs for a Mad King*.

Il ne faut pas voir là le seul trait caractéristique des œuvres du compositeur Maxwell Davies. Comme Britten, il composa un certain nombre de morceaux pour des occasions spécifiques, parfois sociales, et il aima toujours travailler avec les enfants ; ce qu'il fit de plus en plus après s'être installé sur l'île lointaine de Hoy sur l'archipel d'Orkney, au nord de l'Écosse, où il fonda le Festival St. Magnus à Kirkwall en 1977. Ce n'est guère une coïncidence si, à peu près à cette époque, les mouvements violents de sa musique commencèrent à s'adoucir, et une qualité réfléchie, lyrique s'insinua dans ses compositions – souvent dotées de titres plus traditionnels comme Symphonie ou Concerto.

Ce n'est pas que l'on puisse dire, même en faisant un gros effort d'imagination, que les dernières créations de Maxwell Davies étaient d'un abord facile – ce qu'il n'apprécierait d'ailleurs pas. Elles ne dérangent peut-être pas comme les précédentes, ou ne sont pas aussi complexes, mais l'austérité domine, et la vitalité et l'originalité de ses élans créatifs, malgré la paix trouvée dans le calme de la solitude de son île, ne cessent de percer et de surprendre.

Sir Peter Maxwell Davies rehearsing, 13 February 1969.
Sir Peter Maxwell Davies beim Proben, 13. Februar 1969.
Sir Peter Maxwell Davies lors d'une répétition, le 13 février 1969.

HANS WERNER HENZE *1926

As contemporary composers go Henze is one of the least forbidding, but also one of the most bewilderingly diverse. Because his composition teacher happened to be involved in the first course for New Music at Darmstadt, he actually beat Stockhausen, Boulez and Berio to that stronghold of the post-war avant-garde, and a period of indoctrination into the Schoenberg 12-note system inevitably followed. But Henze was never really conquered by the charms of total serialism and soon found ways of bending the rules to his own expressive needs. His position with the avant-garde weakened, but his credibility with the public improved and by the early 1950s Henze was widely regarded as the most gifted of the post-war generation of German composers.

The prodigious output of those early years reveals an insatiable creative talent reaching out eagerly for every available stimulus – Hindemith, Stravinsky, Schoenberg, Berg, Mahler, polytonality, atonality, surrealism, jazz. But Henze was still haunted by old preoccupations, by a perception of music as anti-authoritarian, of the Third Reich as a 'cultural prison', of the new German musical tendencies as suffocatingly doctrinaire. Characteristically he decided on a sudden break, and in 1953 he left Germany for good – settling in Italy, first on the Bay of Naples and later near Rome. His music was anyhow moving in a southern direction, and the impact of the Mediterranean encouraged the romantic and lyrical qualities that were already separating him from his German colleagues.

It also encouraged his interest in opera: the first years in Italy produced the massive, richly imaginative score of *König Hirsch* and the brilliantly italianate *Prinz von Homburg*, but his next opera, *Elegy for Young Lovers*, was written to an English libretto by W. H. Auden and Chester Kallman; when the same librettists undertook the text for *The Bassarids* they insisted that before tackling it Henze should go to a performance of *Götterdämmerung* and 'make his peace with Wagner'. He was ready for the advice, and responded with a fully symphonic drama in the German tradition that created a sensation at the Salzburg Festival of 1966.

But again Henze confounded expectation. 'Be prepared at all times to sacrifice everything to a new stimulus, a new experience', he had written, and though the change now was political rather than geographical, the swing to the New Left and the ideals of the socialist revolution brought with it their own musical effect. And not only musical: the first performance of *The Raft of Medusa* (dedicated to Che Guevara) was stopped by the police in Hamburg in 1968, and soon afterwards Henze left for Cuba, where he spent a year teaching and composing. Score after score continued to pour from his pen, often carrying political messages, always containing moments of great beauty. But opera, the ultimate bourgeois form, was abandoned for a whole decade, until the Royal Opera commissioned an 'Action for Music' and in 1976 *We Come to the River*, with its cast of 127 soloists, brought Marxism at last to the Covent Garden stage. It was not a success, and for many of its audience the less political, more romantic scores of the 1950s and 60s will still be what earns Henze his place in their affections.

Hans Werner Henze gehört sicher zu den umgänglichsten zeitgenössischen Komponisten. Außerdem zeichnet sich sein Werk durch einen faszinierenden Facettenreichtum aus. Seine Lehrer nach dem Krieg engagierten sich in dem ersten „Internationalen Ferienkurs für Neue Musik" in Darmstadt, und so kam es dazu, daß er zusammen mit Stockhausen, Boulez und Berio den Kern der Nachkriegsavantgarde bildete. Darauf folgte eine intensive Auseinandersetzung mit Schönbergs Zwölftonmusik. Henze war jedoch nie ein überzeugter Anhänger der ausschließlich seriellen Musik und fand bald eigene Wege, um die Regeln seinem eigenen Ausdruckswillen anzupassen. Dadurch verlor er zwar immer mehr seine Vorreiterrolle in der Avantgarde, dafür stieg aber seine Bekanntheit, und in den frühen 50er Jahren galt Henze als der begabteste unter den deutschen Komponisten der Nachkriegszeit.

Die gewaltige Produktivität dieser ersten Jahre offenbart ein unersättliches künstlerisches Talent, das bereitwillig jede Anregung aufgreift – Hindemith, Strawinsky, Schönberg, Berg, Mahler, Polytonalität, atonale Musik, Surrealismus, Jazz. Aber Henze wurde auch von anderen Sorgen heimgesucht. Er war davon überzeugt, daß Musik eine anti-autoritäre Kraft sei. Das Dritte Reich war ein „kulturelles Gefängnis" gewesen, und die neuen Strömungen in der deutschen Musik zeigten sich erstickend doktrinär. Er entschloß sich zu einem radikalen Bruch, und wanderte 1953 aus – ließ sich in Italien am Golf von Neapel nieder und lebte später in der Nähe von Rom. Seine Musik war bereits von südlichen Einflüssen inspiriert, und die mediterrane Atmosphäre begünstigte die Entfaltung jener romantischen und poetischen Qualitäten, die ihn immer weiter von seinen deutschen Kollegen entfernte.

Auch sein Interesse an der Oper wurde hierdurch angeregt: In seinen ersten Jahren in Italien schrieb er die umfangreiche, sehr phantasievolle Partitur *König Hirsch* und den wunderbar italienisierten *Prinz von Homburg*. Seine nächste Oper, *Elegie für junge Liebende*, entstand nach dem englischen Libretto von W. H. Auden und Chester Kallmann. Bevor die beiden Autoren den Text für *Die Bassariden* übernahmen, bestanden sie darauf, daß Henze eine Aufführung der *Götterdämmerung* besuche, um sich „mit Wagner auszusöhnen". Henze nahm den Vorschlag an, und 1966 wurde sein symphonisches Drama im Stil der deutschen Tradition zu dem Ereignis der Salzburger Festspiele.

Henze verhielt sich abermals entgegen allen Erwartungen. „Sei jederzeit bereit, alles für eine neue Anregung, eine neue Erfahrung zu opfern", hatte er geschrieben. Diesmal vollzog er keinen geographischen, sondern einen politischen Standortwechsel. Seine Hinwendung zur Neuen Linken und den Idealen der sozialistischen Revolution hatte die entsprechende Auswirkung auf seine Musik und auch auf sein Leben: Als in Hamburg 1968 die Uraufführung von *Das Floß der Medusa* (Che Guevara gewidmet) von der Polizei abgebrochen wurde, brach Henze bald darauf nach Kuba auf, wo er ein Jahr lang lehrte und komponierte. Er schrieb auch weiterhin unermüdlich seine Partituren. Oft enthielten sie eine politische Botschaft, aber immer waren sie von großer Schönheit. Die Oper wurde allerdings als ultimative bürgerliche Form für ein ganzes Jahrzehnt abgelehnt, solange bis die Royal Opera eine „Action for Music" in Auftrag gab und *We Come to the River* 1976 mit einem Ensemble von 127 Solisten den Marxismus schließlich auch auf die Bühne von Covent Garden brachte. Es war kein Erfolg, und für viele Zuhörer werden es Henzes unpolitischere, romantische Stücke der 50er und 60er Jahre sein, die sie in guter Erinnerung halten.

De tous les compositeurs contemporains, Henze est l'un des moins austères, mais également l'un des plus déconcertants de par la variété de ses styles. Après la guerre, parce que son professeur de composition se trouva participer aux premiers cours de New Music à Darmstadt, il forma avec Stockhausen, Boulez et Berio le bastion de la musique d'avant-garde d'après-guerre, et il s'ensuivit inévitablement une période, où il fut fortement attiré par le dodécaphonisme de Schoenberg. Mais Henze ne fut jamais vraiment conquis par les charmes d'une composition totalement sérielle, et il trouva bientôt les moyens d'assouplir les règles pour ses propres besoins d'expression. Sa position dans l'avant-garde s'affaiblit, mais sa crédibilité auprès du public augmenta et au début des années 1950, Henze était considéré comme le compositeur le plus doué de la génération allemande d'après-guerre.

La production prodigieuse de ces premières années reflète un talent créatif insatiable qui s'inspirait de tous les genres – Hindemith, Stravinski, Schoenberg, Berg, Mahler, polytonalité, atonalité, le surréalisme, le jazz. Mais Henze était encore hanté par ses préoccupations premières, c'est-à-dire, d'une part, par une musique anti-autoritaire, d'autre part par l'Allemagne du Troisième Reich qu'il jugeait une « prison culturelle », et enfin par les nouvelles tendances en Allemagne qu'il estimait doctrinaires à en suffoquer. Comme on pouvait s'y attendre, il décida subitement de quitter l'Allemagne pour toujours en 1953 – pour s'installer en Italie, d'abord dans la Baie de Naples, et plus tard près de Rome. Sa musique tendait de toute façon vers le sud, et la Méditerranée eut pour effet de favoriser le romantisme et le lyrisme qui l'éloignaient déjà de ses homologues allemands.

La Méditerranée influença également son goût pour l'opéra : pendant les premières années en Italie, il produisit l'énorme morceau riche et recherché de *König Hirsch*, et, l'italianisant brillamment, le *Prinz von Homburg*, mais son prochain opéra, *Elegy for Young Lovers*, fut écrit pour un livret anglais, par W.H. Auden et Chester Kallman ; lorsque ces mêmes librettistes se chargèrent du texte de *The Bassarids*, ils tinrent à ce que Henze, avant de s'en occuper, assiste à une représentation de *Götterdämmerung*, et qu'il « fasse la paix avec Wagner ». À cette époque-là, Henze était déjà prêt à recevoir un conseil, et ce fut avec un vrai morceau symphonique et suivant la tradition allemande qu'il fit sensation au Festival de Salzbourg en 1966.

Là encore, Henze déçut toutes les attentes. « Soyez disposé à tout moment à tout sacrifier pour un nouvel élan, une expérience nouvelle, » écrivit-il, et bien que le changement ait été plus politique que géographique, ses tendances pour la Gauche Nouvelle et les idéaux de la révolution socialiste influencèrent alors sa musique. Mais pas simplement sa musique : la première représentation de *The Raft of Medusa* (dédié à Che Guevara) fut interrompue par la police à Hambourg en 1968. Peu après Henze partit pour Cuba où il passa une année à enseigner et à composer. Il écrivit partitions sur partitions, souvent porteuses d'un message politique, mais contenant toujours des moments de grande beauté. Cependant, l'opéra, le summum du genre bourgeois, fut abandonné pendant toute une décennie, jusqu'à ce que Le Royal Opera demande une « Action for Music ». En 1976, donc, *We Come to the River*, avec ses 127 solistes, introduisit le marxisme au théâtre de Covent Garden. Ce ne fut pas un succès. Nombreux sont ceux qui apprécieront Henze, en fait, pour ses morceaux, moins politiques et plus romantiques des années 1950 et 1960.

1

2

3

4

(1) Henze in conversation with Margot Fonteyn and Rudolf Nureyev, 14 February 1969. Nearly 11 years earlier Fonteyn had created the title role in Henze's romantic ballet *Ondine* at Covent Garden, choreographed by Frederick Ashton, with the composer conducting. It was the eighth of Henze's ballet scores, and the tale of a water sprite had seemed an unlikely subject for a composer who was then still regarded as a close associate of the European avant-garde. (2, 3, 4) Conducting the English Chamber Orchestra at Morley College, February 1969.

(1) Henze im Gespräch mit Margot Fonteyn und Rudolf Nurejew, 14. Februar 1969. Fast elf Jahre zuvor hatte die Fonteyn in Covent Garden die Titelrolle seines großen romantischen Balletts *Undine* getanzt. Frederick Ashton hatte es choreographiert, und der Komponist hatte die Aufführung selbst dirigiert. Es war Henzes achte Ballettmusik, und das Märchen von der Nixe galt als ein recht ungewöhnliches Thema für einen Komponisten, der damals noch in enger Beziehung zu der musikalischen Avantgarde Europas stand. (2, 3, 4) Henze dirigiert das English Chamber Orchestra am Morley College, Februar 1969.

(1) Henze en grande conversation avec Margot Fonteyn et Rudolf Noureïev le 14 février 1969. Près de 11 années étaient passées depuis que Fonteyn sur la scène de Covent Garden, avait créé le rôle d'*Ondine*, ballet romantique de Henze, et dont la chorégraphie était de Frederick Ashton, et le chef d'orchestre, le compositeur. C'était la huitième musique de ballet de Henze, et l'histoire d'une naïade est un thème des plus inattendus pour un compositeur encore considéré à l'époque comme étant très proche de la musique européenne d'avant-garde. (2, 3, 4) Il dirige ici l'English Chamber Orchestra au Morley Collège en février 1969.

The librettists W. H. Auden (second from right) and Chester Kallman (at left) with Henze in a BBC studio discussion about Henze's opera *Elegy for Young Lovers*, June 1961. When the composer asked Auden and Kallman to write him a libretto, he stipulated a subject suitable for chamber orchestra and the production of 'tender, beautiful noises' – an aspect of the music which seems to have missed the Glyndebourne audience at the first performance in the original language in 1961, though it has won over many audiences since.

Die Schriftsteller und Librettisten W. H. Auden (zweiter von rechts) und Chester Kallmann (links) diskutieren in einem BBC Studio mit Henze seine Oper *Elegie für junge Liebende*. Als Henze die beiden darum bat, ein Libretto für ihn zu schreiben, wünschte er sich ein Thema, das sich für ein Kammerorchester eignen würde und „sanfte, wunderbare Klänge" erlaubte – ein Aspekt, für den das Publikum in Glyndebourne bei der originalsprachigen Erstaufführung 1961 nicht gerade empfänglich gewesen zu sein scheint. Das Stück fand aber seither auf vielen anderen Bühnen großen Anklang.

Les librettistes W. H. Auden (deuxième à partir de la droite) et Chester Kallman (à gauche) avec Henze dans un studio de la BBC en train de parler de l'opéra de Henze, *Elegy for Young Lovers*, en juin 1961. Lorsque le compositeur proposa à Auden et Kallman de lui écrire un livret, il leur demanda de choisir un thème qui convienne à un orchestre de chambre, ainsi que la production de « sons empreints de tendresse et de beauté ». Cet aspect de la musique ne paraît pas avoir frappé le public de Glyndebourne, où la première représentation fut donnée dans la langue d'origine, mais fut depuis très applaudie par de nombreux autres publics.

Hindemith, like his older contemporary Schoenberg, was a refugee from the Nazi regime who sought sanctuary in the United States. Although we tend to think of him now as a rather serious, not to say earnest figure, his first three operas had caused something of a scandal in Germany in the early 1920s, and in 1929 he hit the headlines in Berlin with the opera *Neues vom Tage*, a satirical romp that included a scene for a soprano singing in her bath. Among the audiences at the Kroll Opera there were some who were deeply shocked, including, unfortunately for the composer, Joseph Goebbels – and from the time that Hitler came to power Hindemith was a marked man. In 1934 the production of the opera *Mathis der Maler* was forbidden and, in spite of vigorous defence by Wilhelm Furtwängler (who had already conducted the brilliantly successful première of the symphony that Hindemith extracted from the music of his opera), Hindemith's works were boycotted and the composer himself subjected to personal vilification by Goebbels and the Nazi propaganda machine.

By this time Hindemith had already won a substantial reputation as a professor of music at the Berlin Hochschule für Musik. But in 1937, when all further performances of his music were banned throughout Germany, he finally resigned this post and left his home country for Switzerland, where *Mathis* eventually reached the stage the following year. In 1940 he moved on to the States, where he taught at Yale, Tanglewood and Harvard, and became an American citizen in 1946.

Much of Hindemith's musical life was involved with practical music-making, particularly with chamber music of which he wrote a great deal for many different combinations of instruments. He himself was a viola player, and his first visit to England, in 1929, came about when he undertook to play at very short notice the solo part in Walton's *Viola Concerto* – turned down by Lionel Tertis, for whom it had been written, as 'unplayable'. In spite of his gratitude, Walton's comment on Hindemith's performance was characteristically candid: 'His technique was marvellous, but he was rough – no nonsense about it. He just stood up and played.'

It was this practical, no-nonsense attitude that made Hindemith such a good teacher – and, particularly later in life, so effective a conductor. His professorship at Yale, of the theory of music, was apt to the man, and his view of musical composition was structured and consistent, with no concession to the more drastic revisions of musical technique that were current in his day. Perhaps this is partly why, in any survey of the period in which he worked, his name tends to make less impact than the names of Schoenberg or Berg or Webern or Stravinsky or Bartók. His position was clear and solid. 'Tonality is a natural force, like gravity,' he said; 'there are only 12 tones – you must treat them carefully.' With hindsight, this does sound rather like a warning.

Wie sein älterer Zeitgenosse Schönberg war auch Paul Hindemith vor dem Nazi-Regime geflohen und hatte Zuflucht in den Vereinigten Staaten gesucht. Hindemith gilt heute als ein ernster, wenn nicht strenger Musiker, doch seine ersten drei Opern entfachten in den frühen 20er Jahren in Deutschland einen Skandal. 1929 geriet er mit der Oper *Neues vom Tage*, einer Satire, die auch eine Szene enthält, in der die Sopranistin in der Badewanne singt, in die Berliner Schlagzeilen. Das Publikum in der Kroll Oper reagierte zum Teil zutiefst schockiert – und da zu diesem Teil leider auch Joseph Goebbels gehörte, wurde Hindemith nach Hitlers Machtergreifung geächtet. 1943 wurde die Aufführung der Oper *Mathis der Maler* verboten, und trotz der entschiedenen Fürsprache Wilhelm Furtwänglers (der bereits die ungeheuer erfolgreiche Uraufführung der Symphonie dirigiert hatte, die Hindemiths mit der Musik der Oper geschrieben hatte) wurden seine Werke boykottiert. Der Komponist selbst wurde persönlich von Goebbels und der Propagandamaschinerie der Nazis verschmäht.

Zu diesem Zeitpunkt war Hindemith bereits ein angesehener Musikprofessor an der Berliner Hochschule für Musik. Als 1937 jedoch alle Aufführungen seiner Werke verboten wurden, gab er diese Position auf und wanderte in die Schweiz aus, wo *Mathis* ein Jahr später aufgeführt wurde. 1940 siedelte er in die Staaten über und lehrte in Yale, Tanglewood und Harvard. 1946 wurde er amerikanischer Staatsbürger.

In Hindemiths musikalischem Leben war das Musizieren selbst von großer Bedeutung. Er liebte insbesondere die Kammermusik und schrieb viele Stücke für die unterschiedlichsten Besetzungen. Er selbst beherrschte die Bratsche derart, daß er 1929 zu seinem ersten Besuch nach England eingeladen wurde, um kurzfristig die Solopartie in Waltons *Bratschenkonzert* zu übernehmen. Lionel Tertis, für den es eigentlich geschrieben war, hatte es als „unspielbar" bezeichnet. Trotz seiner Dankbarkeit gegenüber Hindemith kommentierte Walton Hindemiths Darbietung mit der für ihn charakteristischen Offenheit: „Seine Technik war brillant, aber sein Auftreten war ungehobelt – er machte keine Umstände. Er stand einfach auf und spielte."

Es war diese praktische, unkomplizierte Haltung, die Hindemith zu einem ausgezeichneten Lehrer machte – und besonders in seinen späteren Jahren zu einem sehr erfolgreichen Dirigenten. Seine Professur für Musiktheorie in Yale entsprach genau seinen Fähigkeiten, und seine Ansichten zur musikalischen Komposition waren äußerst durchdacht, schlüssig und ohne jede Konzession an die radikaleren musikalischen Strömungen seiner Zeit. Vielleicht liegt es daran, daß die meisten musikwissenschaftlichen Abhandlungen über jene Zeit seinen Namen hinter Schönberg, Berg, Webern, Strawinsky oder Bartók immer etwas zurückstehen lassen. Seine Position war klar und eindeutig: „Tonalität ist ebenso eine Naturkraft wie die Schwerkraft", sagte er, „es gibt nur 12 Töne – man muß sie vorsichtig behandeln." Im nachhinein klingt das fast wie eine Warnung.

Hindemith, comme Schoenberg, plus âgé mais qui fut son contemporain, se réfugia aux États-Unis afin de fuir les nazis. Bien que l'on ait tendance à le considérer comme un personnage grave, pour ne pas dire solennel, ses trois premiers opéras provoquèrent un scandale en Allemagne au début des années 1920, et en 1929 il défraya la chronique à Berlin avec l'opéra *Neues vom Tage*, une farce satirique avec une scène où une soprano chante dans son bain. Parmi les spectateurs du Kroll Opera, certains furent profondément choqués, et malheureusement pour le compositeur, Joseph Goebbels étaient de ceux-là – dès le moment où Hitler prit le pouvoir, Hindemith fut persécuté. En 1934, la production de l'opéra *Mathis le peintre*, fut interdite, et en dépit de sa défense vigoureusement prise par Wilhelm Furtwängler (qui avait déjà dirigé l'excellente première de la symphonie extraite de la musique de l'opéra par Hindemith), les œuvres de Hindemith boycottées, et le compositeur lui-même, a été en butte à une diffamation toute personnelle, de la part de Goebbels et de la machine de propagande nazie.

À cette époque, Hindemith avait déjà une excellente réputation de professeur de musique (titulaire d'une chaire) à la Berliner Hochschule für Musik. Cependant, lorsque toutes ses autres représentations furent interdites en Allemagne, il finit par donner sa démission et quitta sa patrie pour s'installer en Suisse, où, enfin, l'année suivante, il put produire *Mathis le peintre* sur scène. En 1940, il partit aux États-Unis où il enseigna à Yale, Tanglewood et Harvard, et il devint citoyen américain en 1946.

Hindemith joua lui-même beaucoup, surtout de la musique de chambre. Il composa d'ailleurs de nombreux morceaux pour différentes combinaisons d'instruments. Lui-même, jouait de l'alto, et lors de sa première visite en Angleterre, il décida à la dernière minute de jouer le morceau soliste dans le *Viola Concerto* de Walton. Lionel Tertis, pour qui le morceau avait été écrit, l'avait refusé en le qualifiant d'« injouable ». En dépit de sa gratitude, le commentaire de Walton quant à l'interprétation de Hindemith fut, comme on pouvait s'y attendre, d'une grande franchise : « Ses techniques étaient merveilleuses, mais il ne faisait pas de manières. Il s'est simplement levé et a joué ».

C'était ce côté pratique et sérieux qui a fait de Hindemith un si bon professeur – et plus tard dans sa vie un chef d'orchestre aussi valable. Sa chaire à l'université de Yale comme professeur de théorie musicale, lui convenait très bien : ses vues sur la composition musicale étaient structurées et consistantes, et il ne fit pas de compromis avec une technique musicale plus radicale qui était pourtant courante à son époque. C'est peut-être en partie pourquoi, lorsque l'on se penche sur l'époque dans laquelle il a travaillé, on constate que son nom laissa moins d'impact que ceux de Schoenberg, Berg, Webern, Stravinski ou Bartók. Sa position était claire et solide. « La tonalité est une force naturelle, comme la gravité », dit-il, « il n'y a que 12 sons – il faut les traiter du mieux que l'on peut. » Avec le recul, on pourrait croire à un avertissement.

Paul Hindemith with the score of his last full-length opera, *Die Harmonie der Welt*, August 1957.

Paul Hindemith mit der Partitur seiner letzten großen Oper, *Die Harmonie der Welt*, August 1957.

Paul Hindemith avec la partition de son dernier grand opéra, *Die Harmonie der Welt*, août 1957.

Hindemith rehearsing, 23 February 1961.
Hindemith beim Proben, 23. Februar 1961.
Hindemith lors d'une répétition, le 23 février 1961.

Hindemith in jovial mood at a press conference in Munich,
discussing his opera *Die Harmonie der Welt* before its world
première on 11 August 1957.

In entspannter Stimmung spricht Hindemith bei einer
Pressekonferenz in München über seine Oper *Die Harmonie der
Welt* vor ihrer Weltpremiere am 11. August 1957.

Hindemith d'une humeur joviale lors d'une conférence de presse
à Munich, discute de son opéra *Die Harmonie der Welt* avant sa
première mondiale le 11 août 1957.

ZOLTÁN KODÁLY 1882-1967

Even more than Bartók, Kodály was the soul and spirit of Hungarian music in the 20th century. The two men were close friends; they were both enthusiastic pioneers in the collection of folk songs from all parts of ethnic Hungary and from early days collaborated in their joint publication. Like Holst and Vaughan Williams in England, they recognized the wider possibilities that lay untapped in the material they were continually discovering, and from them drew the ideals that were to shape both their lives. 'The vision of an educated Hungary, reborn from the people, rose before us', said Kodály many years later. 'We decided to devote our lives to its realization.'

As their careers progressed, they took rather different directions. Bartók became a very much more original composer, developed a powerfully dissonant style and a more cosmopolitan outlook. Kodály's music remained closer to its ethnic origins: most of the works by which he is best remembered have a strong Hungarian flavour – the orchestral suite from the musical play *Háry János* (which is about a sort of Hungarian Münchhausen), the *Dances of Galánta* (recalling the region where Kodály spent his childhood), the *Dances of Marosszék*, or the *Psalmus hungaricus*, written to celebrate the 50th anniversary of the union of Buda and Pest in 1923, which first established him as a composer of international importance.

Choral music formed a great part of his output, and indeed of his life. The theories of musical education that grew out of his interest in folk music involved much choral singing, and he provided enormous numbers of choruses for young people to sing, as well as larger-scale works for the more sophisticated audience. He engaged with education at every level, from teaching at the Liszt Academy of Music in Budapest to revolutionizing the musical curriculum in local schools: the Singing Youth movement that he founded in the 1930s developed into what became known throughout the world as the Kodály method of music teaching, and he lived to see daily musical education according to his principles introduced into 120 elementary schools thoughout his country.

After the Second World War, and more particularly after Bartók's death in the United States in 1945, Kodály became the elder statesman of Hungarian music. He travelled widely in this capacity, lecturing and conducting his own works: everywhere he was received and admired for the upright, clear-thinking, passionately committed human being that he was. His impact as a composer on the wider world of 20th-century music may not have been immense, but in his own country, whether as a teacher, scholar or composer, he was a profound influence for good.

As one of his pupils, the conductor Antal Dorati, said on being asked what it was like studying with Kodály: 'We never wrote a dirty bar.'

Stärker noch als Bartók repräsentiert Zoltán Kodály die Seele und den Geist der ungarischen Musik des 20. Jahrhunderts. Die beiden waren eng befreundet. Begeistert sammelten sie als erste die Volkslieder aller Ethnien Ungarns und publizierten ihre Sammlungen von Anfang an gemeinsam. Ebenso wie Holst und Vaughan Williams in England erkannten sie die großen Möglichkeiten, die in all dem Material verborgen lagen, das sie nach und nach entdeckten. Daraus entwickelten sie die Ideale, die ihr Leben bestimmen sollten. „Die Vision eines gebildeten Ungarn, wiedergeboren aus dem Volk, entstand vor unseren Augen", sagte Kodály viele Jahre später. „Wir beschlossen, unser Leben ihrer Verwirklichung zu widmen."

Beide Karrieren entwickelten sich jedoch in verschiedene Richtungen. Bartók wurde der sehr viel originellere Komponist, der einen kraftvollen dissonanten Stil und eher kosmopolitische Formen entwickelte. Kodálys Musik blieb mehr seinen Wurzeln verhaftet. Seine bekanntesten Werke haben eine stark ungarische Prägung: die Orchestersuite aus dem Singspiel *Háry János* (eine Art ungarischer Münchhausen), die *Tänze aus Galánta* (wo Kodály seine Kindheit verbrachte), die *Marosszéker Tänze* und auch der *Psalmus hungaricus*, der 1923 zum 50. Jahrestag der Vereinigung von Buda und Pest geschrieben wurde und ihn erstmalig zu einem Komponisten von Weltrang erhob.

Ein großer Teil seiner Arbeiten und auch seines Lebens wurde von der Chormusik bestimmt. Seine Theorien zur Musikerziehung, die sich aus seinem Interesse an der Volksmusik entwickelten, räumten dem Chorgesang eine wichtige Rolle ein. Er schrieb sehr viele Lieder, die von der Jugend gesungen werden sollten, und auch große Chorwerke für eine gebildete Zuhörerschaft. Kodály engagierte sich auf allen Ebenen der Musikerziehung. Er unterrichtete an der Liszt Akademie in Budapest und reorganisierte den musikalischen Lehrplan der regionalen Schulen. Aus der Bewegung „Singende Jugend", die er 1930 ins Leben rief, entwickelte sich seine weltweit bekannte und nach ihm benannte Lehrmethode für den Musikunterricht, und er konnte miterleben, daß seine Methode an 120 Grundschulen im Land eingeführt wurde.

Nach dem Zweiten Weltkrieg, und insbesondere nach Bartóks Tod in den Vereinigten Staaten im Jahre 1945, war Kodály der älteste Vertreter der ungarischen Musik. In dieser Eigenschaft war er viel auf Reisen. Er lehrte und dirigierte seine eigenen Werke. Überall wurde er gern empfangen und für seine Aufrichtigkeit, sein klares Denken und sein leidenschaftliches Engagement geschätzt. Seine Bedeutung als Komponist mag auf dem großen Feld der Musik des 20. Jahrhunderts nicht sehr groß gewesen sein, aber in seinem eigenen Land, ob als Lehrer, Gelehrter oder Komponist, übte er einen starken und guten Einfluß aus. Als einer seiner Schüler, der Dirigent Antal Dorati, einmal gefragt wurde, wie denn das Studium bei Kodály war, antwortete er: „Wir haben keinen einzigen unsauberen Takt geschrieben."

Encore plus que Bartók, Kodály était l'esprit et l'âme de la musique hongroise du XXᵉ siècle. Les deux hommes étaient unis par une amitié étroite ; tous deux étaient de passionnés pionniers dans la collection de chants folkloriques de toutes les régions ethniques de Hongrie, et très tôt, ils collaborèrent à leur publication commune. Tout comme Holst et Vaughan Williams en Angleterre, ils reconnurent l'existence des ressources inexploitées enfouies dans le matériel qu'ils découvraient chaque jour. Ils en tirèrent les idéaux qui allaient déterminer leur destin. « La vision d'une nouvelle Hongrie, éduquée, s'est dressée devant nous », dit Kodály des années plus tard, « nous avons décidé de vouer nos vies à sa concrétisation ».

Quant à leurs carrières, elles prirent des voies plutôt différentes. Bartók devint un compositeur plus original, plus cosmopolite, et il développa un style fortement dissonant. La musique de Kodály demeura plus proche de ses origines ethniques : la plupart de ses œuvres grâce auxquelles il est le plus connu, rendent bien l'atmosphère hongroise. La suite orchestrale de la pièce musicale *Háry János* (un peu le Münchhausen hongrois), les *Dances of Galánta* (qui rappelle la région où Kodály passa son enfance), les *Dances of Marosszék*, ou *Psalmus hungaricus* (composé pour le 50e anniversaire de l'union de Buda et de Pest en 1923), firent de lui un compositeur de valeur sur le plan international.

La musique pour chœurs joua un grand rôle dans sa production, mais aussi dans sa vie. Les théories musicales inspirées par son intérêt pour la musique folklorique, mettaient l'accent sur les chœurs, et il en créa beaucoup destinés à être chantés par les jeunes. D'autres œuvres encore, complètes celles-là, furent composées pour un public plus recherché. Il s'engagea dans l'éducation à tous ses niveaux : il enseigna à l'Académie de musique de Budapest ; il transforma aussi radicalement le programme de musique dans des écoles de la région. The Singing Youth, mouvement qu'il fonda dans les années 1930, fut reconnu dans le monde entier comme la méthode d'enseignement de la musique de Kodály, et il put voir le reste de sa vie, l'enseignement de la musique selon ses principes introduits dans 120 écoles élémentaires au quatre coins de son pays.

Après la Seconde Guerre mondiale, et plus particulièrement après la mort aux États-Unis de Bartók, Kodály devint le plus ancien représentant de la musique hongroise. Cela le mena à travers le monde, comme enseignant ou comme chef d'orchestre de ses propres œuvres : il fut partout reçu et admiré pour son esprit droit, net, totalement engagé. Il n'aura peut-être pas laissé de grandes traces comme compositeur, si l'on considère la musique au sens large du XXᵉ siècle, mais dans son pays, qu'il s'agisse du professeur, de l'érudit ou du compositeur, son influence ne cessera d'être. Comme l'un de ses élèves, le chef d'orchestre Antal Dorati, répondit lorsqu'on lui demanda comment se passaient les cours de Kodály : « Jamais, nous n'avons écrit une barre offensante. »

Zoltán Kodály, a venerable presence, rehearsing his most popular work, the *Háry János suite*, 1 October 1960. Characteristically, he uses no baton.

Zoltán Kodály, eine ehrwürdige Erscheinung, bei der Probe seines bekanntesten Werkes, der *Háry János Suite*, am 1. Oktober 1960. Wie gewöhnlich sieht man ihn ohne Taktstock.

Zoltán Kodály, une présence vénérable, lors de la répétition de son œuvre la plus populaire, la *Háry János suite*, comme d'habitude sans baguette, le 1er octobre 1960.

When he was a small child Ligeti had a dream that he could not reach his cot, 'my safe haven, because the whole room was filled with a dense confused tangle of fine filaments. It looked like the web I had seen silkworms fill their box with as they change into pupas. I was caught up in this immense web together with living things and objects of various kinds.... An indescribable sadness hung over these shifting forms and structure, the hopelessness of passing time and the melancholy of unalterable past events.'

It was quite late in his life before Ligeti had a chance to produce the kind of music he really wanted to write. Until he was 33 years old he lived entirely in Hungary, where the political regime looked askance at progressive tendencies in the arts and experimental composition was rigorously discouraged. So although he studied and became a professor of composition at the Budapest Academy of Music, his creative work was mainly in the Bartók, folk-music tradition; his more experimental scores were composed secretly and never performed or published.

When he left Hungary in 1956 he worked first at the WDR electronic studios in Cologne, but it was with a work for orchestra that he first came to international attention in 1960. *Apparitions* was developed from sketches made in secret before he left Hungary, but in the following years he refined his ideas and later expanded them to include soloists and chorus in the *Requiem* – a work that carried his name to thousands when the Kyrie was used in the soundtrack of the 1968 Stanley Kubrick film *2001*.

Ligeti's own description of *Apparitions*, 'states, events, changes', gives a graphic impression of the nature of his music at this time. He was not interested in the structural possibilities of total serialism, but experimented instead with something altogether more atmospheric, more static, exploring the possibilities of slow change and the 'clustering' of chromatic sound, with practically no melody, harmony or rhythm as distinguishable elements. Everything is texture: swirling complexes of what Ligeti himself called 'micropolyphony' – a web indeed, and one woven out of a tangle of fine filaments, though the confusion of childhood has grown up into an immensely complex and minutely calculated reality.

It is typical of Ligeti that, even as he laboured at these filigree structures, he could send them up mercilessly in a piece like *Fragment* for double bassoon, bass trombone, double-bass tuba, three double basses and percussion. For there is another side to Ligeti's work, where his quizzical humour and sharp sense of satire are given outrageously full rein – as in the *Poème symphonique* for 100 metronomes, set at different tempi, which lasts until they all run down, or the palindromic prelude for motor-car horns which opens his opera *Le grand macabre*. The opera is a wild, surrealistic affair, whose plot turns on whether or not the world will end at midnight, though when midnight comes, nobody is really sure whether it has. It is one of Ligeti's qualities to have shown the ordinary public that not everything in the realm of the avant-garde need be taken with total seriousness, and that there are paths to 20th-century musical salvation other than total serialism.

Als Kind träumte György Ligeti einmal, er könne sein Kinderbett nicht erreichen, diesen „sicheren Hafen, weil das ganze Zimmer voller dicht versponnener, feiner Fäden war. Es sah aus wie das Gewebe, mit dem die Seidenraupen ihre Fächer verspinnen, wenn sie sich verpuppen. Zusammen mit anderen Lebewesen und verschiedenen Gegenständen war ich in diesem riesigen Netzwerk gefangen ... Über diesen schwebenden Formen und Strukturen hing eine unbeschreibliche Traurigkeit, die Hoffnungslosigkeit verrinnender Zeit und die Trauer über vergangene Ereignisse, die nicht mehr zu ändern waren."

Es dauerte recht lange, bis Ligeti die Musik schreiben konnte, die er wirklich komponieren wollte. Bis zu seinem 34. Lebensjahr hat er Ungarn nie verlassen – ein Land, in dem das politische Regime alle progressiven Tendenzen in der Kunst mit Mißtrauen beobachtete und Ansätze zu experimenteller Komposition rigoros unterband. Er hatte zwar Musik studiert und wurde Professor für Kompositionslehre an der Budapester Musikakademie, seine kreative Arbeit orientierte sich aber hauptsächlich an der folkloristischen Tradition im Stile Bartóks. Seine experimentelleren Kompositionen hielt er unter Verschluß und hat sie niemals aufgeführt oder veröffentlicht.

Als er Ungarn 1956 verließ, arbeitete er am Elektronischen Studio des WDR in Köln; internationale Resonanz fand er jedoch 1960 erstmals mit einem Orchesterwerk. *Apparitions* entstand aus Entwürfen, die er heimlich in Ungarn gemacht hatte, in den folgenden Jahren verfeinerte er sein Konzept und erweiterte es zu dem *Requiem*, das Solisten und einen Chor einschloß. Das *Requiem* machte ihn schließlich auch bei einem Massenpublikum bekannt, als Stanley Kubrik 1968 das Kyrie in den Soundtrack seines Films *2001* übernahm.

Ligetis eigene Beschreibung von *Apparitions* – „Zustände, Ereignisse, Veränderungen" – vermittelt deutlich den Charakter seiner damaligen Musik. Allerdings interessierten ihn die strukturellen Möglichkeiten des totalen Serialismus der Avantgarde nicht. Statt dessen experimentierte er mit atmosphärischen, statischen Klängen und untersuchte die Möglichkeiten der langsamen Übergänge und Verflechtungen in der chromatischen Skala, bei denen Melodie, Harmonie und Rhythmus nicht mehr als erkennbare Einzelelemente hervortreten. Alles ist bei ihm Textur: wirbelnde Komplexe, die Ligeti selbst „Mikropolyphonie" nennt – ein Gewebe aus feinen Fäden. Aus der Verworrenheit des Kindertraums ist eine ungeheuer komplexe, aber genau berechnete Wirklichkeit geworden.

Es ist typisch für Ligeti, daß er seine fein ausgearbeiteten Filigranstrukturen dann in einem Stück wie *Fragment* mitleidlos mit Fagott, Posaune, Tuba, drei Kontrabässen und Schlagzeug besetzt. Ligetis Arbeiten haben nämlich auch eine andere Seite, bei der sein wacher Humor und sein Sinn für bissige Satire manchmal überdeutlich Gestalt annehmen – wie in dem *Poème symphonique* für 100 Metronome, die auf verschiedene Tempi eingestellt sind. Das Konzert dauert so lange, bis sie alle zum Stillstand gekommen sind. Das palindromatische Präludium für Autohupen, das seine Oper *Le grand macabre* einleitet, ist ein weiteres Beispiel. Diese Oper ist ein wildes, surrealistisches Werk aus dem Lande Breughels. Die Erzählung kreist um die Frage, ob die Erde um Mitternacht untergehen wird oder nicht. (Um Mitternacht weiß dann niemand, ob es nun geschehen ist oder nicht.) Es zählt zu Ligetis großen Leistungen, dem Publikum einmal vorgeführt zu haben, daß nicht alles aus den Gefilden der Avantgarde bittererernst genommen werden muß. – Vor allem hat er jedoch bewiesen, daß im 20. Jahrhundert noch andere Wege zur Rettung der Musik offenstehen als der totale Serialismus.

Alors qu'il n'était encore qu'un petit enfant, Ligeti rêva qu'il ne pouvait atteindre son petit lit : « mon abri sûr, parce que le reste de la pièce était remplie par un enchevêtrement dense et confus de filaments fins. On aurait dit une toile, comme j'avais vu des vers à soie le faire en remplissant leur cocon pendant qu'ils se transformaient en chrysalides. J'étais pris dans cette immense toile avec d'autres créatures vivantes ainsi que des objets de toute sorte... Une tristesse indescriptible pesait sur cet amas de formes et structures mouvantes, la lassitude du temps qui passe et la mélancolie d'un passé immuable. »

Ce n'est pas tout jeune que Ligeti eut l'occasion de produire le genre de musique qu'il souhaitait vraiment écrire. Il vécut en Hongrie jusqu'à l'âge de 33 ans, où le régime politique regardait d'un œil réprobateur les tendances progressives dans les arts, et la composition expérimentale était rigoureusement découragée. Par conséquent, bien qu'il ait étudié et ait eu une chaire à l'Académie de musique de Budapest comme professeur de composition, ses œuvres relevaient principalement du style de Bartók, c'est-à-dire dans la tradition de la musique folklorique : ses partitions plus expérimentales étaient écrites en cachette, et jamais elles ne furent jouées ou publiées.

Quittant la Hongrie en 1956, il travailla au studios électroniques de WDR à Cologne, mais c'est avec une composition pour orchestre en 1960, que le public international commença à le remarquer. *Apparitions* fut composée à partir de fragments de partition écrits en secret avant qu'il ne quitte la Hongrie, mais les années suivantes, il affina ses idées et inclut des solistes et un chœur dans le *Requiem* – une œuvre qui fit connaître son nom à des milliers de personnes, et sans laquelle, d'ailleurs, il n'aurait sans doute pas été reconnu lorsque le Kyrie fut utilisé pour la musique du film *2001* de Stanley Kubrick en 1968.

Ligeti décrit *Apparitions* comme « des états, événements, transformations, ce qui donne une impression graphique de la nature de sa musique à cette époque. Les possibilités de structure d'une musique totalement sérielle (tellement recherchées par les musiciens d'avant-garde) ne l'intéressaient pas. Il fit des essais avec quelque chose de beaucoup plus atmosphérique, plus statique, tout en explorant les possibilités d'une transformation lente, et l'« assemblement » de sons chromatiques, pratiquement sans que l'on puisse y distinguer mélodie, harmonie ou rythme. Tout est texture : des tourbillons de ce que Ligeti lui-même appelait « micropolyphonie » – une toile, en effet, une toile faite d'un enchevêtrement de filaments fins. La différence, la confusion d'un enfant s'est transformée en une réalité immensément complexe et minutieusement calculée.

Alors même qu'il peinait sur ces structures filigranes, Ligeti n'hésitait pas à les incorporer dans un morceau tel que le *Fragment*, pour contrebasson, trombone basse, contrebasse tuba, trois contrebasses, et instruments de percussion. Il y a une autre facette de Ligeti où son humour moqueur et son sens aigu de la satire s'imprègnent, parfois outrageusement, dans ses œuvres, comme dans le *Poème symphonique à 100 métronomes* (et chacun son tempo), qui ne s'arrête que lorsque le dernier métronome finit par se taire ; ou dans son grand opéra *Le Grand Macabre*, ouvert par un prélude palindromique de klaxons de voiture. L'opéra est de toute façon une histoire sauvage, surréaliste, qui a lieu au pays de Breughel, et ce qui doit arriver arrive, que le monde finisse à minuit ou non. L'une des grandes qualités de Ligeti est d'avoir montré au public ordinaire que l'on ne doit pas nécessairement tout prendre au sérieux en ce qui concerne l'avant-garde, et qu'il y a des chemins autres que celui d'un strict dodécaphonisme qui mènent au salut musical du XXᵉ siècle.

Witold Lutosławski, early 1970s.

Witold Lutosławski, frühe 70er Jahre.

Witold Lutosławski, au début des années 1970.

WITOLD LUTOSŁAWSKI   1913-1994

Until well into the 20th century, Polish music for most people meant Chopin. There had always been a strong musical tradition in Poland, and it was generally recognized that Poland was where all those polonaises and mazurkas came from, but apart from Chopin (who was half-French anyway and really only did it by getting away to Paris as soon as he could and staying there) no Polish composer had achieved international status. Since the First World War three composers have reversed that trend: Karol Szymanowski, Witold Lutosławski and Krzysztof Penderecki. Szymanowski belonged to an earlier generation of late romantics, Penderecki to the radical world of the post-war avant-garde, but Lutosławski commanded the middle ground of reasoned progress and serious musical expression.

Like Ligeti in Hungary, and for the same reasons, Lutosławski developed late – though in his case the relaxation of the Stalinist cultural restraints in 1956 found him ten years older than his Hungarian colleague. Nevertheless he had already managed to produce music that has endured, courting comparison with Brahms and Rachmaninov in an exhilarating set of variations on Paganini's famous *Study in A minor*, and producing one work at least, the brilliant *Concerto for Orchestra*, that carried his name outside Poland. And in addition he had been experimenting in secret with a new harmonic scheme based on the 12 note system (though not on Schoenberg's exploitation of it, which he disliked), so that in the period following the cultural thaw he was ready to develop his ideas – and actually hear the results – in a series of works beginning with the *Funeral Music* of 1958 and leading on to the *Second Symphony* and beyond.

With the relaxation of political restraints came the possibility of travelling freely and communicating with other artists, and in a short space of time Lutosławski had become a world figure, teaching and lecturing in Germany, Sweden, Britain and the United States, and from the mid-1960s onwards appearing as a highly effective conductor of his own works. Loaded with honours, prizes and other distinctions, he became the musical representative of Poland in all the cultural centres of Europe and America.

The list of his compositions remained small, but the quality is consistently high – and he never released a work until he was entirely satisfied with it. The *Third Symphony* lay in a bottom drawer for a decade before he decided to regard it as finished. Even his use of aleatory techniques (that is, allowing chance or the whim of the performer to dictate the course of the music, as pioneered by Cage) is controlled in an entirely un-Cage-like manner – 'I have no wish', he wrote, 'to surrender even the smallest part of my claim to authorship of even the shortest passage of the music which I have written.' Nothing could be clearer than that; it is only what one might expect from a composer whose sense of structure is so highly developed and whose craftsmanship so beautifully calculated. But the recognition that each of his performers 'is gifted with a much greater abundance of potentialities than those required by a purely abstractly conceived musical score', and the desire to harness this human element in the expression of his musical ideas, may have contributed to the later expansion of his style in a less cerebral, more purely expressive direction. In the end it is the sheer beauty of sound that makes Lutosławski, in many of his works, one of the most approachable of contemporary composers.

Bis weit in das 20. Jahrhundert hinein dachten die meisten Menschen bei polnischer Musik allein an Chopin. Es gab immer eine ausgeprägte musikalische Tradition in Polen, von der aber meist nur Polonaisen und Mazurkas erinnert wurden. Außer Chopin (der ohnehin ein halber Franzose war und nur deshalb Anerkennung gewonnen hatte, weil er so früh wie möglich nach Paris ging und dort blieb) hatte kein anderer polnischer Komponist internationalen Status erlangt. Erst die Komponisten Karol Szymanowski, Witold Lutosławski und Krzysztof Penderecki sorgten nach dem Ersten Weltkrieg dafür, daß sich dieses Bild änderte. Szymanowski zählte zu einer früheren Generation später Romantiker, Penderecki gehörte zu der radikalen Welt der Vorkriegsavantgarde, und Lutosławski vertrat den gemäßigten Flügel des vernünftigen Fortschritts und des ernsten musikalischen Ausdrucks.

Ebenso wie Ligeti in Ungarn konnte sich auch Lutosławski erst spät entwickeln, und 1956, als die Entspannung der stalinistischen Kulturrepression einsetzte, war er bereits zehn Jahre älter als sein ungarischer Kollege. Trotzdem war es ihm gelungen, Musik zu schreiben, die die Zeit überdauert hat wie eben seine atemberaubenden Variationen über Paganinis *Thema in a-moll* für zwei Klaviere, die den Vergleich mit Brahms und Rachmaninoff suchen, und das brillante *Konzert für Orchester* von 1970, das ihn über die Grenzen Polens hinaus bekannt machte. Er hatte im stillen mit einem neuen harmonischen System experimentiert, das auf dem Zwölftonsystem basierte (jedoch nicht auf Schönbergs Version, die ihm mißfiel), so daß er dann in der Phase der kulturellen Entspannung bereit war, seine Ideen auszuarbeiten und seine Werke auch wirklich aufzuführen, angefangen bei seiner *Trauermusik* von 1958 bis zur *Zweiten Symphonie*.

Mit der politischen Entspannung kam auch die Möglichkeit, frei zu reisen und sich mit anderen Künstlern auszutauschen, und schon nach kurzer Zeit erreichte Lutosławski internationale Bekanntheit. Er lehrte und unterrichtete in Deutschland, Schweden, England und den USA und trat ab Mitte der 60er Jahre als erfolgreicher Dirigent seiner eigenen Werke auf. Er erhielt viele Ehrungen, Preise und andere Auszeichnungen und galt in allen kulturellen Zentren Europas und Amerikas als Repräsentant der polnischen Musik.

Sein Œuvre ist nicht sehr umfangreich, aber seine Kompositionen sind bis ins letzte ausgearbeitet, denn er veröffentlichte kein Werk zu früh: Seine *Dritte Symphonie* lag zehn Jahre lang in der Schublade, bevor er sie als vollendet ansah. Er steuerte selbst aleatorische Techniken (die dem Zufall oder dem Interpreten Raum geben) auf eine Weise, die Cage, dem Initiator dieser Technik, ganz fremd gewesen wäre. „Es ist nicht mein Wunsch", schrieb er, „auch nur den kleinsten Teil meiner Autorenschaft aufzugeben, und sei es für die kürzeste musikalische Passage, die ich je geschrieben habe". Deutlicher kann es nicht gesagt werden. Was sollte man von einem Komponisten mit einem derartigen Gespür für musikalische Strukturen und einem so ausgeprägten Talent auch anderes erwarten. Die Erkenntnis, daß jeder seiner Interpreten „mit einer wesentlich größeren Fülle von Fähigkeiten begabt ist, als es eine rein abstrakt aufgefaßte Partitur erfordert", erweckte in ihm jedoch den Wunsch, dieses menschliche Vermögen für den Ausdruck seiner musikalischen Ideen zu nutzen. Dies mag zu der späteren Ausweitung seines Stils in eine weniger zeremonielle, expressivere Richtung beigetragen haben. Am Ende bleibt in vielen seiner Werke die reine Schönheit des Klanges, die Lutosławski zu einem der zugänglichsten unter den zeitgenössischen Komponisten gemacht hat.

Jusqu'à une date déjà bien avancée dans le XXᵉ siècle, la musique polonaise était représentée pour beaucoup par Chopin. Il y avait en Pologne une grande tradition musicale, et l'on savait que les polonaises et les mazurkas venaient de ce pays, cependant à part Chopin (qui était d'ailleurs à moitié français, et qui n'a réussi que parce qu'il partit à Paris aussitôt qu'il le put et qu'il y resta), aucun autre compositeur polonais n'atteignit de renommée internationale. À partir de la Première Guerre mondiale trois compositeurs renversèrent la situation : Karol Szymanowski, WitolLutosławski-ki et Krzysztof Penderecki. Szymanowski appartenait à la jeune génération de l'époque de la fin du romantisme, Penderecki au monde radical d'avant-garde de l'après-guerre, paLutosławskitoslawski était au centre d'un terrain d'entente entre un progrès raisonné et une expression musicale sérieuse.

Comme Ligeti en Hongrie, Lutosławski ne put exploiter toutes ses capacités que tardivement – mais il avait quand même dix ans de plus que Ligeti quand les freins mis au développement culturel à l'époque stalinienne se relâchèrent. Il parvint néanmoins à produire des œuvres musicales encore écoutées, que l'on peut peut-être comparer à Brahms et Rachmaninov pour sa superbe série de variations de la célèbre *Étude en la mineur* de Paganini. Il produisit également au moins une œuvre, le brillant *Concerto pour Orchestre*, qui le rendit célèbre hors de la Pologne. En outre, ayant expérimenté en secret un nouveau système harmonique basé sur celui des 12 sons (mais qui ne suit pas la même méthode que Schoenberg qu'il n'aimait pas), il lui fut possible dans la période qui suivit l'assouplissement des restrictions culturelles, de développer ses idées – et d'en entendre les résultats – en une série de compositions, avec d'abord, la *Musique funèbre* en 1958, puis la *Seconde Symphonie* et d'autres encore.

Grâce à la détente politique, il fut possible de voyager librement et de communiquer avec d'autres artistes, et rapidement, Lutosławski fut connu à travers le monde. Il enseigna, aussi à l'université en Allemagne, en Suède, en Grande-Bretagne et aux États-Unis. À partir de la seconde moitié des années 1960, il impressionna le public international en dirigeant ses propres œuvres. Couvert d'honneurs, de prix et autres distinctions, il devint le représentant de la musique polonaise dans tous les centres culturels européens et d'outre-Atlantique. La liste de ses compositions n'est pas longue mais la qualité demeure élevée – il ne publia d'ailleurs aucune œuvre dont il ne fut satisfait. La *Troisième Symphonie* resta au fond d'un tiroir pendant toute une décennie, tant qu'il ne la pensait pas achevée. Même lorsqu'il utilisait des techniques aléatoires (c'est-à-dire, laissant le hasard ou la fantaisie de l'interprète diriger le cours de sa musique, comme l'avait montré Cage initialement), ce fut dans un style totalement différent de celui de Cage – « Je n'ai aucune envie », écrivit-il, « de céder même une partie infiniment petite de mes droits d'auteur du plus petit morceau de musique que j'ai écrit. » On ne pouvait guère être plus clair ; et c'est tout ce qu'on pouvait attendre d'un compositeur dont le sens de la structure est aussi développé, et l'art aussi bien maîtrisé. Mais le fait de voir en chacun de ses musiciens « une profusion de potentialités plus étendues que celles requises par une partition musicale conçue purement dans l'abstrait », et le désir d'exploiter l'élément humain dans l'expression concrète de sa musique, contribuèrent probablement au développement de son style dans une voie moins cérébrale et plus purement expressive. Enfin, la beauté du son fit de Lutosławski, pour un grand nombre de ses œuvres, l'un des compositeurs contemporains les plus accessibles.

Among the musical riches in London during the Festival of Britain in 1951, one outstanding theatrical event caught the popular imagination, a drama of personal despair in the face of political barriers and bureaucratic obstructionism that drove home its message with uncomfortable sincerity and skill. *The Consul*, which had received its première in New York a year earlier, was the American composer Gian Carlo Menotti's first full-length opera, and its unashamed use of the musical style of Puccini and the Italian verismo composers did not find favour with the sterner British critics. But the public flocked to see it: the music was accessible, the story was painfully believable – and besides, who had ever seen a conjuror produce doves out of a hat and bouquets out of thin air on the operatic stage?

Until then Menotti had been known in Britain mainly as the composer of two short but brilliantly accomplished operas, *The Medium*, and the one-act comedy *The Telephone* which became staple fare for the more adventurous amateur operatic societies during the 1950s. They were soon joined by *Amahl and the Night Visitors*, which became a firm Christmas favourite, but *The Saint of Bleecker Street* attracted more critical than popular acclaim.

Meanwhile, he had turned back towards his Italian roots to found the Festival of Two Worlds in the Umbrian town of Spoleto, and from 1958 this highly successful venture – which soon spread to Charleston, South Carolina – took up more and more of his time, to the detriment, some said, of his career as a composer. Nevertheless he continued to produce works for the stage with varying success, and in 1964 was commissioned to write a church opera, *Martin's Lie*, for the Bath Festival. In 1973, sated with the continuous blue skies of Umbria and desperate for a less demanding environment in which to write music, he sold his house in New York and moved to Scotland, where he has made his permanent home ever since.

Von allen musikalischen Kostbarkeiten des Festival of Britain in London im Jahre 1951 beschäftigte besonders eine herausragende Aufführung alle Gemüter. Es handelte sich um ein Drama voll menschlicher Verzweiflung angesichts der Konfrontation mit politischen Grenzen und einer obstruktiven Bürokratie, das seine Botschaft mit unbequemer Ernsthaftigkeit und großem Können vermittelte. Das musikalische Drama *The Consul* wurde ein Jahr zuvor in New York uraufgeführt. Es war die erste große Oper des amerikanischen Komponisten Gian Carlo Menotti. Seine offensichtliche Anlehnung an den Stil Puccinis und den italienischen Realismus mißfiel den ernsteren britischen Kritikern; das Publikum jedoch strömte herbei: Die Musik war eingängig und die Geschichte erschreckend wahr – und außerdem, wer hatte je erlebt, daß ein Magier auf der Opernbühne Tauben aus dem Hut und Blumen aus der Luft zauberte?

Bis dahin war Menotti in England hauptsächlich als Komponist zweier kurzer, aber ausgezeichnet ausgearbeiteter Opern bekannt: *The Medium* und *The Telephone*, letztere eine Komödie in einem Akt, die in den 50er Jahren bei den wagemutigeren unter den Operngesellschaften der Amateursänger hoch im Kurs stand. *Amahl and the Night Visitors*, das kurz darauf folgte, wurde ein beliebtes Weihnachtsstück. *The Saint of Bleecker Street* zog eher die Aufmerksamkeit der Kritiker als den Beifall des Publikums auf sich.

Inzwischen war der Künstler nach Italien zurückgekehrt und hatte im umbrischen Spoleto das „Festival zweier Welten" ins Leben gerufen. Ab 1958 nahm dieses erfolgreiche Unternehmen seine Zeit mehr und mehr in Anspruch, zum Nachteil seiner Laufbahn als Komponist, wie einige behaupten. Trotzdem komponierte er weiterhin Bühnenstücke, wenn auch mit wechselndem Erfolg. 1964 wurde er damit beauftragt, für die Festspiele in Bath die Kirchenoper *Martin's Lie* zu schreiben. 1973 wurde er des stets blauen Himmels von Umbrien überdrüssig, und verkaufte auf der Suche nach einer weniger anstrengenden Umgebung, in der er schreiben konnte, sein Haus in New York, um nach Schottland zu ziehen, wo er seitdem ständig lebt.

Parmi les richesses musicales de Londres, au festival de Grande-Bretagne en 1951, un spectacle exceptionnel conquit le public : le drame d'un désespoir personnel face aux barrières politiques et l'obstructionnisme bureaucratique, communiquant une sincérité pénible avec beaucoup d'habileté. *The Consul*, dont la première fut jouée à New York un an auparavant, est le premier grand opéra de Gian Carlo Menotti. Il avait utilisé, sans se gêner, le style musical de Puccini et des compositeurs véristes italiens, et cela déplut à la critique britannique plus sévère. Mais beaucoup accoururent pour le voir : la musique était accessible, l'histoire si douloureuse était crédible – et d'ailleurs, avait-on jamais vu un prestidigitateur sortir d'un chapeau des colombes et des bouquets de fleurs comme par magie ?

Jusque-là, Menotti avait été en Grande-Bretagne connu comme le compositeur de deux opéras, courts, mais brillamment réalisés, *The Medium*, et la comédie en un acte, *The Telephone*, qui devinrent les éléments de base des compagnies d'opéra amateurs plus aventureuses des années 1950. À ceux-ci vinrent s'ajouter *Amahl and the Night Visitors*, maintenant une chanson de Noël bien établie, et *The Saint of Bleecker Street*, qui s'attira par contre plus de critiques que de popularité.

À cette époque, il se tourna vers ses racines italiennes et fonda le Festival des Deux Mondes, dans la ville de Spolète en Ombrie. À partir de 1958, cette entreprise extrêmement réussie – qui s'étendit à Charleston et à la Caroline du Sud – occupa de plus en plus son temps, au détriment, selon certains, de sa carrière de compositeur. Il continua néanmoins à produire des œuvres pour la scène qui eurent plus ou moins de succès, et en 1964 on le chargea d'écrire un opéra sacré, *Martin's Lie*, pour le Festival de Bath. En 1973, ayant assez du ciel d'azur d'Ombrie, et souhaitant ardemment un endroit plus paisible, qui lui permette de composer, il vendit sa maison de New York et alla vivre en Écosse, maintenant sa résidence permanente.

Gian Carlo Menotti, September 1957.
Gian Carlo Menotti, September 1957.
Gian Carlo Menotti, septembre 1957.

The composer watches from the control room while Schippers conducts the Philharmonia Orchestra.

Der Komponist beobachtet Schippers vom Kontrollraum aus beim Dirigieren des Philharmonia Orchestra.

Le compositeur observe depuis la salle de contrôle, pendant que Schippers dirige le Philharmonia Orchestra.

In the playback room Menotti, the conductor Thomas Schippers and the American soprano Eileen Farrell sing along as they listen to tapes of arias from *The Consul*. Schippers, then at the Metropolitan Opera, New York, had directed the premières of several of Menotti's operas, though he did not conduct this one until it opened in New York two weeks after its first performance in Philadelphia, 25 September 1957.

Menotti, der Dirigent Thomas Schippers und die amerikanische Sopranistin Eileen Farrell singen im Playback-Raum zu Bändern der Arien aus dem *Consul*. Schippers, damals an der Metropolitan Opera in New York, dirigierte mehrere Premieren von Menottis Opern. Diese jedoch dirigierte er erst in New York, zwei Wochen nach der Uraufführung in Philadelphia, 25. September 1957.

Dans la salle de lecture, Menotti, le chef d'orchestre Thomas Schippers, et la soprano américaine Eileen Farrell écoutent les cassettes des arias du *Consul* et chantent en même temps. Schippers, alors au Metropolitan Opera de New York, avait dirigé les premiè-res de plusieurs opéras de Menotti, mais pas celle-ci qu'il ne dirigea à New York, que deux semaines après sa première représentation à Philadelphie, le 25 septembre 1957.

OLIVIER MESSIAEN 1908-1992

Organ music, birdsong and sexual love seem an improbable combination of ingredients for one of the most powerful influences in 20th-century music, especially emanating from a universally respected teacher of profound Catholic religious conviction. But Messiaen's pupils included Boulez, Stockhausen, Jean Barraqué, Iannis Xenakis and many others, and his credentials as the father figure of the European avant-garde in the post war years are unassailable.

He began as an organist, at La Trinité in Paris, where he continued to play regularly for over 40 years. He always claimed that the decisive factor in his determination to become a composer was the gift of a score of Debussy's *Pelléas et Mélisande* at the age of ten, but his musical curiosity was soon leading him in more exotic directions – Hindu rhythms, Greek modes, plainchant, folk music and above all birdsong, a passion that remained with him all his life. His love of nature was second only to his love of love itself: 'In dark hours', he said, 'when my uselessness is brutally revealed to me... I go into the forest, into fields, into mountains, by the sea, among birds.... It is there that music dwells for me; free, anonymous music, improvised for pleasure. Birds alone are the great artists.'

When the war came he was taken prisoner in 1940 and produced his first masterpiece in a Silesian stalag, the hour-long *Quatuor pour la fin du temps* for himself (at the piano) and three fellow prisoners who played the violin, clarinet and cello. Repatriated to France, he took up a position as professor of harmony at the Paris Conservatoire and set out on a teaching career which lasted in one form or another for the rest of his life. But another lifelong attachment dates from this time: at the first performance of the two-piano *Visions de l'amen* in 1943 the second pianist was his pupil Yvonne Loriod; from then on she gave the premières of all Messiaen's piano works and married him in 1961.

His faith was very real and the fundamental inspiration for most of his works was in some way religious. But in the later 1940s love in a more secular sense also began to permeate his music, and its textures became correspondingly more luxuriant. 'The abundance of technical means allows the heart to expand more freely', he said, and put the principle into practice in the *Turangalîla Symphony* – a huge, flamboyant explosion of sensual love, divinity and exotic sound that lasts an hour and a half and has become one of Messiaen's relatively popular compositions. Chief among the exotic sounds is the strange, erotic wail of the ondes martenot, an electronic instrument that he had first used a few years earlier in the *Trois petites liturgies de la présence divine*.

After *Turangalîla*, perhaps feeling the need of a complete change, Messiaen concentrated on clarity of texture and intellectual manipulation of rhythms and systems in works which had a profound effect on composers like Stockhausen and Boulez but had less to offer the general musical public. But later the preoccupation with birds reappears, culminating in the 13 sections of the monumental *Catalogue des oiseaux* for piano solo, and religious themes again predominate. They reached their most dramatic expression in *Et exspecto resurrectionem mortuorum*, an apocalyptic vision for wind, brass and percussion dedicated to the dead of two world wars and first performed in 1965.

Olivier Messiaen with the *Turangalîla* score, Oxford, 28 June 1967.
Olivier Messiaen mit der *Turangalîla*-Partitur, Oxford, 28. Juni 1967.
Olivier Messiaen avec la partition de la *Turangalîla Symphony*, Oxford, le 28 juin 1967.

Orgelmusik, Vogelgezwitscher und Erotik scheinen eine zu verquere Zusammenstellung zu sein, um als Quellen der maßgeblichsten Einflüsse auf die Musik des 20. Jahrhunderts gelten zu können – besonders, wenn sie von einem allgemein respektierten, streng katholischen Lehrer propagiert werden. Zu den Schülern Olivier Messiaens zählten jedoch Boulez, Stockhausen, Jean Barraqué, Iannis Xenakis und viele andere, und seine Stellung als Vaterfigur der europäischen Avantgarde der Nachkriegszeit ist vollkommen unbestreitbar.

Er begann als Organist in La Trinité in Paris, wo er über 40 Jahre lang spielte. Er hat immer behauptet, sein Entschluß, Komponist zu werden, sei auf die Partitur von Debussys *Pelléas et Mélisande* zurückzuführen, die er mit zehn Jahren geschenkt bekommen hatte. Seine musikalische Neugier führte ihn aber bald in exotischere Richtungen – zu Hindurhythmen, griechischen Weisen, Gregorianischem Gesang, Volksmusik und vor allem zum Vogelgezwitscher, das er sein Leben lang geliebt hat. Seine Liebe zur Natur wurde nur von der Liebe zur Liebe selbst übertroffen: „In dunklen Stunden, wenn mir meine Nichtigkeit schonungslos bewußt wird ... gehe ich in den Wald, in die Berge, ans Meer, zu den Vögeln ... Dort ist die Musik für mich zu Hause; freie, selbstlose Musik, improvisiert aus reiner Freude. Nur Vögel sind große Künstler."

1940 geriet er in Kriegsgefangenschaft und schrieb sein erstes Meisterwerk in einem schlesischen Gefangenenlager. Es war das einstündige *Quatuor pour la fin du temps*, das er für sich (am Klavier) und drei Mithäftlinge schrieb, die Violine, Klarinette und Cello spielten. Nachdem er entlassen worden war, nahm er eine Stelle als Professor für Harmonielehre am Pariser Konservatorium an. So begann seine Laufbahn als Lehrer, die er auf die eine oder andere Weise sein Leben lang weiterverfolgte. Auch eine andere Bindung fürs Leben stammt aus dieser Zeit: Seine Schülerin Yvonne Loriod spielte 1943 die Uraufführung des Stückes *Visions de l'amen* für zwei Klaviere mit ihm zusammen; von da an spielte sie alle Uraufführungen seiner Werke für Klavier. 1961 heirateten die beiden.

Sein Glaube war ihm eine Quelle der Inspiration, und die meisten seiner Werke behandeln religiöse Themen. Seit den späten 40er Jahren hielt aber auch die Liebe in ihrer sinnlicheren Gestalt Einzug in seine Musik, die in ihrem Aufbau entsprechend üppiger wurde. „Die Fülle der technischen Möglichkeiten erlaubt dem Herzen einen ungezwungeneren Ausdruck", sagte er und übersetzte diese Idee mit der *Turangalîla Symphonie* in die Praxis – ein groß angelegter, überbordender Ausbruch von Sinnlichkeit, Göttlichkeit und exotischem Klang, der eineinhalb Stunden dauert und zu einer seiner bekanntesten Kompositionen wurde. Das Kernstück unter den exotischen Klängen bilden die fremdartigen, sinnlichen Seufzer der „Ondes Martenot", eines elektronischen Tasteninstruments von Martenot, das Messiaen bereits einige Jahre zuvor in *Trois petites liturgies de la présence divine* eingesetzt hatte.

Nach *Turangalîla* fühlte er das Bedürfnis nach Veränderung und konzentrierte sich auf Arbeiten, deren klarer Aufbau und deren intellektuelle Manipulation der Rhythmen und Tonsysteme eine nachhaltige Wirkung auf Komponisten wie Stockhausen und Boulez ausübten, dem breiteren Publikum aber fremd blieben. Später wendete er sich wieder stärker den Vögeln zu. Die Folge war der dreizehnteilige, monumentale *Catalogue des oiseaux* für Soloklavier. Die religiöse Thematik fand ihren wohl dramatischsten Ausdruck in *Et exspecto resurrectionem mortuorum*, einer apokalyptischen Vision für Wind-, Blas- und Schlaginstrumente. Das Werk ist den Toten der beiden Weltkriege gewidmet und wurde 1965 uraufgeführt.

On a du mal à croire qu'orgue, chant d'oiseau, amour physique puissent être à l'origine d'une des plus grandes influences de la musique du XXᵉ siècle, surtout quand ces éléments sont utilisés par un professeur universellement respecté aux profondes convictions religieuses. Ses élèves regroupèrent Boulez, Stockhausen, Jean Barraqué, Iannis Xenakis et beaucoup d'autres encore, et l'on ne pourrait nier son rôle de père de la musique d'avant-garde des années d'après-guerre.

Il commença comme organiste à La Trinité de Paris, où il devait jouer régulièrement pendant plus de quarante ans. Il déclarait toujours que ce qui le poussa à devenir compositeur fut, à l'âge de dix ans, d'avoir entendu la beauté d'une partition tirée de *Pelléas et Mélisande* de Debussy. Sa curiosité musicale allait cependant lui faire prendre des directions plus exotiques – rythmes hindous, modes grecs, plains-chants, musique folklorique, et surtout des chants d'oiseau, une passion qui jamais ne le quitta. Son amour de la nature ne venait qu'après son amour de l'amour lui-même: « Dans mes sombres moments », dit-il, « lorsque mon inutilité se révèle brutalement à moi, je vais en forêt, dans les champs, sur les montagnes, au bord de la mer, parmi les oiseaux... Pour moi c'est là que vit la musique; libre, anonyme, improvisée pour le plaisir. Seuls les oiseaux sont les grands artistes. »

Pendant la guerre, il fut fait prisonnier en 1940 et compose pour lui-même (au piano) et trois autres prisonniers (un violoniste, un clarinettiste et un violoncelliste), son premier chef-d'œuvre qui dure une heure, *Quatuor pour la fin du temps* dans un stalag de Silésie. Rapatrié en France, il accepta une chaire de professeur d'harmonie au Conservatoire de Paris. Commence alors une carrière d'enseignant à laquelle il devait rester fidèle jusqu'à la fin de sa vie. Un autre attachement devait aussi à partir de là l'accompagner toute son existence: à la première représentation de *Visions de l'amen*, pour deux pianos (1943), son élève Yvonne Loriod était la deuxième pianiste. Elle joua toujours les premières de toutes les œuvres pour piano de Messiaen, et celui-ci l'épousa en 1961.

Sa foi était authentique et l'inspiration fondamentale était à certains égards et pour la plupart de ses compositions, religieuse. À la fin des années 1940, l'amour prit un sens plus profane. Sa musique s'imprégna de cette nouvelle teinte, et ses textures se firent plus luxuriantes. « La profusion des moyens techniques permet au cœur de s'ouvrir plus librement », dit-il. Il mit ce principe en pratique dans la *Turangalîla-Symphonie* – une explosion géante de sensualité, de divinité, et de sons exotiques, qui dure une heure et demie et qui devint une de ses compositions plus populaires. Comme sons exotiques, on entendra principalement l'étrange plainte érotique des ondes martenot, un instrument électronique qu'il utilisa pour la première fois quelques années auparavant dans les *Trois petites liturgies de la présence divine*.

Après *Turangalîla* Messiaen se concentra sur une série d'œuvres dont la clarté de texture et la manipulation intellectuelle des rythmes et systèmes produisirent un effet énorme sur des compositeurs tel que Stockhausen et Boulez, mais eurent moins d'impact sur le grand public. Le thème des oiseaux revint aussi et atteignit son apogée dans les 13 sections du monumental *Catalogue des oiseaux*, pour piano solo. Les thèmes religieux recommencèrent à prédominer. Ils apparurent dans un effet des plus dramatiques dans *Et exspecto resurrectionem mortuorum*, une vision apocalyptique pour des instruments à vent, cuivres et percussions. Cette œuvre est dédiée aux morts des deux guerres mondiales, et une première représentation fut donnée en 1965.

DARIUS MILHAUD   1892-1974

Of the famous French group Les Six, formed round the influential figures of Erik Satie and Jean Cocteau to purge the taint of Wagner from French music and turn it in less solemn directions, only three – Arthur Honegger, Francis Poulenc and Milhaud – ever really achieved the big-time, and of these only Milhaud was captured on camera by Auerbach. Partly at least this was because Honegger was too ill to come to London after the Second World War, and because Poulenc, though he made visits to Britten and the Aldeburgh Festival and was present at the first British performance of his *Dialogues des Carmélites* in 1958, was a very private person, not easy to catch in a moment of public appearance.

Milhaud, on the other hand, was a passionate traveller. He had many friends among writers and painters and at the very outset of his career spent two years in Rio de Janeiro as secretary to the writer Paul Claudel, then French minister in Brazil. The indelible impression left by Latin American music was joined later in his travels by jazz, which together with the countryside of his own native Provence provided some of the most abiding influences in his music. In spite of his rheumatoid arthritis, a continually worsening condition which caused him long periods of intense suffering and in the end more or less confined him to a wheelchair, he continued his activities as a teacher in America and at the Paris Conservatoire until well into his seventies, and his output as a composer was immense, reaching a total of 441 opus numbers. True, some of them were very short, like the three nine-minute operas that he wrote to texts based on Greek mythology, but at the other end of the scale were the imposing collaboration with Paul Claudel, *Christophe Colomb*, and the three large-scale stage works that followed it.

His association with Satie and the provocatively popular flavour of early works like the ballet *Le bœuf sur le toit* gave Milhaud an enfant terrible reputation which was hard to live down, and works which were intended perfectly seriously, like the two song cycles dealing with descriptions of farm machinery (*Machines agricoles*) and extracts from a florist's catalogue (*Catalogue des fleurs*), were laughed off as frivolous. But the best of those days, like the brilliantly successful jazz ballet *La création du monde*, secured his reputation long after 'Les Six' had disintegrated as a group, and have proved more durable than many other attempts to find common ground between 'serious' and 'popular' music.

Aus der berühmten französischen Gruppe Les Six, die sich um die richtungweisenden Künstler Erik Satie und Jean Cocteau bildete, um die französische Musik vom Einfluß Wagners zu befreien und ihr eine größere Leichtigkeit zurückzugeben, schafften nur drei einen wirklichen Durchbruch: Arthur Honegger, Francis Poulenc und Darius Milhaud. Lediglich Milhaud wurde von Auerbach mit der Kamera festgehalten. Das lag sicher auch daran, daß Honegger nach dem Zweiten Weltkrieg zu krank war, um nach London zu kommen, und Poulenc, obwohl er Britten und die Festspiele in Aldeburgh besuchte und bei der ersten englischen Aufführung seiner *Dialogues des Carmélites* 1958 selbst zugegen war, sehr zurückgezogen lebte und selten in der Öffentlichkeit anzutreffen war.

Milhaud hingegen reiste leidenschaftlich gern. Er zählte viele Schriftsteller und Maler zu seinen Freunden, und gleich zu Beginn seiner Laufbahn verbrachte er zwei Jahre in Rio de Janeiro als Sekretär des Dichters Paul Claudel, der damals französischer Botschafter in Brasilien war. Zu dem unauslöschlichen Eindruck der Lateinamerikanischen Musik kam auf späteren Reisen noch der Jazz hinzu. Die neuen musikalischen Erfahrungen und die Landschaft seiner Heimat, die Provence, hatten entscheidenden Einfluß auf die Entwicklung seiner Musik. Trotz seiner rheumatischen Arthritis, die sich zusehends verschlimmerte, ihm lange Leidenszeiten bereitete und ihn schließlich an den Rollstuhl fesselte, setzte er seine Lehrtätigkeit in Amerika und am Pariser Konservatorium fort, bis er die siebzig weit überschritten hatte. Außerdem war er ein unermüdlicher Komponist. Er hinterließ insgesamt 441 Werke. Darunter sind auch einige sehr kurze, wie die drei Miniatur-Opern von insgesamt 30 Minuten, die er zu Themen der griechischen Mythologie schrieb. Das andere Extrem bilden jedoch die beeindruckende Oper *Christophe Colomb* mit dem Text von Claudel und die drei nachfolgenden großen Bühnenwerke.

Seine Verbindung zu Satie und der provokativ populäre Ton seiner frühen Werke wie in dem Ballett *Le bœuf sur le toit* brachten Milhaud jenen Ruf eines enfant terrible ein, der ihm später anhaftete. Werke mit vollständig ernsthaften Absichten wie die beiden Liederzyklen *Machines agricoles*, der landwirtschaftliche Maschinen beschreibt, und *Catalogue des fleurs* mit Auszügen aus einem Floristenkatalog wurden als frivol belächelt. Seine besten Werke jener Tage aber – wie das sehr erfolgreiche Jazzballett *La création du monde* – sicherten ihm seinen Ruf noch lange nachdem Les Six sich aufgelöst hatten. Sie haben die Zeiten besser überdauert als manch anderer Versuch, die Kluft zwischen ernster Musik und Unterhaltungsmusik zu überbrücken.

Du célèbre groupe français Les Six, formé autour des influents Erik Satie et Jean Cocteau, afin d'éliminer toute trace de Wagner dans la musique française et donc de la diriger dans des voies moins formelles, seules trois personnes – Arthur Honegger, Francis Poulenc et Milhaud – connurent la célébrité. De plus, parmi ceux qui ont réussi, seul Milhaud a été saisi sur le film de Auerbach. C'était en partie parce que Honegger était trop malade pour se déplacer jusqu'à Londres après la Deuxième Guerre mondiale. Quant à Poulenc, bien qu'il soit allé voir Britten, se soit rendu au Festival d'Aldeburgh, et qu'il ait assisté à la première représentation de ses *Dialogues des Carmélites* en 1958, c'était quelqu'un de très privé, difficile à approcher lors de ses apparitions en public.

Milhaud, quant à lui, adorait voyager. Il possédait de nombreux amis écrivains et peintres, et au début de sa carrière, il passa deux ans à Rio de Janeiro comme secrétaire de l'écrivain Paul Claudel, alors ministre français au Brésil. La musique latine américaine aura laissé une impression décisive sur son style. À ce genre viendra s'ajouter au cours de ses voyages, le jazz, ainsi que la campagne de sa Provence natale qui aura une influence, elle aussi, indélébile. Milhaud souffrait de polyarthrite chronique qui ne cessa de s'empirer, et qui le jetait dans des périodes de souffrance extrême. Vers la fin de sa vie, il fut plus ou moins consigné à la chaise roulante. Malgré la gravité de sa maladie, il continua d'enseigner en Amérique et au Conservatoire de Paris après avoir même bien dépassé ses soixante-dix ans. Ses compositions furent très nombreuses, atteignant un total de 411 opus. Il est vrai que certaines œuvres étaient fort courtes, comme les opéras de neuf minutes qu'il composa sur des textes tirés de la mythologie grecque. D'un autre côté par contre, il y avait sa collaboration imposante avec Paul Claudel, dans *Christophe Colomb*, et les trois œuvres pour la scène qui suivirent.

Son association avec Satie et le ton populaire et provocant de ses premières œuvres, comme le ballet *Le Bœuf sur le toit* donnèrent à Milhaud une réputation d'enfant terrible dont il lui fut difficile de se débarrasser. C'est pourquoi des compositions qui pour lui étaient parfaitement sérieuses, comme les deux cycles de chansons mettant en scène des *Machines agricoles* et des extraits d'un *Catalogue des Fleurs*, furent jugées frivoles. Cependant, ses meilleures œuvres de cette époque, comme l'excellent ballet jazz, *La Création du monde*, ont protégé sa réputation bien après la désintégration du groupe Les Six, et ont mieux résisté au temps que beaucoup d'autres qui tentèrent de concilier les musiques « sérieuse » et « populaire ».

Darius Milhaud, September 1969.
Darius Milhaud, September 1969.
Darius Milhaud, septembre 1969.

Milhaud, on a rare visit to London, conducting the BBC Symphony Orchestra at the Maida Vale studios in a programme of his own music and works by Erik Satie, 19 September 1969.

Während einem seiner seltenen Londoner Besuche dirigiert Milhaud das BBC Symphony Orchestra in den Studios in Maida Vale in einer Sendung mit Werken von Erik Satie und ihm selbst, 19. September 1969.

Le 19 septembre 1969 : Milhaud, lors de l'une de ses rares visites à Londres, en train de diriger le BBC Symphony Orchestra aux studios de Maida Vale avec un programme contenant ses propres œuvres et quelques-unes d'Erik Satie.

DMITRY SHOSTAKOVICH   DMITRI SCHOSTAKOWITSCH   DIMITRI CHOSTAKOVITCH
1906-1975

Shostakovich was the first of the truly Soviet composers, conditioned by the society in which he lived to see everything 'Western' as decadent and alien to his inner beliefs.

He was a musician of phenomenal natural gifts, and it is a matter for endless debate how much those gifts suffered, or were perversely intensified, by the political and cultural conditions in which he lived so much of his life. What is certain is that they caused him, as a true and patriotic Russian, much soul-searching and deep unhappiness.

His career began with a tremendous splash when his *First Symphony*, written as a graduation piece, achieved instant success and was taken up by star conductors in Europe and America. In those early days, before Stalinism had tightened its cultural grip, the technical brilliance, quirky humour and biting satire of a self-evident *enfant terrible* were smiled on by the regime, and the lack of more popular appeal was not yet a target for criticism. But times were changing: in 1930 his first opera, *The Nose*, was accused of 'bourgeois decadence' and in 1936 its successor, *Lady Macbeth of the Mtsensk District*, which had been an immense success at its first performance two years earlier, was suddenly denounced in *Pravda* as neurotic, coarse and vulgar in a vitriolic article headed 'Chaos instead of music'.

The article, instigated if not written by Stalin himself, had a devastating effect. Shostakovich found himself overnight an enemy of the people: he withdrew his *Fourth Symphony* and his career appeared to be ruined. But after much tough thinking he came to terms with the situation, and in 1937 made a triumphant comeback with the *Fifth Symphony*, a work which was hailed (though not by its composer) as 'the creative reply of a Soviet artist to justified criticism'. Restored to favour, he resumed his career with one difference: with the exception of *Katerina Izmaylova*, a revision of *Lady Macbeth* performed in later, safer days, he never again wrote a full opera. It was as a symphonist that he first became known to the musical public in the West, a process accelerated as chance would have it by one of his less good works, the *Seventh Symphony*, written during the siege of Leningrad and disseminated all over the West as a symbol of the resistance to Nazism. But gradually the works which followed again fell foul of official criticism: with the war over, a new purge was beginning, and in 1948 Shostakovich found himself once more in disgrace for 'formalism' and 'anti-democratic' art.

For the next five years he played safe, sticking to film music and patriotic cantatas for public consumption and keeping works like the *First Violin Concerto* and the *Fourth String Quartet* a secret from the authorities. Only after Stalin's death did he dare to return to his true musical path, producing in that same year a *Tenth Symphony* to add to the series, which would reach 15 before his own death 22 years later. In the absence of the operas that he might have written, it is these works which, along with the 15 string quartets, have established him as the one composer of unquestionable Soviet loyalties to achieve world recognition and status.

Schostakowitsch war einer der ersten wirklich sowjetischen Komponisten, und seine gesellschaftliche Prägung hatte ihn darin geschult, alles „Westliche" als etwas Dekadentes anzusehen, das seinen innersten Überzeugungen fremd war.

Er verfügte über eine außergewöhnliches Begabung. Es gibt endlose Debatten darüber, ob die politischen und kulturellen Bedingungen, unter denen er die meiste Zeit seines Lebens verbrachte, sein Talent eher behindert oder zu einer übernatürlichen Intensität gesteigert haben. Sicher ist, daß er als echter patriotischer Russe viel Seelenpein und tiefes Unglück zu erleiden hatte.

Sein Aufstieg begann sprunghaft mit der *Ersten Symphonie*, der Abschlußarbeit seines Studiums, die sofort von Stardirigenten in Europa und Amerika begeistert aufgeführt wurde. In jenen frühen Tagen, bevor der Stalinismus die Kultur fest im Griff hielt, wurde die technische Perfektion, der spritzige Humor und die beißende Satire eines offensichtlichen *enfant terrible* noch vom Regime belächelt. Der Mangel an Volkstümlichkeit bildete noch keinen Angriffspunkt für die Kritik. Aber die Zeiten änderten sich: 1930 wurde seine erste Oper, *Die Nase*, der „bürgerlichen Dekadenz" beschuldigt, und 1936 wurde *Lady Macbeth von Mzensk*, die zwei Jahre zuvor bei der Uraufführung ein großer Erfolg gewesen war, plötzlich von der Prawda in einem beißenden Artikel mit der Überschrift „Chaos statt Musik" als neurotisch, grob und vulgär geschmäht.

Der Artikel war auf Veranlassung Stalins, wenn nicht gar von ihm selbst, verfaßt worden und das Ergebnis vernichtend: Schostakowitsch galt plötzlich als Volksfeind. Er zog seine *Vierte Symphonie* zurück, und seine Laufbahn schien zu Ende. Nach einigem Grübeln arrangierte er sich jedoch mit der Situation und hatte 1937 mit seiner *Fünften Symphonie* ein glänzendes Comeback. Das Werk wurde als „die kreative Antwort eines sowjetischen Künstlers auf berechtigte Kritik" gelobt. Wieder in der Gunst setzte er seinen Werdegang weiter fort, wenngleich mit einem Unterschied: Abgesehen von *Katerina Ismailowa*, einer Überarbeitung von *Lady Macbeth*, die später in sichereren Zeiten aufgeführt wurde, schrieb er nie wieder eine große Oper, weswegen das westliche Publikum zuerst seine Symphonien kennenlernte. Wie es der Zufall bestimmte, wurde er zuerst mit einem weniger brillanten Werk bekannt: Seine *Siebente Symphonie* entstand während der Belagerung von Leningrad und wurde überall im Westen zum Symbol des Widerstandes gegen die Nazis. Nach und nach fanden seine Werke jedoch wieder das Mißfallen der offiziellen Kritik. Als der Krieg vorbei war, begann eine neue Säuberungswelle, und 1948 fiel Schostakowitsch wegen „Formalismus" und „anti-demokratischer" Kunst erneut in Ungnade.

In den folgenden fünf Jahren setzte er auf Sicherheit, indem er für das Massenpublikum Filmmusiken und patriotische Gesänge schrieb. Seine anderen Arbeiten wie das *Erste Violinkonzert* und das *Vierte Streichquartett* verbarg er dagegen vor der Obrigkeit. Erst nach Stalins Tod, 1953, wagte er sich auf seinen eigentlichen musikalischen Weg zurück und schrieb im gleichen Jahr seine *Zehnte Symphonie*. Als er 22 Jahre später starb, hinterließ er insgesamt 15 Symphonien. In Ermangelung der Opern, die er geschrieben haben könnte, sind es diese Werke und 15 Streichquartette, die ihn zu dem einzigen Komponisten machen, der in seiner zweifellosen Loyalität der Sowjetunion gegenüber weltweit Ruhm und Anerkennung fand.

Chostakovitch fut le premier réel compositeur soviétique, conditionné par une société qui voyait tout ce qui était « à l'Ouest » comme décadent et étranger à ses convictions personnelles.

Il était un musicien aux dons naturels remarquables, et l'on se demandera toujours à quel point ces dons souffrirent ou furent au contraire ironiquement intensifiés par les conditions politiques et culturelles dans lesquelles il vécut pendant si longtemps. Il est incontestable que son sentiment réel pour sa patrie, l'Union Soviétique, lui causa une grande tristesse et l'incita à beaucoup de réflexions sur ses propres motivations intérieures.

Il fit un coup d'éclat au début de sa carrière, quand sa *Première Symphonie*, écrite pour une remise de diplômes, jouit d'un succès immédiat, et fut reprise par des chefs d'orchestre célèbres, comme Bruno Walter à Berlin et Leopold Stokowski en Amérique. À cette époque, avant que Staline n'ai resserré sa poigne sur la culture, la technique remarquable, l'humour excentrique, et la satire mordante d'un enfant terrible faisaient sourire le régime, et le manque de popularité n'était pas encore exposé à la critique. Mais les temps changeaient : en 1930, son premier opéra, *Le Nez*, fut accusé de « décadence bourgeoise », et en 1936, celui qui suivit, *Lady Macbeth du quartier Mtsensk*, qui avait eu un immense succès lors de sa première représentation deux ans plus tôt, fut soudain dénoncé dans la *Pravda* dans un article écrit au vitriol, comme névrotique, grossier et vulgaire, avec en titre, « Le chaos à la place de la musique ».

Que Staline ait influencé son auteur ou qu'il l'ait lui-même écrit, cet article eut un effet dévastateur. Du jour au lendemain, Chostakovitch devint un ennemi du peuple : il retira sa *Quatrième Symphonie* et sa carrière donna l'impression d'être ruinée. Après avoir longuement réfléchi, il finit par accepter la situation et, en 1937, il revint avec la *Cinquième Symphonie* qui le porta au triomphe. Cette composition fut reconnue comme étant « par le moyen de la créativité, la réplique à une critique justifiée ». Ayant retrouvé l'approbation de tous, il continua sa carrière à une différence près : à l'exception de *Katerina Izmaylova*, une révision de *Lady Macbeth*, dont la représentation ne fut donnée que bien plus tard à une époque plus sûre, il n'écrivit jamais plus un grand opéra. En conséquence, ce fut en tant que compositeur d'œuvres pour orchestre, et surtout comme symphoniste, qu'il fut d'abord connu par le public musical de l'Ouest. Le hasard voulut que l'une de ses moins bonnes œuvres, la *Septième Symphonie*, aide à sa renommée. En effet, la partition écrite durant le siège de Leningrad, fut propagée aux quatre coins de l'occident comme le symbole de la résistance contre le nazisme. Les meilleures œuvres qui suivirent subirent à nouveau d'infâmes critiques : après la guerre, une nouvelle purge eut lieu et en 1948 Chostakovitch se trouva encore en proie à la disgrâce pour cause de « formalisme » et d'art « anti-démocratique ».

Les cinq années suivantes, il ne prit aucun risque en ne faisant que des musiques de film et des cantates patriotiques pour le grand public. Il garda secrète la composition d'œuvres comme le *Premier Concerto pour Violon* et le *Quatrième Quatuor à cordes*. Il attendit la mort de Staline pour oser réécrire une musique selon ses vraies aspirations, et il produisit cette année-là, une autre symphonie, la *Dixième Symphonie*, à ajouter aux précédentes. Il en laissa 15 à sa mort, 22 ans plus tard. Ces œuvres ainsi que les 15 quatuors à cordes, le montrèrent comme le seul compositeur dont la loyauté envers l'Union Soviétique est incontestable, à être mondialement reconnu et à avoir sa place parmi les grands de ce monde.

Dmitry Shostakovich, 24 August 1962.
Dmitri Schostakowitsch, 24. August 1962.
Dimitri Chostakovitch, le 24 août 1962.

(1, 2, 3) Shostakovich, at a rehearsal for the London première of his *First Cello Concerto*, in consultation with the soloist, Mstislav Rostropovitch, and Gennady Rozhdestvensky, the conductor of the Leningrad Symphony Orchestra. Royal Festival Hall, 21 September 1960. (4) A lighter moment on the same London visit, 20 September 1960. It was not until the thaw that followed Stalin's death in 1953, when Soviet musicians started to emerge into the West, that Shostakovich went to Edinburgh with Rostropovich and Rozhdestvensky for the British première of his *First Cello Concerto*; at the repeat performance in London he met Benjamin Britten and began the only genuine friendship he ever made with a Western composer.

(1, 2, 3) Schostakowitsch in der London Festival Hall bei einer Probe für die Londoner Erstaufführung seines *Ersten Cellokonzerts* in einer Besprechung mit dem Solisten Mstislaw Rostropowitsch und Gennady Roschdestwenski, dem Dirigenten des Leningrader Symphonieorchesters, 21. September 1960. (4) Ein freundlicherer Augenblick auf der gleichen Reise. Erst als in der Phase der politischen Entspannung nach Stalins Tod im Jahr 1953 viele sowjetische Musiker in den Westen aufbrachen, fuhr Schostakowitsch zusammen mit Rostropowitsch und Roschdestwenski nach Edinburgh zur britischen Erstaufführung seines *Ersten Cellokonzerts*. Bei dessen zweiter Aufführung in London machte er die Bekanntschaft Benjamin Brittens, woraus sich seine einzige wirkliche Freundschaft mit einem westlichen Komponisten entwickelte.

(1, 2, 3) Chostakovitch, pendant une répétition pour la première à Londres de son *Premier Concerto pour Violoncelle*, discutant avec le soliste Mstislav Rostropovitch, et avec Gennadi Rojdestvenski, chef d'orchestre de l'Orchestre Symphonique de Leningrad. Royal Festival Hall, le 21 septembre 1960. (4) Un moment plus détendu, lors de la même tournée à Londres, le 20 septembre 1960. Il fallut attendre l'assouplissement qui suivit la mort de Staline en 1953, pour voir les musiciens soviétiques commencer à apparaître à l'Ouest, et pour permettre à Chostakovitch d'aller assister à Edimbourg avec Rostropovitch et Rojdestvenski, à la première britannique de son *Premier Concerto pour Contrebasse*. Lors de la représentation de cette œuvre à Londres, il rencontra Benjamin Britten, et commença la seule véritable amitié qu'il ait eue avec un compositeur de l'Ouest.

For most people the name of Karlheinz Stockhausen is a great deal more familiar than the music. Few composers (except perhaps John Cage in his later years) have been so hard to approach or comprehend for the average concert-goer – or even to hear, given the size, complexity and practical difficulty of many of his works – but few have made a stronger impact as a modern myth, a sort of ongoing legend whose music it isn't actually necessary to hear to have a view about.

A pupil of Messiaen, friend and colleague of Boulez and mainstay of the redoubtable 'Ferienkurse für Neue Musik' in Darmstadt, Stockhausen placed himself from the start at the centre of the European musical avant-garde, where he has retained a powerful if controversial position ever since. There are few aspects of progressive musical endeavour that he has not touched, but it is probably fair to say that the development of electronic sound, the pursuit of total serialism, the experimental use of physical space and the submission to various forms of mystical discipline have been among the most important.

His student work on musique concrète in France, and later at the WDR electronic studio in Cologne, produced some of the most imaginative of his early compositions, such as the *Gesang der Jünglinge* in which the mixture of tapes with a boy's voice produced magical results. But the preoccupation with serialism that followed, taking Webern's techniques to their logical conclusion and serializing not just pitch, but rhythm, duration, timbre, intensity, even spatial position, has been mainly responsible for the complexity and extraordinary 'difficulty' of his music for the average listener. The complexity is increased when the resulting music is scored for three orchestras, as in *Gruppen*, or four, as in *Carré*, or includes four groups of loudspeakers, as in *Kontakte* – often arranged to surround the audience.

There are smaller-scale pieces too, though no less demanding in a different way: the concentration required to listen to *Stimmung*, a 75-minute meditation on a single series of natural harmonics for six solo voices, is considerable, though rewarding. Works like this, or *Mantra* for two pianists, explore a spiritual dimension involving the virtual suspension of time, and indeed of thought. 'Think NOTHING' warns the instruction on one score. In the end there is almost no limit to the demands, on both performer and listener, in this heroic attempt to fuse the diverse elements of so immensely sophisticated a vision of the world.

Speaking purely personally, the word 'charisma' might have been invented for Stockhausen, and there is no doubt about the charm, any more than the sense of absolute dedication to a spiritual as much as a musical end. 'Who does he think he is, God?' muttered an irate assistant. 'Well, Jesus Christ, minimum', came the answer. It is the image of Wagner that inevitably comes to mind, and there is certainly something Wagnerian about the sheer scope of Stockhausen's vision. Since 1977 he has devoted himself exclusively to the composition of a single work, a cycle of seven operas with the collective title *Licht* ('Light'), each individual opera being named after a day of the week. The essential content is sacred, a summary of all the philosophical and musical concerns of Stockhausen's life. But even the *Ring* takes only four evenings. A *Parsifal* in seven...?

Den meisten ist der Name Karlheinz Stockhausen viel vertrauter als seine Musik. Wenige Komponisten (den späten John Cage vielleicht ausgenommen) sind so schwer zugänglich und für den durchschnittlichen Konzertbesucher so schwer zu verstehen – selbst das Zuhören ist nicht ganz leicht, wenn man an die Länge, die Komplexität und die praktische Schwierigkeit vieler seiner Werke denkt. Kaum einer hat allerdings eine größere Wirkung als moderner Mythos, als eine Art ewige Legende, deren Musik man nicht wirklich hören muß, um eine Meinung dazu zu haben.

Als Schüler von Messiaen, Freund und Kollege von Boulez und einer der Mittelpunkte der Darmstädter „Ferienkurse für Neue Musik", stellte sich Stockhausen von Anfang an ins Zentrum der europäischen musikalischen Avantgarde und behauptet dort bis heute seine machtvolle, wenn auch umstrittene Position. Es gibt nur wenige progressive musikalische Ansätze, mit denen er sich nicht befaßt hat, aber zu seinen wichtigsten Verdiensten zählen die Entwicklung der elektronischen Musik, die Ausarbeitung der vollständig seriellen Musik, der experimentelle Einsatz von Raumklang und die Anwendung verschiedener mystischer Ansätze.

Bei seinen Studien zur Musique concrète beim französischen Rundfunk und später im Elektronischen Studio des WDR in Köln entstanden einige seiner phantasievollsten frühen Kompositionen, wie etwa der *Gesang der Jünglinge*. Dieser Zusammenschnitt von Tonbändern mit der Stimme eines Jungen entfaltet eine ganz eigene Magie. Die anschließende Beschäftigung mit dem Serialismus jedoch, bei der er Weberns Techniken ausarbeitete und nicht nur den Ton, sondern auch den Rhythmus, die Dauer, das Timbre, die Intensität und selbst die Zwischenräume seriell behandelte, macht im wesentlichen die Komplexität und „Schwierigkeit" seiner Musik aus. Die Komplexität steigert sich noch einmal mit der Musik für drei Orchester in seinem Werk *Gruppen*, oder auch für vier wie in *Carré*. *Kontakte* arbeitet mit acht Lautsprechern – die oftmals rund um das Auditorium angeordnet sind.

Einige kleinere Stücke sind auf andere Weise herausfordernd, und es bedarf einer hohen Konzentration, um *Stimmung* zu hören, eine 75minütige Meditation über eine einzelne Reihe natürlicher Harmonien für sechs Solostimmen – aber die Mühe lohnt sich. Werke wie dieses oder *Mantra* für zwei Pianisten erforschen eine geistige Dimension, in der die Zeit virtuell aufgehoben und das Denken wirklich transzendiert wird. „Denke NICHTS" lautet die Anweisung in einer Partitur. Die Ansprüche an Interpreten wie Zuhörer sind grenzenlos bei diesem Versuch, die verschiedensten Elemente einer so unglaublich verfeinerten Vision der Welt zu verschmelzen.

Der Begriff Charisma wurde vielleicht eigens für Stockhausen erfunden, und es gibt keinen Zweifel über seine vollständige Hingabe an ein geistiges und musikalisches Ziel. „Was glaubt er, wer er ist, Gott?", murrte einmal ein verunsicherter Assistent. „Wenigstens Jesus Christus", war die Antwort.

Dabei erinnert man sich unweigerlich an Wagner, und in der radikalen Vision von Stockhausen zeigt sich sicher eine Verwandtschaft. Seit 1977 hat er sich ausschließlich der Komposition eines einzigen Stückes verschrieben, einem Zyklus von sieben Werken mit dem Obertitel *Licht*. Jede der Opern ist nach einem Wochentag benannt und behandelt letzte Inhalte, die Summe aller philosophischen und musikalischen Erfahrungen aus dem Leben des Künstlers. Doch selbst der *Ring* dauert nur vier Abende. Ein *Parsifal* in sieben ... ?

Pour la plupart des gens, le nom de Karlheinz Stockhausen est beaucoup plus connu que sa musique. Peu de compositeurs (à l'exception peut-être de John Cage vers la fin de sa vie) sont aussi difficile à approcher ou à comprendre pour l'habitué ordinaire des concerts – ou plus difficile encore à écouter, étant donné la taille, la complexité et la difficulté pratique de beaucoup de ses œuvres. Pourtant, peu d'œuvres eurent cette réputation de mythe moderne, de légende permanente dont on n'a pas besoin d'entendre la musique pour s'en faire une idée.

Ancien élève de Messiaen, ami et collègue de Boulez et un des piliers du redoutable « Ferienkurse für Neue Musik » à Darmstadt, Stockhausen, se plaça dès le début au centre de la musique d'avant-garde européenne. Il y jouit toujours d'une grande autorité que certains penseront peut-être discutable. Il y a peu d'aspects de la musique progressive qu'il n'ait touchés, mais il est probablement juste de dire que le développement du son électronique, la poursuite d'un dodécaphonisme total, l'utilisation expérimentale de l'espace environnant et la soumission à diverses formes de discipline mystique furent parmi les plus importants.

Alors qu'il était encore étudiant, son travail sur Musique concrète en France, et plus tard, son travail aux studios électroniques de WDR à Cologne, produisirent quelques-unes de ses compositions qui firent le plus appel à l'imagination. On peut citer par exemple, *Gesang der Jünglinge* dont le mixage d'enregistrements de la voix d'un garçon crée un effet magique. Mais son souci du dodécaphonisme qui suivit – il amena les techniques de Webern à leur conclusion logique, appliqua le dodécaphonisme non seulement au ton, mais aussi au rythme, à la durée, au timbre, à l'intensité, même à l'espace – lui doit la complexité et la « difficulté » extraordinaire qui caractérisent ses œuvres. La complexité est accrue lorsque la musique qui en naît est destinée à trois orchestres, comme dans *Gruppen*, ou à quatre, comme dans *Carré*, qui contient quatre groupes d'enceintes, comme dans *Kontakte* – souvent arrangés de telle sorte que le public en est entouré.

Il existe de moins longues compositions, non moins éprouvantes, mais d'une autre manière : la concentration exigée pour écouter *Stimmung*, une méditation qui dure 75 minutes avec des harmoniques naturels pour six voix en solo, est considérable, mais elle en vaut la peine. De telles œuvres, ou encore *Mantra* pour deux pianistes, explorent un univers spirituel qui comprend une suspension virtuelle du temps, et même de la pensée. « Ne pensez à RIEN » est-il inscrit sur la partition. En fin de compte, il n'y a pas de limites aux exigences qui pèsent sur l'interprète et l'auditeur, dans cette tentative héroïque de fusionner les divers éléments de la vision hautement sophistiquée du monde.

Le terme de « charisme » a bien pu être inventé pour Stockhausen. Il n'y a aucun doute quant à sa dévotion absolue à des fins musicales autant que spirituelles. « Qui croit-il être, Dieu ? », bougonna un assistant. « He bien, Jésus- Christ, tout au moins » fut la réponse.

L'image de Wagner vient inévitablement à l'esprit, et il existe à n'en pas douter, quelque chose de wagnérien dans ce que représente Stockhausen. Depuis 1977, il s'est occupé exclusivement de la composition d'une seule œuvre, un cycle de sept opéras dont le titre est *Licht* (la lumière), chacun des opéras étant nommé d'après un jour de la semaine. Le contenu essentiel est sacré, il s'agit d'un résumé des préoccupations philosophiques et musicales de Stockhausen. Mais, même le *Ring* ne prend que quatre soirées. Un *Parsifal* en sept... ?

Karlheinz Stockhausen, complete with score and electronic equipment.

Karlheinz Stockhausen, ausgerüstet mit Partitur und elektronischem Equipment.

Karlheinz Stockhausen, avec partitions et équipement électronique.

In conversation, 2 December 1965.

Im Gespräch, 2. Dezember 1965.

En conversation, le 2 décembre 1965.

(1) Stockhausen conducting the Südwestfunk Symphony Orchestra ▶
and soloist Elisabeth Clarke in the first London performance of
Inori, one of the most substantial of his later compositions, at the
London Coliseum on 23 October 1974. The work had received its
première in Donaueschingen only three days earlier.
(2, 3) Rehearsing in the early 1970s.

(1) Stockhausen dirigiert das Symphonieorchester des Südwest-
funks mit der Solistin Elisabeth Clarke bei der Londoner Erstaufführung von *Inori*, einem seiner wichtigsten Spätwerke, im
London Coliseum am 23. Oktober 1974. Das Werk war erst drei
Tage zuvor in Donaueschingen uraufgeführt worden.
(2, 3) Stockhausen beim Proben, frühe 70er Jahre.

(1) Stockhausen en train de diriger le Südwestfunk Symphony
Orchestra avec la soliste Elisabeth Clarke lors de la première représentation d'*Inori*, l'une de ses dernières œuvres les plus importantes
au London Coliseum le 23 octobre 1974. La première avait été
jouée à Donaueschingen seulement trois jours auparavant.
(2, 3) Répétition au début des années 1970.

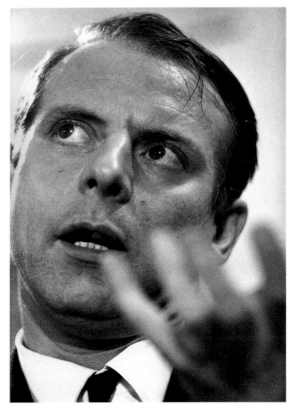

1

2

3

RICHARD STRAUSS 1864-1949

By the time of this photograph, Strauss could look over a career that stretched back for more than 60 years, to a period when Brahms was still alive, Wagner only just dead, and Strauss himself beginning on the series of tone poems that first made his name. He had seen his fame grow, both as conductor and composer, until the scandal of *Salome* and the shock of *Elektra* brought notoriety of a different kind. But after *Elektra* the increasing violence of expression and dissonance were to go no further. With *Der Rosenkavalier* in 1911 he began to mine the inexhaustible vein of rich late romanticism which was to furnish the typical 'Strauss sound' of the last 38 years of his life.

Between the First and Second World Wars, Strauss had sunk into the background of contemporary musical life. The musical world had changed irrevocably, he had no sympathy with the artistic disillusionment of the 1920s and his own style had set: he was content to act the part of a country squire in his luxurious villa in the Bavarian Alps, playing endless games of skat, writing intermittent operas in the well-tried mould, and occasionally appearing for a Grand Old Man demonstration at some festival or other. As a result contemporary critics, and indeed the musical public at large, had begun to regard him as something of a spent force.

They were wrong, as it turned out, for between 1942 and 1948, perhaps as a result of the terrible events that he saw in the world around him, his inspiration returned, and a sort of 'Indian summer' saw the creation of the last opera, *Capriccio*, the *Oboe Concerto*, the deeply poignant *Metamorphosen* and the wonderful *Four Last Songs*.

It was during this last flowering of Strauss's genius that Sir Thomas Beecham, who had been a great champion of the composer in his earlier days, organized a Strauss festival in London, and invited him to attend. At the age of 83, by now a legendary figure, he conducted one of the concerts himself, and at the rehearsal was heard to mutter: 'No, I know what I want, and I know what I meant when I wrote this. After all, I may not be a first-rate composer, but I am a first-class second-rate composer!' It was a sad remark after so long a life of music, and had a grain of truth in it perhaps, but posterity has not endorsed it.

Als dieses Foto aufgenommen wurde, konnte Strauss bereits auf eine mehr als sechzigjährige Karriere zurückblicken – zurück bis in die Zeit, als Brahms noch lebte, Wagner gerade erst gestorben war und Strauss selbst an dem Liederzyklus arbeitete, mit dem er sich zuerst einen Namen machte. Er hatte seinen Aufstieg als Dirigent und Komponist erlebt und war dann mit dem Skandal um *Salomé* und der Schockwirkung der *Elektra* in Verruf geraten. Die intensive Expressivität und Dissonanz erfährt jedoch nach *Elektra* keine weitere Steigerung. Mit dem *Rosenkavalier* von 1911 betrat er das unerschöpfliche Feld der späten Romantik und etablierte damit den für die letzten 38 Jahre seines Lebens „typischen Strauss".

Zwischen den Weltkriegen war Strauss in den Hintergrund der zeitgenössischen Musikwelt getreten. Diese Welt hatte sich unwiderruflich verändert, und er fühlte sich der künstlerischen Entzauberung der 20er Jahre nicht verbunden. Er hatte seinen eigenen Stil gefunden, und war damit zufrieden, in seiner Luxusvilla in den bayrischen Alpen bei ausgedehnten Skatpartien den Landadeligen zu spielen und gelegentlich eine Oper in seiner wohlbekannten Manier zu schreiben. Hin und wieder erschien er als „alte Größe" auf irgendwelchen Festspielen. Dies hatte zur Folge, daß die zeitgenössische Kritik und weite Teile des Publikums glaubten, seine Kräfte hätten sich erschöpft.

Sie irrten sich, wie sich später zeigte. Zwischen 1942 und 1948, möglicherweise aufgerüttelt von den Schrecknissen jener Zeit, erwachte sein Genius erneut. In jenem Herbst seines Schaffens schrieb er seine letzte Oper *Capriccio*, das *Oboenkonzert*, die ergreifenden *Metamorphosen* und die wunderbaren *Vier Letzten Lieder*.

Sir Thomas Beecham, der schon in früheren Tagen ein großer Verehrer von Strauss gewesen war, organisierte damals ein Strauss-Festival in London und lud den Komponisten dazu ein. Im Alter von 83 Jahren und inzwischen eine legendäre Gestalt, dirigierte Strauss selbst eines der Konzerte. Bei der Generalprobe hörte man ihn murmeln: „Nein, ich weiß, was ich will, und ich weiß genau, was ich meinte, als ich dies schrieb. Ich bin vielleicht kein erstklassiger Komponist, aber ich bin ein erstklassiger zweitrangiger Komponist!" Eine traurige Bemerkung gegen Ende einer so langen musikalischen Laufbahn, die vielleicht ein Körnchen Wahrheit enthielt. Die Nachwelt war jedoch anderer Ansicht.

Quand cette photo fut prise, Strauss pouvait contempler une carrière longue de 60 ans, remontant à une époque où Brahms était encore vivant, où Wagner venait de mourir, et où Strauss lui-même commençait à travailler sur les séries de poèmes sonores qui le firent d'abord connaître. Il avait vu sa réputation grandir, à la fois comme chef d'orchestre et comme compositeur, jusqu'au scandale provoqué par *Salomé* et le choc d'*Elektra*, qui le portèrent à une renommée d'un ordre bien différent. Après *Elektra*, la violence croissante de son expression et la dissonance cessèrent. Avec le *Chevalier à la rose* en 1911, il commença à exploiter le filon inépuisable de la fin du romantisme, qui allait alimenter le style musical si caractéristique de Strauss, les 38 dernières années de sa vie.

Pendant l'entre-deux-guerres, Strauss fut refoulé à l'arrière-plan de la vie musicale. Le monde de la musique avait irrévocablement changé, il n'approuvait pas le désillusionnement artistique des années 1920 et son propre style s'était figé : satisfait de jouer le rôle de « châtelain » dans sa somptueuse villa des Alpes bavaroises, il jouait de longues parties de cartes, il écrivait entre deux parties des opéras dans le moule qui avait déjà fait ses preuves, et de temps en temps, il apparaissait en patriarche de la musique, à un festival ou à d'autres manifestations. En conséquence, la critique de l'époque, et même le public en général, commencèrent à considérer ses ressources comme épuisées.

Ils avaient tort. En effet, entre 1942 et 1948, peut-être en raison des événements atroces qui se déroulaient dans le monde autour de lui, il eut un regain d'inspiration et écrivit son dernier opéra, *Capriccio*, le *Concerto pour hautbois*, ainsi que les très poignantes *Métamorphoses* et pour finir, les *Quatre Derniers Chants*.

Ce fut durant ce dernier coup de génie que Sir Thomas Beecham, qui avait toujours défendu ses œuvres, organisa un festival Richard Strauss à Londres, et il demanda au compositeur d'y assister. À l'âge de 83 ans, personnage légendaire, il dirigea l'un des concerts lui-même, et pendant la répétition, on l'entendit marmonner : « Non, je sais ce que je veux, et je sais ce que je voulais dire quand j'ai écrit ceci. Après tout, je ne suis peut-être pas un compositeur de première classe, mais je suis un excellent compositeur de deuxième classe ! » Cette remarque est bien triste si l'on considère une vie où la musique prit tant de place et pour si longtemps. Peut-être recélait-elle un soupçon de vérité, mais la postérité n'est pas de cet avis.

(1) The 83-year-old Richard Strauss at the Theatre Royal, Drury Lane, for a concert by Sir Thomas Beecham and the Royal Philharmonic Orchestra during the Strauss Festival in October 1947. (2) Backstage, the composer talks to one of his most distinguished interpreters, the Viennese conductor Clemens Krauss, who was also the librettist of Strauss's last opera, *Capriccio*, first performed in 1942. (See also page 190)

(1) Der 83jährige Richard Strauss im Theatre Royal, Drury Lane, bei einem Konzert des Royal Philharmonic Orchestra unter der Leitung von Sir Thomas Beecham während des Strauss Festivals im Oktober 1947. (2) Hinter der Bühne des Theatre Royal unterhält sich der Komponist mit einem seiner besten Interpreten, dem Wiener Dirigenten Clemens Krauss, der auch das Libretto für seine 1942 uraufgeführte letzte Oper *Capriccio* schrieb. (Siehe auch S. 190)

(1) Richard Strauss, âgé de 83 ans, au Theatre Royal, à un concert donné par Sir Thomas Beecham et par le Royal Philharmonic Orchestra pendant le Festival Strauss en octobre 1947. (2) Dans les coulisses de Drury Lane, le compositeur parle à l'un de ses interprètes les plus remarquables, le chef d'orchestre viennois Clemens Krauss, qui fut également le librettiste du dernier opéra de Strauss, *Capriccio*, joué pour la première fois en 1942. (voir aussi page 190)

1

2

Appearances can be deceptive. When Stravinsky came to London in May 1954, to conduct a concert at the Festival Hall and receive the gold medal of the Royal Philharmonic Society, it was the first time that a whole generation of concert-goers had seen this giant of 20th-century music in the flesh. And the first impression as he appeared on the platform must have been one of surprise – surprise at how small he was: a slight figure loping through the orchestra, shooting out a long arm and huge hand to grasp the conductor's desk and swing himself up onto the podium, presenting an inconspicuous, crouching back as he turned to address the players. One had to remind oneself that this was the composer of *L'Oiseau de feu* ('The Firebird'), *Petrushka*, *Le Sacre du printemps*, *Oedipus Rex*, *The Symphony of Psalms*, ballets, symphonies and concertos that were the classics of the New Music, a man who had been a pupil of Rimsky-Korsakov, seen Tchaikovsky at the Bolshoy, worked with Nijinsky, Diaghilev, Picasso, Cocteau, Gide, Eliot, Auden, known every musician and artist of consequence in half a century, and was still alive – and, if his latest works were anything to go by, clearly kicking – at 72.

He was to kick for a good deal longer yet, producing in the last 16 years of his life some of his most controversial music and finding in the arcane complexities of post-Webernian serialism a natural beauty of sound that seems to have escaped many of its practitioners. But in spite of the years he spent in Paris, and the many more in Los Angeles, Stravinsky remained a Russian, and nothing could have been more Russian than his early ballets – even, with hindsight, the battering rhythms and ruthless dissonances that sparked the famous riot at the first performance of *Le Sacre du printemps* in 1913. The jazzy, chamber-sized works that followed were unexpected, but the next ballet after the *Sacre* was *Pulcinella*, a delicate score based on Pergolesi, and the 'classical' period which it ushered in seemed so complete a volte-face that some found it impossible to accept. What was the composer of *Petrushka* doing writing oratorios with a Latin text, or concertos in the style of Bach, or even a symphony in the honest, old-fashioned key of C? The *Symphony in Three Movements* in 1946 was hailed as a return to earlier days, but then came *The Rake's Progress*, an opera in 18th-century set numbers which the composer himself declared to have been inspired by Mozart....

What is it that holds together this heterogeneous succession of artistic derniers cris? He was not a great inventor of tunes, and his music allows his listeners no romantic indulgence. But he had at his command an inexhaustible fund of thematic ideas, motifs and scraps of strikingly memorable material, an anarchic rhythmic sense that propelled them with compulsive intensity or sudden inflection, and above all a characteristic sound – an absolutely original blend of harmony and instrumental timbre – that, like Berlioz's in an earlier generation, is instantly recognizable as his own.

In the end it is vitality, sheer, exuberant, all-embracing vitality that fuels Stravinsky, whether the enquiring, sharply human being or the endlessly imaginative, starkly musical mind. It is difficult to believe that in the pictures following he is in his late 70s and early 80s. And he hadn't finished yet.

Die Erscheinung kann täuschen. Als Strawinsky im Mai 1954 nach London kam, um ein Konzert in der Festival Hall zu dirigieren und die Goldmedaille der Royal Philharmonic Society entgegenzunehmen, sah eine ganze Generation von Konzertbesuchern diesen Giganten der Musik des 20. Jahrhunderts zum ersten Mal leibhaftig vor sich. Es muß eine Überraschung gewesen sein, als er die Bühne betrat – Überraschung darüber, wie klein er von Statur war. Eine schlanke Gestalt bahnte sich den Weg durchs Orchester, streckte einen langen Arm und eine große Hand nach dem Dirigentenpult aus, schwang sich hinauf, und präsentierte dem Publikum einen unscheinbaren, gebogenen Rücken, als er sich zur Begrüßung an die Musiker wendete. Man mußte sich ins Gedächtnis rufen, daß dies der Komponist war, der den *Feuervogel*, *Petruschka*, *Le Sacre du printemps*, *Oedipus Rex*, die *Psalmensymphonie*, Ballette, Symphonien und Konzerte geschrieben hatte – Werke, die zu den Klassikern der Neuen Musik gehören; daß er ein Schüler von Rimski-Korsakow gewesen war, Tschaikowsky am Bolschoi Theater erlebt hatte und mit Nijinski, Diaghilew, Picasso, Cocteau, Gide, Eliot und Auden gearbeitet hatte; daß er mit seinen 72 Jahren noch immer quicklebendig und – seinen neuesten Werken nach zu urteilen – äußerst aktiv war.

Er sollte noch eine ganze Zeit lang aktiv bleiben. In seinen letzten 16 Lebensjahren komponierte er einige seiner umstrittensten Werke und entdeckte in der Komplexität des post-webernschen Serialismus eine natürliche Schönheit des Klanges, die vielen Interpreten verborgen geblieben ist. Trotz seiner Jahre in Paris und der langen Zeit in Los Angeles behielt Strawinsky sein russisches Naturell, das in seinen frühen Ballettmusiken besonders deutlich zum Ausdruck kommt, ebenso wie später in den schmetternden Rhythmen und gnadenlosen Dissonanzen, die 1913 bei der Uraufführung von *Le Sacre du printemps* den berühmten Skandal entzündeten. Die darauffolgenden Ragtime-Stücke kamen unerwartet, aber das nächste Ballett nach *Le Sacre* – *Pulcinella*, eine sensible Partitur, die auf Pergolesi basierte – bedeutete die neoklassizistische Wende. Dieser Umschwung schien so radikal, daß er von vielen nicht akzeptiert wurde. Was ging in dem Komponisten der *Petruschka* vor, wenn er Oratorien zu lateinischen Texten, Konzerte im Stile Bachs oder sogar eine Symphonie im guten, altmodischen C-Dur schrieb? Die *Symphony in Three Movements* von 1946 wurde als Rückkehr zu früheren Tagen gepriesen, aber dann folgte *The Rake's Progress*, eine Oper in fünf Aufzügen im Stil des 18. Jahrhunderts, zu der Strawinsky selbst angab, Mozart habe ihn dazu inspiriert.

Was hält diese heterogene Folge avantgardistischer Experimente zusammen? Strawinskys Musik zeichnete sich nicht durch melodische Neuheiten aus, und erlaubt dem Hörer nicht, in romantisches Schwelgen zu geraten. Aber er verfügte über einen unerschöpflichen Fundus an Themen, Motiven und Fragmenten von unvergeßlichem Material und einen anarchischen Sinn für Rhythmik – mit heftiger Intensität hervorgetrieben oder plötzlich moduliert. Vor allem schuf er ein ihm ganz eigenes Klangbild: ein einzigartiges Zusammenspiel von Harmonie und Klangfarbe der Instrumente. Dadurch läßt sich die Musik sofort dem Komponisten zuordnen, wie es auch schon früher bei Berlioz möglich war.

Am Ende bleibt es seine Vitalität, seine reine, überbordende, allumfassende Vitalität, die ihn antrieb, sei es als ständig forschende Intelligenz oder als unendlich schöpferischer musikalischer Geist. Es ist schwer zu glauben, daß Strawinsky auf den folgenden Fotos bereits Ende siebzig/Anfang achtzig war. Und seine Schaffenskraft war noch nicht beendet.

Les apparences sont souvent trompeuses ! En mai 1954, lorsque Stravinski se rend à Londres pour diriger un concert au Festival Hall et recevoir la médaille de la Royal Philharmonic Society, c'est l'occasion pour une jeune génération de mélomanes anglais d'admirer pour la première fois ce monstre sacré du XXᵉ siècle en chair et en os. Quelle surprise ! Ce géant de la musique paraissait si fluet sur la scène : une silhouette frêle voltigeant au milieu des musiciens, lançant un long bras terminé d'une main étonnamment large pour saisir le pupitre de chef d'orchestre et se mettre en place d'un seul bond. Quand il se retournait pour faire face à l'orchestre, on ne distinguait plus qu'à peine ce dos discret qui se ramassait pour mieux diriger. Difficile de croire que c'était bien là le compositeur de l'*Oiseau de feu*, de *Petrouchka*, du *Sacre du printemps*, d'*Œdipus Rex*, de la *Symphonie de psaumes* et de tant d'autres « classiques » de la musique contemporaine : ballets, concertos, œuvres symphoniques... Difficile de réaliser qu'il s'agissait bien de l'élève de Rimski-Korsakov, qu'il avait côtoyé Tchaïkovski au Bolchoï, travaillé avec Nijinski, Diaghilew, Picasso, Cocteau ou Gide, Eliot ou Auden, connu tous les musiciens ou artistes qui avaient marqué ce demi-siècle... Et qu'il était toujours là, bien vivant, ses dernières œuvres faisant ostensiblement la nique à ses 72 ans.

Les seize dernières années de sa vie lui ont inspiré quelques-unes de ses œuvres les plus controversées ; il retrouve dans les arcanes du dodécaphonisme sériel post-webernerien une beauté naturelle des sons qui semble avoir échappé à nombre de ses défenseurs. Il reste russe malgré toutes les années passées à Paris et à Los Angeles. Rien ne saurait être plus russe que ses premiers ballets ainsi que, a posteriori, ces rythmes heurtés et ces cruelles dissonances qui déclenchèrent une mémorable émeute artistique lors de la première du *Sacre du printemps* au Théâtre des Champs-Élysées, en 1913. Les œuvres qui suivirent, conçues pour de plus petites formations et parfois à connotation jazzy, étaient pour le moins inattendues. Après le *Sacre*, vint un autre ballet, *Pulcinella*, d'une écriture toute en finesse, à la manière de Pergolesi. La période de néoclassicisme ainsi annoncée marquait un tel revirement, que beaucoup la trouvèrent inacceptable. Comment osait-il écrire des oratorios en latin, des concertos « à la Bach » ou ne serait-ce qu'une symphonie pour laquelle il choisissait une clef, celle de Ut, idée certes honnête, mais vieillotte ? En 1946, on acclama sa *Symphonie en trois mouvements* ; c'était le retour tant attendu aux premières inspirations ! En 1951 *The Rake's Progress* ramène le compositeur à un opéra structuré comme ceux du XVIIIᵉ et inspiré, comme il l'avoue, de Mozart !

Stravinski n'était pas un génie des mélodies. Impossible pour son public de se laisser aller à un quelconque romantisme sur ses musiques ! Ses sources étaient intarissables ; il puisait à volonté dans des motifs musicaux variés et des matières à composition absolument prodigieuses ; son sens du rythme était très anarchique, mais propulsait le tout avec une irrémédiable intensité ou une intonation inattendue. Il avait surtout un son caractéristique, qui découlait de cette fusion originale entre les harmonies et les timbres des instruments et qui, comme chez Berlioz plus tôt, était immédiatement reconnaissable.

De cette vitalité, Stravinski s'en nourrissait : une vitalité pure, exubérante, totale, qui faisait avancer à la fois l'homme à l'esprit vif sans cesse en quête et le musicien dont l'imagination sans fin conférait à la musique une force sans pareille. Comment croire que ces photos ont été prises alors qu'il avait déjà entre soixante-dix et quatre-vingt-et-quelques années, et qu'il n'en avait pas encore fini avec la vie !

1

2

3

4

Stravinsky follows the score (1) and later takes over himself (2).
His close friend and assistant, Robert Craft, conducts a rehearsal
with the BBC Symphony Orchestra at the Maida Vale studios,
8 December 1958 (3). Stravinsky consults with the orchestra's
harpist, Sidonie Goossens, sister of Eugene and the oboeist Leon (4).

Strawinsky liest die Partitur (1) und dirigiert später auch selbst (2).
Sein enger Freund und Assistent Robert Kraft dirigiert eine Probe
des BBC Symphony Orchestra in den Studios in Maida Vale,
8. Dezember 1958 (3). Strawinsky beratschlagt sich mit der
Harfenistin des Orchesters, Sidonie Goossens, der Schwester des
Komponisten Eugene und des Oboisten Leon Goossens (4).

Stravinsky suit la partition (1) et plus tard dirige lui-même (2).
Robert Craft, son ami proche et assistant, dirige une répétition avec
le BBC Symphony Orchestra aux studios de Maida Vale, le
8 décembre 1958 (3). Stravinsky discute avec la harpiste de
l'orchestre, Sidonie Goossens, sœur d'Eugène et du hautboïste
Leon (4).

Of the same session Auerbach wrote: 'This was my first encounter with the Composer of our Time. He was then almost eighty but had the vitality of a man half his age. I had been forewarned that Stravinsky would be difficult. Yet all through the three-hour rehearsal he was so utterly absorbed and so oblivious of distractions that I was able to work unhindered. This was almost the last shot of a fruitful session.'

Auerbach notierte zu diesen Aufnahmen: „Das war mein erstes Zusammentreffen mit dem großen zeitgenössischen Komponisten. Er war damals beinahe achtzig Jahre alt, aber er hatte die Vitalität eines 40jährigen. Man hatte mich darauf vorbereitet, daß Strawinsky sehr schwierig sein konnte. Die ganze dreistündige Probe über war er jedoch so vollständig in Anspruch genommen, daß ihn nichts ablenken konnte. Ich konnte ganz ungehindert arbeiten. Dies hier ist fast die letzte Aufnahme aus einer gelungenen Serie."

De cette même séance, Auerbach écrivit : « C'était la première fois que je rencontrais le Compositeur de notre Temps. Il avait alors près de quatre-vingts ans, mais il avait la vitalité d'un homme deux fois plus jeune. On m'avait averti que Stravinski serait quelqu'un de difficile. Pourtant pendant les trois heures de la répétition, il était tellement absorbé sans prêter attention au reste, que j'ai pu travailler sans problème. C'était presque la dernière prise de vue d'une séance fructueuse. »

(1) An affectionate greeting for Jean Cocteau, author of the narration, who can also be seen sitting at the left of the chorus in the picture below. (2, 3) Stravinsky recording his oratorio *Oedipus Rex* at the Maida Vale studios, 5 November 1959.

(1) Freundschaftlich begrüßt er Jean Cocteau, den Autor des Dramas, der auch auf dem Foto darunter, links neben dem Chor sitzend, zu sehen ist. (2, 3) Strawinsky bei der Aufnahme seines Opernoratoriums *Oedipus Rex* in den Studios in Maida Vale, 5. November 1959.

(1) Salutations chaleureuses de Jean Cocteau, auteur de la narration, que l'on peut aussi voir à gauche du chœur sur la photo en-bas. (2, 3) Stravinski en train d'enregistrer son oratorio *Oedipus Rex* aux studios de Maida Vale, le 5 novembre 1959.

1

2

1

2

(1-4) Stravinsky at a recording session of his opera *The Rake's Progress* for CBS, 20 June 1964. (5-7) At a concert performance, about 1968.

(1-4) Strawinsky bei der Aufnahme seiner Oper *The Rake's Progress* für CBS, 20. Juni 1964. (5-7) Strawinsky im Konzert, ca. 1968.

(1-4) Stravinski lors de l'enregistrement de son opéra *The Rake's Progress* pour CBS, le 20 juin 1964. (5-7) Pendant un concert, vers 1968.

3

4

5

6

7

2

(1) Stravinsky conducting his arrangement of Bach's *Vom Himmel hoch* at the Royal Academy of Music, 28 June 1964.
(2, 3, 4) Giving a typically Stravinskian interview at the Savoy Hotel, London, 11 September 1965.

(1) Strawinsky dirigiert seine Bearbeitung von Bachs *Vom Himmel hoch* in der Royal Academy of Music, 28. Juni 1964.
(2, 3, 4) Strawinsky gibt im Savoy Hotel in London eines seiner typischen Interviews, 11. September 1965.

(1) Stravinski en train de diriger son arrangement de *Vom Himmel hoch* de Bach au Royal Academy of Music, le 28 juin 1964.
(2, 3, 4) Interview à la Stravinski au Savoy Hotel de Londres, le 11 septembre 1965.

3

4

The years 1929 and 1930 were vintage ones for music in Japan: no less than five distinguished composers were born within a period of 18 months, all of whom were to be influential in the creation of a modern Japanese style. After the 'opening up' of Japan in the last decades of the 19th century Western music had gradually infiltrated the country and, up to the time of the Second World War, had existed more or less side by side with traditional Japanese music, only limited attempts being made to bridge the gap. The few composers who wrote in a Western style tended to follow in the mainstream of German romanticism, with later a dash of French impressionism and an occasional flirtation with Japanese instrumental techniques.

Takemitsu's generation changed all that. Once the war was over, interest in contemporary Western music grew fast: new forms of dissonance, 12-tone systems, musique concrète, electronic music followed one another, and attempts were made to find common ground between these new sounds and the ancient sounds of Japan. The young Takemitsu tried them all, before settling down to a delicately personal style somewhere between Debussy, Messiaen, Boulez and, eventually, Cage. *Requiem for string orchestra*, attracted Stravinsky's admiration in 1959, and as the 60s drew on Takemitsu gradually emerged as the first Asian composer to qualify for international status – a position he established without question in 1967 with *November Steps*, a sort of double concerto for the Japanese biwa and shakuhachi written for the 125th anniversary of the New York Philharmonic Orchestra.

A shy, pensive, diminutive figure, not given to public display, Takemitsu seemed at first sight an unlikely ambassador for Japanese music in the West. But that very private exterior concealed humour, natural curiosity and a great gift for companionship. And it also masked a number of unexpected talents and interests: a passion for the cinema (he claimed to watch 250 films each year, and wrote the music for more than 90), an inventive culinary imagination, and an encyclopedic memory for Western pop songs – words and all.

So just how Japanese is Takemitsu's music? For a Western concert-goer there is so little opportunity for comparison that it is difficult to say. Certainly the poetic sensibility, the meticulous attention to timbre and texture, the sense of a spiritual dimension, fit well enough with the Westerner's expectations, and Takemitsu himself said that his inspiration came from Japanese scroll paintings, haiku verse and (especially for the often random-seeming forms of his music) the formal Japanese garden. Gardens were obviously important to him: 'They never spurn those who enter them', he said, and he tried to give his music the same sort of welcoming character. And gardens have another quality dear to Takemitsu: you can be quiet in them. Many listeners have commented on the silences that occur so frequently in his compositions, of the curious sense of space which they seem to generate in the music. His own explanation, in conversation with a BBC interviewer, came very quietly, very gently: 'I think sirence mudder of music' – there was a long silence – 'no, maybe glandmudder – all light?'

Tōru Takemitsu, May 1973.

Tōru Takemitsu, Mai 1973.

Tōru Takemitsu, mai 1973.

1929 und 1930 waren für die japanische Musik zwei sehr fruchtbare Jahre: Innerhalb von 18 Monaten kamen nicht weniger als fünf ausgezeichnete Komponisten zur Welt. Alle nahmen sie großen Einfluß auf die Entwicklung des modernen japanischen Stils. Nach der Öffnung Japans in den letzten Jahrzehnten des 19. Jahrhunderts hatte die westliche Musik allmählich Eingang in das Land gefunden, und bis zum Zweiten Weltkrieg stand sie mehr oder weniger gleichwertig neben der traditionellen japanischen Musik. Ansätze, die beiden verschiedenen musikalischen Traditionen miteinander zu verbinden, blieben allerdings sehr begrenzt. Die wenigen Komponisten, die Musik im westlichen Stil schrieben, orientierten sich im allgemeinen an der deutschen Romantik. Später kam auch der Einfluß aus dem französischen Impressionismus dazu und vereinzelte Berührungen mit japanischen Instrumentaltechniken.

Die Generation von Takemitsu brachte die Wende. Nach dem Krieg nahm das Interesse an zeitgenössischer westlicher Musik rasch zu: Neue Formen der Dissonanz, Zwölftonsysteme, Musique concrète und elektronische Musik folgten aufeinander, und bald gab es die ersten Versuche, eine gemeinsame Basis für all diese neuen Klänge und die alte japanische Musik zu finden. Der junge Takemitsu experimentierte mit allen, bevor er schließlich seinen eigenen sensiblen Stil entwickelte, der irgendwo zwischen Debussy, Messiaen, Boulez und später auch Cage lag. 1959 zog sein *Requiem für Streichorchester* Strawinskys Bewunderung auf sich, und im Laufe der 60er Jahre entwickelte sich Takemitsu zum ersten asiatischen Komponisten von Weltrang. 1967 festigte er seine Position mit *November Steps*, einer Art Doppelkonzert mit den beiden japanischen Instrumenten Biwa und Shakuhachi, das er zum 125. Jahrestag des New York Philharmonic Orchestra schrieb.

Der schüchterne, nachdenkliche, zierliche und publikumsscheue Takemitsu erschien auf den ersten Blick nicht sehr geeignet für die Rolle eines Botschafters der japanischen Musik in der westlichen Welt. Hinter seiner großen Zurückhaltung verbarg sich jedoch viel Humor, eine gesunde Neugier und eine große Gabe zur Geselligkeit – aber auch eine Reihe unvermuteter Talente und Interessen: seine Leidenschaft für das Kino (er behauptete selbst, jedes Jahr 250 Filme zu sehen; und für über 90 Filme schrieb er die Musik), eine erfinderische kulinarische Phantasie und ein enzyklopädisches Gedächtnis für westliche Schlager – inklusive Text.

Wie japanisch ist denn aber Takemitsus Musik? Ein westlicher Konzertbesucher hat so wenige Vergleichsmöglichkeiten, daß es schwer zu bestimmen ist. Seine Poesie, seine peinlich genaue Beachtung von Klangfarbe und Aufbau und sein Gespür für die spirituelle Dimension der Musik fügen sich gut in die westlichen Erwartungen ein. Takemitsu selbst nennt als Quellen seiner Inspiration die japanischen Rollbilder, die Haikus (besonders bei seinen wie zufällig erscheinenden musikalischen Formen) und die kunstvoll angelegten japanischen Gärten, die für ihn eine große Bedeutung besaßen. „Sie weisen keinen Besucher ab", sagte er und versuchte, seiner Musik dieselbe einladende Qualität zu geben. Takemitsu schätzte an den Gärten aber noch etwas anderes: Man kann dort schweigen. Viele Zuhörer haben die Pausen hervorgehoben, die so oft in seinen Kompositionen zu finden sind und die seiner Musik diese eigentümliche Weite geben. Seine eigene Erklärung dazu in einem BBC Interview kam sehr ruhig und sehr sanft: „Ich halte das Schweigen für die Mutter der Musik" – und nach langem Schweigen – „nein, eher für die Großmutter – verstehen Sie?"

Les années 1929 et 1930 furent fertiles en ce qui concerne la musique japonaise : pas moins de cinq compositeurs naquirent en l'espace de 18 mois, et tous devaient jouer un rôle influent dans la création d'un style japonais moderne. Après « l'ouverture » du Japon dans les dernières décennies du XIXᵉ siècle, la musique occidentale s'infiltra peu à peu dans le pays, et jusqu'à la Deuxième Guerre mondiale, elle vécut plus ou moins côte à côte avec la musique japonaise traditionnelle. Il y eut seulement quelques tentatives pour établir un rapprochement entre les deux genres. Le petit nombre de compositeurs qui écrivaient dans un style occidental le faisaient selon le style du romantisme allemand, en ajoutant plus tard un soupçon d'impressionnisme français, et de temps en temps faisant apparaître des techniques instrumentales japonaises.

La génération de Takemitsu changea tout cela. Une fois la guerre finie, l'intérêt pour la musique occidentale augmenta rapidement : de nouvelles formes de dissonance, des systèmes à 12 tons, de la musique concrète, de la musique électronique se succédèrent, et l'on tenta de trouver un terrain d'entente entre ces nouveaux sons et les anciens sons japonais. Le jeune Takemitsu les essaya tous, avant d'opter pour un style bien personnel que l'on pourrait situer entre Debussy, Messiaen, Boulez, et finalement Cage. *Requiem, pour orchestre à cordes*, s'attira l'admiration de Stravinski en 1959, et au fil des années 1960, Takemitsu devint peu à peu le premier compositeur japonais à atteindre la reconnaissance internationale – une position qu'il consolida en 1967 avec *November Steps*, une sorte de double concerto pour les biwa et shakuhachi japonais écrit pour le 125e anniversaire du New York Philarmonic Orchestra.

Fluet, songeur, timide, Takemitsu ne paraît pas au premier abord être un ambassadeur probant de la musique japonaise en occident. Cette apparence très réservée cachait cependant un certain humour, une curiosité naturelle et une grande cordialité. Il avait aussi d'autre intérêts et talents inattendus : il était passionné de cinéma (il clamait voir 250 films par an, et il composa la musique de 90 films), il avait une grande imagination en matière culinaire, et il possédait une mémoire encyclopédique des chansons occidentales – qu'il s'agisse des paroles ou du reste.

Alors jusqu'à quel point la musique de Takemitsu est-elle japonaise ? Pour un habitué de concerts occidental qui a peu d'occasions de comparer, répondre à cette question est difficile. Il est vrai que la sensibilité poétique, l'attention méticuleuse portée au timbre et à la texture, le sens d'une dimension spirituelle, conviennent bien à ce qu'attendrait un Occidental. Takemitsu dit d'ailleurs qu'il tire son inspiration de toiles japonaises, des haiku et (particulièrement en ce qui concerne les formes paraissant souvent aléatoires de sa musique), du jardin japonais si soigné. Il est évident que les jardins furent pour lui importants : « Ils ne rejettent jamais celui qui y entre », dit-il, en donnant à sa musique ce caractère accueillant. Les jardins avaient une autre qualité, chère à Takemitsu : leur sérénité. De nombreux auditeurs firent des remarques sur les silences qui surviennent si fréquemment dans ses œuvres, sur cette curieuse impression d'espace qu'ils semblent donner à la musique. Son explication donnée dans un entretien à la BBC, intervint très calmement, très doucement : » Poul moi, le silence est mèle de la musique » – il y eut un long silence – « non, peut-être gland-mèle – c'est bon ? »

Kansas City, Missouri, and the organ at the local Baptist church were the background to Virgil Thomson's youth, and the accent acquired from each persisted, the one in his speaking voice and the other in his music, until the end of his life. It was a life that took him far from the popular songs and parlour music of his Midwest origins: in Paris at the age of only 24, at the end of a visit to Europe with the Harvard Glee Club, he was accepted into the circle of Jean Cocteau and Les Six and introduced to Erik Satie, who was to remain perhaps the single most important influence on his development as a composer. On his return to America he reverted to church organist in Boston, but within three years he was back in Paris where he stayed until the outbreak of war in 1940, and where he embarked on the collaboration with the 'progressive' American writer Gertrude Stein that was to make him famous.

The opera they wrote together, *Four Saints in Three Acts*, caused a scandal and made American musical history. It had no plot, much of the text was near-nonsense and the various Saints involved (there are 16 of them in fact) spent most of their time asking unanswered questions, or quoting nursery rhymes, or simply counting. And the music for all this? Instead of being modern-sounding, or noisy, or full of discords, it was made up of plain declamation, simple diatonic tunes with a few spiky harmonies, quotations from popular songs, waltzes, tangos, religious chant and – hymn tunes.

This renunciation of the intellectual complexities of 'modern music', and a continuing obsession with the musical memories of his youth, infuriated many of Thomson's contemporaries, and it has to be admitted that a number of his compositions, including the brilliantly effective scores for films like *The Plow that Broke the Plains* and *Louisiana Story,* remain at entertainment level and seldom rise to any great expressive heights. But then as he said himself, 'Writing music is like giving parties. You make it as good as you can at the time you are doing it. Making it memorable is not the main objective. You merely try to make it interesting and worthy.' A modest credo on which to found such notoriety and Pulitzer Prize prestige.

A considerable part of Thomson's influence came as much from his writings as from his music. Forced back to the States from Paris in 1940, he became music critic of the *New York Herald Tribune* and over a period of 14 years established himself as the most stimulating, provocative, and (at least in his own view) authoritative of American musical columnists. The lucidity and wit is there as it is in the music, with an added sharpness of judgment and intellectual rigour. He was a tireless promoter of 20th-century music, crossed swords willingly, ruthlessly but always stylishly with his opponents, and made many enemies: 'Certainly polemics were my intent', he wrote. Yet he was a man of human warmth and open geniality. He took endless trouble with ordinary readers, penning literally hundreds of personal replies to letters which must often have been tedious to receive, in terms that were iron-fisted but unfailingly courteous: 'Dear Sir, I thank you for your extremely indignant letter. I am afraid I do consider Schumann to be a greater and more original composer than Brahms. Very sincerely yours....'

Virgil Thomson, 28 July 1965.

Virgil Thomson, 28. Juli 1965.

Virgil Thomson, le 28 juillet 1965.

Anyone who has seen Michael Tippett appearing to acknowledge the applause after a performance of one of his works will find it hard to forget the tall, shy, gangling figure, the nervous smile and rather camp wave of the hand to the audience – or the great wall of warmth and admiration that rises from the auditorium as he appears. For behind the reluctant, apparently confused exterior lie an uncompromising honesty, a firmness of purpose, and a dogged determination to find expression that have few equals on the musical scene today.

Tippett was a slow starter. His name is often coupled with Britten's, but their music is very different in character, and although eight years older he was still a background figure when Britten was beginning to be widely recognized as the young hopeful of British music. It is probably true to say that his view of what he wanted was from the beginning very much less precise than Britten's, the goal made more diffuse by his involvement with social and political interests which perhaps encouraged practical music-making at the expense of serious composition.

During the war years his pacifist views got him into trouble: feeling that he could best serve his country as a musician, he refused 'direction' into any aspect of the war effort and in spite of the loyal support of musical colleagues, including the veteran Vaughan Williams, was sentenced to three months in jail. But his concern with the predicament of the ordinary human being in the face of political and social oppression was fundamental to his entire life, and formed the subject of the first of his major successes after the war, the oratorio *A Child of Our Time*. A similar preoccupation with profound truths underlies his first and, some still feel, his greatest opera, *The Midsummer Marriage*, which left the Covent Garden audience in 1952 perplexed and confused, but yet aware that in all this prodigious musical ebullience there was a voice of prophetic individuality. Tippett was clearly a composer to be reckoned with. But how?

The question has not proved easier to answer in the years that have followed. The next opera, *King Priam*, was a highly dramatic and relatively straightforward retelling of classical myth, but its successors were less clear in their structure and message. The orchestral works, the four symphonies, the *Concerto for Orchestra*, the *Triple Concerto*, have fared better and, like the five string quartets, must certainly be counted among the richest and most rewarding scores of the post-war period. There are smaller pieces too, in which Tippett's essential lyricism and humanity come across with greater simplicity. And in 1982 came the monumental oratorio *The Mask of Time*, a huge and comprehensive amalgam of Tippett's musical style which looked like the end of the road but was not – because this amazing old man has gone on producing music into his late 80s, beating even Verdi with a last opera, *New Year*, at the age of 84.

Tippett will never be an easy composer to understand. But for those who are prepared to give themselves to these often forbidding scores, the sheer life-enhancing invention that seemed so bewildering at the first performance of *The Midsummer Marriage* is the driving force through all the work of this very human human being.

Keiner, der erlebt hat, wie Tippett nach der Aufführung seiner Werke auf die Bühne tritt, um den Applaus entgegenzunehmen, wird diese hochgewachsene, schüchterne, schlaksige Gestalt, die nervös lächelt und dem Publikum eher verhalten zuwinkt, wieder vergessen – und auch nicht die Welle der Zuneigung und Bewunderung, die bei seinem Erscheinen aus dem Auditorium aufsteigt. Hinter diesem zurückhaltenden, scheinbar konfusen Auftreten verbirgt sich nämlich eine rückhaltlose Aufrichtigkeit und eine unerschütterliche Standhaftigkeit – beide notwendig für seine Suche nach einem Ausdruck, der unter den heutigen Musikschaffenden kaum seinesgleichen findet.

Tippett hat sich Zeit genommen. Sein Name wird zwar oft zusammen mit Britten genannt, doch ihre Musik ist von sehr unterschiedlichem Charakter. Tippett war acht Jahre älter und kaum bekannt, als Britten bereits als hoffnungsvolles junges Talent der britischen Musik Anerkennung fand. Britten wußte wohl eher als der zögerliche Tippett, was er wollte. Tippetts soziales und politisches Engagement hat ihm die Entscheidung vielleicht erschwert und dazu geführt, daß er das Komponieren lange hinter das praktische Musizieren zurückstellte.

Während der Kriegsjahre brachte ihn sein Pazifismus in Schwierigkeiten: Er fühlte, daß er seinem Land als Musiker am besten dienen konnte, und verweigerte die Beteiligung an jeglicher kriegsdienlichen Aktivität. Trotz der loyalen Unterstützung von seiten seiner Kollegen, einschließlich des greisen Vaughan Williams, wurde er zu drei Monaten Gefängnis verurteilt. Die Leiden der einfachen Bevölkerung angesichts der politischen und sozialen Unterdrückung hatten ihn aber schon immer sehr bewegt, und diese Betroffenheit hat sein Leben fundamental mitbestimmt – und auch das Thema seines ersten großen Erfolges nach dem Krieg, das Oratorium *A Child of Our Time*. Auch in seiner ersten Oper, die einige noch immer für seine beste halten, beschäftigen ihn grundlegende Wahrheiten: *The Midsummer Marriage* ließ 1952 in Covent Garden ein überraschtes und verwirrtes Publikum zurück, das jedoch klar erkannte, daß in all diesem ungeheuren musikalischen Überschwang die Stimme eines Propheten erklang. Tippett war ganz offensichtlich ein Komponist, von dem noch einiges zu erwarten war. Aber was?

Die Frage konnte auch in den folgenden Jahren nicht leicht beantwortet werden. Seine nächste Oper, *King Priam*, war eine hochdramatische und relativ geradlinige Nacherzählung des klassischen Mythos. Struktur und Botschaft der Folgewerke waren jedoch weit weniger klar. Seine orchestralen Werke, die vier Symphonien, das *Concerto for Orchestra*, das *Triple Concerto*, hatten mehr Erfolg und gehören ebenso wie seine fünf Streichquartette unbedingt zu den schönsten und besten Kompositionen der Nachkriegszeit. Es gibt auch kleinere Stücke, die Tippetts besondere Poesie und seine Menschlichkeit mit größerer Schlichtheit zum Ausdruck bringen. 1982 kam dann das monumentale Oratorium *The Mask of Time*, eine stilistisch unglaublich verdichtete Komposition, die fast den Rang eines Vermächtnisses zu haben schien – es aber nicht war. Tippett schrieb weiterhin Musik bis über sein 80. Lebensjahr hinaus – und übertraf in dieser Hinsicht mit seiner letzten Oper, *New Year*, die er im Alter von 84 Jahren schrieb, selbst Verdi.

Tippett wird nie ein leicht verständlicher Komponist sein. All jene aber, die bereit sind, sich diesen oft gewagten Kompositionen zu öffnen, werden erkennen, daß jene reine Lebensintensität, die bei der Uraufführung von *The Midsummer Marriage* so verwunderte, in allen Werken dieses so menschlichen Menschen die eigentlich treibende Kraft ist.

Celui qui a vu Michael Tippett monter sur scène sous les applaudissement du public après un représentation de ses œuvres, n'est pas prêt d'oublier ce personnage timide, grand, déguingandé, ni son sourire nerveux ou sa façon un peu réservée de saluer le public de la main. On n'oubliera pas non plus la chaleur et l'admiration qui se dégagent du public lors de son apparition. En effet, derrière cette hésitation, cette apparence un peu confuse, il y a une honnêteté absolue, une énorme volonté et une résolution tenace dans sa recherche d'expression, qualités que l'on retrouve de nos jours rarement dans le monde musical.

La carrière de Tippett fut longue à démarrer. Son nom est souvent lié à celui de Britten, mais leurs musiques ne se ressemblent pas. De plus, bien que de huit ans son aîné, il était encore au second plan alors que Britten commençait à être considéré un peu partout comme le jeune espoir de la musique britannique. Il est probablement vrai que dès le début, il ne savait pas aussi précisément que Britten ce qu'il voulait. Son engagement politique et social n'a fait que rendre ses buts encore plus diffus. Cela encouragea peut-être le côté musicien de Tippett aux dépens de ses qualités de compositeur.

Pendant la guerre, ses vues pacifistes lui attirèrent des ennuis : il pensait qu'il servirait au mieux son pays en tant que musicien, il refusa de « diriger » quelque aspect que ce soit de l'effort de guerre, et en dépit du soutien loyal de ses collègues, y compris le vétéran Vaughan Williams, il fut condamné à trois mois de prison ferme. Son inquiétude par rapport aux situations difficiles dans lesquelles se trouvaient l'être humain ordinaire face à l'oppression sociale et politique était une composante fondamentale de sa personnalité. Ce souci fut le thème de son premier grand succès après la guerre, l'oratorio *A Child of our Time*. Des préoccupations semblables sont à l'origine de son premier, et pour certains, son meilleur opéra, *The Midsummer Wedding*, qui laissa en 1952 le public de Covent Garden perplexe et déconcerté, mais aussi conscient que dans cette prodigieuse exubérance musicale, résonnait une voix prophétique. C'est clair, Tippett était un compositeur qui réservait encore bien des surprises. Mais à quel point de vue ?

Même dans les années qui suivirent, il fut difficile de répondre à cette question. L'opéra suivant, *King Priam*, reprenait un mythe classique en en faisant une pièce hautement dramatique et relativement simple. Mais ceux qui suivirent n'étaient pas aussi clairs dans leurs structures et dans leur message. Ses œuvres orchestrales, les quatre symphonies, le *Concerto pour Orchestre* et le *Triple Concerto*, eurent plus de succès, et, de même que ses cinq quatuors à cordes, comptent parmi les morceaux les plus riches et les plus valables de l'après-guerre. Il composa aussi des œuvres moins considérables, dans lesquelles son humanité et son lyrisme ressortent plus clairement. En 1982 apparut le monumental oratorio *The Mask of Time*, une composition incroyablement dense sur le plan stylistique et que l'on pensait être sa dernière œuvre, mais non – ce vieil homme impressionnant continue à composer alors qu'il a près de 90 ans, et a battu Verdi avec un dernier opéra, *New Year*, composé à 84 ans.

Il ne sera jamais facile de comprendre Tippett en tant que compositeur. Mais pour ceux qui sont prêts à se donner à ces morceaux souvent sévères, la pure création qui met la vie en valeur, et qui parut si déroutante à la première représentation du *The Midsummer Marriage*, régit toutes les œuvres de cet être si humain.

Michael Tippett, 29 May 1962.

Michael Tippett, 29. Mai 1962.

Michael Tippett, le 29 mai 1962.

Tippett listening to, and evidently commenting on, his *Second Piano Sonata*, at his home near Corsham in Wiltshire, 18 December 1964.

Tippett hört seine *Zweite Klaviersonate* in seinem Haus bei Corsham in Wiltshire (und kommentiert sie offensichtlich auch), 18. Dezember 1964.

Le 18 décembre 1964, chez lui, près de Corsham dans le Wiltshire, Tippett écoute sa *Deuxième Sonate pour Piano*, et de toute évidence fait des commentaires.

Tippett with Benjamin Britten at Tippett's 60th birthday party,
2 January 1965.

Tippett und Benjamin Britten auf Tippetts Feier zu seinem
60. Geburtstag, 2. Januar 1965.

Tippett en compagnie de Benjamin Britten lors du 60e anniversaire
de Tippett, le 2 janvier 1965.

Caught at an odd moment in his garden, 9 January 1966.

Schnappschuß von Tippett in seinem Garten, 9. Januar 1966.

Surpris dans son jardin à un de ses moments perdus,
le 9 janvier 1966.

1

2

(1) Vaughan Williams, always a tremendously loyal supporter of his younger colleagues, shares a score of Tippett's *Second Symphony* with the composer. (2) Sir Adrian Boult directs the London Symphony Orchestra at a rehearsal of the symphony on 4 February 1958. It was at the first performance of this work, on the following day, that the orchestra broke down shortly after the beginning of the first movement and Boult, with characteristic generosity, turned to the audience and said 'My fault entirely, ladies and gentlemen' before starting again. (3) At the rehearsal, from the left: Sir Adrian Boult, Michael Tippett, Ralph Vaughan Williams and his second wife, the poet Ursula Wood, to whom he had been married for five years.

(1) Vaughan Williams, stets ein äußerst loyaler Förderer seiner jüngeren Kollegen, teilt sich mit Tippett eine Partitur von dessen *Zweiter Symphonie*. (2) Sir Adrian Boult dirigiert das London Symphony Orchestra bei einer Probe der Symphonie am 4. Februar 1958. Bei der Uraufführung am folgenden Tag geschah es, daß das Orchester kurz nach Beginn des ersten Satzes durcheinanderkam. Mit der ihm eigenen Großzügigkeit wandte sich Boult vor dem Neuanfang an das Publikum und sagte: „Meine Damen und Herren, das war ganz und gar mein Fehler." (3) Bei der Probe. Von links: Sir Adrian Boult, Michael Tippett, Ralph Vaughan Williams mit seiner zweiten Frau, der Dichterin Ursula Wood, die er fünf Jahre zuvor geheiratet hatte.

(1) Vaughan Williams, toujours totalement loyal envers ses collègues plus jeunes, partage une partition de la *Deuxième Symphonie* de Tippett avec le compositeur. (2) Sir Adrian Boult dirige le London Symphony Orchestra lors d'une répétition, le 4 février 1958. Ce fut à la première représentation de cette œuvre, le lendemain, que l'orchestre s'arrêta de jouer dès le début du premier mouvement, et Boult, toujours généreux, se tourna vers le public et dit « Messieurs-dames, ceci est entièrement de ma faute », puis recommença du début. (3) Lors d'une répétition, à partir de la gauche : Sir Adrian Boult, Michael Tippett, Ralph Vaughan Williams et sa seconde femme, le poète Ursula Wood, avec qui il était marié depuis cinq ans.

3

Tippett in the studio,
4 February 1958.

Tippett im Studio,
4. Februar 1958.

Tippett au studio,
le 4 février 1958.

For many people Elgar is the incarnation of the English spirit in music, and certainly he expresses powerfully the rich assurance, the noble aspirations and the romantic vision of the last days of imperial Britain. Vaughan Williams represents the reverse of the coin: his involvement in folk song, and in the earlier periods of English music, led him back to a pastoral tradition where imperial Britain was unknown, to a mysticism which has its own aspirations, and to the cult of the amateur rather than the practised ease of the professional.

By the 1950s Vaughan Williams, never a dapper figure, had become a bumbling, rather shapeless presence on the musical scene, his hearing all to pieces but his great heart unsullied, a man held in enormous affection by British musicians of virtually every persuasion. Though he lived in and greatly enjoyed London during the last years of his life he still looked the countryman that he never really ceased to be. But he had long outlived the preoccupation with folk song that dominated his early years, and developed from it a musical language, recognizably his own, with which he could explore a spiritual world where innocence, mysticism, lyrical beauty and a rather ungainly humour clashed head-on with the violence he saw in the world around him. It was a mixture that could produce results which startled even the composer himself: as he famously remarked after conducting a rehearsal of the hard-hitting, dissonant *Fourth Symphony*, 'Well, if that's modern music, I don't like it.'

When he was a young man he had a hard struggle fighting the amateurism of his social background – 'that foolish young man, Ralph Vaughan Williams, who would go on working at music when he was so hopelessly bad at it'. As an aunt said, 'He has been playing all his life, and for six months hard, and yet he can't play the simplest thing decently.' Nine symphonies later his technical musicianship and professionalism were no longer in question, but to be fair it has to be said that this expertise was not achieved without effort, and that throughout his life he did his mischievous best to deny this.

Certainly a love of amateur music-making remained with him all his life, and regular sessions of madrigal singing with a few chosen friends continued in London to within months of his death. Indeed, it was the practical experience of vocal music, not only as a singer but as the (rather idiosyncratic) conductor of larger choral groups as well, that underpinned his immensely effective vocal writing, from the *Sea Symphony* to the ravishingly beautiful *Serenade to Music* for 16 soloists and the opera he made out of Bunyan's *Pilgrim's Progress*.

True, there are a good many of VW's works in which pastoral calm and the idyll of the countryside seem inclined to get the upper hand – the kind of music that gave rise to wise-cracks like the one about 'a cow looking over a gate'. And it is also true that, in the end, the resolution of those torments through which any composer must go, if he is to create anything of value, lay for Vaughan Williams somewhere in that world of clear faith and eternal values upon which his humanity was based. The torments were not always resolved, and the cow is not necessarily a happy cow. But Vaughan Williams was a visionary, a dogged, practical visionary who never forgot that music came from people and was made for people, and his greatest achievement was always to take people through the violence to the vision he saw beyond it.

Für viele verkörpert Elgar den Geist der englischen Musik, und sicher brachte er jenes große Selbstvertrauen, die hehren Ziele und die romantischen Visionen der letzten Tage des britischen Empires kraftvoll zum Ausdruck. Vaughan Williams steht für die andere Seite: Seine Beschäftigung mit dem Volkslied und der alten englischen Musik führten zurück in die ländliche Tradition vor der Zeit des Empire, zu einem sehnsuchtsvollen Mystizismus, der eher der Laienmusik zu entstammen schien als einer theoretisierenden Auffassung von Komposition.

In den 50er Jahren war Vaughan Williams, der nie eine gute Figur gemacht hatte, zu einer recht konturlosen Gestalt in der Musikszene geworden. Sein Gehör war ruiniert, aber sein großes Herz war ungebrochen, und tatsächlich verehrten ihn die britischen Musiker aller Sparten sehr. Obwohl er in seinen letzten Lebensjahren gerne in London lebte, sah man ihm immer noch den Mann vom Lande an, der er auch stets blieb. Die Volkslieder seiner frühen Jahre beschäftigten ihn allerdings schon lange nicht mehr, sondern aus ihnen hatte er ein unverkennbar eigenes musikalisches Idiom entwickelt, in dem eine geistige Welt voller Unschuld, Mystik und poetischer Schönheit und ein schlichter Humor mit der Gewalt der realen Welt zusammenstießen. Diese Kombination führte zu Ergebnissen, die den Komponisten selbst erstaunten wie sein berühmter Ausspruch nach dem Dirigieren einer Probe für die vertrackte und dissonante *Vierte Symphonie* beweist: „Also, wenn das moderne Musik ist, dann mag ich sie nicht."

Als junger Mann hatte er einen harten Kampf mit der Ignoranz seiner Umgebung auszufechten – „dieser dumme junge Mann, Ralph Vaughan Williams, der sich immer noch mit der Musik abmüht, wo er doch so schlecht darin ist", wie eine Tante sagte, „er hat sein Leben lang musiziert, und davon sogar sechs Monate sehr intensiv, und trotzdem kann er nicht das einfachste Stück vernünftig spielen." Neun Symphonien später wurden sein technisches Können und seine Professionalität nicht mehr in Frage gestellt. Dies ist ihm allerdings nicht leicht gefallen, obwohl er zeit seines Lebens versuchte, das zu leugnen.

Immer war er ein Liebhaber der Laienmusik, und bis kurz vor seinem Tod traf er sich regelmäßig mit einigen ausgewählten Freunden in London, um Madrigale zu singen. Und in der Tat ist es seine praktische Erfahrung mit dem Gesang – nicht nur als Sänger, sondern auch als (eher eigenwilliger) Dirigent größerer Chöre – die seinen außerordentlich wirkungsvollen Gesangspartituren zugrunde liegt – von der *Sea Symphony* über die bezaubernd schöne *Serenade to Music* für 16 Solo-Stimmen bis zu der Oper, die er aus *The Pilgrim's Progress* von John Bunyan machte.

Wahr ist, daß die friedliche Stille der ländlichen Idylle in vielen seiner Werke die Oberhand bekommt. Diese Art Musik führte zu scherzhaften Bemerkungen wie die von „der Kuh, die über den Gartenzaun sieht." Ebenso wahr ist, daß für Vaughan Williams die Befreiung von den Qualen, die ein Komponist auf sich nehmen muß, wenn er etwas von Bedeutung schaffen will, irgendwo dort in jener Welt des reinen Glaubens und der ewigen Werte lag, die seine Menschlichkeit begründete. Die Qualen ließen ihn nie ganz los, und die friedliche Idylle entsprang nicht unbedingt dem Glück. Aber Vaughan Williams war ein verbissener, praktischer Visionär, der nie vergaß, daß die Musik von Menschen stammt und für Menschen gemacht wird. Seine größte Leistung besteht darin, die Menschen durch die Gewalt hindurch zu der Vision zu tragen, die für ihn dahinter sichtbar war.

Pour beaucoup, Elgar est l'incarnation même de l'âme anglaise de la musique. La riche assurance, les nobles aspirations et les vues romantiques des derniers jours d'une Grande-Bretagne impériale marquent, certes, fortement ses œuvres. Vaughan Williams représente tout le contraire : son engagement pour les chants folkloriques, pour la musique anglaise d'une lointaine époque, le menèrent à une tradition pastorale où l'Angleterre impériale était inconnue, à un mysticisme qui avait ses propres aspirations, et à un culte de l'amateurisme, plus qu'à l'aisance du professionnel.

À l'époque des années 1950, Vaughan Williams, qui n'avait jamais eu beaucoup de présence, était devenu empoté, insignifiant sur scène. Il n'entendait pas bien non plus, mais de par ses grandes qualités de cœur, il fut un personnage aimé des musiciens britanniques de toutes convictions. Bien qu'il ait vécu à Londres dont il aimait la vie, il ressemblait tout de même au campagnard qu'il ne cessa jamais vraiment d'être. Mais il avait laissé de côté les chants folkloriques qui lui étaient si chers autrefois, et inventa à la place, un langage musical, que l'on reconnaît bien comme étant le sien, qui lui permit d'explorer un monde spirituel où l'innocence, le mysticisme, la beauté lyrique et un humour plutôt gauche contrastaient avec la violence qu'il voyait autour de lui. C'était un mélange qui produisit des résultats dont le compositeur lui-même était parfois très surpris : comme il le remarqua si justement après avoir dirigé lors d'une répétition, la *Quatrième Symphonie* : « Hé bien , si ça, c'est de la musique moderne, je n'aime pas du tout. »

Lorsqu'il était jeune, c'est avec beaucoup de mal qu'il essaya de combattre l'amateurisme de son milieu socio-culturel – « ce jeune homme insensé, Ralph Vaughan Williams, il fallait qu'il persiste à travailler sa musique, alors qu'il n'avait absolument aucun don pour ça. » Comme une tante remarqua aussi : « Il a joué toute sa vie, et pendant six mois il a travaillé dur, et pourtant il est incapable de jouer décemment l'air le plus simple. » Neuf symphonies, et plus tard son sens technique de la musique ainsi que son professionnalisme n'étaient pas à remettre en question, mais pour être juste, il faut dire que cette maîtrise ne vint pas sans effort, et que toute sa vie, il fit de son mieux pour prouver le contraire.

Certes, cet amour de l'amateurisme dans la composition musicale persista sa vie entière, et régulièrement, il rencontrait ses amis à Londres pour des sessions de chants madrigaux, jusqu'à une époque proche de sa mort. En effet, c'était son expérience pratique de la musique chantée, pas seulement comme chanteur mais aussi comme chef d'orchestre (plutôt idiosyncratique) de larges chorales, qui aida à obtenir la grande qualité de ses chants, depuis la *Sea Symphony* à la beauté enchanteresse de *Serenade to Music* pour 16 solistes et enfin, l'opéra qu'il tira de *Pilgrim's Progress* de Bunyan.

Dans bon nombre de ses œuvres, en effet, le calme pastoral et une campagne idyllique sont largement présentes – le genre de musique qui donna lieu à des plaisanteries comme « une vache qui regarde par-dessus une barrière ». Il est vrai aussi que l'on trouvera la solution aux tourments par lesquels tout compositeur doit passer s'il veut créer quelque chose de valable, quelque part dans un univers de foi et de valeurs éternelles, sur lesquelles fut basée sa vie. Les tourments ne furent pas toujours résolus, et la vache n'est pas toujours une vache heureuse. Mais Vaughan Williams était un visionnaire, un visionnaire persévérant et pragmatique qui n'oublia jamais que la musique venait des gens et était faite pour les gens, et son plus grand exploit fut de pouvoir amener le public à travers la violence à la vision qu'il voyait au-delà.

(1) Vaughan Williams at the age of 85, listening (with some difficulty) to a rehearsal of his *Ninth Symphony*, which was to receive its première later the same day under the baton of Sir Malcolm Sargent. Sitting next to him is his wife Ursula Wood. (2) Conductor and composer consult during the rehearsal, 2 April 1958.

(1) Vaughan Williams lauscht im Alter von 85 Jahren (mit einiger Mühe) einer Probe seiner *Neunten Symphonie*, die am gleichen Abend unter der Leitung von Sir Malcolm Sargent uraufgeführt werden sollte. Neben ihm sitzt seine Frau Ursula Wood.
(2) Besprechung mit Sir Malcolm Sargent während der Probe, 2. April 1958.

(1) Vaughan Williams âgé de 85 ans, écoute (avec des difficultés) une répétition de sa *Neuvième Symphonie* dont la première allait avoir lieu plus tard le jour-même, sous la direction de Sir Malcolm Sargent. Assise à côté de lui, on voit Ursula Wood, sa femme.
(2) Discussion entre le chef d'orchestre et le compositeur pendant la répétition du 2 avril 1958.

'Drivel they paid to hear' was the headline in one newspaper after the first public performance of Walton's *Façade* in 1922, and it was not an isolated case. The composer was 21 years old, and the scandal made him famous overnight. Much of it was due to the sheer oddity of the piece: avant-garde poetry by Edith Sitwell, declaimed through a megaphone to the accompaniment of a small chamber ensemble concealed behind a painted curtain. The jazzy brilliance of Walton's score was a red rag to an audience for whom English music meant Parry and Elgar, or at the very latest Vaughan Williams, and the reputation of *enfant terrible* was to stick with him for many years.

It was an unlikely label for the pale, shy young man from a modest Lancashire background, an Oxford choirboy who found himself swept into the eccentric, sophisticated circle of the Sitwell family. Perhaps the only work it really suited was the early overture *Portsmouth Point*: in any case, it was because the rhythms and rowdy scoring of this boisterous piece so alarmed contemporary conductors that Walton eventually decided to try his hand at conducting himself. He had already directed *Façade*, 'holding his baton', wrote Osbert Sitwell, 'with something of the air of an elegant and handsome snipe', but *Portsmouth Point* was another matter: he practised long and hard in front of a mirror – after which, he later claimed, 'it was child's play and still is'. He said he didn't enjoy it, and he never conducted any works except his own – but for those he had a quiet authority expressed with a minimum of exertion or fuss, and his performances were models of clarity and vigour.

But the cool, self-deprecating manner, and the caustic wit that accompanied it, were sharply at odds with the romantic nature that ran deep in his music as it did in his life. Sometimes the two worlds collided. When Walton, always a slow worker, was struggling through the *First Symphony*, he got so badly stuck with the last movement that the first three had to be premièred without it. Many serious musical hypotheses were put forward to explain this unusual procedure. But the facts were simpler. As a friend put it: 'The trouble was that Willie changed girl-friends between movements.' A drastic over-simplification, as the passion, anger and despair of the first three movements make abundantly clear: all the same, it was not until the new relationship was under way that the composer was able to work out his original design and complete the most consistently powerful of his works in a blaze of light.

By the time of these pictures Walton had married and made a permanent home on the island of Ischia in the bay of Naples. Suitably enough, the first work written there was the opera *Troilus and Cressida*, and after it a succession of orchestral works – a *Cello Concerto* to add to the two earlier masterpieces in that form for viola and violin, a *Second Symphony*, Variations on themes by Hindemith and Benjamin Britten, all produced with painful slowness and mining the same sources of passionate melancholy and raucous energy that place him somewhere between Elgar and Prokofiev – with a dash of the *vieux terrible* still audible in the mix. The clipped, ironic reserve with wich he treated interviewers seemed curiously at odds with the warm luxuriance of his Italian surroundings,.and indeed with his own music. Strange that all that aggression and potent lyricism should have forced its way out of a character so quintessentially English.

„Der Unsinn, für den man Eintritt zahlt" lautete 1922 eine von vielen ähnlichen Schlagzeilen nach der ersten öffentlichen Aufführung von Waltons *Façade*. Der Skandal machte den 21jährigen Komponisten über Nacht berühmt. Für den Aufruhr war sicher die krasse Eigenwilligkeit dieses Stückes verantwortlich. Über ein Megaphon wurde Avantgardelyrik von Edith Sitwell deklamiert, begleitet von einem kleinen Kammerensemble, das hinter einem Vorhang spielte. Für das Publikum bedeutete englische Musik damals Parry und Elgar und vielleicht noch der späte Vaughan Williams. Die jazzige Brillanz von Waltons Komposition wirkte wie ein rotes Tuch, und der Ruf eines enfant terrible blieb für lange Zeit an ihm haften.

Das war ein ungewöhnliches Prädikat für diesen blassen, schüchternen jungen Mann aus Lancashire, der in Oxford im Chor gesungen hatte und nun in den exzentrischen, gebildeten Kreis um die Sitwells geraten war. Das einzige Werk, das diesem Ruf wirklich entsprach, war die frühe Ouvertüre *Portsmouth Point*. Die Rhythmen und die harten Übergänge dieses pompösen Stückes schreckten die zeitgenössischen Dirigenten jedenfalls soweit ab, daß Walton schließlich versuchte, selbst zu dirigieren. Das hatte er bereits bei *Façade* getan. Osbert Sitwell schrieb: „Er hielt den Taktstock mit der Attitüde eines hübschen, eleganten Heckenschützen." Für *Portsmouth Point* übte er dagegen lange und angestrengt vor dem Spiegel, und danach, so behauptete er, „war es ein Kinderspiel und ist es immer geblieben". Zwar dirigierte er ungern, und auch nur seine eigenen Stücke; das aber tat er mit ruhiger Autorität und einem Minimum an Aufwand und Getue. Seine Aufführungen waren stets von vorbildlicher Klarheit und Kraft.

Waltons abgeklärte, selbstverachtende Art und seine beißende Ironie standen im Mißverhältnis zu seiner romantischen Natur, die seine Musik und sein Leben zutiefst bestimmt hat, und manchmal stießen diese Charakterzüge hart aufeinander. Walton hat nie schnell komponiert, aber als er sich durch seine *Erste Symphonie* kämpfte, hatte er mit dem letzten Satz solche Mühen, daß er die ersten drei Sätze ohne den letzten uraufführen ließ. Viele musiktheoretische Hypothesen wurden aufgestellt, um dieses ungewöhnliche Vorgehen zu deuten; einer seiner Freunde bemerkte dazu jedoch schlicht: „Das Problem war, daß Willie zwischen den Sätzen die Freundinnen wechselte." Eine drastische Vereinfachung, angesichts der Leidenschaft, Wut und Verzweiflung der ersten drei Sätze. Aber in der Tat war der Komponist erst in der Lage, sein ursprüngliches Konzept auszuarbeiten und sein durchgängig ausdrucksstärkstes Werk in einem Lichtblitz zu vollenden, als sich eine neue Beziehung anbahnte.

Als diese Fotos entstanden, war Walton verheiratet und hatte sich auf der Insel Ischia im Golf von Neapel niedergelassen. Das erste Werk, das er dort schrieb, war *Troilus and Cressida*. Darauf folgten einige Orchesterwerke – ein *Cellokonzert*, das die Konzerte für Bratsche und Geige um ein weiteres Meisterwerk ergänzte, eine *Zweite Symphonie* und Variationen über Themen von Hindemith und Britten. Alle Stücke sind von äußerster Langsamkeit, gespeist aus jener leidenschaftlichen Melancholie und rauhen Kraft, die ihn irgendwo zwischen Elgar und Prokofjew ansiedeln – in der Mischung bleibt noch ein leiser Klang des alten enfant terrible zu hören. Walton behandelte Journalisten und Biographen mit einer kurzangebundenen, ironischen Reserviertheit, die in seinem warmen, freundlichen italienischen Umfeld befremdlich unpassend wirkte. Es bleibt erstaunlich, daß diese so außergewöhnlich englischen Charakterzüge die Entfaltung der aggressiven Energie und tiefen Poesie seiner Musik erlaubt haben.

« Ils ont payé pour écouter n'importe quoi », titrait un journal après la première représentation de *Façade* de Walton, en 1922, et ce ne fut pas la seule fois. Il avait alors 21 ans. Le scandale – qui le rendit célèbre du jour au lendemain – venait surtout de l'étrangeté de cette pièce : poésie d'avant-garde d'Edith Sitwell, déclamée à travers un porte-voix, et accompagnée par un petit orchestre de chambre caché derrière un rideau peint. L'éclat tapageur de la partition de Walton fit l'effet d'un chiffon rouge sur un public pour qui la musique anglaise c'était Parry et Elgar, ou, à la limite, Vaughan Williams, et sa réputation d'enfant terrible le suivit pendant des années.

C'était une étiquette mal appropriée à ce jeune homme pâle et timide, issu d'une modeste famille du Lancashire, jeune choriste d'Oxford qui se trouva entraîné dans l'entourage excentrique et élégant des Sitwell. Peut-être pouvait-elle s'appliquer à l'ouverture de Portsmouth Point ; de toute façon, les rythmes et les arrangements tapageurs de cette pièce turbulente inquiétèrent tant les chefs d'orchestre de l'époque que Walton décida, finalement, de s'essayer lui-même à la direction. Il avait déjà dirigé *Façade*, « tenant sa baguette, écrivit Osbert Sitwell, avec l'élégance d'une bécassine de belle allure », mais Portsmouth Point c'était autre chose : il s'entraîna longtemps devant un miroir, et dit plus tard : « C'était un jeu d'enfant et ça l'est resté ». Il dit n'y avoir jamais pris plaisir et ne dirigea que ses propres œuvres, mais, pour elles, il avait une tranquille autorité et ses interprétations étaient un modèle de clarté et d'énergie.

Mais sa froideur, sa tendance à l'autodénigrement et son esprit caustique contrastaient avec la nature romantique de sa musique et de sa vie. Parfois les deux mondes collidaient. Quand Walton, qui travaillait lentement, se débattait avec sa *Première Symphonie*, il resta tellement bloqué sur le dernier mouvement que les trois premiers se sont passés de lui pour la première. De nombreuses et doctes hypothèses furent avancées pour expliquer cette procédure inhabituelle. Mais la cause était toute simple. Comme le dit un ami : « Le problème est que Willie change de petite amie entre les mouvements. » Une simplification excessive, comme la passion, la colère et le désespoir des trois premiers mouvements l'expriment si clairement ; cependant, c'est quand sa nouvelle relation commença que le compositeur put achever, dans un torrent de lumière, la plus puissante de ses œuvres.

À l'époque de ces photographies, Walton était marié et s'était établi sur l'île d'Ischia, dans la baie de Naples. La première œuvre qu'il y écrivit fut l'opéra Troilus and Cressida, suivi d'une succession d'œuvres pour orchestre – un concerto pour violoncelle à ajouter à deux chefs-d'œuvre plus anciens, de même forme, pour alto et violon, une Seconde Symphonie, des Variations sur des thèmes de Hindemith et Benjamin Britten, toutes écrites avec une lenteur douloureuse et exploitant la même mélancolie passionnée, la même rude énergie, qui le placent quelque part entre Elgar et Prokofiev. Walton traita les journalistes et les biographes avec une retenue sèche et ironique qui contrastait avec la luxuriance chaleureuse de son environnement italien et avec sa propre musique. Il est étonnant que toute cette énergie agressive et ce lyrisme puissant aient pu trouver leur voie dans un personnage si parfaitement anglais.

Sir William Walton, 31 December 1965.
Sir William Walton, 31. Dezember 1965.
Sir William Walton, le 31 décembre 1965.

2

3

4

(1) Composer in waiting, 31 December 1965. (2) With the great violinist Jascha Heifetz, Heifetz's wife Frances and the conductor Sir Malcolm Sargent in the stalls at Covent Garden during rehearsals of the opera. Heifetz had commissioned Walton's *Violin Concerto* and first performed it in 1939. (3) Walton conducted his second recording of the cantata *Belshazzar's Feast* with the Philharmonia Orchestra and Chorus, whose founder and general manager Walter Legge is seen here at a recording session with the composer and Legge's wife, Elisabeth Schwarzkopf, 3 February 1959. Walton had intended Schwarzkopf as Cressida but Legge vetoed the idea. (4) Walton at Covent Garden in 1954, rehearsing the Hungarian soprano Magda László, who was to create the role of Cressida in his opera *Troilus and Cressida* on 3 December.

(1) Der Komponist wartet, 31. Dezember 1965. (2) Walton, der große Geiger Jascha Heifetz, dessen Frau Frances und der Dirigent Sir Malcolm Sargent während der Opernproben im Parkett in Covent Garden. Heifetz hatte bei Walton das *Violinkonzert* in Auftrag gegeben und es 1939 uraufgeführt. (3) Walton dirigiert die zweite Aufnahme seines Oratoriums *Belshazzar's Feast* mit dem von Walter Legge gegründeten und gemanagten Philharmonia Orchestra and Chorus. Hier sieht man Legge bei einem Aufnahmetermin zusammen mit dem Komponisten und Legges Frau, Elisabeth Schwarzkopf, 3. Februar 1959. Walton hatte die Schwarzkopf als Cressida haben wollen, aber Legge hatte sein Veto eingelegt. (4) Walton 1954 in Covent Garden bei der Probe mit der ungarischen Sopranistin Magda László, die in seiner Oper *Troilus und Cressida* am 3. Dezember den Part der Cressida singen wird.

(1) Le compositeur en train d'attendre, le 31 décembre 1965. (2) Avec le grand violoniste Jascha Heifetz, l'épouse de ce dernier, Frances, et le chef d'orchestre Sir Malcolm Sargent dans l'orchestre de Covent Garden pendant des répétitions de son opéra. Heifetz avait demandé le *Concerto pour Violon* de Walton et le dirigea pour la première fois en 1939. (3) Walton dirigea son second enregistrement de la cantate *Belshazzar's Feast* avec le Philharmonia Orchestra and Chorus, dont le fondateur et directeur général, Walter Legge, est photographié ici lors d'une séance d'enregistrement avec le compositeur et la femme de Legge, Elisabeth Schwarzkopf, le 3 février 1959. Walton aurait voulu Schwarzkopf dans le rôle de Cressida, mais Legge refusa. (4) Walton à Covent Garden en 1954, en train de faire répéter la soprano hongroise Magda László, qui allait bientôt incarner le rôle de Cressida dans son opéra *Troilus et Cressida*, le 3 décembre.

Walton recording *Belshazzar's Feast* with the Philharmonia
Orchestra, 3 February 1959.

Walton bei der Aufnahme von *Belshazzar's Feast* mit dem
Philharmonia Orchestra, 3. Februar 1959.

Walton enregistrant *Belshazzar's Feast* avec le Philharmonia
Orchestra, le 3 février 1959.

Rehearsing the London Philharmonic Orchestra and Choir in
The Twelve, 31 December 1965. This was the revised version of the
score, originally written for choir and organ earlier the same year;
it received its first performance at Westminster Abbey on 2 January
1966.

Walton probt *The Twelve* mit dem Chor und Orchester des London Philharmonic Orchestra, 31. Dezember 1965. Es handelte sich
um die revidierte Fassung der Partitur, die er zu Beginn des Jahres
ursprünglich für Chor und Orgel geschrieben hatte. Die erste
Aufführung fand am 2. Januar 1966 in Westminster Abbey statt.

Répétition du London Philharmonic Orchestra and Choir dans
The Twelve, le 31 décembre 1965. Ceci était une partition revue et
corrigée, et qui fut à l'origine écrite pour chorale et orgue, plus tôt
cette année-là ; sa première représentation se déroula à Westminster
Abbey le 2 janvier 1966.

CONDUCTORS

DIRIGENTEN

CHEFS D'ORCHESTRE

Leopold Stokowski
(1882-1977).

There was always something a little professorial about Ansermet's appearances on the podium, and this is hardly surprising because he started life as a mathematician and was in fact professor of mathematics at Lausanne University between the ages of 22 and 26. But his interest in music, particularly composition and conducting, and his early friendship with composers such as Debussy, Ravel and Stravinsky shaped his career: as chief conductor of Diaghilev's Ballets Russes he directed the premières of a number of important works including several by Stravinsky. When he founded the Orchestre de la Suisse Romande in Geneva in 1918 he remained faithful to this repertory – to which he added Bartók and, later, Benjamin Britten.

During his 48 years as director of the Suisse Romande orchestra he gave many fine performances of the classical repertory as well, but it was as a champion of the music of his contemporaries that he made his greatest mark. 'Stravinsky is the only true God and Ansermet is his prophet', it was said at the time – and though he couldn't go along with some aspects of Stravinsky's later style, for the earlier works, and the orchestral masterpieces of Debussy, Ravel and Falla, Ansermet remained a touchstone of authenticity for many years.

As a conductor he was not demonstrative – though at rehearsal he was meticulous in his attention to detail. On his many trips abroad as guest conductor, he frequently ran into difficulties with languages, particularly English. He astonished the musicians of one London orchestra by suddenly losing his temper and shouting 'You think I know fuck nothing but you are wrong – I know fuck all!' – a strange outburst for the man who, at about the same time, was writing a philosophical treatise entitled *The fundamentals of music in the human consciousness*.

Ernest Ansermet wirkte auf der Bühne immer etwas akademisch. Das ist kaum verwunderlich, denn eigentlich war er Mathematiker und begann im Alter von 22 Jahren vier Jahre lang Mathematik an der Universität von Lausanne zu lehren. Sein lebhaftes Interesse an der Musik und besonders am Komponieren und Dirigieren sowie seine frühen Freundschaften mit Komponisten wie Debussy, Ravel und Strawinsky lenkten sein Leben jedoch bald in andere Bahnen. Als Chefdirigent von Diaghilews Ballets Russes dirigierte er viele wichtige Uraufführungen, darunter auch einige Werke von Strawinsky. Diesem Repertoire blieb er auch treu, als er 1918 in Genf das Orchestre de la Suisse Romande gründete. Er erweiterte es noch um Bartók und nahm später auch Benjamin Britten ins Programm.

In seinen 48 Jahren als Direktor des Orchestre de la Suisse Romande gab er viele gute Aufführungen aus dem klassischen Repertoire; seine bleibenden Erfolge hatte er jedoch als Meister der zeitgenössischen Musik. „Strawinsky ist der wahre Gott, und Ansermet ist sein Prophet" hieß es damals – und obwohl Ansermet zu dem späteren Strawinsky nicht immer den rechten Zugang fand, galten seine Einspielungen von dessen früheren Werken sowie der Orchester-Meisterwerke von Debussy, Ravel und de Falla jahrelang als verbürgte Authentizität.

Als Dirigent wirkte er zurückhaltend. Bei den Proben achtete er jedoch peinlich genau auf alle Details. Auf seinen vielen Auslandsreisen als Gastdirigent hatte er oft Schwierigkeiten mit den fremden Sprachen, besonders mit dem Englischen. Einmal überraschte er die Musiker eines Londoner Orchesters mit einem plötzlichen Wutausbruch und schrie: „Ihr glaubt wohl, ich wüßte verdammt gar nichts, aber da irrt ihr gewaltig – ich weiß verdammt alles!" Ein etwas irritierender Ausbruch von einem Mann, der zur gleichen Zeit an einer philosophischen Abhandlung mit dem Titel *Die Grundlagen der Musik im menschlichen Bewußtsein* schrieb.

Il y avait toujours quelque chose de professoral dans l'air quand Ansermet apparaissait sur l'estrade, et cela n'a rien d'étonnant puisqu'il fut professeur de mathématiques à l'université de Lausanne de 22 à 26 ans. Son intérêt pour la musique, particulièrement pour la composition et la direction d'orchestre, et son amitié de jeunesse avec des compositeurs comme Debussy, Ravel et Stravinski modelèrent sa carrière : comme chef d'orchestre des Ballets russes de Diaghilev, il dirigea les premières de nombreuses œuvres importantes, plusieurs de Stravinski notamment. Quand il fonda l'Orchestre de la Suisse romande à Genève en 1918, il resta fidèle à son répertoire, auquel il ajouta Bartók et, plus tard, Benjamin Britten.

Pendant ses 48 ans à la tête de l'Orchestre de la Suisse romande, il donna également beaucoup de belles interprétations du répertoire classique, mais c'est avec la musique de ses contemporains qu'il s'imposa. « Stravinski est le seul véritable Dieu et Ansermet est son prophète », disait-on à l'époque. Malgré ses réticences envers les dernières œuvres de Stravinski, Ansermet resta un modèle incontournable dans l'interprétation de ses œuvres plus anciennes et celle des chefs-d'œuvre pour orchestre de Debussy, Ravel et de Falla.

Attentif à chaque détail pendant les répétitions, c'était un chef d'orchestre peu démonstratif. Durant ses nombreux voyages à l'étranger comme chef invité, il eut souvent des problèmes de vocabulaire, particulièrement en anglais. Il surprit les musiciens de l'un des orchestres de Londres en se mettant soudain en colère et en hurlant : « Vous croyez que je sais fichtre rien, mais vous vous trompez ! P..., je sais rien de rien ! ». Étrange éclat pour un homme qui, au même moment, écrivait un traité de philosophie intitulé *Les principes fondamentaux de la musique dans la conscience humaine*…

Ernest Ansermet in 1958. The authentic touch in 20th century music.

Ernest Ansermet im Jahr 1958. Wahrhaftigkeit in der Musik des 20. Jahrhunderts.

Ernest Ansermet en 1958. La touche authentique dans la musique du 20e siècle.

Ernest Ansermet rehearsing the Philharmonia Orchestra,
18 August 1958.

Ernest Ansermet probt mit dem Philharmonia Orchestra,
18. August 1958.

Ernest Ansermet faisant répéter le Philharmonia Orchestra,
le 18 août 1958.

John Barbirolli, born in London to an Italian father and a French mother, became the most wholly English of conductors. In his early days he was very much the coming young man, seen as Beecham's successor, though his very different character did not bode well for their future relationship. But in 1936 he received an invitation to conduct the New York Philharmonic Symphony Orchestra, and in 1937 he was chosen to succeed Toscanini as its chief conductor — an amazing appointment for a relatively unknown candidate only 38 years old. He stuck it for five years, but Toscanini was a difficult act to follow (in spite of the common Italian heritage) and he did not have an easy passage with the New York musicians — or the New York critics. He returned to war-torn England in 1942, and in the following year accepted the formidable job of rebuilding the Hallé Orchestra in Manchester.

It was the love of his life. The Hallé had had no permanent conductor since the great days of Hamilton Harry, who had resigned in 1933. In the interim the orchestra had fallen on bad days: it had practically no money, its concert hall had been destroyed in an air raid and its personnel heavily reduced by military service and an unfortunate deal with the BBC. In his first month in Manchester Barbirolli engaged more than 30 new players, rehearsed wherever space could be found, and starting from scratch rebuilt the orchestra in less than a year into an ensemble that could bear comparison with any in Britain. The understanding which he developed with his musicians was unique: he could be abusive and insistently exacting in rehearsal, but he would share coffee with them in the intervals of work and offer lifts home in his car at the end of the day. His dynamic single-mindedness left no aspect of the Hallé untouched, and as a result he was able to rival Beecham with the best performances outside London. In later years he reduced his commitment a little, allowing himself time to tour with other orchestras and in particular to form a lasting relationship as guest conductor of the Berlin Philharmonic; but it was to the Hallé that he always returned and in 1968 he was appointed its conductor laureate for life. No honour could have pleased him more.

Barbirolli's world was the great, late romantic repertory, which he treated with all the enthusiasm and warmth of a generous Latin temperament. His Mahler compelled the admiration of the Berlin players (he gave more than 70 concerts in West Berlin in the 1960s), and the same glowing attention to detail suffused his performances of Elgar, a composer for whom he had a special passion and with whose music he became closely identified. But even more idiosyncratic, for an Italian, was his attachment to the music of Vaughan Williams, who returned the compliment by dedicating his *Eighth Symphony* to the conductor. It received its first performance in 1956, by the Hallé Orchestra, and when Barbirolli asked the players who had taken part to sign the autograph full score which the composer had just presented to him, Vaughan Williams wrote at the head of the list: 'For glorious John, with love and admiration'. It was a proper and well-deserved tribute to a conductor who has perhaps been underrated by posterity.

John Barbirolli kam als Sohn eines Italieners und einer Französin in London zur Welt und wurde dennoch ein typisch englischer Dirigent. Früh erwartete man von ihm Großes, und er wurde als Beechams Nachfolger gehandelt, obwohl ihre unterschiedlichen Charaktere keine günstige Voraussetzung für eine Zusammenarbeit versprachen. 1936 erhielt er dann jedoch einen Ruf nach New York, um dort das Philharmonic Symphony Orchestra zu dirigieren, und 1937 erkor man ihn zu Toscaninis Nachfolger als Chefdirigent – eine überraschende Entscheidung für den relativ unbekannten Bewerber, der zu dem Zeitpunkt erst 38 Jahre alt war. Er blieb fünf Jahre dort, aber die Fußstapfen Toscaninis waren sehr groß (trotz des gemeinsamen italienischen Erbes), und Barbirolli hatte mit den New Yorker Musikern seine Mühen. 1942 kehrte er in das kriegszerrissene England zurück. Im Jahr darauf bekam er die vielversprechende Aufgabe, das Hallé Orchestra in Manchester wieder aufzubauen.

Es wurde die Liebe seines Lebens. Das Hallé Orchestra hatte seit seiner großen Zeit mit dem 1933 zurückgetretenen Hamilton Harry keine dauerhafte Leitung mehr gehabt. In der Zwischenzeit war es dem Orchester schlecht ergangen. Es hatte praktisch kein Geld, sein Konzerthaus war bei einem Luftangriff zerstört worden, und das Ensemble war durch den Militärdienst und einen ungünstigen Vertrag mit der BBC stark dezimiert. In seinen ersten Monaten in Manchester engagierte Barbirolli mehr als dreißig neue Musiker und probte, wo immer sich Platz fand. Er baute das Orchester von ganz unten wieder auf, und nach kaum einem Jahr hatte er ein Ensemble, das sich mit jedem anderen in England messen konnte. Zwischen ihm und seinen Musikern herrschte ein außergewöhnliches Einverständnis. Bei den Proben konnte er beleidigend und unglaublich kleinlich sein, aber in den Pausen teilte er mit ihnen den Kaffee und bot ihnen an, sie am Schluß in seinem Wagen mitzunehmen. Mit seiner dynamischen Zielstrebigkeit organisierte er das Orchester bis ins kleinste neu und konnte schließlich mit Beecham um die besten Aufführungen außerhalb Londons konkurrieren. In späteren Jahren nahm er sein Engagement etwas zurück, um auch mit anderen Orchestern auf Tourneen gehen zu können. Er wurde ein regelmäßiger Gastdirigent der Berliner Philharmoniker, kehrte aber stets wieder zum Hallé Orchestra zurück. 1968 wurde er zum Ehrendirigenten auf Lebenszeit ernannt. Nichts hätte ihm besser gefallen können.

Barbirollis Welt war das große romantische Repertoire, das er mit aller Begeisterung und aller Wärme seines großzügigen Temperaments behandelte. Sein Mahler trug ihm die Bewunderung der Berliner Musiker ein (in den 60er Jahren gab er in Westberlin über 70 Konzerte). Die gleiche glühende Aufmerksamkeit für jedes Detail zeichnete auch seine Elgar Aufführungen aus, für den er eine besondere Leidenschaft hegte und mit dessen Musik sich sein Name eng verknüpfte. Seine Zuneigung zu Vaughan Williams verwundert vielleicht am meisten, jedoch erwiderte der das Kompliment, indem er dem Dirigenten seine *Achte Symphonie* widmete. 1956 fand die Uraufführung mit dem Hallé Orchestra statt, und als Barbirolli die beteiligten Musiker anschließend bat, die Originalpartitur zu signieren, die der Komponist ihm gerade überreicht hatte, schrieb Vaughan Williams als erster: „Für den famosen John in Liebe und Bewunderung". Es war die deutliche und verdiente Anerkennung für einen Dirigenten, der von der Nachwelt vielleicht unterschätzt wird.

John Barbirolli, né à Londres d'un père italien et d'une mère française, est devenu le plus anglais des chefs d'orchestre. Dans sa jeunesse, c'était un jeune homme plein d'avenir, celui qui allait succéder à Beecham, bien que son caractère ne laissât rien présager de bon pour leurs relations futures. Mais en 1936 il reçut une invitation à diriger l'Orchestre symphonique philharmonique de New York et, en 1937, fut choisi pour succéder à Toscanini, nomination étonnante pour un candidat relativement inconnu, âgé seulement de 38 ans. Il y resta cinq ans, mais il était difficile de succéder à Toscanini (en dépit de l'héritage italien commun) et il eut des difficultés avec les musiciens et les critiques de New York. Il revint vers une Angleterre déchirée par la guerre en 1942 et, l'année suivante, accepta le formidable travail de reconstruction de l'orchestre Hallé à Manchester.

Ce fut l'amour de sa vie. Le Hallé n'avait pas eu de chef permanent depuis les beaux jours d'Hamilton Harry, qui avait démissionné en 1933. Dans l'intérim, l'orchestre avait connu des jours difficiles : peu d'argent, la salle de concerts détruite par un raid aérien, son personnel fortement réduit par le service militaire et un accord malheureux avec la BBC. Dans le premier mois de son arrivée à Manchester, Barbirolli engagea plus de 30 nouveaux instrumentistes, répéta où il pouvait et, partant de rien, fit de l'orchestre, en moins d'un an, un ensemble qui pouvait être comparé à n'importe quel autre en Grande-Bretagne. L'entente qu'il créa avec ses musiciens était unique : il pouvait être grossier et exigeant pendant les répétitions, mais il buvait le café avec eux pendant les pauses et leur proposait de les déposer chez eux en voiture à la fin de la journée. Sa détermination et son dynamisme pour tout ce qui concernait Hallé furent tels qu'il réussit à rivaliser avec Beecham. À la fin de sa carrière, il se désengagea un peu, s'autorisant à partir en tournée avec d'autres orchestres, notamment le Philharmonique de Berlin avec lequel il noua des relations solides ; mais c'était toujours au Hallé qu'il revenait et, en 1968, il en fut nommé chef honoraire à vie. Aucun honneur n'aurait pu lui donner plus de plaisir.

Le monde de Barbirolli était le grand répertoire romantique, qu'il traitait avec tout l'enthousiasme et la chaleur de son tempérament latin. Son Mahler força l'admiration des musiciens de Berlin (il donna plus de 70 concerts à Berlin-Ouest dans les années 60) ; une lumineuse attention pour les détails baignait ses interprétations d'Elgar, compositeur auquel il vouait une passion particulière. Encore plus particulier, pour un Italien, fut son attachement à la musique de Vaughan Williams, qui lui retourna le compliment en lui dédiant sa Huitième Symphonie. Elle fut interprétée pour la première fois en 1956, par l'orchestre Hallé, et quand Barbirolli demanda aux instrumentistes qui l'avaient jouée de signer la partition autographe que le compositeur venait de lui remettre, Vaughan Williams écrivit, tout en haut : « Au merveilleux John, avec affection et admiration. » C'était un hommage authentique et bien mérité, pour un chef d'orchestre peut-être sous-estimé par la postérité.

(1) Sir John Barbirolli conducting the Hallé Orchestra in Guildford Cathedral, 18 January 1962. (2) With his wife, the oboeist Evelyn Rothwell (apparently oblivious of the cigarette smoke), 1949.

(1) Sir John Barbirolli dirigiert das Hallé Orchester in der Guildford Cathedral, 18. Januar 1962. (2) Barbirolli mit seiner Frau, der Oboistin Evelyn Rothwell (die offenbar unempfindlich gegen Zigarettenrauch ist), 1949.

(1) Sir John Barbirolli dirige le Hallé Orchestra dans la cathédrale de Guildford, le 18 janvier 1962. (2) En compagnie de sa femme, la hautboïste Evelyn Rothwell (qui manifestement, n'est pas gênée par la fumée de cigarette) en 1949.

Barbirolli getting a pianissimo out of the Hallé Orchestra, Manchester, 1949.

Barbirolli entlockt dem Hallé Orchester ein Pianissimo, Manchester 1949.

Barbirolli obtenant un pianissimo du Hallé Orchestra, à Manchester en 1949.

SIR THOMAS BEECHAM   1879-1961

His appearances on the concert platform during the 1950s were unforgettable: the stately procession to the rostrum, the patrician manner; the flamboyant performances of the national anthem which opened the concerts; the encores, the speeches, the oracular pronouncements and flashes of wit that closed them. By the time of these pictures Beecham was more than a conductor: he was a national institution, a legend in which we all found ourselves believing.

He had the luck, rare among musicians, to be born into a wealthy family (his father was the proprietor of the Lancashire pharmaceutical company that produced Beecham's Pills), and he lavished this inheritance recklessly on one musical enterprise after another: the Beecham Symphony Orchestra in 1909, the Beecham Opera Company in 1915, the London Philharmonic Orchestra in 1932, the Royal Philharmonic in 1946 – with each creating a new centre of excellence which, in the case of the last two, has endured until the present day. He was much involved in opera: he revived Mozart's *Così fan tutte* and *Die Zauberflöte* after a shameful period of neglect, introduced all the first Strauss operas to London and many British works too, arranged and financed the momentous visits of Diaghilev's Russian ballet and opera company in 1913 and 1914, and directed the Royal Opera at Covent Garden for the last seven years before the war.

As a conductor he was, quite literally, in a class by himself: he was almost entirely self-taught and, unlike his German, Italian or French colleagues, owed nothing to national tradition – in England there was none. Combined with his financial background, this led of course to charges of amateurism. And it is true that he was capable of conducting badly and not unknown to blame somebody else for it afterwards. The goatee beard and the cigar were a familiar presence in the corridors of musical power and the disdainful wit that he bestowed upon his professional fellows made him enemies. But on the whole his orchestras loved him, and there was laughter mixed with the passionate concentration at rehearsals. At his best – and that was most of the time – he gave a greater sense of the enjoyment of music than any other conductor of his day. He may not have had the profundity of Furtwängler or Klemperer, or the demonic intensity of Toscanini, but what he had – the rhythmic buoyancy, the 'lift', the instinctive flexibility of phrasing, the perfect balance of power and elegance, the sheer excitement of the musical sound – these were unique.

Bach didn't interest him much, and from Beethoven on the great German tradition was never really his field, though his Wagner – *Meistersinger, Tristan, The Ring* – could be immensely exciting. His Handel was highly perceptive and sometimes frankly outrageous; Mozart he loved, almost to the point of overstatement in his later years. He championed Haydn, Mendelssohn, all the French from Berlioz onwards, among his own contemporaries Sibelius, Strauss, and above all Delius – whose music only really came alive as the result of Beecham's performances. He more than anyone awoke a generation of Englishmen to the real power of music. 'The English may not like music', he once said, 'but they absolutely love the noise it makes.' The extent to which this situation changed during the course of his lifetime is the measure of his success.

Seine Auftritte in den 50er Jahren hinterließen einen unvergeßlichen Eindruck: sein majestätischer Einzug zum Pult, seine aristokratische Art, die prunkvolle Eröffnung der Konzerte mit der Nationalhymne, die Zugaben und Ansprachen mit ihren orakelhaften Aussprüchen und Bonmots. Zu jener Zeit war Beecham weit mehr als ein Dirigent. Er war zu einer nationalen Institution geworden, zu einer lebendigen Legende.

Er hatte das unter Musikern seltene Glück, einer wohlhabenden Familie zu entstammen (sein Vater besaß die Arzneimittelfirma in Lancashire, die Beecham's Pills herstellte). Unbekümmert verschwendete er dieses Erbe für ein musikalisches Unternehmen nach dem anderen: 1909 gründete er das Beecham Symphony Orchestra, 1915 die Beecham Opera Company, 1932 das London Philharmonic Orchestra, 1946 das Royal Philharmonic Orchestra – und schuf damit jedesmal ein herausragendes musikalisches Zentrum. Die beiden letztgenannten bestehen noch heute. Er engagierte sich stark für die Oper. Nachdem sie lange schändlich vernachlässigt worden waren, brachte er Mozarts *Cosi fan tutte* und die *Zauberflöte* zurück auf die Bühne. Er führte alle Opern von Richard Strauss und auch zahlreiche Werke englischer Komponisten in London auf. 1913 und 1914 arrangierte und finanzierte er die Gastspiele von Diaghilews Russischer Ballett- und Operngesellschaft, und in den letzten sieben Jahren vor dem Krieg leitete er die Royal Opera in Covent Garden.

Als Dirigent bildete er im wahrsten Sinne eine Klasse für sich. Er war fast ausschließlich Autodidakt, und im Gegensatz zu seinen deutschen, französischen und italienischen Kollegen war er keiner nationalen Tradition verpflichtet – in England gab es keine. In Verbindung mit seinem finanziellen Hintergrund brachte ihm dies zwangsläufig den Vorwurf des Dilettantismus ein, manchmal berechtigt. (Und er war durchaus im Stande, hinterher jemand anderem die Schuld dafür zu geben.) Man kannte seinen Spitzbart und seine Zigarre in den einflußreichen musikalischen Kreisen, der hochmütige Spott, mit dem er seine Kollegen bedachte, schuf ihm Feinde. Bei seinen Orchestern war er jedoch trotz allem sehr beliebt, und bei den Proben gab es bei aller leidenschaftlicher Konzentration auch Heiterkeit. Es gelang ihm mehr als jedem anderen Dirigenten, Freude an der Musik zu vermitteln. Er verfügte vielleicht nicht über die Tiefgründigkeit eines Furtwängler oder Klemperer oder über die dämonische Intensität eines Toscanini – seine rhythmische Bewegtheit, sein Schwung, das instinktive Gespür für Phrasierungen, das perfekte Gleichgewicht von Kraft und Anmut und seine begeisternde Art, der Musik ihren Klang zu entlocken, waren jedoch einzigartig.

Bach interessierte ihn nicht sehr, und von Beethoven an war die deutsche Tradition nie wirklich sein Gebiet, obwohl seine Wagnerinterpretationen – *Die Meistersinger, Tristan, Der Ring* – sehr aufregend sein konnten. Er dirigierte Händel äußerst einfühlsam und liebte Mozart – in späteren Lebensjahren fast im Übermaß. Er favorisierte Haydn, Mendelssohn und alle französischen Komponisten, angefangen bei Berlioz. Unter seinen Zeitgenossen schätzte er besonders Sibelius, Strauss und vor allem Delius – dessen Musik eigentlich erst durch Beechams Aufführungen bekannt wurde. Mehr als jedem anderen gelang es ihm, in einer ganzen Generation von Engländern einen Sinn für die wirkliche Kraft der Musik zu erwecken. „Die Engländer mögen vielleicht keine Musik", sagte er einmal, „aber sie haben den Lärm, den sie macht, wirklich gern." Die Reichweite, in der es ihm gelungen ist, dieses musikalische Empfinden im Laufe seines Lebens zu verändern, bestimmt das Maß seines Erfolges.

On ne peut oublier ses apparitions sur la scène des concerts, dans les années 50 : la progression régulière vers l'estrade, l'allure de patricien, les exécutions flamboyantes de l'hymne national, les rappels, les discours, les déclarations sibyllines et les traits d'esprit qui les concluaient. À l'époque de ces photographies, Beecham était plus qu'un chef d'orchestre, il était une institution nationale, une légende vivante.

Il a eu la chance, rare chez les musiciens, de naître dans une famille riche (son père était le propriétaire de la Lancashire Pharmaceutical Company qui produisait les Pastilles Beecham), et il dépensait son héritage, avec prodigalité et insouciance, dans une entreprise musicale après l'autre : le Beecham Symphony Orchestra en 1909, la Beecham Opera Compagny en 1915, le London Philharmonic Orchestra en 1932, le Royal Philharmonic en 1946 – créant avec chacun d'eux un nouveau pôle d'excellence. Les deux derniers sont toujours là pour le prouver. L'opéra lui doit également beaucoup : reprise de *Cosi fan tutte* et de *La Flûte enchantée* de Mozart, présentation de tous les premiers opéras de Strauss à Londres ainsi que de nombreuses œuvres britanniques, mise sur pied et financement des visites capitales des ballets russes et de la troupe d'opéra de Diaghilev en 1913 et 1914, et direction du Royal Opera à Covent Garden durant les sept années précédant la guerre.

En tant que chef d'orchestre, il était unique : presque entièrement autodidacte, il ne devait rien à la tradition nationale (il n'y en avait pas en Angleterre), à l'inverse de ses collègues allemands, italiens ou français. Sa situation financière aidant, cela donna lieu à des accusations d'amateurisme. Et il est vrai qu'il lui arrivait de mal diriger et d'en faire porter la responsabilité à tout autre qu'à lui-même. Sa barbichette et son cigare étaient omniprésents dans les couloirs du pouvoir musical, et le regard dédaigneux qu'il portait sur ses confrères lui fit plus d'un ennemi. Mais, dans l'ensemble, ses orchestres l'aimaient, et pendant les répétitions, le rire se mêlait à la concentration passionnée. Au mieux de sa forme – et c'était le plus souvent –, il surpassait tous les chefs de son époque par son sens du plaisir de la musique. Il n'avait peut-être pas la profondeur d'un Furtwängler ou d'un Klemperer, ou l'intensité démoniaque d'un Toscanini, mais il avait d'uniques le ressort rythmique, la flexibilité instinctive du phrasé, le parfait équilibre de la puissance et de l'élégance, la pure sensation du son musical.

Bach ne l'intéressait qu'assez peu et, à partir de Beethoven, la tradition allemande ne fut jamais vraiment son domaine, bien que ses Wagner – *Les Maîtres chanteurs, Tristan*, le *Ring* – aient pu être extrêmement captivants. Son interprétation d'Haendel était parfois franchement excessive ; il adorait Mozart, presque jusqu'à l'exagération dans ses dernières années. Il soutenait Haydn, Mendelssohn, tous les Français à partir de Berlioz ; parmi ses contemporains, Sibelius, Strauss et par-dessus tout Delius, dont la musique ne prit réellement vie qu'à la suite des représentations de Beecham. Plus que quiconque, il éveilla une génération d'Anglais au pouvoir réel de la musique. « Les Anglais n'aiment peut-être pas la musique, dit-il un jour, mais ils adorent le bruit qu'elle fait ». Le réel changement intervenu dans cet état de fait au cours de sa vie est la marque de son succès.

◀ Sir Thomas Beecham, cigar in hand, listens to his own voice in a playback of his talk on Delius (sponsored by a soap company for Canadian commercial radio), 1949.

Sir Thomas Beecham hört sich mit einer Zigarre in der Hand die Wiedergabe seines Vortrags über Delius an (Sponsor war eine Seifenfirma im Auftrag des privaten Kanadischen Rundfunks), 1949.

Sir Thomas Beecham, un cigare à la main, réécoutant son discours sur Delius (parrainé par un fabricant de savons pour une radio commerciale canadienne), en 1949.

Beecham rehearsing the Royal Philharmonic – the orchestra he
founded in 1946 – on 13 October 1958.

Beecham bei einer Probe mit dem 1946 von ihm selbst gegründeten Royal Philharmonic Orchestra, 13. Oktober 1958.

Beecham en répétition avec le Royal Philharmonic – l'orchestre
qu'il fonda en 1946 – le 13 octobre 1958.

KARL BÖHM 1894-1981

Böhm was very much a central European figure – Austrian-born, he studied in Graz and Vienna, and was invited as an assistant to the Munich Opera by Bruno Walter, later progressing to the opera houses at Darmstadt, Hamburg and eventually Dresden, where his nine years as music director established him as one of the foremost interpreters of the great German operatic tradition. He became a close friend of Richard Strauss and directed the first performances of *Die schweigsame Frau* and *Daphne* (of which he was the dedicatee), meanwhile laying the foundations of a relationship with the Vienna Philharmonic Orchestra which bore fruit when he was appointed director of the Staatsoper in 1943. The appointment came to an end two years later when the opera house received a direct hit during an Allied air raid, but at the reopening in 1954 Böhm was there again to conduct a gala performance of *Fidelio* before a distinguished audience including practically all Europe's heads of state.

Until the end of the war he had made comparatively few appearances outside the German-speaking countries, unless it was with his own orchestra, as when he visited London with the Staatskapelle Dresden in 1936. But during the post-war period, while the Vienna Staatsoper was being rebuilt, he had no stable position and for the first time in his life was forced to find freelance work where he could; for three years he directed the German opera seasons in Buenos Aires, and the attractions of travel, guest conducting and recording became more evident as he advanced into his 60s. Inevitably the Viennese didn't like it: he was criticized for his continued absences and in 1956, announcing publicly that he was not prepared to sacrifice an international career for the sake of the Vienna Opera, he tendered his resignation as Generalmusikdirektor of the most prestigious opera house in the German-speaking world.

He made up for it to some extent in New York, where he became a visiting stalwart of the Metropolitan Opera for the next 22 years, but mainly he still restricted his activities to Europe, returning year after year to the Salzburg Festival, to Bayreuth, to Munich, and of course to Vienna and Berlin. He has made occasional visits to Milan and Paris, and a few to London, where his reputation was sufficient to gain him the position of president of the London Symphony Orchestra for the last four years of his life. But he never attained the kind of familiarity with British audiences enjoyed by Kleiber or Klemperer or Monteux.

Böhm was one of the last survivors of a great generation of Austro-German conductors. His world was the world of the great Viennese and German classics, and he treated them as if he had known them intimately all his life – as indeed he had – with an authority, sense of proportion and in later years a wise maturity that had nothing of the 'performer' about it, everything of the musician. There were no flamboyant gestures, no conductor's mannerisms, just a skilful and perfectly judged presentation of the music. It was a world in which clarity and a sense of structure served him well, in Wagner as in Berg, but above all in Richard Strauss, of whose music he was probably the best conductor of his day. And there are many for whom, in the deeply rooted, idiomatic Viennese tradition, Böhm is the best Mozart conductor of all.

Karl Böhm war im wesentlichen ein Musiker Mitteleuropas. Er war gebürtiger Österreicher und studierte in Graz und Wien. Bruno Walter holte ihn als Assistenten zu sich an die Münchner Oper. Später war er in den Opernhäusern von Darmstadt, Hamburg und schließlich Dresden tätig, wo er neun Jahre lang Musikdirektor war. In dieser Zeit entstand sein Ruf als einer der besten Interpreten der deutschen Operntradition. Böhm wurde ein enger Freund von Richard Strauss und dirigierte die Uraufführungen von *Die schweigsame Frau* und *Daphne* (die ihm gewidmet war). Dabei entwickelte sich seine Beziehung zu den Wiener Philharmonikern, die 1943 in seiner Ernennung zum Direktor der Staatsoper mündete. Diese Tätigkeit endete zwei Jahre später, als das Opernhaus bei einem Angriff der Alliierten zerstört wurde. (Bei der Galaveranstaltung zur Wiedereröffnung 1954 dirigierte Böhm vor einem illustren Publikum, zu dem praktisch alle Staatsoberhäupter Europas zählten, den *Fidelio*.)

Bis zum Kriegsende trat Böhm verhältnismäßig selten außerhalb der deutschsprachigen Länder auf, es sei denn mit seinem eigenen Orchester wie bei seinem Besuch in London mit der Staatskapelle Dresden im Jahre 1936. In der Nachkriegszeit jedoch, als sich die Wiener Staatsoper noch im Wiederaufbau befand, hatte er keine feste Anstellung und mußte zum ersten Mal in seinem Leben freiberuflich arbeiten. Drei Jahre lang dirigierte er die deutsche Opernsaison in Buenos Aires und fand zunehmend Gefallen an den Reisen, den Auftritten als Gastdirigent und der Arbeit in Aufnahmestudios. In seinen 60er Jahren zeigte sich das immer deutlicher, und es mußte den Wienern mißfallen. Sie kritisierten seine ständige Abwesenheit, und als er 1956 öffentlich erklärte, er sei nicht bereit, eine internationale Karriere für die Wiener Oper zu opfern, nahm er damit Abschied von seiner Position als Generalmusikdirektor eines der angesehensten Opernhäuser im deutschsprachigen Raum.

Bis zu einem gewissen Grad fand er in New York einen Ausgleich dafür, wo er für die nächsten 22 Jahre ein regelmäßiger Gast an der Metropolitan Opera wurde. Seine Aktivitäten blieben aber weiterhin auf Europa konzentriert. Jahr für Jahr kehrte er zu den Salzburger Festspielen zurück, nach Bayreuth, München und natürlich nach Wien und Berlin. Gelegentlich besuchte er Mailand oder Paris und manchmal auch London. Seine Reputation trug ihm – für die letzten vier Jahre seines Lebens – die Präsidentschaft des London Symphony Orchestra ein. Er wurde jedoch mit dem englischen Publikum nie so vertraut wie Kleiber, Klemperer oder Monteux.

Böhm war einer der letzten aus der großen Tradition deutsch-österreichischer Dirigenten. Er lebte in der Welt der großen Deutschen und Wiener Klassik, und er bewegte sich darin, als habe er sie sein Leben lang persönlich gekannt – was ja auch zutraf. Er behandelte sie mit einer Autorität, einem Sinn für das richtige Maß und in seinen späteren Jahren mit einer gereiften Weisheit, die sich von der reinen „Interpretation" immer mehr zur Kunst selbst wandelte. Er verzichtete sich statt dessen auf eine meisterhafte und perfekte musikalische Darbietung. In der Welt dieser Musik kam sein Sinn für Klarheit und Aufbau außerordentlich gut zur Geltung. Das gilt für Wagner und Berg, aber wohl besonders für Strauss, dessen Musik er vielleicht von allen seinen Zeitgenossen am besten dirigiert hat, und viele halten ihn, wegen des tief in ihm verwurzelten Wiener Ausdrucks, für den überzeugendsten Dirigenten der Werke Mozarts.

Karl Böhm, un musicien considérable en Europe, est né en Autriche où il étudie à Graz et à Vienne. Invité comme assistant à l'Opéra de Munich par Bruno Walter, il œuvre par la suite à l'opéra de Darmstadt, de Hambourg et, enfin, de Dresde, où ses neuf années en tant que directeur musical l'ont consacré comme l'un des interprètes de premier plan de la grande tradition allemande de l'opéra. Ami intime de Richard Strauss, il dirigea les premières représentations de *Die schweigsame Frau* et de *Daphne* (qui lui était dédié), posant alors les bases de ses relations avec l'Orchestre philharmonique de Vienne, qui portèrent leurs fruits quand il fut nommé directeur du Staatsoper en 1943, fonction qui prit fin deux ans plus tard, quand l'opéra fut touché par un raid aérien allié, mais, à sa réouverture en 1954, Böhm était présent pour diriger une représentation de gala de *Fidelio*, devant un public comprenant la quasi-totalité de tous les chefs d'État européens.

Il fit relativement peu d'apparitions hors des pays germanophones, sauf avec son propre orchestre, comme à Londres, en 1936, avec la Staatskapelle Dresden. Mais, durant l'après-guerre, tandis que l'on reconstruisait l'Opéra de Vienne, n'ayant plus de situation fixe, pour la première fois de sa vie il fut obligé de travailler en indépendant, là où il trouvait à se produire : pendant trois ans, il dirigea les saisons d'opéra allemand à Buenos Aires. Puis, dans les années 60, l'attrait des voyages, de la direction d'orchestre en tant qu'invité et des enregistrements se fit plus manifeste, ce qui bien sûr déplut aux Viennois qui lui reprochèrent ses absences prolongées. En 1956, annonçant publiquement qu'il n'était pas prêt à abandonner une carrière internationale pour l'Opéra de Vienne, il remit sa démission de directeur général de la musique de l'Opéra le plus prestigieux du monde germanophone.

Il devint l'invité régulier du Metropolitan Opera de New York pendant les vingt-deux années suivantes, mais il concentra principalement ses activités en Europe, retournant chaque année au festival de Salzbourg, à Bayreuth, à Munich, et bien sûr à Vienne et à Berlin. Il fit des visites ponctuelles à Milan et à Paris, quelques-unes à Londres, où sa réputation suffit à lui obtenir le poste de président de l'Orchestre symphonique de Londres, pour les quatre dernières années de sa vie. Toutefois il n'obtiendra pas du public anglais la confiance accordée à celui-ci à Kleiber, Klemperer ou à Monteux.

Böhm fut l'un des derniers survivants d'une grande génération de chefs d'orchestre austro-allemands. Son monde était celui des grands classiques viennois et allemands, et il les traitait avec une autorité, un sens de la proportion et, dans les dernières années, une sage maturité qui n'avaient rien de l'interprète, mais tout du musicien. Ni gestes extravagants ni affectations de chef d'orchestre, seulement une présentation habile et parfaitement mesurée de la musique. C'était un monde dans lequel la clarté et le sens de la structure le servirent, autant pour Wagner que pour Berg, mais, par-dessus tout, pour Richard Strauss, dont la musique n'a sans doute pas encore trouvé de meilleur chef. Et ils sont nombreux ceux pour qui, dans la tradition viennoise profondément enracinée, Böhm est le meilleur de tous pour diriger Mozart.

Karl Böhm in the orchestra pit at Salzburg rehearsing *Cosí fan tutte*, 4 August 1963.

Karl Böhm im Orchestergraben in Salzburg bei der Probe von *Cosí fan tutte*, 4. August 1963.

Karl Böhm dans la fosse d'orchestre à Salzbourg, répétant *Cosí fan tutte*, le 4 août 1963.

Some of Auerbach's last conducting studies – Karl Böhm
rehearsing in 1975.

Einige von Auerbachs letzten Dirigentenstudien – Karl Böhm
beim Proben, 1975.

Quelques-unes des dernières études de Auerbach sur la direction
d'orchestre – Karl Böhm répétant en 1975.

Conducting the Philharmonia Orchestra at a recording of *Cosí fan tutte* in the Kingsway Hall, London, 11 September 1962.

Böhm dirigiert das Philharmonia Orchestra bei einer Aufnahme von *Cosí fan tutte* in der Kingsway Hall in London, 11. September 1962.

Dirigant le Philharmonia Orchestra, lors d'un enregistrement de *Cosí fan tutte* au Kingsway Hall, à Londres, le 11 septembre 1962.

If Thomas Beecham typified for many music lovers the flamboyant, eccentric side of the English character, Adrian Boult, ten years his junior, was always the correct English gentleman – erect bearing, military moustache, courteous manner, impeccable self-control. No conductor was ever less of a showman, or less interested in cultivating an 'image' – but that is not to say that rehearsals were free of explosions, or performances devoid of passion. Boult was a dangerously easy conductor to underrate.

His earliest successes were with English music – Elgar, Vaughan Williams, Holst (he conducted the first performance of *The Planets* in 1918) – and he remained throughout his life a discerning champion of contemporary British composers. But he made his name in the 1930s when he was appointed musical director of the BBC and principal conductor of the newly formed BBC Symphony Orchestra. As an orchestra trainer Boult was second to none, and in a few years he had created an ensemble that attracted eminent conductors from all over the world and in 1935 became the first British orchestra to be conducted by Toscanini. At the same time he tirelessly expanded his own repertory, not only to include the whole range of the classics but a constant flow of contemporary works as well.

In a life so full and so dependent on routine, it was perhaps inevitable that there should have been moments when the creative inspiration didn't run at quite the usual level. But Boult's commitment and absolute fidelity to any composer he was conducting were never in doubt, and the precision of his stick technique and the integrity of his interpretation ensured that performances never fell below a certain standard. It was this reliability, which so endeared him to the musical establishment, combined with the familiarity of his immaculate appearance on the concert platform (he never conducted opera), that led to his being taken for granted by the cognoscenti.

But Boult confounded them. In old age, released from the administrative responsibilities of official appointments, the understanding and clarity of vision which had always been at the heart of his music-making matured and developed, and he became, particularly in the works of his own countrymen, a great rather than just a respected conductor.

Für viele Musikliebhaber repräsentierte Thomas Beecham den Typ des auffälligen, exzentrischen Engländers. Demgegenüber verkörperte der zehn Jahre jüngere Adrian Boult mit seiner aufrechten Haltung, dem militärischen Oberlippenbart, seiner Höflichkeit und der makellosen Selbstdisziplin den Inbegriff des englischen Gentleman. Kaum ein Dirigent interessierte sich weniger für glanzvolles Auftreten und Imagepflege – was aber nicht heißt, daß es bei seinen Proben immer harmonisch zuging oder daß es seinen Aufführungen etwa an Leidenschaft fehlte. Boult war ein Dirigent, der leicht unterschätzt wurde.

Seine ersten Erfolge errang er mit englischer Musik – Elgar, Vaughan Williams, Holst (1918 dirigierte er die Uraufführung von *The Planets*) – und blieb sein Leben lang ein überzeugter Anhänger der zeitgenössischen britischen Komponisten. Berühmt wurde er jedoch erst in den 30er Jahren als Musikdirektor der BBC und Chefdirigent des neu gegründeten BBC Symphony Orchestra. Boult hatte ein besonderes Talent für die Orchesterarbeit, und schon nach wenigen Jahren hatte er ein Ensemble geschaffen, das berühmte Dirigenten aus aller Welt anzog und 1953 als erstes britisches Orchester von Toscanini dirigiert wurde. Gleichzeitig arbeitete er beständig an der Erweiterung seines eigenen Repertoires, das schließlich nicht nur die gesamte Klassik umfaßte, sondern sich auch ständig um zeitgenössische Werke erweiterte.

In einem von Alltagsroutine bestimmten Leben waren Einbrüche der kreativen Inspiration wohl unvermeidlich. Boults Engagement und seine vollkommene Werktreue standen jedoch nie in Zweifel. Die Präzision, mit der er den Taktstock führte, und die Integrität seiner Einspielungen sicherten den Aufführungen stets einen zuverlässigen Standard. Diese Zuverlässigkeit und seine stets makellose Erscheinung auf der Konzertbühne (er dirigierte nie eine Oper) sicherten ihm die Beliebtheit in der etablierten Musikwelt und führten dazu, daß die „cognoscenti" ihn als eine Selbstverständlichkeit ansahen.

Aber in ihm steckte noch mehr. Im Alter, befreit von organisatorischen Verantwortlichkeiten und offiziellen Terminen und mit einem gereiften Verständnis, entfaltete sich klar die Vision, die immer im Herzen seiner Musik gelegen hatte. Insbesondere mit Werken seiner eigenen Landsleute entwickelte sich Boult von einem respektablen zu einem wirklich großen Dirigenten.

Si Sir Thomas Beecham symbolisait, pour de nombreux amateurs de musique, le côté brillant et excentrique du caractère anglais, Sir Adrian Boult, de dix ans son cadet, fut toujours le type même du parfait gentleman : port altier, moustache militaire, manières courtoises, contrôle de soi sans faille. Jamais aucun chef d'orchestre ne fut moins comédien, moins intéressé par le fait de cultiver une « image », mais cela ne veut pas dire que les répétitions étaient exemptes d'éclats de voix, ou les représentations vides de passion.

Il obtint ses premiers succès avec la musique anglaise – Elgar, Vaughan Williams, Holst (il dirigea la première représentation de *The Planets* en 1918) – et resta sa vie durant un défenseur avisé des compositeurs britanniques contemporains. Mais il se fit un nom dans les années 30, quand il fut nommé directeur musical de la BBC et premier chef d'orchestre de l'Orchestre symphonique de la BBC, nouvellement formé. Pour faire répéter les orchestres, Boult était un maître ; en quelques années, il créa un ensemble qui attirait d'éminents chefs d'orchestre du monde entier et qui fut, en 1935, le premier orchestre britannique dirigé par Toscanini. Dans le même temps, il étendit sans relâche son propre répertoire, non seulement pour intégrer la totalité des classiques, mais aussi un flux constant d'œuvres contemporaines.

Dans une vie si riche et si dépendante de la routine, il était peut-être inévitable qu'il y eut des moments où l'inspiration créatrice n'atteignît pas tout à fait le plus haut niveau. Mais l'engagement et la fidélité absolue de Boult envers tout compositeur dont il dirigeait les œuvres n'étaient jamais remis en cause, la précision de sa technique de direction et l'honnêteté de ses interprétations garantissaient que les représentations ne tombaient jamais au-dessous d'une certaine qualité. C'était cette fiabilité, qui l'a tant fait apprécier du monde musical, combinée à son habituelle impeccable présentation sur les scènes de concert (il n'a jamais dirigé d'opéra), qui lui ont permis d'être accepté par les cognoscenti.

À la fin de sa vie, débarrassé désormais des responsabilités administratives de ses charges officielles, la compréhension et la clarté de vision qui avaient toujours été au cœur de ses interprétations mûrissant et se développant, il devint, particulièrement pour les œuvres de ses compatriotes, un grand chef d'orchestre, plutôt qu'un chef d'orchestre simplement respecté.

Sir Adrian Boult in the audience at the Royal Festival Hall, London, at a concert given by Elisabeth Schwarzkopf, January 1958.

Sir Adrian Boult im Publikum der Royal Festival Hall in London bei einem Konzert von Elisabeth Schwarzkopf, Januar 1958.

Sir Adrian Boult dans le public au Royal Festival Hall, à Londres, lors d'un concert donné par Elisabeth Schwarzkopf, en janvier 1958.

Boult rehearsing, 12 October 1972.
Boult bei einer Probe, 12. Oktober 1972.
Boult en répétition, le 12 octobre 1972.

'Charisma? That's not my style' ran the headline of a recent newspaper interview with Colin Davis. Certainly few conductors have more consistently avoided publicity. Davis is a very private person: he leads a quiet and intensely personal family life, reads a lot, thinks extensively about and around the music that he is going to perform, and pours white-hot energy into the performance of it. And his behaviour on the platform is in character. No flamboyant entry, no playing to the gallery: at the end of a concert performance of Berlioz's four-hour epic *Les Troyens* he was to be seen wandering around the orchestra shaking hands with the players before climbing on to the rostrum to face the audience himself. The passion, the intense commitment, are reserved for the music – to waste it on anything less would be pointless.

It was not always like that. 'I was a very wild and arrogant young man', he said recently, and it is true that he could be abrasive with orchestras and temperamental with management. He was a clarinettist by training, and does not play the piano, so that many of the normal routes to a conducting career were closed to him, and as a conductor he was entirely self-taught. He hit the headlines in 1959 when Otto Klemperer, who was due to direct a concert performance of *Don Giovanni* at the Festival Hall in London, was suddenly taken ill: Davis stepped in at short notice and achieved one of those spectacular successes for which the history of music is notorious. From then on his career took off; in 1961 he was appointed musical director of Sadler's Wells Opera (now the English National Opera), eight years later he moved on to the BBC Symphony Orchestra (becoming the idol of the young Prom audience in the process) and, after a spell abroad with the Boston Symphony Orchestra, succeeded Georg Solti as musical director at Covent Garden, where he stayed for 15 years.

The Covent Garden period was not altogether easy, and as it neared its end he turned down an offer from Cleveland, Ohio, in favour of a long and happy relationship with the Bavarian Radio Symphony Orchestra – a less glossy appointment, but for Davis a musically satisfying one. But the nine years in Germany did little for his public image and, until his return to the London Symphony Orchestra in 1995, removed him somewhat from the concert-goer's eye. It was the concert-goer's loss.

From the start the foundation of his repertory was Mozart. Asked what it was that originally attracted him to the Mozart symphonies, his answer was not about melody, or harmony, or divine inspiration, but about energy – the immense energy contained in such compact form – and it is an answer very much in line with his own musical temperament. In the early days he was criticized for driving performances too hard, but as his musical views broadened, and philosophical concepts enlarged his outlook, the fresh, vivid quality that never left him took its proper place in his work. Sensitivity and warmth there is in plenty, but no place for sentimentality or emotional wallowing: that is why he is so well suited to Stravinsky, or so utterly convincing in Berlioz, the composer with whom his name is most closely associated. And it explains his success with Tippett, whose dense textures and rhythmic complexities need above all clarity and projection. In some ways Tippett is the composer with whom Davis has most in common – they share many attitudes of mind. Which of them was it who said: 'Every piece of music is a rehearsal of one's own life, it comes out of nothing and disappears into nothing'?

„Charisma? Das ist nicht mein Stil." titelte kürzlich ein Zeitungsinterview mit Colin Davis. Nur wenige Dirigenten haben die Öffentlichkeit so konsequent gemieden wie er. Davis lebt sehr zurückgezogen im Kreise seiner Familie, die ihm viel bedeutet. Er liest viel, denkt ausgiebig über die Musik nach, die er dirigieren wird, und steckt alle Energie in die Aufführungen. Sein Auftritt auf die Bühne fügt sich ins Bild. Kein aufsehenerregender Einzug, keine Werbung um das Publikum: Nach dem vierstündigen Epos *Les Troyens* von Berlioz sah man ihn zuerst den Musikern die Hände schütteln, bevor er sich vor dem Publikum verbeugte. Seine Energie, seine Leidenschaft und sein ganzes Engagement gehören nur der Musik – er würde sie nie auf etwas anderes verschwenden.

Das war nicht immer so. „Ich war ein ungebärdiger und arroganter junger Mann", gab er vor kurzem zu, und wirklich konnte er für das Orchester sehr aufreibend sein und der Konzertleitung gegenüber äußerst temperamentvoll auftreten. Er spielte eigentlich die Klarinette und nicht das Piano, so daß seine – autodidaktische – Ausbildung nicht die üblichen Wege einer Dirigentenlaufbahn beschritt. Seinen Durchbruch erlebte er 1959, als Otto Klemperer, der eine Konzertaufführung des *Don Giovanni* in der Londoner Festival Hall dirigieren sollte, plötzlich erkrankte. Davis sprang kurzfristig für ihn ein und errang einen jener spektakulären Erfolge, die in der Musikgeschichte berüchtigt sind. Damit begann sein Aufstieg. 1961 wurde er zum Musikdirektor der Sadler's Well Opera ernannt (heute die English National Opera). Acht Jahre später zog er zum BBC Symphony Orchestra weiter (und wurde dabei zum Idol des jungen „Prom"-Publikums), und später, nach einem Ruf an das Boston Symphony Orchestra, löste er Georg Solti als Musikdirektor in Covent Garden ab, wo er 15 Jahre lang blieb.

Am Ende seiner recht schwierigen Zeit in Covent Garden lehnte er ein verlockendes Angebot aus Cleveland in Ohio ab zugunsten einer langen und fruchtbaren Zusammenarbeit mit dem Symphonieorchester des Bayrischen Rundfunks – eine weniger glanzvolle, aber für Davis musikalisch sehr befriedigende Tätigkeit. Die neun Jahre in Deutschland waren jedoch nicht allzu öffentlichkeitswirksam, und bis zu seiner Rückkehr zum London Symphony Orchestra 1995 verlor ihn das Publikum etwas aus den Augen.

Von Anfang an war Mozart Mittelpunkt seines Repertoires. Nach dem Grund dafür gefragt, sprach er nicht von Melodie, Harmonie und göttlicher Inspiration, sondern von Kraft, von der ungeheuren Kraft einer so geschlossenen Form – eine Antwort, die seinem eigenen musikalischen Temperament entspricht. Anfangs wurde er wirklich für seine Vehemenz kritisiert, aber sein musikalischer Horizont weitete sich, und philosophische Ideen bereicherten seinen Blick. So fand die für ihn so charakteristische Frische und Lebhaftigkeit in seiner Arbeit schließlich das rechte Maß. Seine Interpretationen zeichnen sich durch Sensibilität und Wärme aus, aber Sentimentalität oder Gefühlsduselei haben dort keinen Platz. Vielleicht liegt ihm Strawinsky deshalb so gut, und vielleicht überzeugt er gerade deshalb so sehr mit Berlioz, dem Komponisten, den man mehr als alle anderen mit dem Namen Davis verbindet. Es erklärt auch seinen Erfolg mit Tippett, dessen dichte Strukturen und rhythmische Komplexität besonderer Klarheit bedürfen. Tippett ist derjenige Komponist, mit dem Davis eine geistige Verwandtschaft empfindet. Welcher von ihnen sagte doch: „Mit jedem Musikstück probt man das eigene Leben; es kommt aus dem Nichts und verschwindet im Nichts"?

« Le charisme ? Ce n'est pas mon style », titrait un journal lors d'un récent entretien avec Colin Davis. Peu de chefs d'orchestre ont évité la publicité avec plus de constance. Très secret, Davis mène une tranquille vie de famille, lit beaucoup, se concentre sur la musique qu'il va interpréter et, dans les représentations, dépense une énergie chauffée à blanc. Et sa conduite sur scène est à l'unisson : pas d'entrée fracassante, pas de jeu pour la galerie ; à la fin de la représentation en concert des quatre heures de l'épopée de Berlioz *Les Troyens*, on l'a vu passant dans les rangs de l'orchestre pour serrer la main des musiciens avant de monter lui-même sur l'estrade pour saluer le public. Sa passion, son engagement, sont réservés à la musique, rien qu'à la musique.

Il n'en fut pas toujours ainsi. « J'étais un jeune homme très farouche et arrogant », a-t-il récemment déclaré, et il est vrai qu'il pouvait être acerbe avec les orchestres et capricieux avec l'administration. Sa formation de clarinettiste et son absence de pratique du piano lui fermèrent la plupart des routes normales vers la carrière de chef d'orchestre, ce qui fit de lui un chef d'orchestre entièrement autodidacte. Il fit la une des journaux en 1959 quand Otto Klemperer, qui devait diriger une version en concert de *Don Giovanni* au Festival Hall de Londres, tomba brusquement malade : Davis le remplaça au pied levé et obtint l'un de ces succès spectaculaires dont l'histoire de la musique est prodigue. En 1961, il fut nommé directeur musical du Sadler's Wells Opera (actuellement l'English National Opera), huit ans plus tard, on le trouve à l'Orchestre symphonique de la BBC (devenant alors l'idole du jeune public des Promenade Concert) et, après une courte période à l'étranger avec l'Orchestre symphonique de Boston, il succède à Sir Georg Solti comme directeur musical de Covent Garden, où il reste quinze ans.

Au terme de cette période à Covent Garden – qui ne fut pas toujours facile –, il refusa une offre de Cleveland, en Ohio, en faveur d'une longue et heureuse collaboration avec l'Orchestre symphonique de la Radio bavaroise, position moins brillante mais satisfaisante pour Davis, sur le plan musical. Ces neuf ans en Allemagne firent peu pour son image publique, et, jusqu'à son retour à l'Orchestre symphonique de Londres en 1995, le soustrairent quelque peu au regard du public des concerts.

Dès le début, Mozart a été la base de son répertoire. Quand il lui fut demandé ce qui l'avait d'abord attiré dans les symphonies de Mozart, il ne parla pas de mélodie, d'harmonie ou d'inspiration divine, mais de l'énergie intense contenue dans une forme si compacte ; cette réponse est totalement en accord avec son propre tempérament musical. Au début de sa carrière, on lui reprochait de mener ses représentations trop durement, mais tandis que ses vues musicales s'élargissaient et que les concepts philosophiques enrichissaient ses perspectives, la fraîcheur et la vivacité qui ne l'ont jamais quitté trouvèrent leur place véritable dans son travail. Sensibilité et chaleur sont là, mais nulle sentimentalité ou débauche d'émotion, c'est pourquoi il convient très bien à Stravinsky, est si convaincant avec Berlioz, le compositeur auquel son nom est le plus étroitement associé. Cela explique également son succès avec Tippett, dont les textures denses et les complexités rythmiques nécessitent avant tout clarté et dynamisme. Tippett est le compositeur avec lequel Davis a le plus en commun, ils partagent de nombreuses manières de penser. Lequel des deux a dit : « Chaque morceau de musique est une répétition de sa propre vie, il vient du néant et disparaît dans le néant » ?

◄◄ Colin Davis at the last night of the Promenade Concerts, Royal Albert Hall, 1970. Note the typical piece of Last Night humour at the time of the Apollo moon landings.

Colin Davis am letzten Abend der Promenadenkonzerte in der Royal Albert Hall, 1970. Man beachte die ausgelassene Stimmung – typisch für den „Letzten Abend" der Promenadenkonzerte zur Zeit der ersten Mondlandungen.

Colin Davis lors de la dernière nuit des Promenade Concerts au Royal Albert Hall, en 1970. A remarquer : l'humour de la Dernière Nuit au même moment de l'alunissage d'Apollo.

The young Colin Davis in the pit at Sadler's Wells Theatre,
22 October 1959, conducting *Don Giovanni*, the opera with which
he had made his name earlier in the year. A rare series of studies at
an actual performance.

Der junge Colin Davis im Orchestergraben des Sadler's Wells
Theatre am 22. Oktober 1959. Er dirigiert *Don Giovanni*, die
Oper, mit der zu Beginn des Jahres seinen großen Erfolg hatte.
Die Fotosequenz entstand direkt bei einer Aufführung und hat
deshalb Seltenheitswert.

Le jeune Colin Davis dans la fosse du Sadler's Wells Theatre,
le 22 octobre 1959, dirigeant *Don Giovanni*, l'opéra qui l'avait fait
connaître la même année. Une rare série d'études lors d'une représentation.

ANTAL DORATI 1906-1988

Dorati was one of a distinguished group of Hungarian conductors, including Fritz Reiner, Eugene Ormandy, George Szell and Georg Solti, who made their careers in the United States and (with the exception of Solti, who became a British citizen) ended up by taking American nationality. In Budapest after the First World War Dorati was a composition pupil of Kodály, and later described his own style of musical composition as being 'recognizably contemporary but unafraid of melody'. As a conductor he was a lifelong champion of the music of Kodály's friend and compatriot Béla Bartók, and with Yehudi Menuhin he made the première recording of the Bartók *Violin Concerto* (as it was called before the discovery of an earlier one) when he was principal conductor of the Dallas Symphony Orchestra in the 1940s.

Dorati's early conducting experience was in ballet – with the Ballets Russes de Monte Carlo in the 1930s and as musical director of the American Ballet Theater when he moved to the United States – and it was during the four years he spent at Dallas after the war that he had his first real opportunity to get to grips with the orchestral repertory and develop his gifts as an orchestra trainer. When he took over the Minneapolis Symphony Orchestra in 1949 he had to his hand an instrument already well attuned to the kind of late romantic and contemporary repertory that he most enjoyed, and he found himself perfectly placed to embark on a programme of gramophone recording which took full advantage of the LP explosion of the 50s and made his name known on an international scale.

The big difference between recording on 78 r.p.m. discs and LP was that, with 78s, a performance was recorded directly on to the master disc and so had to be interrupted every 4.5 minutes to allow for transfer to a new master, whereas LPs were recorded first onto electronic tape which could be played back and assessed on the spot, allowing unsatisfactory passages to be re-recorded or patched up from previous takes. This process, in the wrong hands, later came to be sadly abused, but Dorati was a past-master and used it in its early days to ensure recorded performances of great perfection and reliability without any loss of artistic integrity.

A warmly human personality, Dorati was not an infallible conductor from the technical point of view. Missed cues were not unknown – and he could be irascible with the orchestra. 'I have a short circuit', he used to say, and would storm off in the middle of a rehearsal (muttering as he passed the last desk of violins 'I'll be back in three minutes'). But the rich colouring and rhythmic buoyancy of his performances made him an ideal interpreter for the masterpieces of the early 20th century (his own Hungarian background being well represented). He had other areas of interest as well: in 1973 he completed the first ever recording of all the 104 Haydn symphonies with the Philharmonica Hungarica, an orchestra of Hungarian refugees of which he eventually became honorary president. His four years as principal conductor of the BBC Symphony Orchestra made him a familiar figure on the London concert platform and on air in the 1960s, a musician of broad sympathies – as a conductor, perhaps, as he was as a composer, 'recognizably contemporary but unafraid of melody'.

Antal Dorati rehearsing the BBC Symphony Orchestra at the Maida Vale studios, 25 September 1962.

Antal Dorati bei einer Probe mit dem BBC Symphony Orchestra in den Studios in Maida Vale, 25. September 1962.

Antal Dorati faisant répéter le BBC Symphony Orchestra aux studios Maida Vale, le 25 septembre 1962.

Antal Dorati gehört zusammen mit Fritz Reiner, Eugene Ormandy, George Szell und Georg Solti zu jener bestimmten Gruppe ungarischer Dirigenten, die ihren Aufstieg in den Vereinigten Staaten erlebten und schließlich alle (mit Ausnahme von Solti, der britischer Staatsbürger wurde) die amerikanische Staatsbürgerschaft annahmen. Nach dem Ersten Weltkrieg studierte Dorati bei Kodálys Komposition. Später beschrieb er seine eigenen Kompositionen als „erkennbar zeitgenössisch, aber melodisch unbekümmert". Als Dirigent schätzte er zeitlebens die Musik von Kodálys Freund und Landsmann Béla Bartók. In den 40er Jahren, als Dorati Chefdirigent des Dallas Symphony Orchestra war, machte er mit Yehudi Menuhin die erste Aufnahme von Bartóks *Violinkonzert* (das solange so hieß, bis ein früheres entdeckt wurde).

Seine ersten Erfahrungen als Dirigent sammelte Dorati beim Ballett: in den 30er Jahren mit den Ballets Russes de Monte Carlo und in den USA später als Generalmusikdirektor des American Ballet Theater. Erst während der vier Jahre, die er nach dem Krieg in Dallas zubrachte, erhielt Dorati die Gelegenheit, sich wirklich mit der Orchesterliteratur vertraut zu machen. Dort entfaltete sich auch sein Talent für die Orchesterarbeit. Als er 1949 das Minneapolis Symphony Orchestra übernahm, stand ihm ein Ensemble zur Verfügung, das bereits gut auf jenes Repertoire aus später Romantik und zeitgenössischer Musik eingestimmt war, das ihm selbst die größte Freude bereitete, so daß gleich daranging, eine Reihe von Schallplatten aufzunehmen. Mit dem Boom der Langspielplatte in den 50er Jahren wurde Dorati zu einer internationalen Größe.

Zwischen den alten Aufnahmen mit 78 Umdrehungen pro Minute und der Langspielplatte gab es einen entscheidenden Unterschied: Mit der alten Technik wurde direkt auf die Platte aufgenommen, und deshalb mußte die Aufführung alle viereinhalb Minuten unterbrochen werden, um die Platte zu wechseln. Bei der Langspielplatte dagegen wurde das Original zuerst auf ein Band aufgenommen, das man sofort abhören und prüfen konnte. Alle unbefriedigenden Passagen konnten erneut aufgenommen oder aus früheren Aufnahmen eingespielt werden. Die Technik wurde später traurigerweise mißbraucht, Dorati jedoch war ein Meister des Einkopierens und nutzte diese Technik in ihren Anfängen ohne jede Einbuße an künstlerischer Integrität, um perfekte und zuverlässige Aufnahmen zu erzielen.

Dorati war ein warmherziger, umgänglicher Mensch, aber kein unfehlbarer Dirigent. Verpaßte Einsätze waren nicht selten – ebenso wie Zornesausbrüche vor dem Orchester. „Ich habe eine kurze Leitung", pflegte er zu sagen und mitten in der Probe davonzustürmen (bei den letzten Violinenpulten hörte man ihn brummen: „Bin gleich wieder da"). Seine reiche Ausdruckskraft und der rhythmische Schwung seiner Aufführungen machten ihn jedoch zum idealen Interpreten der Meisterwerke des frühen 20. Jahrhunderts (unter denen sein eigener ungarischer Hintergrund gut repräsentiert war). Er interessierte sich aber auch für andere musikalische Bereiche. Mit der Philharmonica Hungarica, einem Orchester aus ungarischen Flüchtlingen, dessen Ehrenpräsident er später wurde, schloß er 1973 die erste vollständige Aufnahme aller 104 Symphonien von Haydn ab. In den vier Jahren als Chefdirigent des BBC Symphony Orchestra wurde er zu einer bekannten und beliebten Erscheinung auf der Londoner Konzertbühne, und in den 60er Jahren auch im Rundfunk. Er war ein Musiker, der als Dirigent breite Sympathien genoß – als Komponist war er wohl „erkennbar zeitgenössisch, aber melodisch unbekümmert".

Dorati faisait partie d'un groupe éminent de chefs d'orchestre hongrois, comprenant Fritz Reiner, Eugene Ormandy, George Szell et Georg Solti, qui firent leur carrière aux États-Unis et finirent par prendre la nationalité américaine (à l'exception de Solti, qui devint citoyen britannique). Ayant étudié composition avec Kodály à Budapest après la Première Guerre mondiale, Dorati décrivit plus tard son style musical comme étant « manifestement contemporain, mais sans peur de la mélodie ». En tant que chef d'orchestre, il fut toute sa vie le défenseur de la musique de l'ami et compatriote de Kodály, Béla Bartók et, avec Yehudi Menuhin, enregistra la première du *Concerto pour violon* de Bartók (comme on l'appela avant d'en découvrir un précédent) quand il était premier chef d'orchestre de l'Orchestre symphonique de Dallas, dans les années 40.

Il mena ses premières expériences de chef d'orchestre avec des ballets – les Ballets russes de Monte-Carlo dans les années 30 et en tant que directeur musical de l'American Ballet Theater, quand il partit aux États-Unis – et ce fut pendant les quatre ans qu'il passa à Dallas, après la guerre, qu'il eut vraiment la première occasion de s'attaquer au répertoire pour orchestre et put développer son talent pour faire travailler les orchestres. Quand il prit la direction de l'Orchestre symphonique de Minneapolis en 1949, il avait en main un instrument déjà bien accordé au répertoire qu'il appréciait le plus : fin du romantique et contemporain, et il se trouva parfaitement placé pour se lancer dans un programme d'enregistrements pour gramophone, qui profita pleinement de l'explosion des 33 tours dans les années 50, et rendit son nom célèbre au plan international.

Contrairement aux 78 tours, où l'interprétation était enregistrée directement sur le master et devait donc être interrompue toutes les quatre minutes et demie pour permettre le transfert vers un autre master, les 33 tours étaient d'abord enregistrés sur une bande électronique qui pouvait être repassée et immédiatement estimée, ce qui laissait la possibilité de réenregistrer les passages peu satisfaisants ou d'y inclure des prises antérieures. Ce procédé fut plus tard largement mal utilisé, mais Dorati était un expert et ne s'en servit, au début, que pour assurer aux enregistrements perfection et fiabilité sans rien perdre de leur intégrité artistique.

D'une personnalité chaleureuse, Dorati n'était pas un chef d'orchestre infaillible du point de vue technique. Les départs manqués n'étaient pas rares et il pouvait être irascible avec l'orchestre. « J'ai un court circuit », avait-il l'habitude de dire, et, comme un ouragan, il quittait la répétition (murmurant, en passant près des derniers rangs des violons : « Je reviens dans trois minutes »). Mais ses interprétations hautes en couleur et au rythme entraînant en faisaient un interprète idéal pour les chefs-d'œuvre du début du XXᵉ siècle (ses origines hongroises y étaient bien représentées). Il avait également d'autres centres d'intérêt : en 1973, il acheva le tout premier enregistrement des 104 symphonies de Haydn, avec le Philharmonique hongrois, un orchestre de réfugiés hongrois dont il devint, par l'occasion, le président d'honneur. Ses quatre ans comme premier chef d'orchestre de l'Orchestre symphonique de la BBC en firent un familier des scènes de concert et de la radio de Londres dans les années 60, un chef aux sympathies musicales étendues : n'avait-il pas été un compositeur « manifestement contemporain, mais sans peur de la mélodie »…

In the memory of post-war London opera-goers the Royal Opera House *Don Carlos* of 1958 remains one of the glories of the 1950s. Luchino Visconti's magisterial production ensured the success of the staging, but it was Carlo Maria Giulini's treatment of the musical score that was the real revelation. The piece was not well known, and generally thought to be uneven and difficult to bring off, with regrettable lapses into 'early Verdi'. Yet under Giulini's baton the lapses just seemed to disappear, and what emerged was a consistent and convincing masterpiece of astonishing lyrical power.

Not much was known about Giulini in Britain at the time. A comparatively late starter, he had been 'noticed' by Toscanini and Victor de Sabata in the early 50s and conducted at La Scala, Milan, for five years, where colleagues like Callas, Visconti and Franco Zeffirelli, had helped him to develop his ideas about the relationship of music and the stage in operatic performance. But in the year after *Don Carlos* he was invited by the Gramophone Company's legendary producer Walter Legge to record *Don Giovanni* and *Figaro* with Legge's own orchestra, the Philharmonia, and casts that were unmatched in their day. The association with the Philharmonia flourished since leaving the Scala he had had no fixed appointment, his growing disillusion with the conditions in which it was necessary to work was already undermining his commitment to opera, and the orchestral repertory became more and more his field of activity.

It was never a large repertory, because he will not conduct a work with which he doesn't feel completely in tune. It was this utter integrity and dedicated perfectionism that produced the quality which came to be expected as a matter of course by the Philharmonia audiences in the 1960s – in Schubert, Brahms, Dvořák, Tchaikovsky, Debussy, Ravel, brilliant Rossini overtures and memorable performances of the Verdi *Requiem*. There was not much Beethoven (perhaps because this was the accepted preserve of Otto Klemperer, at that time the revered principal conductor of the Philharmonia Orchestra) and little contemporary music. Meanwhile he made three returns to Covent Garden during the 60s, but in 1967 announced his intention of leaving opera entirely – and kept his word for the next 14 years.

For those whose memories of Giulini are relatively recent the sense of grandeur, the other-worldliness, the sometimes exaggeratedly slow tempi may have left a rather different impression from the Giulini of these photographs. The energy was more obvious in those days, the passion less contained, there was a brilliance of orchestral effect that interested him less in later years. But the performances were never other than deeply considered, and there was a tranquillity at the heart of the music that is not always found in an artist of such dynamic temperament.

As a man Giulini is kindly, courteous, utterly sincere and deeply religious. It is no surprise that in later years his taste has moved more and more to the serious end of the repertory – Beethoven in particular. At performances of the great religious works he loved conducting best the word 'spiritual' always seemed to be hovering in the air. After a holiday on a Greek island he told an orchestral player that he was sad not to be able to stay there as a hermit, 'but one would have to be very simple', he said, 'which I am not, or a saint, which I also am not.' 'He's nearer to being one than any other conductor I met,' commented the player.

Die Aufführung von *Don Carlos* im Royal Opera House blieb den Londoner Opernbesuchern der Nachkriegszeit als ein Glanzlicht der 50er Jahre im Gedächtnis. Luchino Viscontis meisterhafte Inszenierung sicherten den Bühnenerfolg, die eigentliche Offenbarung war jedoch Carlo Maria Giulinis Interpretation der Partitur. Das Stück war nicht sehr bekannt und galt mit seinen bedauerlichen Anleihen beim „frühen Verdi" allgemein als unausgewogen und schwierig vorzutragen. Unter Giulinis Taktstock schienen die Fehlgriffe jedoch zu verschwinden, und ein geschlossenes, überzeugendes Meisterwerk von überraschender poetischer Kraft trat hervor.

Zu jener Zeit hatte man in England noch nicht viel von Giulini gehört, denn seine Laufbahn begann verhältnismäßig spät. In den frühen 50er Jahren war er von Toscanini und Sabata „entdeckt" worden und dirigierte fünf Jahre lang die Mailänder Scala, wo ihm Kollegen wie Callas, Visconti und Franco Zeffirelli halfen, seine Vorstellungen zum Verhältnis von Musik und Bühnendarstellung in der Oper zu entwickeln. Aber ein Jahr nach *Don Carlos* lud ihn Walter Legge, der legendäre Produzent der Gramophone Company, dazu ein, mit Legges eigenem Orchester, der Philharmonia, und einer zu jener Zeit unübertroffenen Besetzung den *Don Giovanni* und den *Figaro* aufzunehmen. Die Zusammenarbeit mit der Philharmonia war ein Erfolg. Seine wachsende Desillusionierung über die Arbeitsbedingungen hatten bereits dazu geführt, daß sich seine Verbundenheit mit der Oper lockerte. Mehr und mehr verlagerte er seine Aktivitäten auf das orchestrale Repertoire.

Es war nie ein großes Repertoire, denn er dirigiert nie ein Werk, mit dem er sich nicht völlig im Einklang fühlt. Diese unantastbare Integrität und der entschiedene Perfektionismus führte die Philharmonia auf jenes Niveau, an das sich das Publikum in den 60er Jahren dann ganz selbstverständlich gewöhnt hatte – sei es bei Schubert, Brahms, Dvořák, Tschaikowsky, Debussy, Ravel, den brillanten Ouvertüren von Rossini oder den großartigen Aufführungen von Verdis *Requiem*. Beethoven war selten zu hören (vielleicht blieb dies ein anerkanntes Vorrecht von Otto Klemperer, der damals Chefdirigent des Philharmonia Orchestra war) und auch wenig zeitgenössische Musik. Giulinis Opernlaufbahn klang allmählich aus. Dreimal kehrte er nach Covent Garden zurück, aber 1967 gab er seine Absicht bekannt, sich von der Oper zurückzuziehen – und hielt für die nächsten vierzehn Jahre Wort.

Alle, die Giulini aus jüngster Zeit kennen, werden an jene Aura von Größe und Jenseitigkeit und an die übertrieben langsamen Tempi denken. Diese Fotos spiegeln eine andere Zeit. Seine Energie trat damals noch deutlicher hervor, die Leidenschaftlichkeit kam stärker zum Ausdruck. Später interessierten ihn die glanzvollen Orchestereffekte nicht mehr so sehr. Seine Aufführungen waren jedoch immer tief durchdacht, und im Herzen der Musik gab es eine Ruhe, die man bei einem so dynamischen, temperamentvollen Musiker nicht erwarten würde.

Giulini ist ein freundlicher, höflicher, sehr ernsthafter und tief gläubiger Mensch. Es überrascht nicht, daß er sich in späten Jahren immer stärker den ernsten Werken zuwendet – besonders Beethoven beschäftigt ihn. Bei seinen Aufführungen der großen geistlichen Werke, die er am liebsten dirigierte, breitete sich stets eine durchgeistigte Atmosphäre im Saal aus. Nach dem Urlaub auf einer griechischen Insel erzählte er einem Orchestermusiker, er sei traurig, daß er nicht als Einsiedler dort bleiben könne, „aber dazu braucht man ein sehr schlichtes Gemüt, das mir fehlt, oder man muß ein Heiliger sein, und das bin ich nicht." Der Musiker bemerkte dazu: „Er kommt dem näher als jeder andere Dirigent."

Dans la mémoire des amateurs d'opéra du Londres de l'après-guerre, le *Don Carlos* de 1958 au Royal Opera House reste l'une des splendeurs des années 50. La production magistrale de Luchino Visconti, assura le succès de la mise en scène, mais la véritable révélation fut le traitement de la partition musicale par Carlo Maria Giulini. Cette œuvre n'était pas bien connue, et on pensait généralement qu'elle était inégale et difficile à réaliser, avec de regrettables retours vers « le jeune Verdi ». Cependant, sous la baguette de Giulini, les retours semblaient avoir disparu, et ce qui émergea fut un chef-d'œuvre cohérent et convaincant, d'une puissance lyrique étonnante.

Ayant commencé relativement tard, il avait été « remarqué » par Toscanini et Victor de Sabata au début des années 50, et avait dirigé à la Scala de Milan pendant cinq ans, où Callas, Visconti et Franco Zeffirelli, l'aidèrent à développer ses idées sur les relations entre la musique et la scène pour les représentations d'opéras.

Dans l'année après *Don Carlos*, il fut invité par le producteur légendaire de la Gramophone Company, Walter Legge, pour enregistrer *Don Giovanni* et *Figaro* avec le propre orchestre de Legge, le Philharmonia, et les meilleurs chanteurs de l'époque. Son association avec le Philharmonia était appelée à un bel avenir. En effet, depuis son départ de la Scala, il était sans situation fixe, et de mauvaises conditions de travail minaient son engagement pour l'opéra, aussi le répertoire pour orchestre devint-il son champ d'activité principal.

Ce répertoire n'a jamais été très large, son principe étant de ne diriger une œuvre que s'il ne se sente pleinement en accord avec elle. Cette extrême intégrité et ce perfectionnisme ont produit la qualité que, tout naturellement, le public attendait du Philharmonia, dans les années 60 : Schubert, Brahms, Dvořák, Tchaïkovski, Debussy, Ravel, les brillantes ouvertures de Rossini et les représentations mémorables du *Requiem* de Verdi. Peu de Beethoven (peut-être parce que considéré comme le domaine réservé d'Otto Klemperer, premier et vénéré chef du Philharmonia Orchestra) et peu de musique contemporaine. Pendant ce temps il revint trois fois à Covent Garden dans les années 60, mais en 1967 annonça son intention de quitter complètement l'opéra, ce qu'il fit pendant les quatorze années suivantes.

Pour ceux dont les souvenirs de Giulini sont relativement récents, le sens de la grandeur, le dépouillement, des tempos parfois exagérément longs, ont pu laisser une impression assez différente du Giulini de ces photographies où l'énergie est plus évidente, la passion moins contenue, le souci de l'éclat orchestral manifeste, éclat qu'il recherchera moins par la suite. Mais les représentations ont toujours été mûrement réfléchies, et il y avait une tranquillité au cœur de la musique que l'on ne trouve pas toujours chez un artiste au tempérament si dynamique.

En tant qu'homme, Giulini est amical, courtois, extrêmement sincère et profondément religieux. Il n'est pas surprenant que, ces dernières années, il ait abordé de plus en plus la partie grave du répertoire, Beethoven en particulier. Pendant les représentations des œuvres religieuses qu'il préférait diriger, le mot « spirituel » semblait toujours planer dans les airs. Après des vacances dans une île grecque, il a dit à un musicien d'orchestre qu'il était triste de ne pouvoir rester là-bas en ermite, mais, dit-il, « il faudrait être très simple, ce que je ne suis pas, ou un saint, ce que je ne suis pas non plus ». « Il en est plus proche qu'aucun autre chef d'orchestre que j'ai rencontré », commenta le musicien.

For the classic recording of *Don Giovanni* produced by Walter Legge at EMI in 1959, Giulini replaced Klemperer at short notice. He is here seen talking to his Donna Anna, the young Joan Sutherland, just starting on her international career.

Bei der klassischen Aufnahme des *Don Giovanni*, die Walter Legge 1959 bei EMI produzierte, sprang Giulini kurzfristig für Klemperer ein. (1) Hier sieht man ihn im Gespräch mit Donna Anna, der jungen Joan Sutherland, die damals gerade am Anfang ihrer internationalen Karriere stand.

Pour l'enregistrement classique de *Don Giovanni*, produit par Walter Legge pour EMI en 1959, Giulini remplaça Klemperer à la dernière minute. Ici, il parle à Donna Anna, la jeune Joan Sutherland, qui commençait à peine sa carrière internationale.

Giulini looks on as Sutherland receives
guidance from Walter Legge.
14 October 1959.

Giulini schaut zu, wie der erfahrene
Walter Legge der Sutherland ein paar
Tips gibt. 14. Oktober 1959.

Giulini regarde Sutherland écoutant
les conseils avisés de Walter Legge.
14 octobre 1959.

BERNARD HAITINK　* 1929

Haitink is a conductor who believes in continuity. His association with the Concertgebouw Orchestra in Amsterdam lasted for 30 years, 23 of them as its principal conductor and artistic director; his 11 years with the London Philharmonic Orchestra transformed that orchestra's fortunes, and another ten as music director at Glyndebourne ended only when he took over from Colin Davis at the Royal Opera House, Covent Garden – a post which he still holds at the time of writing nine years later. He has toured in many parts of the world with both the Concertgebouw and the London Philharmonic, but in contrast to the jet-setting antics of many of his colleagues his appearances as a guest conductor with other orchestras are comparatively rare. He likes to work with players he knows, and as a result the players he knows like to work with him.

His repertory has never been very adventurous, avoiding the more far-out areas of the avant-garde at one end and anything much before Mozart at the other. At the centre of it has always been the great romantic tradition of the 19th and early 20th centuries, with a particular emphasis on Bruckner and Mahler – two composers who have been a part of his musical experience from his earliest concert-going days, when the Concertgebouw Orchestra was conducted by that great Bruckner pioneer, Eduard van Beinum, and, before him, by Mahler's friend and champion Willem Mengelberg. In music of this kind, where care and precise craftsmanship are of the first importance in holding a work together and too much emotion can sink it, Haitink's essentially level-headed approach pays golden dividends. It is no chance that Shostakovich also figures regularly in his programmes, and his recent performances of Wagner's *Ring* cycle at Covent Garden have demonstrated the value of sympathetic attention to orchestral detail combined with long-sighted control of structure.

He is not a demonstrative conductor in performance – he doesn't need to be, given the relationship he has already established between himself and his orchestra – and for those who look for flamboyance or balletic expertise on the podium he perhaps has little to offer. He simply conducts very well indeed, and in such a way that you cannot miss the conviction lying at the heart of everything he does. He is one of the few conductors who really achieve that most elusive of objectives – the expression of passion through restraint.

Bernard Haitink ist ein Dirigent, der an Kontinuität glaubt. Dreißig Jahre lang blieb er dem Amsterdamer Concertgebouw Orchester treu, 23 Jahre lang war er dort Chefdirigent und künstlerischer Leiter. Seine elf Jahre mit dem London Philharmonic Orchestra steigerten dessen Qualität erheblich. Seine zehnjährige Tätigkeit als Musikdirektor in Glyndebourne endete erst, als er von Colin Davis das Royal Opera House in Covent Garden übernahm – eine Position, die er auch jetzt, neun Jahre später, noch innehat. Mit dem Concertgebouw und auch mit dem London Philharmonic Orchestra ging er in vielen Teilen der Welt auf Tournee, aber verglichen mit der Reisefreudigkeit vieler seiner Kollegen sieht man ihn sehr selten als Gastdirigenten fremder Orchester. Er arbeitet gerne mit Musikern, die er kennt, und aus diesem Grund diese auch gern mit ihm.

Die Zusammenstellung seines Repertoires war nie sehr gewagt, er hat immer sowohl die Randzonen der Avantgarde als auch den Zeitraum vor Mozart gemieden. Im Zentrum seiner Kunst stehen die große romantische Tradition des 19. und 20. Jahrhunderts mit besonderem Schwerpunkt auf Bruckner und Mahler – zwei Komponisten, die seit der Zeit seiner ersten Konzertbesuche zum festen Bestandteil seiner musikalischen Erfahrung gehören – damals, als das Concertgebouw Orchester noch von Eduard van Beinum, dem großen Entdecker Bruckners, dirigiert wurde und noch davor von Mahlers Freund und Vorkämpfer Willem Mengelberg. Diese Art von Musik, deren Spannungsbogen sich nur durch größte Sorgfalt und präzises Können halten läßt und bei der sich zu starke Akzentuierungen verbieten, kann durch Haitinks musikalische Ausgewogenheit nur gewinnen. Es ist kein Zufall, daß auch Schostakowitsch häufig auf seinem Programm steht, und seine neuerliche Aufführung von Wagners *Ring* in Covent Garden hat gezeigt, was eine einfühlsame Achtsamkeit auf musikalische Details zusammen mit einer weitsichtigen Kontrolle des Gesamtaufbaus zu leisten vermögen.

Haitink ist kein besonders lebhafter Dirigent – da er mit seinem Orchester gut vertraut ist, kann er auf eine übertriebene Gebärdensprache verzichten. Wer eine besondere Darstellung auf dem Podium erwartet, wird enttäuscht sein. Haitink beschränkt sich darauf, gut zu dirigieren, und es gelingt ihm dabei, die tiefe Überzeugung zu vermitteln, die ihn trägt. Er gehört zu den wenigen Dirigenten mit jener flüchtigen, schwer zu fassenden Gabe, die Leidenschaft durch Zurückhaltung zum Ausdruck zu bringen.

Haitink est un chef d'orchestre qui croit en la continuité. Son association avec l'Orchestre du Concertgebouw d'Amsterdam dura trente ans, dont vingt-trois en tant que premier chef et directeur artistique ; ses onze années avec l'Orchestre philharmonique de Londres en changèrent le destin, et son travail de directeur musical de Glyndebourne ne prit fin, au bout de dix autres années, que quand il succéda à Colin Davis au Royal Opera House de Covent Garden, un poste qu'il occupe toujours au moment où ces lignes sont écrites, neuf ans plus tard. Il a fait des tournées dans une grande partie du monde avec le Concertgebouw et le Philharmonique de Londres, mais contrairement à nombre de ses collègues habitués des jets, il est comparativement peu apparu en tant que chef invité : il aime travailler avec des interprètes qu'il connaît et ces derniers aiment travailler avec lui.

Évitant les œuvres les plus avant-gardistes et ne s'aventurant que peu avant Mozart, son répertoire n'a jamais été très audacieux. Au cœur de celui-ci, il y a toujours eu la grande tradition romantique du XIXᵉ siècle et du début du XXᵉ, l'accent étant mis sur Bruckner et Mahler, compositeurs qui ont fait partie de son expérience musicale de jeune spectateur de concert, quand l'Orchestre du Concertgebouw était dirigé par le grand chef brucknérien, Eduard van Beinum et, avant lui, par l'ami et le soutien de Mahler, Willem Mengelberg. L'approche avant tout équilibrée de Haitink fait merveille dans l'exécution de cette musique, qui demande attention et connaissance précise du métier pour assurer l'unité de l'œuvre, quand trop d'émotion peut la faire sombrer. Ce n'est pas un hasard si Chostakovitch figure aussi régulièrement dans ses programmes, et ses récentes représentations du cycle complet du *Ring* de Wagner à Covent Garden ont démontré la valeur de l'attention pour le détail orchestral, alliée à un contrôle prévoyant de la structure.

Sur scène, il n'est pas un chef démonstratif – il n'a pas besoin de l'être, étant donné la qualité de la relation qu'il a déjà établie avec son orchestre – et, à ceux qui recherchent la flamboyance ou l'adresse d'un danseur de ballet, il a peu à offrir. Simplement, il dirige extrêmement bien et d'une telle façon que vous ne pouvez pas ne pas remarquer la conviction qui est au cœur de tout ce qu'il fait. Il est l'un des rares chefs d'orchestre qui atteint vraiment l'un des objectifs les plus insaisissables : l'expression de la passion à travers la retenue.

Bernard Haitink rehearsing, 12 November 1966.
Bernard Haitink beim Proben, 12. November 1966.
Bernard Haitink en répétition, le 12 novembre 1966.

HERBERT VON KARAJAN   1908-1989

With Karajan it is difficult to know where to start. By the end of his life he had become the most successful, most publicized, most recorded and wealthiest conductor in Europe. For years he had held the reins of musical power in his hands: the Berlin Philharmonic, the Vienna Staatsoper, La Scala, Milan, the Salzburg Festival and an unassailable contract with Deutsche Grammophon, which sold over 100 million copies of his recordings – these were the elements of a musical empire on which the sun was not going to set in Karajan's lifetime.

Until 1948 his activities had been confined entirely to Austria and Germany. He made a brilliant start at Aachen and used it as the crucial stepping stone to Berlin, where his first *Tristan* at the Staatsoper in 1938 precipitated the notorious headline 'Das Wunder Karajan'. True, he had been obliged to become a member of the Nazi Party in order to get the Aachen job, but he wanted the position desperately – 'so I said what the hell and signed'. His success in Berlin earned him the undying hatred of Furtwängler, 20 years his senior and for nearly as long the revered figurehead of the Berlin Philharmonic and the rivalry between them was exploited by feuding politicians. In the end Karajan fell out with the Nazi authorities, but he still had to face a denazification tribunal at the end of the war and was not able to conduct in public until 1947.

It was at this not altogether happy moment in his career that he met Walter Legge, the *éminence grise* of the Gramophone Company, who had just created an all-star orchestra in the London Philharmonia and was looking for someone to conduct it on a permanent basis – and particularly to record with it. Karajan grabbed the opportunity, and his future was sealed.

There are many opinions about Karajan as a conductor, varying from hero worship via grudging admiration to the plain unprintable. But three things are beyond dispute: he was a superb orchestra trainer, he was a fanatical perfectionist, and he consistently aimed at – and achieved – absolute beauty of sound. Over the last 35 years of his life he created in the Berlin Philharmonic Orchestra the most opulently perfect music-making machine, possibly in the world, certainly in Europe; but the seamless legato line, the smooth elasticity of rhythm and the brilliant splashes of effect served a musical temperament that was more emotional than intellectual and produced interpretations that could be seen as over-indulgent and lacking in depth. His later preoccupation with the huge romantic symphonic edifices of Bruckner and Mahler provides rich material for either point of view.

The methods by which he got his results were flamboyant on and off the podium, and his arrogance and desire for applause were too evident for some tastes. He could be charming, helpful to his soloists and brilliant in moulding them to his musical concepts, but raised hackles with his assumptions of authority and the demands he made on them as human beings.

A difficult man to place, then, and more difficult as he became ever more and more immersed in the music industry that he played so large a part in creating. But at the time of these photographs he was still the new man of 'hair-raising' energy and vitality who had astonished Legge in Vienna, and who more than anyone else made the Philharmonia Orchestra what it was in its great days. Sheer beauty of sound is not so common a commodity, after all.

Bei Herbert von Karajan weiß man nicht recht, wo man beginnen soll. Am Ende seines Lebens war er der erfolgreichste, meistpublizierte, reichste Dirigent Europas. Von niemandem gibt es mehr Aufnahmen. Lange Zeit dominierte er die Musikwelt. Die Berliner Philharmoniker, die Wiener Staatsoper, die Mailänder Scala, die Salzburger Festspiele und ein unkündbarer Vertrag mit der Deutschen Grammophon, die über 100 Millionen Aufnahmen von ihm verkaufte, gehörten zu den Bausteinen seines musikalischen Imperiums, in dem die Sonne zu seinen Lebzeiten nicht unterging.

Bis 1948 waren seine Aktivitäten ausschließlich auf Österreich und Deutschland beschränkt. Sein brillanter Start in Aachen öffnete ihm den Weg nach Berlin. 1938 gab seine erste Aufführung des *Tristan* an der Staatsoper den Anlaß zu der berühmten Schlagzeile: „Das Wunder Karajan". Es ist wahr, daß er der NSDAP beitrat, um das Engagement in Aachen zu bekommen, aber er wünschte es sich um jeden Preis – „also sagte ich, ‚zum Teufel', und unterschrieb." Der um zwanzig Jahre ältere Furtwängler, der nahezu ebenso lange ein verehrter Repräsentant der Berliner Philharmonie gewesen war, verzieh ihm seinen Erfolg in Berlin nie und verfeindete Politiker nutzten die Rivalität zwischen den beiden für sich. Am Ende überwarf sich Karajan zwar mit den Naziherrschern, fiel aber trotzdem nach dem Krieg den Entnazifizierungs-Kampagnen zum Opfer und konnte bis 1947 nicht öffentlich auftreten.

In dieser weniger glücklichen Zeit traf er auf Walter Legge, die graue Eminenz der Gramophone Company, der gerade aus hervorragenden Musikern die Londoner Philharmonia zusammengestellt hatte und jemanden suchte, der sie auf Dauer dirigieren konnte – insbesondere bei Plattenaufnahmen. Karajan ergriff die Gelegenheit, und seine Zukunft war besiegelt.

Es gibt die verschiedensten Reaktionen auf den Dirigenten Karajan – vom angebeteten Helden über unwillige Bewunderung bis hin zu direkten Beleidigungen ist alles vertreten. Drei Dinge stehen jedoch außer Zweifel: Er leistete ausgezeichnete Orchesterarbeit; er war ein fanatischer Perfektionist; und er strebte stets nach der vollendeten Schönheit des Klanges – und es gelang. In den letzten 35 Jahren seines Lebens machte er die Berliner Philharmoniker zu dem perfektesten Ensemble Europas, vielleicht sogar der Welt, obwohl die unkonturierten Legati, die weiche Elastizität der Rhythmen und die brillant eingestreuten Effekte ein musikalisches Temperament charakterisieren, das eher emotional als intellektuell bestimmt war. Seine Interpretationen können als übertrieben und zu flach erlebt werden. Karajans spätere Hinwendung zu den großen romantischen Symphonien von Bruckner und Mahler bieten den geteilten Meinungen reiches Material.

Seine Arbeitsmethoden sowohl auf als hinter der Bühne zeichnen sich allerdings durch Übertreibung aus. Seine Arroganz und seine Sucht nach Applaus waren vielen gar zu offensichtlich. Er konnte charmant sein, seinen Solisten helfen und sie sehr erfolgreich in sein musikalisches Konzept einbinden. In Fragen der Autorität war er jedoch unerbittlich, und seine Forderungen an die Musiker konnten eine Zumutung sein.

Es fällt nicht leicht, ihn einzuordnen, und mit zunehmender Verschmelzung mit dem Musikgeschäft, zu dessen Entwicklung er soviel beigetragen hat, wurde es immer schwieriger. Als diese Fotos entstanden, war er allerdings noch der energiegeladene, vitale neue Mann, der Legge in Wien in Erstaunen versetzte und der das Philharmonia Orchester zu dem machte, was es in seinen größten Tagen war – und die reine, perfekte Schönheit des Klanges entfaltet sich keineswegs von selbst.

Avec Karajan, il est difficile de savoir par où commencer. À la fin de sa vie, il était devenu le chef d'orchestre le plus couronné de lauriers, celui dont on parlait le plus, le plus enregistré et le plus riche d'Europe. Pendant des années, il avait tenu les rênes du pouvoir musical : le Philharmonique de Berlin, le Staatsoper de Vienne, la Scala de Milan, le Festival de Salzbourg et un contrat à vie avec la Deutsche Grammophon – qui a vendu plus de 100 millions d'exemplaires de ses enregistrements –, tels étaient les éléments d'un empire musical sur lequel le soleil ne devait pas se coucher durant la vie de ce chef.

Jusqu'en 1948, ses activités furent entièrement restreintes à l'Autriche et à l'Allemagne. Il fit de brillants débuts à Aachen et s'en servit comme tremplin décisif pour Berlin, où son premier *Tristan* au Staatsoper, en 1938, fut à l'origine de la fameuse manchette des journaux « Das Wunder Karajan » (Le prodige Karajan). C'est vrai, il a été obligé de devenir membre du parti nazi pour obtenir le poste d'Aachen, mais il le voulait désespérément – « Alors j'ai dit peu importe et j'ai signé ». Son succès à Berlin lui valut la haine éternelle de Furtwängler, de vingt ans son aîné et depuis presque aussi longtemps figure de proue vénérée du Philharmonique de Berlin et leur rivalité fut exploitée par des politiciens dans leurs propres querelles. Pour finir, Karajan se brouilla avec les autorités nazies, mais dut passer devant un tribunal de dénazification à la fin de la guerre, et il n'eut plus le droit de diriger en public jusqu'en 1947.

C'est à ce moment de sa carrière qu'il rencontra Walter Legge, l'éminence grise de la Gramophone Company, qui venait juste de créer un orchestre entièrement composé de vedettes de la Philharmonia de Londres et qui cherchait quelqu'un pour le diriger en permanence, et particulièrement pour enregistrer avec lui. Karajan saisit cette occasion, et son avenir fut réglé.

Les avis sont nombreux sur Karajan chef d'orchestre, allant de l'adoration aux propos impubliables, en passant par une admiration réticente. Mais trois faits sont incontestables : il était magnifique dans la direction d'opéras, c'était un fanatique du perfectionnisme et il visait constamment – et l'atteignait – la beauté absolue du son. Pendant les trente-cinq dernières années de sa vie, il créa, avec l'Orchestre philharmonique de Berlin, la plus opulente et parfaite machine à faire de la musique, peut-être du monde, sans aucun doute d'Europe. Il est vrai que les sons liés intimement, la douce élasticité du rythme et les brillantes gerbes d'effets servaient un tempérament musical plus émotionnel qu'intellectuel et donnaient des interprétations pouvant être jugées trop complaisantes et manquant de profondeur. Son intérêt postérieur pour les énormes édifices symphoniques romantiques de Bruckner et Mahler procure un riche matériau pour étayer chaque point de vue.

Les méthodes par lesquelles il obtenait ses résultats étaient hautes en couleur sur et hors de scène, et son arrogance et sa soif d'applaudissements étaient trop évidentes au goût de certains. Il pouvait être charmant, d'un grand secours pour ses solistes et brillant pour les former à ses concepts musicaux, mais il les mettait en fureur avec ses crises d'autorité et ce qu'il exigeait d'eux, en tant qu'êtres humains.

Donc, un homme difficile à situer et de plus en plus immergé dans l'industrie musicale qu'il avait tant contribué à créer. Au moment de ces photographies, il était encore le nouvel homme à l'énergie et à la vitalité « à dresser les cheveux sur la tête », qui avait étonné Legge à Vienne, et fit du Philharmonia ce qu'il était à sa grande époque. La pureté, la beauté absolue d'un son ne sont pas des articles si courants, après tout.

◀ Herbert von Karajan with the Vienna Philharmonic Orchestra at the Royal Festival Hall, London, 24 April 1963.

Herbert von Karajan mit dem Wiener Philharmonieorchester in der Royal Festival Hall, London, 24. April 1963.

Herbert von Karajan avec l'Orchestre philharmonique de Vienne au Royal Festival Hall à Londres, le 24 avril 1963.

Karajan recording Liszt and Tchaikovsky with the Philharmonia Orchestra at the Kingsway Hall, London, 17 January 1958.

Karajan bei Aufnahmen von Liszt und Tschaikowsky mit dem Philharmonia Orchestra in der Kingsway Hall, London, 17. Januar 1958.

Karajan enregistrant Liszt et Tchaïkovski avec le Philharmonia Orchestra au Kingsway Hall à Londres, le 17 janvier 1958.

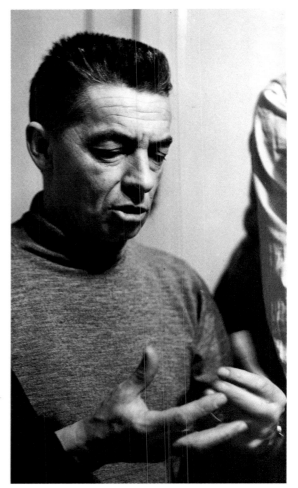

Karajan listening to the playback of the recording (see previous pages), 17 January 1958.

Karajan hört sich die Bänder der Aufnahmen an (siehe vorige Seiten), 17. Januar 1958.

Karajan réécoutant son enregistrement (voir pages précédentes), le 17 janvier 1958.

In rehearsal – the full Karajan treatment, 6 April 1962.

Bei der Probe – Karajan in Aktion, 6. April 1962.

Karajan en répétition, le 6 avril 1962.

There is very little to say about Kempe because he said so very little about himself. The least demonstrative of conductors, he was also the least demonstrative of people – shy, private and the last person to talk about the art that he practised so supremely well.

He rose from the ranks as an oboist, spending six years as principal oboe in the Leipzig Gewandhaus Orchestra before becoming a répétiteur and junior conductor with the same orchestra in 1936. In 1942 he left, electing to join the German army rather than obey a Nazi command to dismiss a valued orchestral player, but much of his military service was occupied with musical duties at Chemnitz, where he became conductor and musical director as soon as the war was over. After two more posts in East Germany, at Weimar and at Dresden, and a brilliant success opening the Vienna season in 1951, he finally crossed the border into Western Europe and succeeded Georg Solti as general music director of the Bavarian Staatsoper in Munich.

It was in this capacity that he made his London début, with Strauss's *Arabella*, when the Bavarian company visited the Royal Opera House in 1953. He was an idiomatic and deeply sensitive Strauss conductor (perhaps something of the Böhm tradition had got into him during his three years at Dresden) and when the Covent Garden company invited him as guest conductor in the year after the Bavarian visit it was in *Salome*, *Elektra* and *Der Rosenkavalier* that he was admired. But his field was the whole of the German romantic repertory, and in the following season he returned to direct *Tristan* and two complete cycles of the *Ring*; after the more overtly emotional interpretations of previous Wagner conductors at Covent Garden, Kempe's restrained approach took a little time to adjust to, but what was lost in sheer impact was more than regained in overall satisfaction. The relaxed clarity and warm understanding of his direction earned him the affection of singers and orchestra, the unbounded admiration of the critics, and with the public an immense musical and personal success.

At this time Covent Garden was looking desperately for a new musical director, but in spite of urgent entreaties Kempe could not be persuaded to take on the job and in the end the post went to Rafael Kubelík, Kempe continuing as a welcome guest conductor for many years to come. Four years later, however, he did accept a London appointment, when at Beecham's request he became associate conductor of the Royal Philharmonic Orchestra (a position more than merited by his purely musical qualities – though one cannot help feeling that Sir Thomas may not have been averse to an associate whose quiet public image would not threaten his own).

After Beecham's death in the following year he stayed on with the orchestra as artistic director and was appointed 'conductor for life' in 1970. When finally he was appointed principal conductor of the BBC Symphony Orchestra in 1975 great things were expected of him, but alas before he could take up the job he died at the relatively early age of 66. Few conductors have been so deeply and so genuinely mourned.

Von Rudolf Kempe gibt es wenig zu erzählen, denn er gab sehr wenig von sich preis. Seine äußerst zurückhaltende Gestik beim Dirigieren entsprach ganz und gar seiner Person. Scheu und sehr zurückgezogen sprach er niemals über die Kunst, die er so meisterhaft beherrschte.

Sein Aufstieg aus den Rängen des Orchesters begann an der Oboe. Sechs Jahre lang spielte er die erste Oboe im Leipziger Gewandhausorchester, bevor er 1936 Korrepetitor und Kapellmeister des Orchesters wurde. 1942 verließ er es, da er es eher bevorzugte, in die deutsche Armee einzutreten, als auf Weisung der Nazis einen geschätzten Musiker entlassen zu müssen. Einen großen Teil seiner Militärzeit verbrachte er jedoch, betraut mit musikalischen Aufgaben, in Chemnitz, wo er sofort nach Kriegsende Dirigent und Musikdirektor wurde. Nach zwei weiteren Engagements in Ostdeutschland (in Weimar und Dresden) und einem strahlenden Erfolg bei der Eröffnung der Wiener Saison im Jahre 1951, siedelte er schließlich in den Westen über und wurde Georg Soltis Nachfolger als Generalmusikdirektor der Bayrischen Staatsoper in München.

In dieser Eigenschaft gab er auch sein Debüt in London. 1953 reiste er mit dem Bayrischen Ensemble an und dirigierte im Royal Opera House die *Arabella* von Strauss. Er präsentierte den Komponisten sehr ausdrucksvoll und einfühlsam (vielleicht hatte er in seinen drei Dresdener Jahren etwas von der Tradition Böhms angenommen). Ein Jahr später lud ihn Covent Garden als Gastdirigenten ein, und er erntete mit *Salome*, *Elektra* und dem *Rosenkavalier* große Bewunderung. Sein Feld war jedoch die gesamte Tradition der deutschen Romantik, und in der nächsten Saison kehrte er zurück, um den *Tristan* und zwei vollständige *Ring*-Zyklen zu dirigieren. In Covent Garden kannte man eher gefühlsbetonte Wagner-Interpretationen und mußte sich erst an Kempes verhaltenen Ansatz gewöhnen. Anstatt sich wie bisher von der Musik schlicht überwältigen zu lassen, erlebte man nun einen ausgewogenen Genuß. Die entspannte Klarheit und das innige Verständnis seiner Interpretation sicherten ihm die Zuneigung des Orchesters und der Sänger, die grenzenlose Bewunderung der Kritiker und den ungeheuren musikalischen und persönlichen Erfolg beim Publikum.

Zu dieser Zeit suchte Covent Garden verzweifelt nach einem neuen Musikdirektor, aber trotz dringlicher Bitte konnte Kempe nicht dazu bewegt werden, das Engagement anzunehmen. Schließlich übernahm Rafael Kubelík den Posten. Kempe blieb viele Jahre lang ein willkommener Gastdirigent. Vier Jahre später nahm er dennoch ein Engagement in London an: Auf Beechams Ersuchen kam er als Dirigent zum Royal Philharmonic Orchestra (eine Position, die seinen rein musikalischen Qualitäten mehr als angemessen war – es drängt sich jedoch der Verdacht auf, daß Beecham gern jemanden an seiner Seite wußte, dessen stilles öffentliches Auftreten ihn selbst nicht in den Schatten stellen würde).

Ein Jahr später starb Beecham, und Kempe blieb als künstlerischer Leiter bei den Philharmonikern. 1970 wurde er zum „Dirigenten auf Lebenszeit" ernannt. Als er 1975 schließlich Chefdirigent des BBC Symphony Orchestra wurde, erwartete man große Dinge von ihm. Noch bevor er jedoch seinen Posten antreten konnte, verstarb er unerwartet im Alter von 66 Jahren. Selten wurde ein Dirigent so tief und aufrichtig betrauert.

Il y a peu de choses à dire sur Kempe, parce qu'il en disait très peu sur lui-même. Le moins démonstratif des chefs d'orchestre, il était également le moins démonstratif des hommes – timide, secret, et le dernier à parler de l'art qu'il pratiquait suprêmement bien.

Il sortit du rang en tant que hautbois, restant six ans premier hautbois dans le Gewandhaus de Leipzig, avant de devenir répétiteur et second chef d'orchestre du même orchestre en 1936. Il le quitta en 1942, préférant rejoindre l'armée plutôt que d'obéir à l'ordre des nazis de renvoyer un musicien de l'orchestre, mais pendant la plus grande partie de cette période il occupa des fonctions musicales à Chemnitz, où il devint chef d'orchestre et directeur musical dès la fin de la guerre. Après deux autres postes en Allemagne de l'Est, à Weimar et à Dresde, et un brillant succès à l'ouverture de la saison viennoise en 1951, il passa finalement à l'Ouest et succéda à Georg Solti en tant que directeur général de la musique au Staatsoper bavarois à Munich.

C'est en tant que tel qu'il fit ses débuts à Londres, avec *Arabella* de Strauss, quand la Compagnie bavaroise fut invitée au Royal Opera House en 1953. Il parlait la même langue que Strauss et était très sensible à son œuvre (quelque chose de la tradition de Böhm l'avait peut-être imprégné pendant ses trois ans à Dresde), et quand la compagnie du Covent Garden lui proposa d'être chef invité, un an après la visite de la Compagnie bavaroise, on l'admira dans *Salomé*, *Elektra* et *Le chevalier à la rose*. Mais la totalité du répertoire romantique allemand constituait son domaine, et pendant la saison suivante il repartit diriger *Tristan* et deux cycles complets du *Ring*. À Covent Garden, après les interprétations de Wagner plus manifestement émotionnelles des chefs précédents, l'approche tout en retenue de Kempe mit quelque temps à gagner la faveur du public, mais ce qui fut perdu en impact fut plus que regagné en satisfaction générale. La calme précision et la compréhension chaleureuse de sa direction lui ont valu l'affection des chanteurs et de l'orchestre, l'admiration sans borne des critiques et, auprès du public, un immense succès musical et personnel.

À cette époque, Covent Garden cherchait désespérément un nouveau directeur musical, mais en dépit des demandes pressantes, Kempe ne se laissa pas convaincre et le poste fut finalement attribué à Rafael Kubelík, Kempe restant chef invité pendant de nombreuses années. Quatre ans après, cependant, il accepta un engagement à Londres, devenant, à la demande de Sir Thomas Beecham, chef associé du Royal Philharmonic Orchestra (un statut plus que mérité par ses qualités purement musicales, bien que l'on ne puisse s'empêcher de penser que Sir Thomas avait été favorable à un associé dont l'image publique si calme ne menaçait pas la sienne).

Après la mort de Beecham l'année suivante, il resta auprès de l'orchestre comme directeur artistique et fut nommé « chef d'orchestre à vie » en 1970. Quand il fut finalement nommé premier chef de l'Orchestre symphonique de la BBC en 1975, on attendait beaucoup de lui, mais hélas, il mourut avant d'avoir pu occuper le poste, à l'âge de 66 ans. Peu de chefs d'orchestre ont été si profondément et si sincèrement pleurés.

Rudolf Kempe rehearsing Strauss's *Ein Heldenleben*, August 1974.

Rudolf Kempe bei einer Probe von Strauss' *Ein Heldenleben*, August 1974.

Rudolf Kempe répétant *Ein Heldenleben* de Strauss, en août 1974.

Kempe at rehearsal, 14 June 1961. He had become principal conductor of the Royal Philharmonic Orchestra after Beecham's death earlier in the year.

Kempe beim Proben, 14. Juni 1961. Seit Beechams Tod Anfang des Jahres war er der Chefdirigent des Royal Philharmonic Orchestra.

Kempe en répétition, le 14 juin 1961. Il était devenu chef d'orchestre en titre du Royal Philharmonic Orchestra après la mort de Beecham, au début de l'année.

Klemperer's appearances in London after the Second World War represented a new lease of life for this monumental figure from the past. Originally a protégé of Mahler's, he had built up a reputation between the wars as a conductor of fierce independence, with a special sympathy for the modern repertory and a less than traditional approach to the great German classics. In Berlin his work as first director of the new Kroll Opera was controversial and immensely influential, but the Kroll did not long survive in the German political climate then current, and after its closure in 1931 Klemperer, who was of Jewish birth, emigrated to the United States. An operation for a brain tumour in 1939 put a severe check on his career and when, after several years of ill health and semi-retirement, he did return to conducting, it was with a relatively obscure directorship at the Budapest Opera. So his appointment, at the age of 70, as principal conductor of the Philharmonia Orchestra in London was a huge new step for a conductor who had been almost forgotten in the cultural centres of Europe.

Meanwhile his misfortunes had continued. A broken hip in 1951 put him in hospital for eight months and forced him to conduct sitting down. He was back on his feet by the time he faced the Philharmonia Orchestra, but not for long: a stroke was followed by an appendix operation, and then by a near-fatal accident in his hotel bedroom, involving a cigarette which set light to the Bible on his knees and an unfortunate recourse to alcohol instead of water to extinguish the conflagration. In the end his physical resources were so reduced that even that formidable constitution had to bow to the inevitable. Still a towering figure, he walked slowly onto the platform with the help of a thick walking stick (which he handed to the leader as soon as he reached the rostrum) and sat down to conduct.

He did not so much conduct as preside. The arm and hand movements were stiff and awkward, the body immobile, the broad back (from the audience's point of view) black and impenetrable. But to the orchestra his whole figure exuded music, and above all authority: the eyes were piercing, the discipline at rehearsals harsh, the wit at the expense of miscreants acid. His intellectual grasp was profound and the power and intensity of his performances could be overwhelming: in the years after the death of Wilhelm Furtwängler, Klemperer came to be seen as the ultimate interpreter of the great Austro-German repertory from Haydn to Mahler – above all Beethoven. His performances of the *Ninth Symphony* reached almost cult status.

If in later years his tempi became obsessively slow, there still remained a rock-like integrity of structure and a total absence of sentimentality. It was these qualities which particularly distinguished his performances of Mahler. In this he was the exact opposite of Mahler's other famous protégé, Bruno Walter, whose warmer, more nostalgic approach to his mentor's music was for years accepted as the only authentic one. Klemperer, who disliked Walter intensely, was well aware of the difference, personal as well as musical: 'He is a moralist, I am an *im*-moralist', he said in one of his more restrained comments about his eminent colleague. It may be that that is how he would best like to be remembered.

Seine Auftritte in London nach dem Zweiten Weltkrieg stellten für den in der Vergangenheit so bedeutenden Otto Klemperer einen hoffnungsvollen Neuanfang dar. Ursprünglich ein Schützling von Mahler, hatte er sich zwischen den Weltkriegen einen Ruf als äußerst eigenständiger Dirigent mit einer Vorliebe für die Moderne und einem unkonventionellen Zugang zur großen deutschen Klassik erworben. Seine Arbeit als Generalmusikdirektor der Kroll Oper war umstritten, aber unglaublich einflußreich. Die Kroll Oper konnte sich jedoch in dem politischen Klima Deutschlands nicht lange halten. Nach ihrer Schließung 1931 emigrierte Klemperer, der jüdischer Abstammung war, in die USA. Die Operation an einem Gehirntumor 1939 bedeutete einen schweren Einbruch in seiner Karriere, die er erst nach mehreren Jahren fortsetzen konnte – in einer relativ unbedeutenden Position als Musikdirektor an der Oper in Budapest. Als er im Alter von 70 Jahren zum Chefdirigenten des Philharmonia Orchestra London wurde, war das ein neuer großer Schritt für einen Dirigenten, der in den Metropolen Europas fast vergessen war.

Zwischenzeitlich hatte ihn das Unglück weiter verfolgt. 1951 fesselte ihn ein Oberschenkelhalsbruch für acht Monate ans Krankenbett. Danach war er gezwungen, im Sitzen zu dirigieren. Als er dann nach London kam, war er zwar wieder auf den Beinen, jedoch nicht für lange. Auf einen Schlaganfall folgte eine Blinddarmoperation. Später entging er bei einem Unfall in seinem Hotelzimmer nur knapp dem Tode. Eine brennende Zigarette hatte die Bibel auf seinen Knien entzündet, und er hatte versehentlich Alkohol anstatt Wasser auf die Flammen geschüttet. Schließlich waren seine Kraftreserven trotz der unglaublichen Konstitution so erschöpft, daß er darauf Rücksicht nehmen mußte. Immer noch eine eindrucksvolle Gestalt, betrat er die Bühne nun langsam und auf einen Stock gestützt (den er, am Pult angelangt, sofort dem ersten Geiger übergab) und dirigierte sitzend.

Er führte eher den Vorsitz, als daß er dirigierte. Hand und Arm bewegten sich steif und ungelenk; der Körper blieb unbewegt, und sein breiter Rücken wirkte (vom Publikum aus gesehen) schwarz und undurchdringlich. Für das Orchester jedoch strahlte seine ganze Erscheinung Musik aus – und vor allem Autorität. Seinen Augen entging nichts. Bei den Proben hielt er eiserne Disziplin und ahndete Mißgriffe mit beißendem Spott. Er verfügte über ein tiefgründiges musikalisches Verständnis. Die Kraft und Intensität seiner Aufführungen konnte überwältigend sein. In den Jahren nach Furtwänglers Tod begann man Klemperer als den größten Interpreten des deutsch-österreichischen Repertoires von Haydn bis Mahler anzusehen – und insbesondere von Beethoven. Seine Aufführungen der *Neunten Symphonie* genossen fast kultische Verehrung.

Wenn sich seine Tempi in späteren Jahren auch extrem verlangsamten, so blieb doch die Integrität der Komposition stets vollkommen gewahrt, und es fehlte jedes Anzeichen von Sentimentalität. Gerade diese Eigenschaften zeichneten besonders seine Mahler-Einspielungen aus. In dieser Hinsicht stand Klemperer ganz im Gegensatz zu Bruno Walter, Mahlers anderem Protégé. Walters gefühlvollerer, nostalgischerer Zugang zum Werk seines Mentors galt jahrelang als einzig authentische Interpretation. Klemperer, der Walter gar nicht mochte, war sich dieser musikalischen und persönlichen Unterschiede deutlich bewußt. „Er ist ein Moralist, ich bin ein Immoralist", bemerkte er einmal in einem seiner zurückhaltenderen Kommentare über den berühmten Kollegen. So möchte er vielleicht am liebsten in Erinnerung bleiben.

Les apparitions de Klemperer à Londres, après la Seconde Guerre mondiale, donnèrent un regain de vitalité à cette monumentale figure du passé. Protégé de Mahler à ses débuts, il s'était forgé, entre les deux guerres, une réputation de chef d'orchestre farouchement indépendant, qui appréciait particulièrement le répertoire moderne et une approche moins que traditionnelle des grands classiques allemands. À Berlin, son travail comme premier chef du nouveau Kroll Opera était à la fois controversé et extrêmement prestigieux. Mais le Kroll ne survécut pas longtemps dans le climat politique allemand de cette époque et, après sa fermeture en 1931, Klemperer, qui était d'origine juive, émigra aux États-Unis. Une opération d'une tumeur au cerveau, en 1939, mit un frein sévère à sa carrière et, quand après plusieurs années de mauvaise santé et de semi-retraite, il revint à la direction d'orchestre, ce fut à un poste relativement obscur à l'Opéra de Budapest. Donc sa nomination, à l'âge de 70 ans, comme premier chef d'orchestre du Philharmonia de Londres fut un nouveau départ pour ce chef pratiquement oublié des centres culturels d'Europe.

En 1951, une hanche brisée le conduisit à l'hôpital pour huit mois et l'obligea à rester assis pour diriger. Il était à nouveau sur pied quand il arriva au Philharmonique, mais pas pour longtemps : une attaque fut suivie d'une opération de l'appendicite, puis d'un accident presque fatal dans sa chambre d'hôtel : une cigarette ayant mis le feu à la Bible qu'il tenait sur ses genoux, il voulut éteindre les flammes avec de l'alcool ! En fin de compte, ses ressources physiques étaient tellement diminuées que même cette constitution formidable dut s'incliner devant l'inévitable. Toujours d'une silhouette imposante, il marchait lentement sur la scène à l'aide d'une canne épaisse (qu'il tendait au premier violon dès qu'il avait atteint l'estrade) et s'asseyait pour diriger.

Ce n'est pas tant qu'il dirigeait, il présidait. Les mouvements de ses bras et de ses mains étaient raides et peu élégants, son corps immobile, son large dos (du point de vue du public) noir et impénétrable. Mais pour l'orchestre, toute sa personne n'était que musique et autorité : le regard était perçant, la discipline sévère aux répétitions, les remarques contre les incapables mordantes. Sa compréhension intellectuelle était profonde et la puissance et l'intensité de ses représentations pouvaient être bouleversantes : après la mort de Wilhelm Furtwängler, on en vint à considérer Klemperer comme l'ultime interprète du grand répertoire austro-allemand de Haydn à Mahler — et surtout Beethoven. Ses interprétations de la *Neuvième Symphonie* sont quasi mythiques.

Même si, dans ses dernières années, et de façon obsédante, ses tempi étaient devenus lents, restaient cependant une intégrité de structure inébranlable et une absence totale de sentimentalité. Ce sont ces qualités qui distinguèrent particulièrement ses interprétations de Mahler. Il était, en cela, l'exact opposé de l'autre célèbre protégé de ce compositeur, Bruno Walter, dont l'approche plus chaleureuse, plus nostalgique de la musique de son mentor fut, pendant des années, regardée comme la seule authentique. Klemperer, qui détestait cordialement Walter, était bien conscient de cette différence, autant personnelle que musicale : « C'est un moraliste, je suis un immoraliste », dit-il dans l'une de ses remarques les plus sobres sur son éminent collègue. C'est peut-être comme cela qu'il souhaiterait que l'on se souvienne de lui.

Otto Klemperer rehearsing, 26 October 1964.

Otto Klemperer beim Proben, 26. Oktober 1964.

Otto Klemperer en répétition, le 26 octobre 1964.

2

3

4

(1) Klemperer recording the last movement of Beethoven's *Ninth Symphony* with the Philharmonia Orchestra at the Kingsway Hall, London, November 1957. The soloists (top left) were Hans Hotter, Waldemar Kmentt, Christa Ludwig and Aase Nordmo-Lövberg. (2, 3, 4) 18 August 1958.

(1) Klemperer bei der Aufnahme des letzten Satzes von Beethovens *Neunter Symphonie* mit dem Philharmonia Orchestra in der Kingsway Hall in London im November 1957. Die Solisten (oben links) waren Hans Hotter, Waldemar Kmentt, Christa Ludwig und Aase Nordmo-Lövberg. (2, 3, 4) 18. August 1958.

(1) Klemperer enregistrant le dernier mouvement de la *Neuvième Symphonie* de Beethoven avec le Philharmonia Orchestra au Kingsway Hall à Londres, en novembre 1957. Les solistes (en haut à gauche) étaient Hans Hotter, Waldemar Kmentt, Christa Ludwig et Aase Nordmo-Lövberg. (2, 3, 4) Le 18 août 1958.

Another *Ninth Symphony*, 26 October 1964. Earlier in the year Walter Legge, for commercial reasons, had decided to disband the Philharmonia Orchestra, but the players, refusing to be disbanded, reformed themselves as the New Philharmonia Orchestra. Otto Klemperer agreed to stay on as principal conductor, and the new venture was launched with a tremendous performance of the Beethoven symphony at the Royal Albert Hall on the day after this rehearsal (1, 2, 3).

Noch einmal die *Neunte Symphonie*, 26. Oktober 1964. Zu Beginn des Jahres hatte sich Walter Legge aus finanziellen Gründen dazu entschlossen, das Philharmonia Orchestra aufzulösen. Die Musiker verweigerten jedoch die Auflösung und gründeten sich selbst neu als das New Philharmonia Orchestra. Otto Klemperer war damit einverstanden, ihr Chefdirigent zu bleiben, und das neue Unternehmen startete einen Tag nach dieser Probe (1, 2, 3) mit einer großartigen Aufführung von Beethovens Symphonie in der Royal Albert Hall.

Une autre *Neuvième Symphonie*, le 26 octobre 1964. Plus tôt dans l'année, Walter Legge, pour des raisons commerciales, avait décidé de dissoudre le Philharmonia Orchestra, mais les interprètes, refusant leur dispersion, fondèrent le New Philharmonia Orchestra dont Otto Klemperer accepta d'être le chef, et la nouvelle entreprise fut lancée avec une représentation mémorable de la symphonie de Beethoven au Royal Albert Hall (1, 2, 3), le lendemain de cette répétition.

1

(4) Klemperer, who was ill and desperately tired, being helped by his daughter Lotte and his personal assistant Otto Ehrenthal after the rehearsal. (5, 6, 7) Hugh Bean, leader of the New Philharmonia Orchestra, doing his best to raise a smile from the exhausted conductor.

(4) Tochter Lotte und sein persönlicher Assistent Otto Ehrenthal kümmern sich nach der Probe um den erkrankten und furchtbar müden Klemperer. (5, 6, 7) Hugh Bean, der Konzertmeister des New Philharmonia Orchestra, gibt sich alle Mühe, dem erschöpften Dirigenten ein Lächeln abzuringen.

(4) Klemperer, malade et très fatigué, aidé par sa fille Lotte et son secrétaire particulier Otto Ehrenthal, après la répétition. (5, 6, 7) Hugh Bean, premier violon du New Philharmonia Orchestra, faisant son possible pour faire sourire le chef d'orchestre épuisé.

4

2

3

5

6

7

To a generation conditioned to regard Carlos Kleiber as an almost mythical figure on the contemporary conducting scene it may come as a surprise to find that he had a father who was as great as, if not greater than, his son. Erich Kleiber, a Viennese by birth with youthful memories of Mahler at the Court Opera, hit the headlines in Berlin in 1923 when he made a spectacular début with *Fidelio* at the State Opera after only one rehearsal, and was appointed general music director three days later.

This was a fabulous period for music in the German capital: Furtwängler was at the Philharmonic, Klemperer at the Kroll Opera, Bruno Walter at the Charlottenburg – yet even in this company Kleiber's 11 years at the Staatsoper turned into one of the most brilliant directorships in its history. Most celebrated among the many new operas that he introduced was Alban Berg's *Wozzeck* after an incredible total of 137 rehearsals. But times were changing and the new music in Germany was finding less and less favour with current political and ideological trends. It soon became clear that Berg's second opera *Lulu* was heading for the same fate as Hindemith's works: at the end of 1934 Kleiber gave the first performance of the *Suite* which Berg had compiled from the music of *Lulu* and four days later resigned his post at the Berlin State Opera.

After Berlin he never took another permanent appointment. Instead he made himself a new home in Buenos Aires, where he appeared frequently at the Teatro Colón and undertook pioneering tours as a guest conductor in South America, Mexico and Cuba, as well as more conventional trips to Europe and the USA. After the war his visits to London were memorable, breathing new life into the post-war company at Covent Garden, though he could not be persuaded to stay on as musical director. Plans for his appointment to a similar position in Vienna fell through and when he was finally tempted back to the Berlin Staatsoper, now in the eastern zone of the city, he resigned before he even took up the job, in protest at political interference.

Utterly uncompromising and in every sense demanding, Kleiber was feared and often hated by administrators but loved by his orchestral players, whose part he constantly took in any brush with management. As a conductor he was a perfectionist, sensitive to every nuance of the score – a fanatic at rehearsal and an autocrat on the rostrum or in the pit. Never did operatic performances begin with less fuss: the sudden impetuous passage of that bullet head through the orchestra, the merest nod of a bow as he turned to face the players, applause cut short as it began, *Carmen* off like a bomb, *Rosenkavalier* like a sky rocket. From the first bar on the whole performance was a single act of concentration, with no room for anything but the meaning of the opera itself. Yet he looked after everybody. Faced by a nervous and unimaginative bass singing Sarastro for the first time, he was able to coax a fine performance by fixing him with a beady eye and phrasing the entire role with his left hand – from inside the jacket of his tail-coat, so that the audience couldn't see what was happening. These things were not forgotten by the artists he worked with.

Eine Generation, für die Carlos Kleiber eine nahezu mythische Figur unter den zeitgenössischen Dirigenten ist, mag es überraschen, daß sein Vater mindestens ebenso berühmt war: Der gebürtige Wiener Erich Kleiber erlebte in seiner Jugend noch Mahler selbst an der höfischen Oper. Als er 1923 in Berlin mit *Fidelio* sein Debüt an der Staatsoper gab, erregte er großes Aufsehen, und drei Jahre später wurde er dort Generalmusikdirektor.

Es war eine große Zeit in der Berliner Musikgeschichte – mit Furtwängler an der Philharmonie, Klemperer an der Kroll Oper und Bruno Walter in Charlottenburg. Doch selbst in diesem Kreis behauptet sich Kleibers elfjährige Leitung der Staatsoper als eine glanzvolle Phase. Von all den neuen Opern, die er auf den Spielplan setzte, wurde Alban Bergs *Wozzeck* nach der unglaublichen Anzahl von 137 Proben am meisten gefeiert. Aber die Zeiten änderten sich, und die neue Musik geriet in Deutschland immer mehr in Widerspruch zu den herrschenden politischen und ideologischen Strömungen. Es zeichnete sich bald ab, daß Bergs zweite Oper *Lulu* demselben Schicksal entgegenging wie die Werke Hindemiths. Ende 1934 gab Kleiber die erste Aufführung der *Suite*, die Berg aus der Musik von *Lulu* zusammengestellt hatte. Vier Tage später trat er von seinem Posten an der Berliner Staatsoper zurück.

Danach nahm er nie wieder ein festes Engagement an. Er ließ sich in Buenos Aires nieder, wo er regelmäßig am Teatro Colón auftrat. Er stieß mit seinen Tourneen nach Südamerika, Mexico und Kuba vor, unternahm aber auch konventionelle Reisen nach Europa und in die USA. Seine erinnerungswürdigen Besuche in London nach dem Krieg brachten neuen Schwung nach Covent Garden. Er war jedoch nicht dazu zu bewegen, als Musikdirektor zu bleiben. Auch die Wiener konnten ihn nicht für sich gewinnen, und als es schließlich gelang, ihn an die nun im Ostteil der Stadt gelegene Berliner Staatsoper zurückzuholen, trat er aus Protest gegen politische Einmischung zurück, bevor er die Arbeit überhaupt aufgenommen hatte.

Völlig kompromißlos und in jeder Hinsicht fordernd wurde Kleiber von den Orchesterverwaltungen oft gefürchtet und gehaßt. Die Musiker aber, deren Interessen er in jedem Streit mit der Leitung vertrat, verehrten ihn. Als Dirigent war er ein Perfektionist und reagierte sensibel auf jede Nuance der Partitur. Bei den Proben war er ein Fanatiker. Am Dirigentenpult und im Orchestergraben herrschte er uneingeschränkt. Um den Auftakt zu seinen Opernaufführungen machte er überhaupt kein Aufheben: Er schritt rasch auf seinen Platz, machte die leiseste Andeutung einer Verbeugung vor dem Orchester und brach den Eingangsapplaus ab. *Carmen* wurde ein durchschlagender Erfolg, und der *Rosenkavalier* war eine Sensation. Vom ersten Takt an waren seine Aufführungen voller Konzentration, ohne jeden Raum für etwas anderes als die Bedeutung der Oper selbst. Trotzdem kümmerte er sich um jeden einzelnen seiner Künstler. Einem nervösen, uninspirierten Baß, der den Sarastro zum ersten Mal sang, entlockte er eine gute Vorstellung, indem er ihn mit großen Augen ansah und ihm die gesamte Rolle phrasierte – mit der linken Hand, die er in seinem Frack verbarg, damit das Publikum nicht sah, was er tat. Seine Künstler haben es ihm nie vergessen.

Pour une génération habituée à considérer Carlos Kleiber comme un personnage quasi mythique de la direction d'orchestre, il peut être surprenant d'apprendre qu'il avait un père aussi grand, sinon plus, que lui. Erich Kleiber, Viennois de naissance, avec des souvenirs de jeunesse de Mahler au Court Opera, fit les manchettes des journaux de Berlin en 1923 quand il débuta, de façon spectaculaire, avec *Fidelio* au Staatsoper, après une seule répétition, et fut nommé directeur général de la musique trois jours plus tard.

C'était une période fabuleuse pour la musique dans la capitale allemande : Furtwängler était au Philharmonique, Klemperer au Kroll Opera, Bruno Walter au Charlottenburg. Les onze années de Kleiber au Staatsoper furent l'une des plus brillantes périodes de direction d'orchestre de l'histoire de cette salle. Parmi les nombreux opéras qu'il y présenta, le plus acclamé fut *Wozzeck* d'Alban Berg, après un total incroyable de 137 répétitions. Mais les temps changeaient et, en Allemagne, la nouvelle musique se heurtait de plus en plus à des résistances, en raison des tendances politiques et idéologiques du moment. Il devint rapidement évident que le second opéra de Berg, *Lulu*, allait subir le même sort que les œuvres d'Hindemith : à la fin de 1934, Kleiber donna la première représentation de la *Suite* que Berg avait composée à partir de la musique de *Lulu*. Quatre jours plus tard, il démissionnait de son poste au Staatsoper de Berlin.

Après Berlin, il n'accepta plus aucun poste fixe et s'installa à Buenos Aires, où il apparut fréquemment au Teatro Colón, et entreprit des tournées comme chef invité en Amérique du Sud, Mexico et Cuba, ainsi que des voyages plus traditionnels en Europe et aux États-Unis. Après la guerre, ses visites à Londres furent mémorables, insufflant une nouvelle vie dans la compagnie de Covent Garden, mais il ne se laissa pas persuader de rester comme directeur musical. Les projets pour le nommer à un poste similaire à Vienne échouèrent, et lorsqu'il fut finalement tenté de retourner au Staatsoper de Berlin, désormais dans la partie orientale de la ville, il démissionna avant même d'avoir commencé, pour protester contre l'ingérence politique.

Totalement inflexible et, dans tous les sens, exigeant, Kleiber était craint et souvent détesté des administrateurs, mais aimé de ses musiciens, dont il prenait constamment le parti dans tout démêlé avec l'administration. En tant que chef d'orchestre c'était un perfectionniste, sensible à chaque nuance de la partition, un fanatique à la répétition et un autocrate sur l'estrade ou dans la fosse. Jamais les représentations d'opéras n'ont commencé avec aussi peu de cérémonie : le passage soudain et impétueux de sa tête ronde à travers l'orchestre, un simple signe de tête en guise de salut quand il se retournait vers ses musiciens, les applaudissements coupés court, *Carmen* explosant comme une bombe, *Le chevalier à la rose* comme une fusée volante. De la première à la dernière mesure, toute la représentation n'était qu'un seul acte de concentration, ne laissant place à rien d'autre que la signification de l'opéra lui-même. Néanmoins, il prenait grand soin de tout le monde. Confronté à un chanteur nerveux et sans imagination, qui chantait Sarastro pour la première fois, il put l'amener à donner une belle interprétation en le guidant du regard et en lui indiquant le phrasé avec sa main gauche – de l'intérieur de la veste de son habit, pour que le public ne se doute de rien. Ce sont des choses que les artistes avec lesquels il a travaillé n'oublièrent pas.

Erich Kleiber in Prague, 1937.

Erich Kleiber in Prag, 1937.

Erich Kleiber à Prague, 1937.

Josef Krips – Viennese charm, September 1962.
Josef Krips – Wiener Charme, September 1962.
Josef Krips ou le charme viennois, septembre 1962.

JOSEF KRIPS   1902-1974

Krips was a very Viennese conductor. He was born in Vienna, studied there with Weingartner, got his first conducting job at the Volksoper under Weingartner and, after gaining experience at various opera houses in Germany, returned to Vienna as a resident conductor at the Staatsoper in 1933. A couple of years later he became a professor at the Vienna Academy, and the same year made his début at the Salzburg Festival in *Der Rosenkavalier* with the Vienna ensemble.

But at the age of 35 this promising career was suddenly blocked. On 12 March 1938 German troops marched into the Austrian capital and on the following day Krips, being partly Jewish, was dismissed from his post at the Staatsoper. He managed one more season of conducting with the Belgrade opera, but after it he was banned by the Nazis from all musical activities and, unable to leave Austria, was forced to find employment as an industrial clerk for the duration of the war.

He must have been a proud man when, three weeks after the capitulation of Germany, he raised his baton for the overture to *Le nozze di Figaro* and re-launched the Vienna Staatsoper on its post-war career. The opera house on the Ring having been destroyed during an Allied air raid only a few months earlier, the performance took place in the Theater an der Wien, where Mozart himself had conducted the first performance of *Die Zauberflöte*, and it set the stage for a five-year period during which Krips, as much as anybody, was responsible for rebuilding Vienna's worldwide reputation as a centre of musical life. Later in 1945 it was Krips again who presided over the resumption of concerts by the Vienna Philharmonic Orchestra, and in the following year he reopened the Salzburg Festival with *Don Giovanni* – taking over from Karajan, whose planned appearance had been vetoed by the United States military authorities.

As he told Adrian Boult in 1948, his post-war years in Vienna were a little soured by what he saw as 'the restoration of the local (and artistic) Nazis of the Furtwängler and Karajan order', but he was already making contacts abroad, especially in London where he made a highly successful visit with the Staatsoper to Covent Garden in 1947 – and eventually accepted the appointment of principal conductor of the London Symphony Orchestra. His four years in this post made a crucial contribution to the recovery of the orchestra after its lean period during the war. Later he moved on to America – Buffalo, Cincinnati, San Francisco, the Metropolitan – while still appearing regularly as an admired guest at the great European centres.

But always, wherever he went, Krips remained a Viennese, and it is as a conductor of the great classics of Viennese music, above all Mozart and Richard Strauss, that he will be remembered. It is a position he shares to some extent with Karl Böhm, but because of his association with the Viennese renaissance after the war, and the marvellous Mozart casts he could call upon for performance and recording in those crucial years, it is probably Krips who will be remembered by the post-war generation of music lovers as the ultimate Viennese Mozartian.

Josef Krips war von Grund auf ein Wiener Dirigent. Er war gebürtiger Wiener, hatte dort bei Weingartner studiert und bekam sein erstes Engagement als Dirigent an der Volksoper unter Weingartner. Nachdem er an verschiedenen deutschen Opernhäusern Erfahrungen gesammelt hatte, kehrte er 1933 als ständiger Dirigent an die Staatsoper nach Wien zurück. Einige Jahre später wurde er Professor an der Wiener Akademie. Im gleichen Jahr debütierte er mit dem Wiener Ensemble bei den Salzburger Festspielen mit dem *Rosenkavalier*.

Im Alter von 35 Jahren wurde diese vielversprechende Karriere jäh unterbrochen. Am 12. März 1938 marschierten deutsche Truppen in die österreichische Hauptstadt ein, und bereits am nächsten Tag verlor Krips, der auch jüdische Vorfahren hatte, seine Stelle an der Staatsoper. Er konnte noch eine Saison an der Oper in Belgrad dirigieren, dann wurde ihm jede musikalische Tätigkeit verboten. Da er Österreich nicht verlassen konnte, war er für die Dauer des Krieges gezwungen, als Angestellter in der Industrie zu arbeiten.

Es muß ihn mit Stolz erfüllt haben, als er drei Wochen nach der Kapitulation Deutschlands seinen Taktstock zur Ouvertüre des *Figaro* erheben und damit die Nachkriegskarriere der Wiener Staatsoper einleiten konnte. Das Opernhaus auf dem Ring war nur wenige Monate zuvor den Luftangriffen der Alliierten zum Opfer gefallen, und deshalb fand die Vorstellung im Theater an der Wien statt, wo Mozart seinerzeit selbst die Uraufführung der *Zauberflöte* dirigiert hatte. Damit begann die fünfjährige Aufbauphase, in der Krips mit vielen anderen gemeinsam die Aufgabe zufiel, Wiens Weltrang als ein Zentrum des musikalischen Lebens neu zu begründen. Später im Jahre 1945 leitete Krips die Wiederaufnahme der Konzerte der Wiener Philharmoniker und im darauffolgenden Jahr die Wiedereröffnung der Salzburger Festspiele mit *Don Giovanni* anstelle Karajans ein, dessen geplanter Auftritt am Veto der amerikanischen Militärbehörden scheiterte.

1948 erzählte er Adrian Boult, „der Wiederaufstieg lokaler und (künstlerischer) Nazigrößen vom Schlage Furtwänglers und Karajans" habe ihm die Nachkriegsjahre in Wien etwas verdorben. Da verhandelte er aber bereits mit dem Ausland, besonders mit London, wo er 1947 mit der Wiener Staatsoper sehr erfolgreich in Covent Garden gastierte. Schließlich nahm er die Ernennung zum Chefdirigenten des London Symphony Orchestra an. In den vier Jahren seiner Leitung leistete das Orchester Entscheidendes zur Wiederherstellung seines Rufes, der in den Kriegsjahren gelitten hatte. Später ging Krips nach Amerika – Buffalo, Cincinnati, San Francisco, die Metropolitan Opera – doch er blieb ein regelmäßiger und gern gesehener Gast in den großen europäischen Musikzentren.

Krips blieb Wiener, wo auch immer er war; und vor allem als Dirigent der großen Wiener Klassik – insbesondere der Musik Mozarts und Richard Strauss' – wird er in Erinnerung bleiben. Dieses Prädikat teilt er in gewisser Weise mit Karl Böhm. Seine Bedeutung für den Wiener Wiederaufbau in der Nachkriegszeit und die wunderbaren Mozartbesetzungen, die er in diesen entscheidenden Jahren auf die Bühne und ins Aufnahmestudio brachte, werden aber vermutlich dazu führen, daß die Musikliebhaber der Nachkriegsgeneration Krips hauptsächlich als den besten Wiener Mozartianer im Gedächtnis behalten werden.

Krips était un chef d'orchestre viennois jusqu'au bout de la baguette. Né à Vienne, il y poursuit ses études avec Weingartner, y effectue ses premiers pas à la tête de l'orchestre du Volksoper sous la direction de Weingartner et, après avoir acquis plus d'expérience dans de nombreuses maisons allemandes, revient à Vienne en 1933 comme chef d'orchestre permanent de l'Opéra national, le célèbre Staatsoper. Quelques années plus tard, il devient professeur à l'Académie de Vienne et fait ses débuts avec l'ensemble de Vienne au Festival de Salzbourg, dans le *Chevalier à la rose*.

Le nazisme met soudainement un terme provisoire à sa carrière prometteuse. Il n'a que 35 ans lorsque les troupes allemandes s'emparent de la capitale autrichienne, le 12 mars 1938, et le jour suivant, il est démis de ses fonctions en raison de ses origines juives. Il réussit à rester une saison de plus à la tête de l'Opéra de Belgrade, mais les nazis lui interdisent ensuite définitivement toute activité musicale. N'étant plus autorisé à quitter l'Autriche, il se voit contraint de travailler dans l'industrie pendant toute la durée de la guerre.

Mais, Krips avait sa fierté. Trois semaines après la capitulation de l'Allemagne, sa baguette animait déjà l'orchestre du Staatsoper où l'on donnait pour l'ouverture *Les noces de Figaro*. Sa carrière d'après-guerre prenait, elle aussi, un nouveau départ. Les bombardements alliés ayant détruit l'Opéra du Ring quelques mois plus tôt, le concert eut lieu au Theater an der Wien, où Mozart lui-même avait dirigé la première de *La Flûte enchantée*. L'événement était annonciateur : pendant cinq ans, Krips allait, plus que tout autre, contribuer à redonner à Vienne sa réputation de ville mondiale de la musique. Vers la fin de 1945, c'est en effet encore lui qui préside à la reprise des concerts de l'Orchestre philharmonique de Vienne et, l'année suivante, à la réouverture du Festival de Salzbourg, avec *Don Giovanni*, les autorités militaires des États-Unis ayant opposé leur veto à la présence de Karajan.

Comme il le confia à Adrian Boult en 1948, ces années d'après-guerre viennoises furent quelque peu gâchées par ce qu'il considérait comme la « restauration des nazis locaux (et artistiques) à la botte de Furtwängler et Karajan ». Il prenait d'ailleurs déjà des contacts à l'étranger, notamment à Londres, où il fit une première visite remarquable et remarquée à Covent Garden avec le Staatsoper, en 1947, et où il accepta finalement le poste de premier chef d'orchestre du London Symphony Orchestra. Pendant ses quatre années de fonction, il contribua à redonner à cet orchestre ses lettres de noblesse au sortir d'une longue période de déclin due à la guerre. Il s'envola ensuite pour les États-Unis (Buffalo, Cincinnati, San Francisco, New-York) avec le Metropolitan, continuant d'apparaître régulièrement comme invité d'honneur, fort apprécié, dans les grandes salles européennes.

Où qu'il ait pu se rendre, Krips était resté viennois. On se souviendra de lui comme étant le Chef d'orchestre des grands classiques de Vienne, et plus particulièrement des œuvres de Mozart et de Richard Strauss. Il partage certes ce privilège avec Karl Böhm, mais son engagement dans la renaissance de Vienne après la Seconde Guerre mondiale, et ce souffle merveilleux dont il emplissait les lieux lorsqu'il dirigeait du Mozart pendant ces années primordiales – sur scène ou pour des enregistrements – font que c'est probablement lui, Josef Krips, qui restera dans la mémoire des amoureux de la musique comme le « Mozartien » de Vienne par excellence.

Most good conductors are respected by the orchestras who play under them, some are hated, some are feared. Rafael Kubelík was loved – for his enthusiasm, his uncompromising idealism and the warmth of his generous human personality.

He was born with a name that was already famous in the musical world. His father was a virtuoso violinist of international celebrity, and the son was launched on the Prague musical scene at an early age, becoming a regular conductor of the Czech Philharmonic Orchestra at only 22, and its principal conductor five years later. But in 1948, when the Communists seized power in Czechoslovakia, he knew his days in his own country were numbered: taking advantage of an invitation to conduct in Edinburgh that summer, he left Czechoslovakia permanently, vowing never to return under a Communist regime.

A period of wandering took him to Australia and South and North America, but after three unhappy years as director of the Chicago Symphony Orchestra he returned to London, where he had already established a good relationship with the Philharmonic Orchestra, in 1953. His first real impact on London came with the revival of Janáček's opera *Katya Kabanova* at Sadler's Wells in 1954. The sensation caused by this blazing performance did not go unnoticed at Covent Garden, where London's senior opera company was desperately in search of a new musical director – and in the following year Kubelík accepted the appointment.

The company he took over had been without a permanent director for four years and was in need of direction and a sense of purpose. Kubelík believed passionately in building up a genuine ensemble of British singers and was not prepared to tolerate film-star behaviour. He sacked Tito Gobbi when he failed to turn up for rehearsals of the opening *Otello*, but scored a resounding success on the first night even so. He introduced Janáček's *Jenůfa* to London, conducted the first ever full stage performance of Berlioz's gigantic masterpiece *Les Troyens*, and gave the British première of Poulenc's *Dialogues des Carmélites*. With singers, orchestra and public he created a warm personal bond, and as a musical director he made up in enthusiasm what he lacked in brute strength. But, sadly, he allowed himself to be unsettled by a chauvinistic witch-hunt (with Beecham at its head) and after only three years the new and promising regime was allowed to lapse. It was ironic, too, that his successor was the Hungarian Georg Solti.

After London his main centre of activity was Munich, where he was principal conductor of the Bavarian Radio Symphony Orchestra for 18 happy and fruitful years, building up a relatively young ensemble into one of the finest orchestras in Europe. Many of his best and most characteristic performances were recorded in these years – Dvořák, Smetana, Janáček, Bartók, all the Mahler symphonies and, with the Berlin Philharmonic, some of the greatest Schumann of all. By this time a guest conductor with all the world's finest orchestras, he continued to be warmly welcomed in that capacity until heart disease and rheumatoid arthritis forced him into unwilling retirement at the relatively early age of 71.

Only one thing could have tempted him out of it. He had kept his vow for 41 years, and in 1989, on the day of the first free election in Czechoslovakia, in spite of acute physical suffering, he returned to Prague and conducted the Czech Philharmonic Orchestra in three complete performances of Smetana's *Ma vlást*. 'My Fatherland', indeed.

Die meisten guten Dirigenten werden von ihren Orchestern respektiert, einige werden gehaßt, andere gefürchtet. Kubelík wurde geliebt – denn er war enthusiastisch, ein kompromißloser Idealist und ein warmherziger, großzügiger Mensch.

Er war mit einem berühmten Namen zur Welt gekommen. Sein Vater war ein virtuoser Geiger von internationalem Rang, und der Sohn wurde schon früh in die Prager Musikszene eingeführt. Bereits mit 22 Jahren wurde er Dirigent des Tschechischen Philharmonieorchesters und fünf Jahre später dessen Chefdirigent. Als 1948 die Kommunisten die Macht ergriffen, wußte er, daß seine Tage in seinem Heimatland gezählt waren. In jenem Sommer nahm er eine Einladung als Gastdirigent nach Edinburgh an und verließ die Tschechoslowakei. Er schwor, niemals in ein kommunistisch regiertes Land zurückzukehren.

Seine Wanderjahre führten ihn nach Australien und Süd- und Nordamerika, doch nach drei unglücklichen Jahren als Direktor des Chicago Symphony Orchestra kehrte er 1953 nach London zurück, wo er bereits gute Beziehungen zum Philharmonic Orchestra aufgebaut hatte. Seinen ersten großen Durchbruch in London hatte er 1954 am Sadler's Wells mit der Wiederaufnahme von Janáčeks Oper *Katja Kabanowa*. Die Nachricht von dem sensationellen Erfolg dieser großartigen Aufführung verbreitete sich auch in Covent Garden, wo man gerade verzweifelt nach einem neuen Musikdirektor suchte – und im folgenden Jahr nahm Kubelík die Stelle an.

Damit übernahm er ein Ensemble, das seit vier Jahren keinen ständigen Leiter mehr gehabt hatte. Voller Enthusiasmus machte sich Kubelík daran, ein solides Ensemble britischer Sänger aufzubauen. Dabei duldete er keine Starallüren, und als Tito Gobbi nicht zu den Proben für den *Othello* erschien, der die Saison eröffnen sollte, entließ er ihn. Trotzdem wurde der erste Abend ein glänzender Erfolg. Er führte Janáčeks *Jenufa* in London ein, dirigierte die erste vollständige Aufführung des gigantischen Meisterwerks *Les Troyens* von Berlioz und gab die britische Uraufführung von Poulencs *Dialogues des Carmélites*. Sänger, Orchester und Publikum waren ihm freundschaftlich verbunden, und was ihm als Musikdirektor an Durchsetzungsvermögen fehlte, glich er durch Enthusiasmus aus. Leider geriet seine Position jedoch durch eine chauvinistische Hexenjagd (angeführt von Beecham) ins Wanken, und nach nur drei Jahren ließ man es geschehen, daß diese neue und vielversprechende Leitung abgelöst wurde. Die Ironie des Schicksals wollte es, daß ausgerechnet der Ungar Georg Solti sein Nachfolger wurde.

Von London ging er nach München. Achtzehn fruchtbare Jahre lang war er dort Chefdirigent des Symphonieorchesters des Bayrischen Rundfunks und baute das Ensemble zu einem der herausragendsten Orchester Europas auf. Viele seiner besten und charakteristischsten Aufführungen wurden damals aufgenommen – Dvořák, Smetana, Janáček, Bartók, Mahler und, zusammen mit den Berliner Philharmonikern, einige der besten Einspielungen von Schumann, die wir kennen. Zu diesem Zeitpunkt war er bei allen Orchestern von Weltrang Gastdirigent und reiste in dieser Eigenschaft umher, bis ihn Herzbeschwerden und rheumatische Arthritis in dem relativ jungen Alter von 71 Jahren dazu zwangen, sich zurückzuziehen.

Nur ein Ereignis vermochte es, ihn nochmals auf die Bühne zu locken. Nach 41 Jahren kehrte er 1989 am Tag der ersten freien Wahlen in der Tschechoslowakei trotz akuter körperlicher Leiden nach Prag zurück und dirigierte das Tschechische Philharmonieorchester in drei vollständigen Aufführungen von Smetanas *Ma vlást*, Mein Vaterland.

La plupart des bons chefs d'orchestre sont respectés par les orchestres qu'ils dirigent, certains sont détestés, d'autres encore sont craints. Rafael Kubelík était adoré – pour son enthousiasme, son idéalisme auquel il se donnait sans faire de compromis, et pour la chaleur qui se dégageait de sa personnalité humaine et généreuse.

Il naîtra avec un nom déjà célèbre dans le monde de la musique. Son père était un virtuose du piano connu dans le monde entier. Rafael fut lancé sur la scène musicale de Prague à un âge très jeune ; il dirigea régulièrement l'Orchestre Philharmonique Tchèque dès l'âge de 22 ans, et en devint le premier chef d'orchestre cinq ans plus tard. Lorsqu'en 1948 les Communistes s'emparèrent du pouvoir en Tchécoslovaquie, il sut que les jours dans son pays étaient comptés : il profita d'une invitation à diriger un orchestre à Edinbourg cet été-là pour quitter la Tchécoslovaquie pour toujours, jurant qu'il n'y retournerait pas tant que règnerait un régime communiste.

Voyageant beaucoup, il se rendit en Australie et en Amérique du Sud et du Nord. Après trois années malheureuses comme directeur musical de l'Orchestre Symphonique de Chicago il rentra en 1953 à Londres, où il avait établi une relation positive avec le Philharmonia Orchestra. Il s'imposa pour la première fois à Londres en 1954, avec la reprise de l'opéra de Janáček, *Katya Kabanova* à Sadler's Wells. Le succès de cette représentation éblouissante ne passa pas inaperçu à Covent Garden où l'une des plus anciennes compagnies d'opéra londonniennes était à la recherche d'un nouveau directeur musical – et l'année suivante, Kubelík accepta le poste.

Cet opéra était resté quatre ans sans directeur permanent et avait besoin de direction et qu'on lui donne un but. Kubelík croyait passionnément à l'importance de la formation d'un ensemble de chanteurs britanniques, et ne tolérait pas les caprices de star. Il congédia Tito Gobbi qui ne venait pas régulièrement aux répétitions d'*Otello*. Cela n'empêcha pas le succès retentissant à la première. Il fit connaître le *Jenufa* de Janáček à Londres, dirigea la toute première représentation du gigantesque chef d'œuvre de Berlioz, *Les Troyens* et donna la première britannique des *Dialogues des Carmélites* de Poulenc. Il noua des liens chaleureux avec les chanteurs, l'orchestre et le public ; dans sa qualité de chef d'orchestre, il compensa sa force brutale par son enthousiasme. Malheureusement il se laissa destabiliser par une chasse aux sorcières chauviniste (avec à la tête, Beecham), et après trois ans seulement, le nouveau régime si prometteur ne put que déchoir. Ironiquement, le Hongrois Georg Solti fut son successeur.

Après Londres, il fut le principal dirigeant de l'Orchestre Symphonique de la Radio Bavaroise à Munich, pendant 18 années fructueuses. Il fit de cet ensemble relativement jeune l'un des plus remarquables d'Europe. Beaucoup de ses meilleures et plus caractéristiques représentations de ces années-là, furent enregistrées – Dvořák, Smetana, Janáček, Bartók, toutes les symphonies de Mahler, et avec le Philharmonique de Berlin quelques-uns des plus grands morceaux de Schumann. A cette époque-là, les orchestres les plus considérables l'aimaient tous pour ses qualités de chef d'orchestre. Il jouit de cet accueil jusqu'à ce qu'une maladie de cœur et de polyarthrite chronique le poussent à un isolement qu'il eut du mal à accepter, à l'âge relativement jeune de 71 ans.

Une chose seulement aurait pu le faire partir. En 1989, le jour de la première élection libre en Tchécoslovaquie, malgré une extrême fatigue physique, il retourna à Prague et dirigea l'Orchestre Philharmonique Tchèque dans trois représentations de Smetana, *Ma vlást*. « Ma Patrie », oui en effet.

LORIN MAAZEL   *1930

Maazel was the conductor with everything. Born in France but brought up in America, he made his first appearance with the New York Philharmonic Orchestra at the age of nine, and at 11 achieved the distinction of conducting Toscanini's orchestra, the NBC Symphony, and the even greater distinction of earning the commendation of its dreaded director. At 15 he formed his own string quartet, and while reading philosophy and mathematics at Pittsburgh University (and becoming fluent in four languages) studied the violin to virtuoso level. His first professional job was in the comparatively humble capacity of orchestral violinist but he couldn't be kept off the podium for long: in Italy on a research scholarship in Baroque music, he made his adult conducting début in Catania, followed it up with other appearances in Europe and in 1960, at the age of 30, became the youngest conductor, and the first American, ever to raise a baton at Bayreuth. Five years later he was appointed music director of the Deutsche Oper in West Berlin, combined it with being chief conductor of the Berlin Radio Orchestra (only just across the road from Karajan at the Berlin Philharmonic), and in 1972 succeeded Georg Szell as music director of the Cleveland Orchestra, one of the most coveted positions in the orchestral world.

You could call it meteoric, and Maazel would probably not disagree with you. He is a superbly confident, technically brilliant conductor with a powerful sense of musical style and the ability to inspire an orchestra – qualities which, as he himself confessed in 1978, he felt that he shared only with Karajan and Solti among his contemporaries. In some ways, perhaps, he is almost too gifted; he rises to the challenge of rehearsal but, as one player observed, 'gets bored when it comes to the concert'. It is a temperament that can produce variable results, yet when it works, in Mahler, Prokofiev, Verdi, Gershwin, the warmth and energy are compelling.

Curiously enough, given so intractable a personality, Maazel has an instinctive ability to establish easy communication with his players. After ten years at Cleveland, when he moved on to become general and artistic director of the Vienna Staatsoper, it was not with the orchestra (the venerable Vienna Philharmonic) that he had trouble, but with the management and the public. American efficiency and self-assurance were not well received in an organization where tradition was so highly prized, and his insistence on staging the full version of Alban Berg's *Lulu* in that bastion of reaction was the last straw. After fulfilling only half of his contract at one of the unquestioned summits of his profession, he left Vienna and in due course found his way back to Pittsburgh as music director in the town where he had started.

Yet the fickle Viennese applauded him again when he returned for later guest visits, and he has maintained flourishing contacts with all the great European orchestras, in Berlin, Paris and London. He has appeared regularly at La Scala, Milan. His recording career has gone from strength to strength, and he has been much involved in filmed opera: Joseph Losey's *Don Giovanni*, Francesco Rosi's *Carmen* and Franco Zeffirelli's *Otello* were all conducted, and brilliantly conducted, by Maazel. The meteor is still well placed in the musical firmament.

Lorin Maazel ist ein Dirigent aller Sparten. Er wurde in Frankreich geboren und wuchs in Amerika auf. Im Alter von neun Jahren hatte er seinen ersten Auftritt mit dem New York Philharmonic Orchestra. Mit elf Jahren wurde ihm die Auszeichnung zuteil, Toscaninis Orchester, die NBC Symphoniker, dirigieren zu dürfen, und er verdiente sich dabei sogar das Lob des gefürchteten Leiters. Mit 15 gründete er sein eigenes Streichquartett. Er studierte Philosophie und Mathematik in Pittsburgh (außerdem beherrscht er vier Sprachen fließend) und erlernte das Geigenspiel bis zur Virtuosität. Seine erste Stelle als Musiker war die eines einfachen Orchesterviolinisten, doch lange konnte er nicht vom Dirigentenpult ferngehalten werden: Während eines Forschungsaufenthaltes über Barockmusik gab er sein Erwachsenen-Debüt im italienischen Catina. Weitere Auftritte in Europa folgten, und 1960 wurde er mit dreißig Jahren der jüngste und zudem der erste amerikanische Dirigent, der je in Bayreuth seinen Taktstock erhoben hatte. Fünf Jahre später wurde er Musikdirektor an der Deutschen Oper in Westberlin und zugleich Chefdirigent des Berliner Rundfunkorchesters (in direkter Nachbarschaft zu Karajan an der Berliner Philharmonie). 1972 löste er George Szell als Musikdirektor des Cleveland Orchestra ab und errang damit eine der begehrtesten Positionen in der musikalischen Welt.

Man könnte das einen kometenhaften Aufstieg nennen – und Maazel würde wohl nicht widersprechen. Er ist ein äußerst sicherer, technisch brillanter Dirigent mit einem ausgeprägten Sinn für musikalischen Stil, und er besitzt die Gabe, ein Orchester zu begeistern – Qualitäten, die er, wie er 1978 selbst zugab, unter seinen Zeitgenossen nur mit Karajan und Solti teilt. Vielleicht ist er sogar zu begabt. Er stellt sich zwar der Herausforderung der Probe, aber – wie ein Musiker beobachtete – „wenn es zum Konzert kommt, langweilt er sich". Ein solches Temperament führt zu ganz unterschiedlichen Ergebnissen, wenn es jedoch gelingt – bei Mahler, Prokofjew, Verdi und Gershwin – dann entfaltet es eine überwältigende Kraft und Gefühlstiefe.

Maazel ist zwar eine eigensinnige Persönlichkeit, aber es fällt ihm leicht, ein gutes Verhältnis zu seinen Musikern aufzubauen. Als er Cleveland nach zehn Jahren verließ, um Generalmusikdirektor und künstlerischer Leiter der Wiener Staatsoper zu werden, hatte er dort keine Schwierigkeiten mit dem Orchester (den ehrwürdigen Wiener Philharmonikern), sondern mit dem Management und dem Publikum. Amerikanische Effektivität und Selbstgewißheit wurden von einer Organisation, die sich der Tradition verpflichtet sah, nicht gut aufgenommen. Daß er darauf bestand, in dieser konservativen Bastion die vollständige Fassung von Bergs *Lulu* auf die Bühne zu bringen, brachte das Faß zum Überlaufen. Auf diesem fraglosen Gipfelpunkt seiner Laufbahn verließ er Wien, nachdem er seinen Vertrag erst zur Hälfte erfüllt hatte. Bald fand er seinen Weg zurück nach Pittsburgh und wurde Musikdirektor in jener Stadt, in der seine Karriere begonnen hatte.

Bei seinen späteren Gastauftritten überschütteten ihn die wankelmütigen Wiener wieder mit Applaus, und Maazel blieb mit allen großen europäischen Orchestern in Berlin, Paris und London in gutem Kontakt. Er trat auch regelmäßig an der Mailänder Scala auf. Zunehmend wichtiger wurde seine Arbeit in Aufnahmestudios, und er beteiligte sich intensiv an Opernverfilmungen. Joseph Loseys *Don Giovanni*, Francesco Rosis *Carmen* und Zeffirellis *Othello*, alle wurden sie von Maazel auf brillante Weise dirigiert. Der Komet leuchtet noch immer am musikalischen Firmament.

Lorin Maazel peut tout diriger. Né en France, mais élevé aux États-Unis, il fit sa première apparition avec le New York Philarmonic Orchestra à l'âge de neuf ans. À 11 ans il se voyait accorder par Toscanini lui-même l'honneur de diriger ses musiciens, l'Orchestre symphonique de la NBC. Ce directeur tant redouté lui fit un second honneur en le couvrant d'éloges. À 15 ans, Lorin Maazel forme son propre quatuor à cordes et, pendant qu'il révise sa philosophie et les mathématiques à l'université de Pittsburgh (il parle couramment quatre langues), il étudie le violon et se montre un soliste d'une grande virtuosité. Son premier emploi comme second violon paraissait bien modeste par rapport à son talent et ne pouvait le tenir plus longtemps éloigné du pupitre de chef d'orchestre. En Italie, où une bourse d'études lui est accordée pour poursuivre des recherches sur la musique baroque, il fait ses débuts d'adulte dans la direction d'orchestre à Catane, en Sicile, puis continue sur sa lancée par une série de concerts en Europe pour devenir en 1960, à 30 ans seulement, le plus jeune chef et le premier Américain à diriger au Festival de Bayreuth. Cinq ans plus tard, il est nommé directeur musical à l'Opéra de Berlin-Ouest, fonction qu'il allie à celle de premier chef de l'Orchestre de la radio de Berlin (juste en face du Philharmonique de Karajan). En 1972, il succède à George Szell comme directeur musical pour l'Orchestre de Cleveland, l'un des postes les plus convoités dans le monde.

Éblouissant, foudroyant ! Ce sont sans doute les termes qui conviennent pour le décrire, et ce n'est probablement pas lui qui nous contredira. Superbement sûr de lui, techniquement brillant, doté d'un sens magistral du style et capable d'inspirer tout un orchestre, Lorin Maazel avoua lui-même en 1978 n'avoir rencontré ces qualités que chez ses contemporains Karajan et Solti. Il est peut-être même trop doué ! Comme le fit remarquer un musicien, s'il relève avec éclat le défi que constituent pour lui les répétitions, « il s'ennuie au concert ». Ses humeurs peuvent produire les résultats les plus variés, mais lorsque tout fonctionne comme il l'entend, comme c'est le cas, par exemple, pour ses interprétations de Mahler, Prokofiev, Verdi ou Gershwin... Quelle chaleur, quelle puissance !

Aussi bizarre que cela puisse paraître, son caractère difficile ne l'a jamais empêché d'avoir un sens inné de la communication ni de s'entendre facilement avec ses musiciens. Après dix ans passés à Cleveland, lorsqu'il devint directeur artistique et directeur général du Staatsoper de Vienne, ce n'est pas avec l'orchestre qu'il eut des problèmes, mais avec l'administration et le public. Son efficacité et son assurance toute américaine furent très mal perçues dans ce temple de la tradition. Son insistance à vouloir donner, dans son intégralité, l'opéra *Lulu* d'Alban Berg au sein de ce bastion réactionnaire fit déborder le vase. Seulement arrivé à mi-contrat, mais atteignant alors sans conteste l'un des sommets de sa carrière, il quitte Vienne et retrouve naturellement le chemin de Pittsburgh pour devenir directeur de la musique dans cette ville même où il débuta.

Le public viennois, dans son inconstance, l'applaudira toutefois à nouveau lors de ses divers passages en tant qu'invité dans la capitale autrichienne. Maazel a d'ailleurs toujours gardé d'excellents contacts avec les grandes formations européennes de Berlin, Londres ou Paris, et s'est aussi souvent rendu à la Scala de Milan. Sa discographie n'a fait qu'aller de succès en succès et il a participé aux plus grands des opéras filmés. Le *Don Giovanni* de Losey, *La Carmen* de Rosi ou l'*Otello* de Zefirelli... Tous étaient dirigés, et de main de maître, par un Lorin Maazel qui continue à frapper le monde de la musique de ses géniales étincelles.

Lorin Maazel in performance, November 1970.

Lorin Maazel im Konzert, November 1970.

Lorin Maazel en concert, novembre 1970.

IGOR MARKEVICH IGOR MARKEWITSCH IGOR MARKÉVITCH
1912–1983

Markevich was Diaghilev's last discovery. He had been born of Russian parents who moved to Switzerland when he was only two years old, and he began playing the piano and composing when he was still a child. One of his early compositions was heard by the great French pianist Alfred Cortot, and at the age of 14 he was sent to Paris where he studied the piano with Cortot and composition with Nadia Boulanger, the most inspiring and influential teacher of her day.

It was at this stage, 'youthful, birdlike and brittle', that he attracted the attention of the great Russian impresario, then nearing the end of his stormy and eventful life. Diaghilev had unbounded confidence in the talents of his new protégé, and did his best to stimulate the interest of his many influential colleagues. He commissioned a piano concerto from him and arranged for it to be performed as an interlude in one of the Ballets Russes programmes at Covent Garden: its tepid reception disappointed him bitterly but he continued his support for Markevich who responded by composing a ballet for Diaghilev's company. But Diaghilev died before it was ready to be performed.

By this time, however, Markevich had become known in progressive musical circles as the latest boy wonder, and the works which followed were received with interest and sometimes enthusiasm. In 1930, at the age of 18, he made his professional début as a conductor, and from then on divided his time between composing and conducting. He took time off to study advanced conducting technique with that formidable champion of contemporary music, Hermann Scherchen, and made occasional appearances as a pianist as well. But his own compositions never really reached the level that was expected of him in his earlier years. They were brilliantly accomplished, technically interesting and full of imaginative ideas in a generally French, rather Stravinskian way. Diaghilev had thought them 'very exceptional stuff – still very green, but enormously gifted', but maybe Prokofiev was nearer the mark when he said, 'It's as if someone were engaged in acoustical experiments with the instruments of the orchestra.'

Whatever the reason, Markevich's composing career more or less petered out at the end of the 1930s, and after the war (which he spent in Italy) he concentrated instead on conducting and teaching, becoming director of the Maggio Musicale at Florence and later holding resident appointments in Stockholm, Montreal, Havana, Paris, Madrid and Monte Carlo. These were not big star jobs, any of them, but then Markevich was never a big star conductor. Instead he developed an enviable reputation as a musician of exceptional intelligence, vigorous temperament and great integrity in his treatment of instrumental detail. Though his repertory was surprisingly wide ranging, and his many recordings cover the whole of the romantic 19th and early 20th centuries (with an unexpected Haydn *Creation* or Cherubini *Requiem* thrown in for good measure), he was very much a contemporary conductor, utterly unsentimental, and a magnificent interpreter of Stravinsky. His recording of *Le sacre du printemps* remains one of the great classics of its day.

Igor Markevich rehearsing a Mozart piano concerto with the London Symphony Orchestra, 23 February 1965.

Igor Markevich probt mit dem London Symphony Orchestra ein Klavierkonzert von Mozart, 23. Februar 1965.

Igor Markevich répétant un concerto pour piano de Mozart avec le London Symphony Orchestra, le 23 février 1965.

Igor Markewitsch war Diaghilews letzte Entdeckung. Markewitsch war russischer Abstammung (seine Familie siedelte in die Schweiz über, als er zwei Jahre alt war), und schon als Kind begann er, Klavier zu spielen und zu komponieren. Nachdem eine seiner frühen Kompositionen dem großen französischen Pianisten Alfred Cortot zu Ohren gekommen war, wurde Markewitsch im Alter von vierzehn Jahren nach Paris geschickt, um bei Cortot zu lernen und Kompositionslehre bei Nadia Boulanger, der anregendsten und einflußreichsten Lehrerin ihrer Zeit, zu studieren.

In diesem Stadium, „jung, vogelartig und zerbrechlich", zog er die Aufmerksamkeit des großen russischen Impresario auf sich, der sich bereits dem Ende seines stürmischen und ereignisreichen Lebens näherte. Diaghilew hatte unbegrenztes Vertrauen in die Talente seines neuen Schützlings und tat sein Bestes, um seine vielen einflußreichen Kollegen für ihn zu interessieren. Er ließ ihn ein Klavierkonzert schreiben und sorgte dafür, daß es als Zwischenspiel im Programm seiner Ballets Russes in Covent Garden aufgeführt wurde: Die zurückhaltende Rezeption enttäuschte ihn sehr, aber er unterstützte Markewitsch weiterhin. Der antwortete mit einer Ballett-Komposition für Diaghilews Truppe. Bevor sie jedoch aufgeführt werden konnte, starb Diaghilew.

Dennoch war Markewitsch inzwischen in progressiven musikalischen Kreisen als das neueste Wunderkind bekannt geworden, und seine folgenden Arbeiten wurden mit Interesse und gelegentlich sogar mit Begeisterung aufgenommen. Im Alter von achtzehn Jahren gab er 1930 sein professionelles Debüt als Dirigent und teilte von da an seine Zeit zwischen dem Komponieren und dem Dirigieren auf. Er machte sich schließlich von seinen Verpflichtungen frei, um beim Meister der zeitgenössischen Musik, Hermann Scherchen, fortgeschrittene Dirigier-Technik zu studieren. Gelegentlich trat er auch als Pianist auf. Seine eigenen Kompositionen erreichten jedoch nie das Niveau, das man in jüngeren Jahren von ihm erwartet hatte. Sie waren brillant aufgebaut, technisch interessant und voller kreativer Ideen in einer eher französischen, an Strawinsky erinnernden Manier. Diaghilew hatte sie für „sehr außergewöhnlich – noch sehr grün, aber unglaublich begabt" gehalten, aber Prokofjew traf es vielleicht genauer als er sagte: „Es klingt, als mache jemand akustische Experimente mit den Orchesterinstrumenten."

Aus welchem Grund auch immer, Markewitschs Laufbahn als Komponist lief Ende der 30er Jahre aus. Nach dem Krieg (den er in Italien verbrachte) konzentrierte er sich statt dessen auf das Dirigieren und die Lehre und wurde Direktor des Maggio Musicale in Florenz. Später hatte er vorübergehende Verträge mit Stockholm, Montreal, Havanna, Paris, Madrid und Monte Carlo. Es waren keine großen Starauftritte, aber Markewitsch war auch nie ein Stardirigent. Statt dessen erwarb er sich den beneidenswerten Ruf eines Musikers von außergewöhnlicher Intelligenz, lebhaftem Temperament und großer Integrität in seinem kenntnisreichen Umgang mit den einzelnen Orchesterstimmen. Obwohl sein Repertoire erstaunlich weit gefächert war und seine vielen Platteneinspielungen alle romantischen Werke des 19. und frühen 20. Jahrhunderts abdeckten (mit überraschenden Einsprengseln wie der *Schöpfung* von Haydn und Cherubinis *Requiem*), war er doch hauptsächlich ein Dirigent zeitgenössischer Werke, gänzlich unsentimental, und ein hervorragender Interpret von Strawinsky. Seine Aufnahme von *Le sacre du printemps* gehört zu den großen Klassikern seiner Zeit.

Markévitch fut la dernière découverte de Diaghilev. Né de parents russes émigrés en Suisse alors qu'il n'avait que deux ans, il commença à jouer du piano et à composer dès son plus jeune âge. À l'écoute de l'une de ses premières pièces, Alfred Cortot, pianiste fondateur de l'École normale de musique, le prend pour élève. Il a quatorze ans et part ainsi à Paris étudier le piano avec Cortot et la composition avec Nadia Boulanger, l'une des professeurs les plus influentes de l'époque.

Encore « petit oiseau fragile », il attire déjà l'attention du grand mécène russe, Diaghilev, arrivé au crépuscule d'une vie riche et mouvementée. Diaghilev vouait une confiance sans limites aux talents de son jeune protégé. Il fit tout ce qui était en son pouvoir pour aiguiser l'intérêt de ses nombreux et influents confrères. Il organisa, par exemple, pour lui un concerto pour piano en s'arrangeant pour qu'il soit donné en interlude des Ballets russes à Covent Garden et, si l'accueil mitigé du public londonien le déçut profondément, il n'en continua pas moins à soutenir Markévitch, qui lui rendit ce dévouement en composant pour lui un ballet. Malheureusement, le créateur des Ballets russes mourut avant que l'œuvre ne puisse être montée.

Entre-temps, Markévitch était peu à peu devenu le dernier petit génie des cercles de musique progressistes. Les œuvres qui allaient suivre étaient maintenant accueillies avec plus d'intérêt, voire avec enthousiasme. Il fait ses débuts en tant que chef d'orchestre professionnel à 18 ans, en 1930, année à partir de laquelle il partagera désormais son temps entre la composition et la direction. Il s'accorda quelques congés « sabbatiques » pour mieux étudier les techniques novatrices de direction avec ce formidable bienfaiteur de la musique contemporaine qu'était Hermann Scherchen, fit occasionnellement des apparitions au piano, mais ses propres compositions n'atteignirent jamais les espérances qu'il avait éveillées dans sa jeunesse. Elles étaient certes brillamment écrites, techniquement intéressantes et pleines d'imagination, d'un style globalement français relevé d'une petite touche de Stravinski, et Diaghilev les trouvait tout à fait exceptionnelles, encore si jeunes, mais si talentueuses. Prokofiev était cependant peut-être plus près de la vérité lorsqu'il disait : « C'est un peu comme si quelqu'un faisait des expériences acoustiques avec tous les instruments de l'orchestre. »

Quelle qu'en soit la raison, sa carrière de compositeur fit plus ou moins long feu à la fin des années 30 et, une fois la guerre terminée, il se consacra à la direction et à l'enseignement, devenant directeur du Mai musical de Florence (il avait passé les années de guerre en Italie), puis occupant divers postes de résident à Stockholm, Montréal, La Havane, Paris, Madrid et Monte-Carlo. Il ne s'agissait sûrement pas de prestigieuses fonctions réservées aux stars de la musique classique, mais Markévitch n'a jamais été une star. Il s'est simplement forgé une solide réputation, que beaucoup pourraient lui envier, celle d'un musicien intelligent, au tempérament vif et d'une grande intégrité dans son travail méticuleux des instruments. Même si son répertoire était étonnamment varié et si ses nombreux enregistrements couvrent toute la période romantique du XIXe et le début du XXe siècle (avec, en surprise, *Die Schöpfung* de Haydn et le *Requiem* de Cherubini), il aura surtout marqué l'histoire de la musique en tant que chef d'orchestre contemporain, totalement asentimental et interprétant à merveille Stravinski. Son enregistrement du *Sacre du printemps* reste d'ailleurs l'un des grands classiques de notre temps.

PIERRE MONTEUX 1875-1964

In 1961, at the age of 86, Pierre Monteux became chief conductor of the London Symphony Orchestra on a 25-year contract – renewable by agreement – and for the last three years of his life his portly, Poirot-esque figure and luxuriant French moustache became familiar features of the London concert platform. By this time the immense number of his recordings, made mainly during his 16 years at San Francisco (he became an American citizen in 1942) as well as in Boston, Paris, Amsterdam and Vienna, had already established a formidable reputation in Europe. But for longer still his name had been deeply embedded in musical legend as the conductor of Diaghilev's Ballets Russes, responsible in that capacity for the first performances of Stravinsky's *Petrushka*, Ravel's *Daphnis et Chloé*, Debussy's *Jeux* and, above all, *Le sacre du printemps* ('The Rite of Spring').

The uproar which broke out at this famous 'succès à scandale' in Paris has been described by many people, but Stravinsky himself remembered Monteux at the conductor's desk 'apparently impervious and as nerveless as a crocodile', adding, 'it is still almost incredible to me that he actually brought the orchestra through to the end'. To the end of his life Monteux retained the same undemonstrative, compact manner before an orchestra, preferring to expend time and concentration at rehearsals in order to produce results. But Stravinsky later described how, after the extremely successful first concert performance of *Le sacre* which Monteux also conducted, he jumped on to the stage and hugged the conductor 'who was a river of perspiration; it was the saltiest hug of my life' – which shows that an undemonstrative manner does not necessarily indicate lack of energy.

A man who enjoyed the good things of life, he had the common touch: in San Francisco the trolley-car drivers all greeted him by name, and wherever he conducted he was regarded with respect. He was unfailingly considerate to players, and always eager to encourage young talent: he set up two schools of conducting, one in Paris, and later another at his home in the United States. His own performances retained the freshness of youth and, in spite of the hundreds of recordings that he made, he hated the recording process for its lack of spontaneity.

He hated to be type-cast. He loved the great German repertory, particularly Beethoven and Brahms (though his Mozart was not to every critic's taste) and he gave powerful accounts of the Tchaikovsky symphonies. All the same, it is with the French school, and with Stravinsky, that his name is inevitably linked, and anybody who heard him conduct Berlioz's *Symphonie fantastique*, or Debussy's *La Mer*, or *Daphnis et Chloé* will understand why. This, after all, was the soil from which he sprang. He was born in the same year as Ravel, seven years before Stravinsky and only 13 after Debussy; one can only record with amazement and delight that he conducted a performance of *Le sacre du printemps* in London on the 50th anniversary of its première in 1963.

Pierre Monteux after the 50th anniversary performance of *Le sacre du printemps* at the Royal Festival Hall, London, 29 May 1963.

Pierre Monteux nach der Jubiläumsaufführung von *Le sacre du printemps* zum 50. Jahrestag der Uraufführung in der Royal Festival Hall, 29. Mai 1963.

Pierre Monteux après la représentation du cinquantenaire du *Sacre du printemps*, au Royal Festival Hall à Londres, le 29 mai 1963.

1961, im Alter von 86 Jahren, unterzeichnete Pierre Monteux einen Vertrag mit 25jähriger Laufzeit als Chefdirigent des London Symphony Orchestra – verlängerbar nach Vereinbarung. In den letzten drei Jahren seines Lebens wurde seine stattliche Erscheinung mit dem großen französischen Schnurrbart, die ein bißchen an Poirot erinnerte, ein vertrauter Anblick auf der Londoner Konzertbühne. Zu dieser Zeit war er bereits mit zahlreichen Aufnahmen in Europa berühmt geworden. Die meisten davon entstanden in San Francisco (er lebte 16 Jahre dort; 1942 wurde er amerikanischer Staatsbürger), aber auch in Boston, Paris, Amsterdam und Wien. Sein Name war jedoch bereits viel früher aufs engste mit der Musikgeschichte verwoben, denn er dirigierte seinerzeit Diaghilews Ballets Russes und war verantwortlich für die ersten Aufführungen von Strawinskys *Petruschka*, Ravels *Daphnis et Cloé*, Debussys *Jeux* und vor allem *Le sacre du printemps*.

Der Aufruhr nach diesem berühmten „succès à scandale" in Paris ist vielfach beschrieben worden. Strawinsky selbst erinnerte sich, daß Monteux „offensichtlich unzugänglich und ungerührt wie ein Krokodil" am Dirigentenpult gestanden habe, und er fügte hinzu: „Ich kann es immer noch kaum glauben, daß er das Orchester tatsächlich bis zum Ende geführt hat." Bis zuletzt bewahrte sich der Dirigent diese Ruhe und Festigkeit gegenüber dem Orchester während der Aufführungen. Er zog es vor, Zeit und Energie auf die Proben zu verwenden, um die entsprechenden Ergebnisse zu erzielen. Strawinsky erzählte jedoch später, wie er nach der außerordentlich erfolgreichen ersten Konzertaufführung von *Le sacre* auf die Bühne sprang, um den Dirigenten zu umarmen, „der ein einziger Strom aus Schweiß war; es war die salzigste Umarmung meines Lebens". Das beweist, daß eine ruhige Art noch lange nichts über die Anstrengung aussagt.

Als ein Mann, der die guten Dinge des Lebens genoß, hatte er auch ein umgängliches Wesen. Die Taxifahrer in San Francisco grüßten ihn mit Namen, und überall wo er auftrat, wurde er respektvoll empfangen. Seinen Musikern gegenüber war er stets aufmerksam, und er bemühte sich immer, junge Talente zu ermutigen. Er eröffnete zwei Schulen für Orchesterleitung, eine in Paris und später eine zweite in seiner Residenz in den USA. Seine eigenen Aufführungen bewahrten sich eine jugendliche Frische, und selbst nach Hunderten von Platteneinspielungen verabscheute er diese wegen der fehlenden Spontaneität.

Er ließ sich nicht gern einordnen. Er liebte das große deutsche Repertoire, besonders Beethoven und Brahms (sein Mozart fand jedoch nicht bei allen Kritikern Anklang), und er beeindruckte mit kraftvollen Interpretationen der Symphonien Tschaikowskys. Dennoch bleibt sein Name unweigerlich mit der französischen Schule und mit Strawinsky verbunden. Jeder, der ihn die *Symphonie fantastique* von Berlioz, Debussys *La Mer* oder *Daphnis et Cloé* dirigieren hörte, wird verstehen warum. Dies war der Stoff, aus dem er gemacht war. Er kam im selben Jahr zur Welt wie Ravel, sieben Jahre vor Strawinsky und nur dreizehn Jahre nach Debussy. Nur mit Erstaunen und Bewunderung bleibt zu berichten, daß er 1963 in London *Le sacre du printemps* zum 50. Jahrestag der Uraufführung dirigierte.

En 1961, à l'âge de 86 ans, Pierre Monteux devint premier chef d'orchestre de l'Orchestre symphonique de Londres, avec un contrat de 25 ans, renouvelable d'un commun accord, et, pendant les trois dernières années de sa vie, sa silhouette corpulente, style Hercule Poirot, et sa luxuriante moustache française devinrent familières sur la scène musical londonienne. À cette époque, le nombre impressionnant de ses enregistrements, réalisés surtout durant ses seize ans passées à San Francisco (il devint citoyen américain en 1942), ainsi qu'à Boston, Paris, Amsterdam et Vienne, avait déjà solidement établi sa réputation en Europe. Mais depuis plus longtemps encore son nom était inscrit de façon indélébile dans la légende musicale comme chef d'orchestre des Ballets russes de Diaghilev, artisan, en cette qualité, des premières représentations de *Petrouchka* de Stravinski, de *Daphnis et Chloé* de Ravel, des *Jeux* de Debussy et, surtout, du *Sacre du printemps*.

Le tumulte qui éclata lors de ce fameux « succès à scandale » à Paris a été souvent décrit, mais Stravinski lui-même se souvient de Monteux au pupitre, « apparemment indifférent et aussi inerte qu'un crocodile », ajoutant : « Je n'arrive toujours pas à croire qu'il a vraiment mené l'orchestre jusqu'au bout. » À la fin de sa vie, Monteux conservait la même attitude peu démonstrative et « compacte » devant un orchestre, lors des représentations, préférant dépenser du temps et de l'énergie aux répétitions, pour obtenir des résultats. Pourtant, Stravinski raconta plus tard comment, après le grand succès de la première représentation en concert du *Sacre*, également dirigée par Monteux, il sauta sur la scène et serra dans ses bras le chef d'orchestre, « qui était en nage ; ce fut l'étreinte la plus salée de ma vie » – ce qui prouve qu'un comportement peu démonstratif n'implique pas nécessairement un manque d'énergie.

C'était un homme qui aimait les bonnes choses de la vie et qui était connu du grand public : à San Francisco, tous les conducteurs de trolley le saluaient par son nom et, où qu'il dirigeât, il était regardé avec respect. Il portait une considération sans faille aux musiciens et avait toujours le désir d'encourager les jeunes talents : il fonda deux écoles de direction d'orchestre, l'une à Paris et, plus tard, une autre chez lui aux États-Unis. Ses propres représentations gardaient la fraîcheur de la jeunesse et, en dépit des centaines d'enregistrements qu'il réalisa, il détestait le fait d'enregistrer à cause du manque de spontanéité qu'il entraîne.

Il avait horreur d'être catalogué. Il aimait le grand répertoire allemand, particulièrement Beethoven et Brahms (son Mozart n'était pas du goût de tous les critiques) et il donnait de puissantes interprétations des symphonies de Tchaïkovski. Son nom était, tout de même, inévitablement lié à l'école française et à Stravinski, et quiconque l'a entendu diriger La *Symphonie fantastique* de Berlioz, *La Mer* de Debussy ou *Daphnis et Chloé* comprendra pourquoi. Il est né la même année que Ravel, sept ans avant Stravinski et seulement treize après Debussy ; on peut se souvenir avec étonnement et délectation qu'il dirigea une interprétation du *Sacre du printemps* à Londres, en 1963, lors du cinquantième anniversaire de la première.

1

(1) Monteux rehearsing the London Symphony Orchestra in a piano concerto with the eminent British pianist Dame Myra Hess, 13 April 1960, and (2, 3) a year later with the Hungarian Lili Kraus at the piano, 6 April 1961. In later years Monteux had to wear spectacles while conducting, though he always said that his wife objected to his being photographed in them (so did he, actually). Doris Monteux, an American from Hancock, Maine (where Monteux eventually made his home and founded a conducting school), always spoke of him as 'the maestro'; he referred to her affectionately as 'the Eroica'.

(1) Monteux leitet eine Probe des London Symphony Orchestra für ein Klavierkonzert mit der berühmten englischen Pianistin Myra Hess, 13. April 1960. (2, 3) Ein Jahr später probt er für ein Konzert mit der ungarischen Pianistin Lili Krauss, 6. April 1961. In späteren Jahren mußte Monteux beim Dirigieren eine Brille tragen; er erzählte zwar immer, seine Frau sei dagegen, daß er damit fotografiert werde, aber das war wohl ein Vorwand. Doris Monteux, eine Amerikanerin aus Hancock, Maine (wo sich Monteux schließlich niederließ und eine Schule für Dirigiertechnik gründete) nannte ihn stets „Maestro", und er titulierte sie liebevoll als „die Eroica".

(1) Monteux en répétition avec le London Symphony Orchestra et l'éminente pianiste britannique Myra Hess, le 13 avril 1960 et (2,3) avec la Hongroise Lili Kraus, le 6 avril 1961. Dans les dernières années de sa vie, Monteux devait porter des lunettes pour diriger. Il prétendait que sa femme s'opposait à ce qu'on le photographie quand il les portait, en fait lui aussi. Doris Monteux, une Américaine de Hancock, dans le Maine (où Monteux s'installa et fonda une école de direction d'orchestre), parlait toujours de lui comme du « maestro » ; il l'appelait affectueusement « l'Héroïque ».

2

3

There are plenty of conductors who have started out as solo instrumentalists, but not many who have risen from the ranks of the orchestra itself, and very few who have been orchestral players for any length of time. Until he was 41 years old Charles Munch's entire performing experience had been as an orchestral violinist, though a very distinguished one as leader of the Leipzig Gewandhaus Orchestra under Furtwängler and Bruno Walter. When he did make his conducting début it was not in response to any professional invitation but by scraping together all the money he could and risking it on a concert for himself.

Munch (with an umlaut over the u in those days) was born in Strasbourg, so he was a German citizen at the time of the First World War, in which he fought and was wounded. But when Alsace was restored to France after the war he acquired French citizenship, and it was at least partly the fear of losing it again in the rising tide of German nationalism that decided him to give up his post in Leipzig and launch his new career in Paris. As he admitted later, that first concert in November 1932 scared the daylights out of him. But he need not have worried. His next, with the Lamoureux Orchestra, was an even greater success, and over the next 15 years he established a formidable reputation, conducting virtually all the main Parisian orchestras, forming one of his own, the Philharmonique de Paris, in 1935, and reaching the summit of French musical achievement with the appointment as director of the Société des Concerts du Conservatoire only five years into his conducting career.

Although he had toured in Europe before the war it was not until 1947 that he made his first appearance in the United States, and only two years later he was invited to succeed the veteran Serge Koussevitzky as chief conductor of the Boston Symphony Orchestra. Following Koussevitzky was not easy, but at least the orchestra Munch inherited had been drilled and bullied into an unrivalled state of technical perfection, and the players took readily to this shy, mild-mannered Frenchman, and to the freshness and spontaneity of his approach, after so many years of overbearing Russian flamboyance.

Munch was a marvellous conductor. For all his unassuming manner and relaxed attitude at rehearsal, there was a dynamism and a powerful creative urgency about his performances, combined with an acute ear for orchestral balance and a sensitive feeling for tone colour and clarity of detail and line. His repertory was broad – his Beethoven, Schubert, Brahms and Strauss could be masterly – but inevitably it was with the French composers that his particular blend of intensity, brilliance and passionate conviction found its most natural outlet. He was unrivalled in Debussy and Ravel, and he was one of the great Berlioz conductors of all time. 'The predominant features of my music', wrote Berlioz, 'are passionate expression, inward intensity, rhythmic impetus, and a quality of unexpectedness... To perform my works well... requires a combination of irresistible verve and the utmost precision, a controlled vehemence, a dreamlike sensitivity, an almost morbid melancholy, without which the essential character of my phrases is falsified or even obliterated.' It might be a description of Munch conducting.

Viele Dirigenten haben als Solisten angefangen, aber wenige sind aus den Orchesterrängen selbst aufgestiegen, und noch seltener waren sie über einen längeren Zeitraum Orchestermusiker. Charles Munch war bis zu seinem 42. Lebensjahr ausschließlich Orchestergeiger, allerdings ein sehr renommierter als Konzertmeister des Leipziger Gewandhausorchesters unter Furtwängler und Bruno Walter. Als er schließlich sein Debüt als Dirigent gab, tat er dies nicht auf eine Einladung hin, sondern indem er all seine finanziellen Mittel ausschöpfte und ein eigenes Konzert riskierte.

Munch (damals noch Münch) wurde in Straßburg geboren, war also zur Zeit des Ersten Weltkriegs deutscher Staatsbürger. Er wurde als Soldat verwundet. Als das Elsaß nach dem Krieg an Frankreich zurückfiel, nahm er die französische Staatsbürgerschaft an. Seine Furcht, sie in dem wachsenden deutsch-nationalen Trend wieder zu verlieren, trug sicher mit dazu bei, daß er sich entschloß, seine Stelle in Leipzig aufzugeben und in Paris einen Neubeginn zu wagen. Wie er später zugab, hatte er bei seinem ersten Konzert im November 1932 furchtbare Angst. Aber er hätte sich nicht sorgen müssen. Sein nächstes Konzert, mit dem Lamoureux Orchester, wurde ein noch größerer Erfolg, und in den nächsten fünfzehn Jahren erwarb sich Munch einen hervorragenden Ruf. Er dirigierte alle wichtigen Pariser Orchester, gründete 1935 die Philharmonique de Paris, und bereits nach einer fünfjährigen Dirigentenlaufbahn erreichte er die Spitze der französischen Musikhierarchie – er wurde Direktor der Société des Concerts du Conservatoire.

Vor dem Krieg ging er zwar in Europa auf Tournee, trat aber erst 1947 in den USA auf. Nur zwei Jahre später erhielt er das Angebot, den greisen Serge Kussewitzky als Chefdirigenten des Boston Symphony Orchestra abzulösen. Die Nachfolge von Koussewitzky war nicht leicht. Munch übernahm jedoch ein Orchester, das auf einen makellosen Stand technischer Perfektion getrimmt war, und die Musiker lernten diesen schüchternen, umgänglichen Franzosen bald schätzen. Nach so vielen Jahren anmaßender russischer Extravaganz gingen sie gern auf seinen frischen, spontanen musikalischen Ansatz ein.

Munch war ein hervorragender Dirigent. Bei aller Bescheidenheit und seiner entspannten Haltung bei den Proben entfalteten seine Aufführungen doch eine Dynamik und einen kraftvollen schöpferischen Schwung, der sich mit einem wachen Ohr für die Ausgewogenheit der Stimmen und einem sensiblen Gespür für Klangfarbe und Klarheit in Detail und Aufbau verband. Er verfügte über ein breites Repertoire – Beethoven, Schubert, Brahms und Strauss dirigierte er meisterhaft –, aber bei den französischen Komponisten fand seine einzigartige Verbindung von Intensität, Brillanz und leidenschaftlicher Überzeugung ihren natürlichsten Ausdruck. Sein Debussy und sein Ravel waren unübertroffen, und er gehört zu den größten Dirigenten der Werke von Berlioz. Berlioz schrieb: „Die wichtigsten Eigenschaften meiner Musik sind leidenschaftlicher Ausdruck, innere Intensität, rhythmischer Schwung und ein gewisser Überraschungseffekt ... Um meine Werke gut aufzuführen ... bedarf es einer Kombination von unwiderstehlicher Energie und äußerster Präzision, einer kontrollierten Vehemenz, einer traumhaften Sensibilität und einer fast morbiden Melancholie, ohne der der wesentlichste Charakterzug meiner Sätze verfälscht oder gar zerstört würde." Es klingt, als habe er Munch beim Dirigieren beschrieben.

De nombreux chefs d'orchestre commencèrent comme instrumentistes solistes, par contre peu sortirent des rangs de l'orchestre lui-même, moins encore furent à leur début exécutants orchestraux. Jusqu'à ce qu'il ait 41 ans, la seule expérience professionnelle de Charles Munch avait été celle d'un violoniste orchestral, quoique excellent premier violon, au Leipzig Gewandhaus Orchestra sous la direction de Furtwängler et de Bruno Walter. Lorsqu'il débuta comme chef d'orchestre, ce ne fut pas parce qu'il avait été professionnellement invité, mais grâce à de l'argent économisé sou par sou qu'il risqua afin de s'offrir un concert.

Munch (à l'époque Münch) est né à Strasbourg et était donc citoyen allemand au temps de la Première Guerre mondiale dans laquelle il se battit et fut blessé. Lorsqu'après la guerre, l'Alsace fut rendue à la France, il acquit la nationalité française. Ayant peur de la reperdre au moment de la montée du nationalisme allemand, il abandonna son poste à Leipzig et tenta une nouvelle carrière à Paris. Comme il l'avoua plus tard, il redouta énormément le premier concert donné en novembre 1932. Pourtant sans raison. Le suivant, avec l'Orchestre Lamoureux, eut encore plus de succès, et les quinze années suivantes lui assurèrent une énorme réputation. Il dirigea pratiquement tous les orchestres principaux de Paris, en créa un, le Philhamonique de Paris en 1935. Il atteignit le summum de toute réussite dans le monde de la musique française, lorsqu'il fut nommé directeur de la Société des Concerts du Conservatoire, seulement cinq ans après avoir commencé sa carrière de chef d'orchestre.

Bien qu'il fit des tournées en Europe avant la guerre, il dut attendre 1947 pour aller aux États-Unis. Deux ans plus tard seulement on lui demanda de remplacer le vétéran Serge Koussevitzky comme premier chef d'orchestre de l'Orchestre Symphonique de Boston. Succéder à Koussevitzky n'était pas chose aisée. L'orchestre dont hérita Munch était contraint à goûter la pure perfection technique, et les joueurs sympathisèrent tout de suite avec ce Français timide, aux manières douces, et avec la fraîcheur et la spontanéité de son approche musicale, en contraste avec leur expérience de tant d'années d'impérieuse extravagance russe.

Munch fut un chef d'orchestre exceptionnel. A toute modestie et à toute attitude détendue qui régnaient sur les répétitions, correspondaient un dynamisme et un fort besoin de création dans ses représentations, sans oublier qu'il avait l'oreille pour maîtriser l'équilibre de l'orchestre, et une sensibilité quant aux nuances de ton, à la clarté de chaque détail et ligne. Son répertoire était vaste – Beethoven, Schubert, Brahms et Strauss étaient excellents sous sa baguette – pourtant inévitablement, ce fut avec les compositeurs français que l'une de ses caractéristiques, une fusion d'intensité, d'éclat et de conviction passionnée trouva son débouché le plus naturel. Il fut incomparable dans Debussy et Ravel, et le plus grand chef d'orchestre de tous les temps pour les œuvres de Berlioz. « Les traits prédominants de ma musique », écrivit Berlioz, « sont caractérisés par une expression de passion, de profonde intensité, d'impulsions rythmiques et par de l'imprévu... Pour rendre correctement mes œuvres... il faut un mélange de brio irrésistible, et d'une extrême précision, une véhémence contrôlée, une sensibilité onirique, une mélancolie presque morbide, sans lesquelles le caractère fondamental de mes phrases serait falsifié ou même effacé. » Cela pourrait être une description de l'art de diriger de Munch.

Charles Munch with the New Philharmonia Orchestra,
3 January 1965.

Charles Munch mit dem New Philharmonia Orchestra,
3. Januar 1965.

Charles Munch avec le New Philharmonia Orchestra,
le 3 janvier 1965.

It is not often that a conductor's career is linked with a single orchestra for upwards of 40 years, but this was the case with Eugene Ormandy, who was appointed joint director with Stokowski of the Philadelphia Orchestra in 1936 and remained its sole director, and almost sole conductor, from 1938 until 1980.

Stokowski's was not an easy act to follow, and Ormandy wisely avoided the showmanship and razzmatazz of his extrovert predecessor. There was less flamboyance in the approach to musical interpretation – no more show-stopping Bach arrangements or 'improved' orchestrations of Beethoven or Stravinsky – but the romantic repertory remained his staple diet and the orchestra he inherited was the ideal instrument for its performance. It was an instrument in amazingly perfect condition, and it was Ormandy's achievement that he preserved the qualities for which it was famous, the richness of tone, the seamless texture, the plush elegance and power which Stokowski had developed during the preceding 26 years, through decades of change and decay with scarcely a blemish on its immaculately polished surface.

Though he did not have Stokowski's flair for unleashing novelties on the Philadelphian public, he continued the tradition of Philadelphia premières (notably Rachmaninov's last orchestral work, the *Symphonic Dances*, and Bartók's *Third Piano Concerto* a few months after the composer's death), and in 1965 gave the first American performance of Deryck Cooke's performing version of Mahler's *Tenth Symphony*. There was, perhaps, a certain sameness in the sound of his performances, but never any question about the technical wizardry or the satisfyingly opulent orchestral colour. If it was Stokowski who created, it was Ormandy who caressed, preserved and embalmed the Philadelphia legend.

Es kommt nicht häufig vor, daß die Laufbahn eines Dirigenten über 40 Jahre lang mit dem gleichen Orchester verbunden ist. Eugene Ormandy bildet die Ausnahme: Seit 1936 leitete er mit Stokowski das Philadelphia Orchestra und blieb von 1938 bis 1980 beinahe der einzige Dirigent des Orchesters.

Die Nachfolge von Stokowski war keine leichte Aufgabe, und Ormandy vermied klugerweise die Selbstdarstellung und den Rummel seines extravertierten Vorgängers. Seine musikalischen Interpretationen waren weniger spektakulär. Es gab keine weiteren aufsehenerregenden Bach-Arrangements oder „verbesserte" Orchestrierungen von Beethoven und Strawinsky. Ormandys Grundlage war das romantische Repertoire, und er übernahm mit dem Orchester ein Instrument, das ausgezeichnet darauf vorbereitet war. Dieses Instrument war erstaunlich perfekt eingespielt, und es ist Ormandys Verdienst, daß die Qualität dieses Orchesters konstant blieb, das für seine Klangfülle, seine Geschmeidigkeit, seine vollendete Eleganz und Kraft berühmt war. Stokowski hatte es in den vorangegangenen 26 Jahren dazu aufgebaut, und Ormandy hat es durch Jahrzehnte der Veränderung und des Niedergangs so gut geführt, daß es kaum einen Kratzer auf der makellos polierten Oberfläche erlitt.

Ormandy teilte zwar nicht Stokowskis Gespür für bahnbrechende Neuheiten, aber er führte dennoch die Premierentradition von Philadelphia fort (besonders zu nennen sind Rachmaninovs letztes Orchesterwerk *Symphonische Tänze* und Bartóks *Drittes Klavierkonzert* wenige Monate nach dem Tod des Komponisten). 1965 führte er Deryck Cookes Bearbeitung der *Zehnten Symphonie* von Mahler zum ersten Mal in Amerika auf. Vielleicht gab es da eine gewisse Gleichförmigkeit im Stil seiner Aufführungen, aber seine meisterliche Perfektion und seine virtuose klangvolle Orchestrierung standen niemals in Zweifel. War Stokowski der Schöpfer, so war Ormandy der Hüter, und er hat die Legende von Philadelphia wohl bewahrt und konserviert.

Il n'est pas fréquent que la carrière d'un chef soit liée à un seul orchestre pour plus de quarante ans ; ce fut le cas pour Eugene Ormandy, qui fut nommé directeur associé, avec Stokowski, de l'Orchestre de Philadelphie en 1936 et resta son seul directeur, et presque son seul chef, de 1938 à 1980.

Le modèle de Stokowski n'était pas facile à suivre et Ormandy évita sagement le sens de la mise en scène et le côté « tape-à-l'œil » de son prédécesseur extraverti. Il mettait moins d'éclat dans son approche de l'interprétation musicale – plus d'arrangements de Bach comme « clou du spectacle » ni d'orchestrations « améliorées » de Beethoven ou de Stravinski –, mais le répertoire romantique demeura sa « nourriture de base », et l'orchestre dont il hérita en était l'instrument idéal. C'était un ensemble en parfaite condition, et ce fut l'œuvre d'Ormandy de préserver ces qualités qui l'avaient rendu célèbre – richesse de tons, structure lisse, élégance somptueuse et puissance –, et que Stokowski avait développées les vingt-six années précédentes, au cours de décennies de changements et de déclin, sans pratiquement aucun défaut sur sa surface impeccablement polie.

Bien qu'il n'ait pas eu la perspicacité de Stokowski pour lancer des nouveautés sur le public de Philadelphie, il continua la tradition des premières (notamment l'ultime œuvre pour orchestre de Rachmaninov, les *Danses symphoniques*, et le *Troisième Concerto pour piano* de Bartók, quelques mois après la mort du compositeur) et donna, en 1965, la première représentation américaine de la version de Deryck Cooke de la *Dixième Symphonie* de Mahler. Il y avait, peut-être, une certaine similitude dans le son de ses interprétations, mais aucune critique n'est possible sur la magie technique ou la couleur orchestrale, dont la richesse faisait plaisir. Si Stokowski créa la légende de Philadelphie, c'est Ormandy qui la caressa, la préserva et l'embauma.

Eugene Ormandy rehearses the London Symphony Orchestra in Deryck Cooke's performing version of Mahler's *Tenth Symphony*, 4 November 1966.

Eugene Ormandy probt mit dem London Symphony Orchestra Deryck Cookes' Konzertfassung von Mahlers *Zehnter Symphonie*, 4. November 1966.

Eugene Ormandy fait répéter la *Dixième Symphonie* de Mahler par le London Symphony Orchestra, dans la version de Deryck Cooke, le 4 novembre 1966.

Here (3, 4, 5) Ormandy rehearses the London Symphony Orchestra in Deryck Cooke's performing version of Mahler's *Tenth Symphony*, 4 November 1966. (1) He consults Deryck Cooke at rehearsal. (2) Ormandy meets the great Russian violinist David Oistrakh after a concert by the Philadelphia Orchestra in London, 12 April 1958. Mahler's *Tenth* had been a source of romantic conjecture for many years. It was known that at his death in 1911 the composer had left substantial sketches, some more or less complete, and that he had wanted the manuscript burnt if he was unable to finish it before he died. His widow could not bring herself to do this: Alma Mahler allowed the two completed movements to be performed, and even canvassed the possibility of a performing version by such distinguished figures as Schoenberg or Shostakovich – but for the rest she jealously defended the draft score against would-be 'completers' until the English musicologist Deryck Cooke came up with a version that eventually convinced even this redoubtable lady. She gave permission for the performance of Cooke's score on condition that the American première was given by Ormandy and the Philadelphia Orchestra; this took place in November 1965.

Hier (3, 4, 5) sieht man Ormandy mit dem London Symphony Orchestra bei den Proben zu Deryck Cookes Konzertfassung von Mahlers *Zehnter Symphonie*, 4. November 1966. (1) Ormandy bespricht sich während der Proben mit Deryck Cooke. (2) Nach einem Konzert mit dem Philadelphia Orchestra in London trifft Ormandy den großen russischen Geiger David Oistrach, 12 April 1958. Mahlers *Zehnte Symphonie* hatte die Gemüter jahrelang beschäftigt. Man wußte, daß der Komponist, als er 1911 starb, einen vollendeten und einen fast vollendeten Satz sowie eine Menge Skizzen und Partiturentwürfe hinterlassen hatte und daß er darum gebeten hatte, das Manuskript zu verbrennen, falls es unvollendet bliebe. Seine Witwe konnte sich jedoch nicht dazu entschließen. Alma Mahler ließ die vollendeten Sätze aufführen und erwog sogar die Möglichkeit, eine Konzertfassung von Größen wie Schönberg und Schostakowitsch vervollständigen zu lassen – ansonsten verteidigte sie die Fragmente jedoch eifersüchtig gegen alle Übergriffe potentieller „Vollender" oder Interpreten – bis der Musikwissenschaftler Deryck Cooke seine Konzertfassung vorlegte. Sie bewies soviel Verständnis für Mahlers Stil, daß die streitbare Dame schließlich ihre Einwilligung zu der Aufführung gab – unter der Bedingung, daß die Premiere in Amerika mit dem Philadelphia Orchestra unter der Leitung von Eugene Ormandy stattfände. Im November 1965 war es soweit.

Ici (3, 4, 5) Ormandy fait répéter la *Dixième Symphonie* de Mahler par le London Symphony Orchestra, dans la version de Deryck Cooke, le 4 novembre 1966. (1) Il consulte Deryck Cooke pendant la répétition. (2) Ormandy rencontre le grand violoniste russe David Oïstrakh après un concert de l'Orchestre de Philadelphie à Londres, le 12 avril 1958. La *Dixième* de Mahler a été la source de conjectures romantiques pendant des années : on savait qu'à sa mort, en 1911, le compositeur avait laissé des ébauches substantielles, plus ou moins complètes, et qu'il voulait que le manuscrit soit brûlé s'il ne pouvait le finir avant sa mort. Alma Mahler ne put se résoudre à le faire et accepta que les deux mouvements complets soient joués et envisagea même la possibilité de les faire interpréter par deux personnages aussi distingués que Schoenberg ou Chostakovitch. Mais, pour le reste, elle défendit jalousement le brouillon de la partition contre de prétendus « compléteurs », jusqu'à ce que le musicologue anglais Deryck Cooke lui présente une version qui finit par la convaincre. Elle autorisa l'interprétation de la partition de Cooke, à condition que la première américaine soit donnée par Ormandy et l'Orchestre de Philadelphie ; ce qui fut fait en novembre 1965.

1

3

2

4

5

ANDRÉ PREVIN *1929

September in the rain, *Just one of those things*, a handful of brilliantly inventive jazz piano recordings on 10-inch 78s – that was all we knew of André Previn in London in the 1950s. So it was something of a surprise, some 15 years later, to find him turning up as principal conductor of London's oldest established and most respected symphony orchestra.

His name may have sounded French but he was an American citizen, from a family of Russian-Jewish origin, actually born Andreas Ludwig Priwin in Berlin. (As a child he heard Furtwängler conduct the Berlin Philharmonic.) But when he was ten the family emigrated to the United States, where an uncle was music director for Universal Studios in Hollywood. By then Andreas had already studied the piano at both the Berlin Hochschule für Musik and the Paris Conservatoire; in California he studied composition (writing film scores before he left school), made a name for himself as a jazz pianist and became what must have been the youngest ever musical director for MGM. A brief period of study under the great French conductor Pierre Monteux awakened ambitions dormant perhaps since Berlin, but film continued to dominate his life during the 1950s; it was not till 1962 that he made his professional conducting début with the St Louis Symphony Orchestra.

St Louis lasted five years, and then, when he was only a year into a new job at Houston, came the London offer. It was a surprise appointment, this cosmopolitan whizz-kid from Hollywood with his jazzy background and film-star wife (he had married Mia Farrow along the line), but the London Symphony Orchestra had already had some experience of him in recordings – particularly in the romantic Russian masterpieces in which he specialized – and were anyhow in urgent need of a high-profile music director to help rebuild a faltering commercial image. And he certainly gave them value for money.

His experience of the wider orchestral repertory was limited: there were stories of symphonic scores being desperately studied on night flights between Houston and London, and not all his earlier London concerts were free of criticism. But Previn has always been a workaholic, and his instinctive grasp of idiom and style has stood him in good stead. Surprisingly, he became a great advocate for contemporary English music; he was the first conductor in the generation after Vaughan Williams's death to tackle the symphonies with fresh dedication and understanding, and his performances of Walton, particularly the *First Symphony*, earned him the composer's warm approval and friendship. Above all, his name and the publicity that somehow always seemed to surround him attracted a new and enthusiastic audience for 'classical' concerts – he came across with terrific effect on television.

Previn may not be the most profound of conductors, but he is a wonderful music-maker. In his hands the score comes alive, with a freshness and vividness that compel you to listen. And he remains an astonishing all-round musician: it is not every jazz pianist, after all, who is invited to conduct Mozart concertos from the keyboard by the Vienna Philharmonic Orchestra – or indeed to record the whole series of the Strauss tone poems by the same venerable organization. His later conducting appointments in Pittsburgh and Los Angeles have not interrupted his relationship with London, where he has maintained another long association with the Royal Philharmonic Orchestra and the British public.

September in the rain, *Just one of those things*, eine handvoll brillant innovativer Jazzstücke am Klavier auf alten Singles – das war alles, was wir in den 50er Jahren in London von André Previn kannten. Ihn etwa fünfzehn Jahre später als Chefdirigenten des ältesten und respektabelsten Londoner Symphonieorchesters zu erleben war also eine Überraschung.

Sein Name klingt zwar französisch, aber Previn war amerikanischer Staatsbürger und stammte aus einer russisch-jüdischen Familie. Geboren wurde er als Andreas Ludwig Priwin in Berlin (als Kind hörte er die Berliner Philharmoniker unter der Leitung von Furtwängler). Als er zehn Jahre alt war, emigrierte die Familie in die USA. Ein Onkel war dort Musikdirektor der Universal Studios in Hollywood. Andreas hatte damals bereits Klavier studiert, sowohl an der Berliner Hochschule für Musik als auch am Pariser Konservatorium. In Kalifornien studierte er Kompositionslehre (und schrieb schon damals Filmmusiken), machte sich einen Namen als Jazzpianist und wurde der wohl jüngste Musikdirektor von MGM. Eine kurze Zeit bei dem großen französischen Dirigenten Pierre Monteux weckte Ambitionen, die vielleicht seit Berlin schlummerten. Während der 50er Jahre blieb sein Leben aber weiterhin vom Film bestimmt. Erst 1962 gab er mit dem St. Louis Symphony Orchestra sein Dirigentendebüt.

Er blieb fünf Jahre dort, bevor er nach Houston ging. Er hatte die neue Stelle erst ein Jahr, da kam ein Angebot aus London. Die Offerte an diesen Weltenbummler aus Hollywood mit seiner Jazzvergangenheit, der obendrein einen Filmstar geheiratet hatte (Mia Farrow), war überraschend, aber das London Symphony Orchestra hatte ihn schon bei mehreren Aufnahmen kennengelernt – insbesondere mit den Meisterwerken der russischen Romantik, auf die er spezialisiert war – und brauchte in jedem Fall dringend einen namhaften Musikdirektor, um sein bröckelndes Image wiederherzustellen. Previn enttäuschte ihre Erwartungen nicht.

Seine Erfahrungen mit dem größeren Orchesterrepertoire waren begrenzt. Es gibt Geschichten über eifrig studierte Symphoniepartituren auf den Nachtflügen zwischen Houston und London, und nicht all seine frühen Londoner Konzerte blieben frei von Kritik. Previn konnte jedoch verbissen und sehr konzentriert arbeiten, und seine natürliche Stilsicherheit und sein Einfühlungsvermögen standen ihm zur Seite. Überraschenderweise entwickelte er sich zu einem großen Fürsprecher der zeitgenössischen englischen Musik. Er war der erste Dirigent in der Generation nach Vaughan Williams Tod, der die Symphonien mit Hingabe und Verständnis behandelte. Seine Aufführungen von Waltons Werken, besonders der *Ersten Symphonie*, trugen ihm den zustimmenden Applaus und die Freundschaft des Komponisten ein. Vor allem aber interessierten sein Name und seine Bekanntheit ein neues begeisterungsfähiges Publikum für „klassische" Konzerte – im Fernsehen feierte er gewaltige Erfolge.

Previn gehört vielleicht nicht zu den tiefgründigsten Dirigenten, aber er ist ein wunderbarer Musiker. Unter seinen Händen erwachen die Partituren zum Leben, und die Musik entfaltet eine Frische und Lebendigkeit, die zum Zuhören zwingt. Previn bleibt ein erstaunlicher Allround-Musiker. Nicht jeder Jazzpianist wird dazu eingeladen, vor den Wiener Philharmonikern Mozart zu dirigieren – oder gar mit diesem ehrwürdigen Orchester alle Lieder von Strauss aufzunehmen. Später dirigierte er auch in Pittsburgh und Los Angeles, aber sein Kontakt zu London brach nicht ab, so daß ihn eine langjährige Beziehung mit dem Royal Philharmonic Orchestra und dem englischen Publikum verbindet.

September in the rain, *Just one of those things*, une poignée de superbes morceaux de jazz originaux pour piano enregistrés sur des 30 cm – c'était tout ce qu'on connaissait d'André Prévin à Londres dans les années 1950. Ce fut donc une surprise de le voir quelque 15 ans plus tard, premier chef d'orchestre de l'orchestre symphonique le plus ancien et le plus respecté de Londres.

Son nom aurait pu sembler français, mais il était citoyen américain, d'origine juive russe, né en fait à Berlin avec le nom d'Andreas Ludwig Priwin. (Enfant il entendit Furtwängler diriger le Philharmonic de Berlin.) Il avait dix ans quand sa famille émigra aux États-Unis où un oncle était directeur musical des Universal Studios à Hollywood. À cette époque-là, Andreas avait déjà étudié le piano à la Hochschule für Musik de Berlin et au Conservatoire de Paris ; en Californie, il étudia la composition (il écrivit des musiques de films alors même qu'il était encore à l'école), se fit un nom comme pianiste de jazz, et il devint probablement le plus jeune directeur musical de MGM. Après avoir brièvement étudié avec le grand chef d'orchestre français, Pierre Monteux, ses ambitions latentes, peut-être depuis Berlin se réveillèrent, mais les films continuèrent à avoir une place prépondérante dans sa vie dans les années 1950. Il fallut attendre 1962 pour le voir faire son début de chef d'orchestre avec le St Louis Symphony Orchestra.

Il resta cinq ans à St Louis, et ce fut seulement un an après avoir commencé son nouveau travail à Houston, qu'on lui offrit un poste à Londres. Embaucher ce cosmopolite personnage hollywoodien qui avait comme formation le jazz, et comme épouse une vedette de cinéma (Mia Farrow) provoqua de l'étonnement. Cependant le London Symphony Orchestra avait déjà travaillé avec lui pour des enregistrements – d'œuvres romantiques russes – et ils avaient un besoin urgent d'un directeur musical célèbre afin de redonner du tonus à une image commerciale vacillante. Ils ne devaient pas le regretter.

Son expérience quant à un répertoire pour orchestre plus large était assez limitée : on laissait entendre qu'il étudiait avec acharnement des morceaux pendant ses voyages de nuit en avion entre Houston et Londres, et les critiques de ses premiers concerts à Londres ne furent pas toujours chaleureuses. Previn vivait pour travailler et son habileté à sentir les particularités et le style lui rendit un grand service. Il devint un grand défenseur de la musique anglaise contemporaine. Il fut le premier chef d'orchestre dans la génération qui suivit la mort de Vaughan Williams à aborder les symphonies avec une telle compréhension. Il gagna l'approbation chaleureuse et l'amitié du compositeur grâce à ses interprétations de Walton, surtout de la *Première Symphonie*. Par-dessus tout, son nom et la publicité dont il semblait toujours être l'objet attirèrent un public nouveau et enthousiaste de concerts « classiques » – ses passages à la télévision eurent un effet prodigieux.

Previn n'est peut-être pas le meilleur chef d'orchestre, mais c'est un extraordinaire créateur de musique. Dans ses mains, les partitions prennent vie, avec une fraîcheur et un éclat qui vous forcent à écouter. Il reste aussi un impressionnant musicien sur toute la ligne : tous les pianistes de jazz ne sont pas invités par l'Orchestre philharmonique de Vienne, à diriger des concertos de Mozart – et tous ne sont pas non plus invités par ce même vénérable établissement, à enregistrer tous les poèmes symphoniques de Strauss. Lorsque plus tard il dirigea des orchestres de Pittsburgh et de Los Angeles, ses contacts avec Londres ne furent pas coupés, et il y maintint une autre association durable avec le Royal Philharmonic Orchestra et le public britannique.

GENNADY ROZHDESTVENSKY   GENNADI ROSCHDESTWENSKI   GENNADI ROJDESTVENSKI
* 1931

Among the first wave of musicians to emerge from Soviet Russia during the mid-1950s came David Oistrakh, Emil Gilels, Leonid Kogan, Mstislav Rostropovich and Gennady Rozhdestvensky. Of these Rostropovich and Rozhdestvensky were the youngest, and there was sometimes almost a sense of escapade when they were together during their first visits to Britain. In common with all Soviet artists at this time their public appearances were strictly monitored by the authorities back home (and no doubt on the spot as well), and at the Edinburgh Festival in 1960, when they were invited to take part in an unscheduled performance of the Haydn *Toy Symphony*, they were obviously doubtful whether they ought to accept. Eventually they did, limiting their contribution to a joint performance on the triangle (Rozhdestvensky held it and Rostropovich hit it) and obviously enjoying themselves – but at the party afterwards they were to be seen hurrying nervously away before anybody could accuse them of participation in such capitalist junketings.

Although he has toured abroad a lot since then, Rozhdestvensky never severed links with his home country, where his musical roots were formed and where he spent the first 19 years of his career as conductor and then principal conductor at the Bolshoy Theatre in Moscow. It was Mussorgsky's opera *Boris Godunov* at Covent Garden in 1970 that gave him his first experience of British orchestral players, and he had time to develop the relationship further during his three years as chief conductor of the BBC Symphony Orchestra from 1978.

On the whole they liked one another. Rozhdestvensky does not set great store by rehearsal, which often goes down well with orchestral players, but coming after Pierre Boulez and Rudolf Kempe his relaxed manner and minimal beat could sometimes cause difficulties for the BBC musicians. An instinctive, warm-hearted, essentially spontaneous artist, he relies on personal communication. 'Could you please raise your hands a little higher, we can't see your beat,' requested one player. 'What do you want to see my beat for?' replied Rozhdestvensky, 'it's all together isn't it?' Asked whether he taught conducting, 'Yes,' he said, 'but not how to wave the hands in the air!' There have been times when a little more waving might have been welcome.

Yet to see him on the rostrum, like a genial field marshal urging on his troops with gestures of encouragement, there is no doubt about his authority, or the musical intelligence that lies behind it. He was born to music (both his parents were professional musicians), and married the pianist Victoria Postnikova with whom he plays piano duets – she taking the top part, as he points out. His repertory is vast, and he is always adding to it. Along with richly idiomatic performances of the Russian classics, he has brought much little-known Russian music to the West, particularly that of the younger Soviet composers. And he has learned much in return, courageously undertaking performances of Elgar, Delius, Britten and other British composers on home ground with convincing success. But that is only natural to Rozhdestvensky. As he says, 'Music has occupied all my life, all my brain, all my heart, everything.'

David Oistrach, Emil Gilels, Leonid Kogan, Mstislaw Rostropowitsch und Gennadi Roschdestwenski gehörten zu den ersten Musikern, die Mitte der 50er Jahre aus der UdSSR kamen. Rostropowitsch und Roschdestwenski waren die Jüngsten unter ihnen, und bei ihren ersten gemeinsamen Besuchen in England konnte man zuweilen so etwas wie verhaltene Streiche beobachten. Ihre öffentlichen Auftritte, wie auch die aller anderen sowjetischen Künstler, wurden zu jener Zeit von den russischen Autoritäten (zweifellos auch vor Ort) streng überwacht. Als man die beiden während der Edinburgher Festspiele 1960 einlud, an einer unplanmäßigen Aufführung der *Spielzeugsymphonie* von Haydn teilzunehmen, waren sie offensichtlich im Zweifel, ob sie annehmen sollten oder nicht. Schließlich sagten sie zu, begrenzten ihren Beitrag jedoch auf eine gemeinsame Darbietung an der Triangel (Roschdestwenski hielt sie und Rostropowitsch schlug sie an). Sie hatten offenkundig ihren Spaß dabei – die anschließende Party sah man sie jedoch nervös und hastig verlassen, bevor irgend jemand sie für die Teilnahme an derartigen kapitalistischen Extratouren tadeln konnte.

Roschdestwenski hat seither viele Tourneen unternommen, aber die Verbindung zu seiner Heimat hat er nie abgebrochen, dort liegen seine musikalischen Wurzeln. Die ersten neunzehn Jahre seiner Laufbahn verbrachte er erst als Dirigent und später als Chefdirigent am Bolschoi Theater in Moskau. Seine ersten Erfahrungen mit britischen Orchestermusikern machte er 1970 mit Mussorgskis Oper *Boris Godunow* in Covent Garden, und 1978 erhielt er die Gelegenheit, diese Bekanntschaft zu vertiefen, als er für drei Jahre Chefdirigent des BBC Symphony Orchestra wurde.

Alles in allem war es eine harmonische Beziehung. Roschdestwenski hält nicht viel vom Proben, was für Orchestermusiker meistens kein Problem ist, allerdings hatte das BBC Ensemble mit seiner entspannten Art und dem minimalen Taktschlag nach Boulez und Kempe manchmal Schwierigkeiten. Roschdestwenski ist ein natürlicher, warmherziger und spontaner Künstler, dem persönlicher Kontakt sehr wichtig ist. „Könnten Sie bitte ihre Hände etwas höher halten, wir können Ihren Taktschlag nicht sehen", bat ein Spieler. „Warum wollen Sie ihn sehen?" antwortete Roschdestwenski, „es ist doch alles ein Ensemble, oder nicht?" Als er gefragt wurde, ob er Orchesterleitung lehre, antwortete er: „Ja, aber nicht, wie man mit den Händen in der Luft fuchtelt!" Etwas mehr Gefuchtel hätte vielleicht hin und wieder nicht geschadet.

Sieht man ihn aber am Dirigentenpult stehen wie einen genialen Feldmarschall, der seine Truppen mit Gesten antreibt, bleibt kein Zweifel an seiner Autorität, geschweige denn an der Musikalität, auf der sie gründet. Er wurde für die Musik geboren (beide Elternteile waren professionelle Musiker), und er heiratete die Pianistin Victoria Postnikowa. Mit ihr spielt er vierhändig am Klavier – wobei sie die Führung übernimmt, wie er betont. Sein Repertoire ist sehr umfangreich, und er erweitert es beständig. Im Zuge seiner ausdrucksvollen Aufführungen der russischen Klassiker brachte er auch viele weniger bekannte russische Werke in den Westen und förderte damit insbesondere jüngere sowjetische Komponisten. Aber er lernte auch vom Westen und führte in Rußland mutig und mit überzeugendem Erfolg Elgar, Delius, Britten und andere britische Komponisten auf. Für Roschdestwenski ist das nur natürlich. Er sagt es selbst: „Mein Leben, mein Verstand, mein Herz, einfach alles gehört der Musik."

La première vague de musiciens émergeant de la Russie soviétique au milieu des années 50 comprenait David Oïstrach, Emil Gilels, Leonid Kogan, Mstislav Rostropovitch et Gennadi Rojdestvenski. Rostropovitch et Rojdestvenski étaient les plus jeunes et leurs premières visites en Grande-Bretagne avaient parfois comme un goût de fugue. Une fois rentrés (et sans doute également sur le lieu même), ils étaient strictement contrôlés par les autorités – ce qui était le cas de tous les artistes soviétiques de cette époque. Aussi, quand au Festival d'Édimbourg, en 1960, ils furent conviés à prendre part à une représentation non prévue de la *Symphonie des jouets* de Haydn, ils se demandèrent s'ils devaient accepter. En fin de compte ils le fire, se limitant à une contribution commune au triangle (Rojdestvenski le tenait et Rostropovitch le frappait) et visiblement ils s'amusèrent beaucoup ; mais, à la réception qui suivit, on les vit se dépêcher de partir avant que quiconque puisse les accuser de participer à de telles « bombances » capitalistes.

Bien que, depuis, il ait effectué de nombreuses tournées à l'étranger, Rojdestvenski n'a jamais coupé les liens avec son pays, où sont nées ses racines musicales et où il passa les dix-neuf premières années de sa carrière comme chef d'orchestre, puis premier chef d'orchestre du théâtre du Bolchoï de Moscou. Il fit sa première expérience des musiciens d'orchestre britanniques avec l'opéra *Boris Godounov* de Moussorgski à Covent Garden en 1970, et il eut le temps d'approfondir cette relation pendant ses trois ans comme premier chef d'orchestre de l'Orchestre symphonique de la BBC, à partir de 1978. Dans l'ensemble, le courant passait entre les musiciens et Rojdestvenski.

Rojdestvenski fait peu de cas des répétitions, qui se passent souvent bien avec les musiciens, mais arrivant après Pierre Boulez et Rudolf Kempe, son attitude détendue et ses battements minimaux posaient parfois des problèmes aux musiciens de la BBC. Artiste instinctif, chaleureux, avant tout spontané, il compte sur la communication personnelle. « Pourriez-vous, s'il vous plaît, lever un petit peu plus vos mains, nous ne voyons pas vos battements », demanda un musicien. « Pourquoi voulez-vous voir mon battement ?, répondit Rojdestvenski, c'est un ensemble non ? » À la question de savoir s'il enseignait la direction d'orchestre, il répondit : « Oui, mais pas comment agiter les mains en l'air ! » Parfois, un peu plus d'agitation aurait été apprécié…

Cependant, à le voir sur l'estrade comme un général chaleureux encourageant ses troupes d'un geste, on n'a aucun doute sur son autorité, ou sur l'intelligence musicale qui la sous-tend. Il est né pour la musique (ses parents étaient des musiciens professionnels) et a épousé la pianiste Victoria Postnikova avec laquelle il joue des duos de piano – dont elle prend la portée supérieure, comme il se plaît à le faire remarquer. Son répertoire est vaste et il l'enrichit toujours. En même temps que de riches interprétations des classiques russes, il a apporté à l'Ouest beaucoup de musiques russes méconnues, surtout celles de jeunes compositeurs. Mais il a aussi beaucoup appris, interprétant courageusement Elgar, Delius, Britten et autres compositeurs britanniques sur leur sol, avec un succès convaincant. Mais tout cela est naturel pour Rojdestvenski. Comme il le dit, « La musique a occupé toute ma vie, tout mon esprit, tout mon cœur, tout. »

Gennady Rozhdestvensky, 17 August 1966.
Gennadi Roschdestwenski, 17. August 1966.
Gennadi Rojdestvenski, le 17 août 1966.

Gennady Rozhdestvensky, 17 August 1966.

Gennadi Roschdestwenski, 17. August 1966.

Gennadi Rojdestvenski, le 17 août 1966.

Rozhdestvensky with the Moscow Radio Symphony Orchestra,
of which he was at the time principal conductor, at a Promenade
Concert in the Royal Albert Hall, London, 1968.

Roschdestwenski, damaliger Chefdirigent des Symphonieorchesters
des Moskauer Rundfunks, mit seinem Orchester bei einem
Promenadenkonzert in der Royal Albert Hall, London 1968.

Rojdestvenski avec l'Orchestre symphonique de la Radio de Moscou, dont il était à l'époque le chef d'orchestre en titre, lors d'un
Promenade Concert au Royal Albert Hall à Londres, en 1968.

Sargent's musical background was the English choral tradition. His father was an organist and choirmaster, and his own first appointment was for ten years in a similar position at a small parish church in the English Midlands. And throughout his life, alongside the glossy conducting schedule in London, the social career with its recurring overtones of royalty, and the beloved role of 'Britain's musical ambassador' on his travels abroad, the relationship with the great choirs and choral societies of northern England continued unabated. He was at his best with amateurs, who lavished on him a devotion he could never inspire in professional orchestras and where half the ladies of the chorus were in love with him – with the result that his control of the huge forces assembled on these spectacular occasions was second to none.

On the London concert scene his slim, elegant figure, always immaculately turned out, with the ever-black hair impeccably groomed, was probably familiar to more concert-goers than that of any other conductor. His work as a popularizer of classical music began with the foundation of the Courtauld-Sargent concerts in 1928, and reached its natural climax with his appointment as chief conductor of the Henry Wood Promenade Concerts in 1948, a position he held until the end of his life. He quickly became the hero of an enormous, comparatively unsophisticated musical public, and it was under his guidance that the last night of the Proms developed into the jamboree it is today. He loved every moment of it, even if it didn't always endear him to his colleagues: when Beecham called him 'Flash Harry' the nickname stuck.

His repertory was unadventurous, with a tendency towards the standard romantics, and an occasional foray into the more spectacular choral regions. He gave the first performance of Walton's oratorio *Belshazzar's Feast*, not altogether to the composer's satisfaction, and upset him still more by his cavalier treatment of the score of *Troilus and Cressida* at its première in 1954. He did better with Vaughan Williams, whose ninth and last symphony he conducted for the first time, but generally he was not much interested in contemporary music. He was never one to agonize over musical complexities or novel ideas – at least, not of the intellectual kind.

Yet the things he did well he did very well indeed: at his best, his performances could be brilliant and exciting, and his energy and personal enthusiasm were infectious. And his personal appeal was not without its importance. There are plenty of people around today who owe their first experience of classical music to Malcolm Sargent.

Sargents musikalischer Hintergrund basierte auf dem englischen Chorgesang. Sein Vater war Organist und Chorleiter, und auch er hatte zuerst zehn Jahre lang diese Position in einer kleinen Pfarrkirche in den englischen Midlands inne. Trotz seiner glänzenden Londoner Erfolge als Dirigent, seines steilen gesellschaftlichen Aufstiegs und seiner Lieblingsrolle als „Britanniens musikalischer Botschafter" auf seinen vielen Auslandsreisen riß seine enge Beziehung zu den Chören und Gesangsvereinigungen des nördlichen Englands niemals wirklich ab. Am wohlsten fühlte er sich bei Laienmusikern, die ihn mit einer Bewunderung überschütteten, die er einem professionellen Orchester nie entlocken konnte. Besonders die weiblichen Mitglieder verehrten ihn – mit dem Resultat, daß es ihm nicht mehr gelang, diese gewaltigen Kräfte bei den entsprechenden Gelegenheiten erfolgreich zu bändigen.

Seine schlanke, elegante und stets makellos gekleidete Gestalt war dem Publikum der Londoner Konzerte vielleicht vertrauter als die jedes anderen Dirigenten. Er machte die Klassik populär. Der erste Schritt dazu war die Einführung der Courtauld-Sargent Konzerte 1928. Den konsequenten Höhepunkt dieser Entwicklung bildete seine Ernennung zum Chefdirigenten der Henry Wood Promenadenkonzerte im Jahre 1948, eine Position, die er bis zu seinem Lebensende behielt. Schnell wurde er zum Helden eines riesigen, musikalisch verhältnismäßig ungebildeten Publikums, und unter seiner Leitung entwickelte sich die letzte Nacht einer jeden „Proms"-Saison zu dem immer noch existierenden Spektakel. Er liebte es, selbst wenn ihm dies nicht immer die Wertschätzung seiner Kollegen eintrug, und als Beecham den Spitznamen „Flash Harry" (Blitzlicht-Harry) für ihn prägte, blieb er an ihm haften.

Sein Repertoire war nicht sehr wagemutig. Es hatte seinen Schwerpunkt in der bekannten Romantik mit gelegentlichen Ausflügen in die interessanteren Regionen der Chormusik. Die Uraufführung von Waltons Oratorium *Belshazzar's Feast* geriet ihm nicht ganz zur Zufriedenheit des Komponisten, und Sargents sorgloser Umgang mit der Partitur von *Troilus and Cressida* bei der Premiere 1954 enttäuschte diesen noch mehr. Mit der ersten Aufführung von Vaughan Williams neunter und letzter Symphonie hatte er mehr Erfolg, aber im allgemeinen war er an zeitgenössischer Musik nicht sehr interessiert. Er quälte sich nicht mit Problemen musikalischer Komplexität oder neuen Ideen – jedenfalls nicht auf intellektuelle Weise.

Aber wenn er Erfolg hatte, dann war es ein großer Erfolg. Seine Aufführungen konnten brillant und aufregend sein, und seine Energie und seine eigene Begeisterung wirkten ansteckend. Sein persönliches Engagement blieb ganz und gar nicht wirkungslos. Noch heute verdanken viele Sargent ihre erste Begegnung mit der klassischen Musik.

Les bases de l'éducation musicale de Sargent sont constituées par la tradition anglaise du chœur. Son père était organiste et chef de chœur, et il fit de même, pendant dix ans, dans une petite église paroissiale des Midlands anglais. Durant toute sa vie, à côté de son brillant programme de direction d'orchestre à Londres, de sa carrière mondaine – il fréquentait régulièrement les membres de la famille royale –, et de son rôle apprécié d'« ambassadeur britannique de la musique » lors de ses voyages à l'étranger, sa relation avec les grands chœurs et les chorales du nord de l'Angleterre resta inchangée. C'est avec les amateurs qu'il était le meilleur, ces derniers lui manifestant un attachement qu'il n'a jamais pu inspirer aux orchestres professionnels, aussi était-il imbattable pour contrôler les énormes effectifs rassemblés dans ces occasions spectaculaires.

Sur la scène des concerts de Londres, sa silhouette mince et élégante, toujours impeccable, aux cheveux noirs parfaitement bien coiffés, était probablement plus familière aux amateurs de concerts que celle de tout autre chef d'orchestre. Son travail de vulgarisateur de la musique classique a commencé avec la création des concerts Courtauld-Sargent en 1928, et a atteint son apogée avec sa nomination comme premier chef d'orchestre des Henry Wood Promenade Concerts en 1948, poste qu'il occupa jusqu'à la fin de sa vie. Il devint bientôt le héros d'un immense public populaire, et c'est avec lui que la dernière nuit des Promenade Concerts est devenue le grand rassemblement qu'elle est aujourd'hui. Il en adorait chaque minute, même si cela ne l'a pas toujours fait apprécier de ses collègues : quand Beecham l'a appelé « Flash Harry », le surnom lui est resté.

Son répertoire était sans surprise, avec une préférence pour les standards romantiques et quelques incursions occasionnelles du côté plus spectaculaire des chœurs. Il donna la première représentation de l'oratorio de Walton, *Belshazzar's Feast*, dont le compositeur ne fut pas complètement satisfait, et finit de le mécontenter par son traitement cavalier de la partition de *Troilus and Cressida* pour la première, en 1954. Il fit mieux avec Vaughan Williams, dont il dirigea la neuvième et dernière symphonie pour la première fois, mais il s'intéressait généralement peu à la musique contemporaine. Il n'était pas du genre à s'interroger sur les complexités de la musique ou sur les idées nouvelles – du moins, pas de façon intellectuelle.

Pourtant, ce qu'il faisait bien il le faisait vraiment très bien : quand il était très bon, ses représentations pouvaient être brillantes et passionnantes ; son énergie et son enthousiasme étaient contagieux. Son charme personnel n'était pas sans importance. Nombreux sont ceux qui, aujourd'hui, doivent leur première expérience de la musique classique à Malcolm Sargent.

Sir Malcolm Sargent in his element at the Royal Albert Hall: the Last Night of the Proms, 1966 season.

Sir Malcolm Sargent in seinem Element: beim Abschlußkonzert der „Proms" in der Royal Albert Hall, 1966.

Sir Malcolm Sargent dans son élément au Royal Albert Hall : la Dernière Nuit des Promenade Concerts, en 1966.

Sargent at a concert with the Sydney Symphony Orchestra and the Royal Choral Society at the Royal Festival Hall, 19 June 1965.

Sargent bei einem Konzert mit dem Sydney Symphony Orchestra und der Royal Choral Society in der Royal Festival Hall, 19. Juni 1965.

Sargent lors d'un concert avec l'Orchestre symphonique de Sydney et la Royal Choral Society au Royal Festival Hall, le 19 juin 1965.

(1, 3) Conducting the Hallé Orchestra at Rochdale, 1951;
(2) 1951, at the Belle Vue, Manchester – a venue more usually
occupied by a local circus. Any reference to its temporary
incumbent is purely coincidental.

(1, 3) Sargent dirigiert 1951 das Hallé Orchestra in Rochdale und,
ebenfalls 1951, im Belle Vue in Manchester, einer Zirkusarena (2).
Jede Ähnlichkeit mit der normalen Nutzung des Ortes ist natürlich
rein zufällig.

(1, 3) Dirigeant l'orchestre Hallé à Rochdale, en 1951 ; (2) au
Belle Vue, à Manchester, un lieu habituellement occupé par un
cirque local. Toute référence à son occupant temporaire n'est que
pure coïncidence.

WOLFGANG SAWALLISCH * 1923

In these days of the glossy musical supermarket there are not many conductors left who still represent the great German Kapellmeister tradition, for centuries the backbone of German musical life and the mainstay of German provincial opera. In a jet-driven age, when conductors, singers and instrumentalists can fly from one performance to another and back again within a matter of hours, the resident Generalmusikdirektor who concentrates his energies on his own company or orchestra and labours at home to produce well rehearsed, seriously good performances of a comprehensive repertory is becoming something of a rarity. Conductors like this were essentially enablers of first-class performances rather than star figures in themselves – though that is not to say that they didn't in some cases go on to make great careers. Hans Knappertsbusch, Clemens Krauss, Karl Böhm, Eugen Jochum, Rudolf Kempe were products of the Kapellmeister tradition, and Sawallisch is one of its last representatives.

Until his most recent appointment, with the Philadelphia Orchestra in America in 1992, his career was almost entirely confined to Germany: after studying in Munich, where he was born, he spent six years in Augsburg (rising rapidly from répétiteur to principal conductor), and the next ten as music director successively in Aachen, Wiesbaden, and Cologne – along the way becoming, in 1957, the youngest conductor to appear at Bayreuth (a record that was wrested from him three years later by Lorin Maazel). The next decade was more purely orchestral, divided between the Vienna Symphony Orchestra and the Hamburg Philharmonic, but in 1972 the lure of the opera house drew him back again to his home town, where he spent the next 22 years as Generalmusikdirektor of the Bavarian State Opera.

Although he is first and foremost a conductor, he is a brilliant pianist as well and has appeared often as accompanist to eminent singers – Elisabeth Schwarzkopf, Dietrich Fischer-Dieskau, Margaret Price, Hermann Prey. This ability to accompany, to cooperate with singers rather than command them, is the secret of his success: they love working with him, he likes and understands them, knows their strengths and weaknesses, breathes with them, and as a result they sing well for him. As one of them said: 'With Sawallisch, if something goes wrong on the stage in the first five minutes of an opera, you can be sure it's going to be a good performance. With many conductors it would be the opposite, but with Sawallisch it's a challenge, it puts him on his mettle. And it's very reassuring for a singer, to see Sawallisch down there in the pit, beaming and trying to help.'

He is at his best in the Viennese classics (he has recorded all the Schubert sacred choral works), the romantic 19th century, Wagner, Bruckner, maybe Hindemith, and above all Strauss – he gave virtually all the Strauss operas during his period in Munich (which is Strauss territory, after all) and his recording of *Capriccio* with Schwarzkopf as the Countess is unlikely to be superseded. Not an adventurous repertory perhaps, but one that he does marvellously well.

In der heutigen Zeit des schillernden musikalischen Supermarkts gibt es nicht mehr viele Dirigenten, die noch immer in der großen deutschen Tradition der Kapellmeister stehen, die jahrhundertelang das Rückgrat der deutschen Musikwelt und die Stützpfeiler der deutschen Provinzoper gewesen sind. Im Zeitalter des Jet-Set, wo Dirigenten, Sänger und Musiker innerhalb weniger Stunden von einer Vorstellung zur anderen und wieder zurück fliegen können, ist der ortsansässige Musikdirektor eine Seltenheit geworden – jener Musikdirektor, der seine Energien auf sein eigenes Ensemble und Orchester konzentriert und zu Hause mit ihnen an gut geprobten, wirklich hervorragenden Aufführungen und einem umfangreichen Repertoire arbeitet. Diese Dirigenten stehen weit mehr im Dienst erstklassiger Aufführungen, als daß sie selbst als Stars hervortreten – das heißt aber nicht, daß sie nie eine eigene große Laufbahn hatten. Hans Knappertsbusch, Clemens Krauss, Karl Böhm, Eugen Jochum und Rudolf Kempe kamen aus der Kapellmeistertradition, und Sawallisch gehört zu ihren letzten Repräsentanten.

Bis zu seiner erst kürzlich – 1992 – aufgenommenen Arbeit mit dem Philadelphia Orchestra in Amerika beschränkte sich der Wirkungskreis von Wolfgang Sawallisch fast ausschließlich auf Deutschland. Nach einem Studium in seiner Geburtsstadt München verbrachte er sechs Jahre in Augsburg (wo er rasch vom Korrepetitor zum Chefdirigenten aufstieg). In den nächsten zehn Jahren wurde er Musikdirektor in Aachen, Wiesbaden und Köln. Zwischendurch, im Jahre 1957, war er der jüngste Dirigent in der Geschichte Bayreuths (ein Rekord, den Lorin Maazel drei Jahre später brach). In den folgenden zehn Jahren konzentrierte er sich fast ausschließlich auf Orchestermusik und arbeitete mit dem Wiener Symphonieorchester und den Hamburger Philharmonikern. 1972 rief ihn jedoch die Oper zurück in seine Heimatstadt, und für die nächsten 22 Jahre war er Generalmusikdirektor der Bayrischen Staatsoper.

Sawallisch ist zwar in erster Linie Dirigent, aber er ist auch ein brillanter Pianist. Oft trat er als Begleitung berühmter Sängerinnen und Sänger auf – Elisabeth Schwarzkopf, Dietrich Fischer-Dieskau, Margaret Price und Hermann Prey. In dieser Fähigkeit zur Begleitung liegt das Geheimnis seines Erfolges: Er arbeitet mit den Sängern zusammen, anstatt sie zu kommandieren. Die Künstler lieben die Arbeit mit ihm, denn er mag und versteht sie, er kennt ihre Stärken und Schwächen, er ist einer von ihnen – und deshalb singen sie auch gut für ihn. Einer von ihnen sagte: „Mit Sawallisch ist es so: Wenn in den ersten fünf Minuten einer Oper auf der Bühne etwas schiefgeht, kann man sicher sein, daß es eine gute Aufführung wird. Bei vielen Dirigenten wäre es genau umgekehrt, aber für Sawallisch ist es eine Herausforderung; es ruft ihn auf den Plan. Und es ist sehr vertrauenerweckend für einen Sänger, Sawallisch da im Orchestergraben zu sehen, wie er strahlt und versucht, zu helfen."

Seine Stärken liegen in der Wiener Klassik (es gibt Aufnahmen der gesamten geistlichen Chormusik Schuberts) und der Romantik des 19. Jahrhunderts, bei Wagner, Bruckner, vielleicht Hindemith und vor allem bei Strauss. In seiner Münchner Zeit brachte er tatsächlich alle Strauss-Opern auf die Bühne, und seine Aufnahme von *Capriccio* mit der Schwarzkopf in der Rolle der Fürstin ist kaum zu übertreffen. Sein Repertoire ist vielleicht nicht gewagt, aber er beherrscht es vollkommen.

Dans cette ère de la musique clinquante de supermarché, on pourrait presque compter sur les doigts de la main les derniers représentants de la vieille tradition allemande des Kapellmeister, qui furent de tout temps les véritables piliers de la vie musicale allemande et des opéras de province germaniques. À l'heure du Concorde et des voyages effrénés des musiciens, chanteurs et chefs d'orchestre, qui volent d'un concert à l'autre, avec retour au point de départ en moins de temps qu'il ne faut pour le dire, le Generalmusikdirektor résident se fait rare, qui concentre son énergie sur son ensemble ou sa troupe et persévère dans les répétitions jusqu'à recréer pour sa ville un répertoire auquel il aura conféré sa propre beauté et sa propre richesse. Plutôt que de se mettre eux-mêmes en avant, ces hommes-là préféraient se mettre au service de la qualité des représentations qu'ils donnaient, ce qui n'exclut pas que certains aient aussi pu mener de front une belle carrière. Knappertsbusch, Krauss, Böhm, Jochum et Kempe étaient de purs produits de cette tradition, et Sawallisch est sans doute l'un des derniers à faire briller cette flamme.

Jusqu'à ce qu'il soit nommé en 1992 à la tête de l'Orchestre de Philadelphie, il se confine à l'Allemagne : il étudie à Munich, où il est né, passe ensuite rapidement du poste de répétiteur à celui de premier chef d'orchestre au cours de ses six années d'exercice à Augsbourg, puis occupe durant les dix années suivantes plusieurs postes de directeur musical – Aix-la-Chapelle, Wiesbaden et Cologne – devenant en 1957 le plus jeune chef d'orchestre à monter sur la scène du Festival de Bayreuth, un record que Lorin Maazel lui soufflera trois ans plus tard. Partageant ses talents entre l'Orchestre symphonique de Vienne et le Philharmonique d'Hambourg, il consacre la décennie qui suit à la musique purement orchestrale, jusqu'en 1972, lorsque l'opéra l'attire à nouveau dans sa ville natale. Là, il devient Generalmusikdirektor de l'Opéra national de Bavière, un poste qu'il chérira pendant 22 ans.

Wolfgang Sawallisch est avant tout un chef d'orchestre, mais il brille également au piano et on l'a souvent vu accompagner de grands chanteurs lyrique : Elisabeth Schwarzkopf, Dietrich Fischer-Dieskau, Margaret Price, Hermann Prey etc. Cette faculté qu'il a d'aller avec eux, de les suivre plutôt que de les diriger... C'est cela qui a fait son succès. Ils adorent travailler avec lui ; lui les aime, les comprend. Il connaît leurs forces, leurs faiblesses et respire avec ses chanteurs. Eux se surpassent pour leur accompagnateur. Comme disait l'un d'eux : « Avec Sawallisch, si quelque chose ne va pas dans les cinq premières minutes d'un opéra, vous pouvez être sûr que le spectacle sera excellent, tandis qu'avec la plupart des autres chefs d'orchestre, ce serait justement le contraire. Pour lui, cela devient un défi, un stimulant. Et puis, c'est très rassurant pour un interprète de voir Sawallisch rayonnant, là, dans la fosse, faisant tout son possible pour vous aider. »

Il excelle dans les classiques de Vienne – et a d'ailleurs gravé sur sillon toutes les œuvres chorales de musique sacrée de Schubert, se montre admirable avec les romantiques du XIXe tels que Wagner et Bruckner et, dans une moindre mesure, Hindemith, mais c'est surtout à Strauss qu'il offre toutes ses qualités. Generalmusikdirektor à Munich, il a dirigé pratiquement tous les opéras de Richard Strauss, ce qui est bien normal puisqu'il se trouvait sur les terres du grand compositeur. Il a notamment enregistré *Capriccio*, avec Elisabeth Schwarzkopf dans le rôle de la Comtesse, un enregistrement d'une beauté qui ne se fanera sûrement pas de si tôt. Son répertoire n'est peut-être pas très audacieux, mais il le sert merveilleusement bien.

Wolfgang Sawallisch, September 1957.

Wolfgang Sawallisch, September 1957.

Wolfgang Sawallisch, septembre 1957.

Sawallisch with the Philharmonia Orchestra, recording Strauss's last opera, *Capriccio*, with soloists (left to right) Dietrich Fischer-Dieskau, Hans Hotter, Eberhard Waechter, Christa Ludwig and Elisabeth Schwarzkopf (only just visible in this picture, but unforgettable as the Countess in this classic performance). Kingsway Hall, London, 6 September 1957.

Sawallisch und das Philharmonia Orchestra bei den Aufnahmen der letzten Oper von Strauss, *Capriccio*. Die Solisten sind (v. l. n. r.): Dietrich Fischer-Dieskau, Hans Hotter, Eberhard Wächter, Christa Ludwig und Elisabeth Schwarzkopf (auf dem Foto kaum zu erkennen, aber unvergeßlich in ihrer Rolle als Gräfin bei dieser klassischen Aufführung), Kingsway Hall, 6. September 1957.

Kingsway Hall, à Londres: Sawallisch avec le Philharmonia Orchestra enregistrant le dernier opéra de Strauss, *Capriccio*, en compagnie de (de g. à dr.) Dietrich Fischer-Diskau, Hans Hotter, Eberhard Waechter, Christa Ludwig et Elisabeth Schwarzkopf, à peine visible sur cette photo, mais inoubliable dans son interprétation de la Comtesse, le 6 septembre 1957.

1

(1) Going over the recording in the playback room, (left to right) Fischer-Dieskau, Elisabeth Schwarzkopf, Walter Legge, Wolfgang Sawallisch. (2) On the following evening, while Legge and Schwarzkopf entertain the cast of *Capriccio* at their home in Hampstead, Schwarzkopf listens with Sawallisch and Eberhard Waechter to her performance of the role of the Marschallin in Karajan's recently completed recording of *Der Rosenkavalier*.

(1) Überarbeitung der Aufnahmen im Playback-Studio (von links nach rechts): Fischer-Dieskau, Elisabeth Schwarzkopf, Walter Legge, Wolfgang Sawallisch. (2) Am nächsten Abend bei einer Party für die *Capriccio*-Besetzung im Haus der Legges in Hampstead. Die Schwarzkopf hört sich zusammen mit Sawallisch und Eberhard Wächter ihren Part der Marschallin aus der gerade fertiggestellten Aufnahme des *Rosenkavaliers* unter der Leitung von Karajan an.

(1) Repassant l'enregistrement dans la salle de lecture, (de gauche à droite), Fischer-Dieskau, Elisabeth Schwarzkopf, Walter Legge, Wolfgang Sawallisch. (2) Le soir suivant, pendant que Legge et Schwarzkopf recevaient chez eux à Hampstead, ceux qui avaient joué dans *Capriccio*, Schwarzkopf écoute avec Sawallisch et Eberhard Waechter, sa performance dans le rôle de la Maréchale du *Chevalier à la Rose* que Karajan avait récemment fini d'enregistrer.

2

There is probably no conductor today whose name is more widely known than Solti's. As principal of the Chicago Symphony Orchestra for 22 years he had to his hand one of the finest orchestral ensembles in the world; he gave with it the best part of 1,000 concerts, as well as making innumerable recordings and appearing regularly with orchestras in Vienna, Paris and London. Though a very different character and a very different type of conductor, he was the only figure who could seriously rival Karajan in the musical supermarket of the 1970s and 80s.

He got to the top the hard way. He studied in Budapest, became a rehearsal pianist at the Opera, and on a visit to Salzburg in 1937 got himself taken on by Toscanini as an assistant at the Festival. Only months later he made his operatic début in Budapest with *The Marriage of Figaro*, but during the second act news reached the theatre that Hitler had invaded Austria (with a predictable effect on the audience). Being Jewish, within a few months he was out of a job. Hoping for help from Toscanini, he went to Switzerland but found himself unable to get away, and also unable to get a work permit to conduct. So he took up the piano again and, winning a Geneva piano competition in 1942, managed to get enough teaching work to keep the wolf from the door.

The war over, he used a connection in the US occupation forces to land the appointment of musical director at the bombed-out Bayerische Staatsoper in Munich. Apart from that unhappy début in Budapest, he had never conducted opera before – 'it was several years before they realized that I was conducting everything for the first time', he commented later – but hard work kept him just ahead of his players, and after eight tough years led to his appointment as Generalmusikdirektor in Frankfurt. And then in 1959 came his London début with *Der Rosenkavalier* and two years later he became musical director at the Royal Opera, Covent Garden.

'I have only one wish,' he said when he first arrived, 'to make Covent Garden the best opera house in the world.' He certainly came nearer than anybody else to doing so – though not without blood and tears, his own as well as the company's. After the strict discipline of German theatres he found the easy-going atmosphere in London unbearable, and lost no time in saying so, in a thick Hungarian accent and with a bluntness that the orchestra found hard to accept. They nicknamed him 'The Screaming Skull'. But gradually the humanity that underlies Solti's fierce, aggressive exterior began to emerge, and the respect of the orchestra and singers increased as they saw that here was a man who really knew what it meant to be a director.

Not everybody agreed about his interpretations. The Strauss was gorgeous (including the first *Die Frau ohne Schatten* in London), there was a stunning British première for Schoenberg's *Moses und Aron* (with a naked orgy round the Golden Calf that risked apoplexy in the grand tier), fine performances of Britten, and a memorable cycle of *The Ring* (at much the same time as he was making the first ever, now classic, complete recording in Vienna). But the strong, decisive, urgent style can sound hard-driven (youthful memories of Toscanini, perhaps?), the enormous energy and unflagging search for the richest sonorities can go over the top. 'Too much control and you lose intensity,' he has said; 'too little control, and you - become rhapsodic and abandoned.' For a musician with so much power at his command the balance is not easy to achieve. But when he gets it right, in Strauss or Mahler, or the Elgar of his adopted country, the conviction and passionate involvement still carry the day.

Es gibt heute vielleicht keinen bekannteren Dirigenten als Sir Georg Solti. 22 Jahre lang leitete er das Chicago Symphony Orchestra, eines der besten Orchesterensembles der Welt, gab ca. 1000 Konzerte mit ihm und machte zahllose Aufnahmen. Er gastierte bei Orchestern in Wien, Paris und London. Obwohl er einen ganz anderen Charakter hat und anders dirigiert, war er der einzige, der im musikalischen Supermarkt der 70er und 80er Jahre ernsthaft mit Karajan konkurrieren konnte.

Solti hatte es schwer auf dem Weg nach oben. Er studierte in Budapest und wurde Probenpianist an der Oper. Bei einem Besuch in Salzburg 1937 stellte ihn Toscanini als Assistenten für die Festspiele an. Schon wenige Monate später gab er in Budapest mit dem *Figaro* sein Operndebüt, aber beim zweiten Akt drang die Nachricht in das Theater, daß Hitler in Österreich einmarschiert war (die Wirkung kann man sich vorstellen). Als Jude verlor Solti innerhalb weniger Monate seine Arbeit. Er hoffte auf Hilfe von Toscanini und ging in die Schweiz, kam aber von dort nicht weiter und erhielt auch keine Arbeitserlaubnis als Dirigent. Also spielte er wieder Klavier, und nachdem er 1942 einen Genfer Klavierwettbewerb gewonnen hatte, konnte er genug Unterricht geben, um zu überleben.

Nach Kriegsende nutzte er Beziehungen zu den amerikanischen Besatzungstruppen, um als Musikdirektor an die ausgebombte Münchner Staatsoper zu kommen, obwohl er, abgesehen von seinem unglücklichen Debüt in Budapest, nie zuvor eine Oper dirigiert hatte. „Es dauerte einige Jahre, bis sie bemerkten, daß ich alles zum ersten Mal dirigierte", kommentierte er später: durch harte Arbeit war er seinen Musikern immer etwas voraus. Der Erfolg nach acht schwierigen Jahren war seine Ernennung zum Generalmusikdirektor in Frankfurt. 1959 gab er an der Royal Opera in Covent Garden mit dem *Rosenkavalier* sein Londoner Debüt und wurde dort zwei Jahre später Musikdirektor.

„Ich habe nur einen Wunsch", sagte er bei seiner Ankunft, „ich will Covent Garden zum besten Opernhaus der Welt machen." Er kam diesem Ziel sicher näher als alle anderen, die es versucht hatten – allerdings nicht ohne Mühen und Kämpfe auf seiner Seite und auch auf seiten des Ensembles. Nach der strikten Disziplin der deutschen Bühnen fand er die lockere Atmosphäre in London unerträglich und beeilte sich damit, das auch zu sagen – mit seinem schweren ungarischen Akzent und einer Offenheit, die das Orchester nur schwer hinnahm. Sie gaben ihm den Spitznamen „Der Schreihals". Allmählich kam aber Soltis Herzlichkeit hinter der heftigen, aggressiven Außenseite zum Vorschein, und das Orchester und die Sänger respektierten ihn um so mehr, als sie erkannten, daß er wirklich verstand, was es bedeutet, Musikdirektor zu sein.

Nicht alle sind mit seinen Interpretationen einverstanden. Sein Strauss war wundervoll; es gab eine glänzende britische Erstaufführung von Schönbergs Oper *Moses und Aaron* (mit einer nackten Orgie rund um das goldene Kalb), sensible Interpretationen von Britten und einen bemerkenswerten *Ring*-Zyklus (etwa zeitgleich zu seiner ersten, inzwischen klassischen Aufnahme des gesamten Werks in Wien). Sein vehementer, entschiedener, drängender Stil kann jedoch sehr hart klingen (jugendliche Erinnerungen an Toscanini vielleicht). Die Kraft und die Bemühung um größte Klangfülle können auch übertrieben wirken. „Zuviel Kontrolle, und man verliert die Intensität" sagte er, „zuwenig Kontrolle, und es wirkt rhapsodisch und verloren." Einem Musiker mit dieser Energie fällt die Balance nicht immer leicht; ist sie jedoch gelungen – z. B. bei Strauss, Mahler oder dem Engländer Elgar –, ist das Ergebnis überzeugend und leidenschaftlich.

De nos jours, il n'y a probablement pas d'autres chefs d'orchestre dont le nom soit si connu que celui de Solti. Premier chef d'orchestre à l'Orchestre symphonique de Chicago pendant 22 ans, il avait alors l'un des meilleurs ensembles orchestraux du monde ; il donna avec celui-ci près de 1000 concerts ainsi que de nombreux enregistrements et dirigea en tant qu'invité des orchestres à Vienne, Paris et Londres. Malgré un tempérament très différent et une autre façon de diriger, il fut le seul qui pourrait sérieusement rivaliser avec Karajan dans le monde musical des années 1970 et 1980.

Sa carrière ne fut pas sans embûches. Il étudia à Budapest, fut co-répétiteur à l'opéra, et lors d'une visite à Salzbourg en 1937, fut embauché par Toscanini comme assistant du Festival. Seulement quelques mois plus tard il fit ses débuts à l'opéra de Budapest dans *Le Mariage de Figaro*. Pendant le second acte, on annonça au théâtre qu'Hitler avait envahi l'Autriche. Il était juif, et en quelques mois, il se retrouva sans travail. Espérant de l'aide de la part de Toscanini, il partit pour la Suisse mais se trouva dans une position d'immobilité et incapable d'avoir un permis de travailler comme chef d'orchestre. Il recommença alors le piano, remporta un prix lors d'un concours de piano à Genève en 1942. Il réussit à trouver assez de cours à donner pour rester à l'abri du besoin.

La guerre finie, il utilisa une de ses relations dans les forces armées de l'occupation américaine afin d'obtenir un poste de chef d'orchestre au Bayerische Staatsoper de Munich, détruit par un bombardement. Outre son triste début à Budapest, il n'avait encore jamais dirigé d'opéra . « Ce ne fut que des années plus tard qu'ils réalisèrent que je dirigeais tout pour la première fois », commenta-t-il plus tard – son acharnement au travail le rendit juste un peu meilleur que ses joueurs, et après huit années difficiles il obtint le poste de Generalmusikdirektor à Francfort. Puis vint 1959 et ses débuts à Londres avec *Le Chevalier à la rose*, et deux ans après son poste de directeur musical au Royal Opera de Covent Garden .

« Je n'ai qu'un souhait, » avait-il dit à son arrivée, « faire de Covent Garden le meilleur opéra du monde ». Il fut bien le seul à presque y parvenir, non sans que lui ou la compagnie ne verse de larmes. Après la stricte discipline des salles allemandes, il ne put supporter l'atmosphère complaisante de Londres. Il n'hésita pas à le dire avec un fort accent hongrois et sans mâcher ses mots. L'orchestre eut du mal à l'accepter. Il le surnomma « le Crâne hurlant ». Mais peu à peu la chaleur humaine enfouie sous cet extérieur agressif et implacable commença à faire surface, et le respect de l'orchestre grandit au fur et à mesure qu'il réalisèrent que Solti était un homme qui savait vraiment ce que signifiait être chef d'orchestre.

Tous ne sont pas d'accord quant à ses interprétations. Celle de Strauss était superbe ; il dirigea une éblouissante première de *Moïse et Aron* de Schoenberg (une orgie de nus autour du Veau d'Or) ; ses interprétations de Britten, ainsi que le cycle mémorable du *Ring* (tout en en faisant à Vienne, le tout premier enregistrement de l'œuvre complète). Cependant son style fort, décidé, et pressant peut paraître dur à l'oreille (souvenirs de jeunesse avec Toscanini, peut-être ?), et son énorme énergie et sa recherche infatigable de sonorités riches peuvent parfois aller trop loin. « Trop de contrôle, et vous perdez de l'intensité, » dit-il, « trop peu de contrôle, et vous devenez rhapsodique et délaissé ». Pour quelqu'un qui a tellement d'énergie à sa disposition, l'équilibre n'est pas facile à ajuster. Mais quand il y arrive, dans Strauss ou Mahler par exemple, ou encore dans l'Elgar, on croit en lui. Ceci, plus son engagement passionnel resteront des traits gravés dans les mémoires.

◄ Georg Solti in thoughtful mood.

Georg Solti in Gedanken.

Georg Solti perdu dans ses pensées.

Georg Solti rehearsing, 23 January 1961.

Georg Solti bei einer Probe, 23. Januar 1961.

Georg Solti lors d'une répétition, le 23 janvier 1961.

1

Solti rehearsing the cast of Mozart's *Le nozze di Figaro* at the Royal
Opera House, Covent Garden, 19 May 1963, with (2, seated, left
to right) Geraint Evans, Tito Gobbi, Mirella Freni and Ilva
Ligabue. Some of these pictures (1, 3, 4) indicate how he acquired
his nickname of 'The Screaming Skull'. (4) With James Gibson at
the piano.

Solti probt mit der Besetzung für Mozarts *Hochzeit des Figaro* im
Royal Opera House in Covent Garden, 19. Mai 1963. (2) Von
links nach rechts: Geraint Evans, Tito Gobbi, Mirella Freni und
Ilva Ligabue. Auf einigen Fotos (1, 3, 4) sieht man, wie Solti zu
seinem Spitznamen „Der Schreihals" gekommen ist. (4) Mit James
Gibson am Klavier.

Solti en répétition avec la troupe des *Noces de Figaro* de Mozart au
Royal Opera House à Covent Garden, le 19 mai 1963, avec (2,
assis de gauche à droite) Geraint Evans, Tito Gobbi, Mirella Freni
et Ilva Ligabue. Certaines de ces photos (1, 3, 4) montrent pourquoi il avait le surnom de « crâne hurlant ». (4) Avec James Gibson
au piano.

Conductors often die old, but none die older than Stokowski. By the time these photographs were taken the Old Magician was already coming up to 90; it was nearly 70 years since his first appointment as organist at St James's, Piccadilly, and over 60 since he had deserted the organ to become conductor of the Cincinnati Symphony Orchestra. Although in the United States he liked to jazz up his international image by claiming to have been born in a forest in Pomerania, Stokowski was a Londoner by birth and musical upbringing. Nevertheless he had become a US citizen in 1915; his reputation had been made entirely in America, and as far as his country of origin was concerned it was not unmixed.

The fact is, Stokowski was an incorrigible showman, and the showmanship overshadows the achievement. His artistic success in Philadelphia in building up over a quarter of a century one of the greatest and most accomplished of all American orchestral ensembles was real and lasting, a tribute both to his musicianship and to the power of his personality. But he craved worldly success as well, and the Philadelphia Orchestra became the base for a whole series of sensational musical occasions in which he was the star figure. He made national headlines in 1916 with the first American performance of Mahler's colossal *Eighth Symphony*, and followed it among many others with Stravinsky's *Rite of Spring*, Schoenberg's *Gurrelieder*, Berg's *Wozzeck* and Rachmaninov's *Rhapsody on a theme of Paganini* – attention grabbers, all of them, with the romantically handsome figure on the podium grabbing as much of it as the music.

He was quick to recognize the power of the gramophone, and the advent of electrical recording soon carried the brilliance of the Philadelphia sound, the warm, seamless opulence of string tone that Stokowski so much loved, to the living rooms of the world. The prodigious orchestral transcriptions he made to show it off sold in their millions, and however much the purists may sneer arrangements like the famous *Toccata and Fugue in D minor* of Bach are amazingly effective. More controversial was his tinkering with the scores of the classics, but always the object was a clearer and more powerful orchestral effect, and though we may take a different attitude today there is no doubt that what Stokowski wanted he got.

Some say that he was never happy after he left Philadelphia in 1938, and it is true that his career from then on did not have the single-mindedness of earlier days. But his achievements were by no means over: after a brief flirtation with Hollywood, of which the main results were the movie *100 Men and a Girl* with Deanna Durbin, the collaboration with Walt Disney and Mickey Mouse in *Fantasia*, and a romantic affair in Rome with Greta Garbo, he moved on to the orchestra of the Hollywood Bowl, married Gloria Vanderbilt, founded the All-American Youth Orchestra, shared the NBC Symphony with Toscanini, and turned up everywhere as an indefatigable champion of new music. In 1962 he founded the American Symphony Orchestra and three years later, at the age of 83, conducted it in an epoch-making first performance of Charles Ives's wildly complex and immensely difficult *Fourth Symphony*. By 1971 it was calculated that he had given over 2000 first performances in about 7000 concerts.

Returning to London, he continued conducting into his 90s with the same wizardry, the same caressing hand for a soloist, the same unshakeable belief in the human power of music that had illuminated his whole career.

Dirigenten erreichen oft ein hohes Alter, aber keiner wurde so alt wie Stokowski: Als diese Fotografien entstanden, war der alte Hexenmeister schon beinahe 90 Jahre alt. Sein erstes Engagement als Organist von St. James's in Piccadilly lag beinahe 70 Jahre zurück, und vor mehr als 60 Jahren hatte er die Orgel verlassen, um das Cincinnati Symphony Orchestra zu dirigieren. Obwohl er in den USA gerne vorgab, aus dem hintersten Pommern zu stammen, um sich damit ein noch interessanteres internationales Image zu geben, war Stokowski doch geborener Londoner. Das bestimmte auch seinen musikalischen Hintergrund. Trotzdem nahm er 1915 die amerikanische Staatsbürgerschaft an. In Amerika war er berühmt geworden, in England gab es gewisse Vorbehalte.

Stokowksi hatte eine unbezwingbare Neigung zur Selbstdarstellung, die seine Leistungen überschattete. In Philadelphia hatte er über ein halbes Jahrhundert das größte und beste amerikanische Orchester aufgebaut. Dieser künstlerische Erfolg war real und dauerhaft und bezeugt seine Leistung als Musiker und auch die Kraft seiner Persönlichkeit. Er strebte jedoch auch nach weltlichem Ruhm und inszenierte mit dem Philadelphia Orchestra eine ganze Reihe musikalischer Sensationen, bei denen er selbst die Hauptrolle spielte. 1916 errang er landesweite Aufmerksamkeit mit der ersten Aufführung von Mahlers grandioser *Achter Symphonie*. Darauf folgten unter anderem Strawinskys *Le sacre du printemps*, Schönbergs *Gurrelieder*, Bergs *Wozzeck* und Rachmaninows *Rhapsodie über ein Thema von Paganini* – alles Aufmerksamkeit heischende Aufführungen mit einer romantisch-hübschen Gestalt auf der Bühne, die davon ebenso profitierte wie die Musik.

Schnell erkannte er die Macht der Schallplatte, und die neue elektronische Aufnahmetechnik trug den brillanten Philadelphia-Klang, die warme, geschmeidige Fülle der Streicher bald in die Wohnzimmer in aller Welt. Die gewaltigen Transkriptionen der Orchesterstimmen, die er dabei vornahm, verkauften sich in Millionenhöhe, und so sehr es die Puristen auch verstimmen mochte, Arrangements wie Bachs berühmte *Toccata und Fuge in d-moll* waren äußerst wirkungsvoll. Umstrittener bleiben seine Experimente mit den Partituren der Klassiker. Sein Ziel war es, dem Orchester eine größere Klarheit und Kraft zu geben. Auch wenn wir heute andere Schwerpunkte setzen – Stokowski hat zweifellos erreicht, was er wollte.

Manchmal wird behauptet, nachdem er Philadelphia 1938 verlassen habe, sei er nicht mehr glücklich geworden, und in der Tat fehlt seiner Laufbahn von da an die frühere Stringenz. Sie brach jedoch keineswegs ab. Er machte einen kurzen Abstecher nach Hollywood und arbeitete dort an Filmen wie *100 Men and a Girl* (mit Deanna Durbin) oder Walt Disney's *Fantasia* mit. Nach einer Romanze mit Greta Garbo in Rom zog er weiter zum Orchester der Hollywood Bowl. Schließlich heiratete er Gloria Vanderbilt. Er gründete das All-American Youth Orchestra, teilte sich die NBC Symphoniker mit Toscanini und erwies sich überall als ein unermüdlicher Meister der neuen Musik. 1962 gründete er das American Symphony Orchestra, und drei Jahre später, im Alter von 83 Jahren, dirigierte er es bei der epochemachenden Erstaufführung von Charles Ives unglaublich komplexer und überaus schwieriger *Vierter Symphonie*. 1971 errechnete man, daß er in circa 7000 Konzerten über 2000 Erstaufführungen dirigiert hatte.

Zurück in London schwang er den Taktstock bis über sein 90. Lebensjahr hinaus mit ungeminderter Zauberkraft, kümmerte sich um Solisten und bewahrte sich seinen unerschütterlichen Glauben an die menschliche Macht der Musik, der seine ganze Karriere überstrahlt hatte.

Les chefs d'orchestre meurent souvent âgés, mais aucun ne mourut plus vieux que Stokowski. Au moment où ont été prises ces photographies, le « vieux magicien » avait presque 90 ans ; son premier engagement comme organiste à St James de Piccadilly datait d'environ soixante-dix ans et plus de soixante s'étaient écoulés depuis qu'il avait abandonné l'orgue pour devenir chef de l'Orchestre symphonique de Cincinnati. Il aimait dire qu'il était né dans une forêt de Poméranie, en réalité, Stokowski était londonien de naissance et d'éducation musicale. Devenu citoyen des États-Unis en 1915, c'est dans ce pays qu'il a acquis sa renommée.

Stokowski était un incorrigible comédien et le cabotinage peut faire de l'ombre à la réussite. Néanmoins, son succès artistique à Philadelphie, à la tête, pendant plus d'un quart de siècle, de l'un des ensembles américains les plus prestigieux et les plus accomplis, fut réel et durable, hommage à la fois à sa maestria et au pouvoir de sa personnalité. Pour satisfaire sa soif de célébrité, il utilisa l'Orchestre de Philadelphie pour monter une série d'événements musicaux sensationnels dont il était la vedette. Il fit les gros titres du pays, en 1916, avec la première représentation américaine de la colossale *Huitième Symphonie* de Mahler et la fit suivre, entre autres, du *Sacre du printemps* de Stravinski, des *Gurrelieder* de Schoenberg, du *Wozzeck* de Berg et de la *Rhapsodie sur un thème de Paganini* de Rachmaninov – sa belle silhouette romantique, sur l'estrade, attirant l'attention autant que la musique.

Il ne tarda pas à comprendre le pouvoir du phonographe et l'avènement du disque porta bientôt l'éclat du son du Philadelphie, la chaude et lisse opulence des cordes, que Stokowski aimait tant, jusqu'aux salons du monde entier. Ses prodigieuses transcriptions orchestrales se vendirent par millions et même si les puristes ricanent, elles sont d'une indéniable efficacité ; ce qu'il fit de la fameuse *Toccata et Fugue en ré mineur* de Bach en est un exemple. Son bricolage des partitions des classiques était plus controversé, mais l'objectif était toujours un effet orchestral plus clair et plus puissant, et Stokowski l'obtenait toujours.

Certains disent qu'il n'a jamais été heureux après avoir quitté Philadelphie en 1938, et il est vrai qu'à partir de là il conduisit sa carrière avec moins de détermination qu'auparavant. Mais il avait encore du chemin à faire: après une courte idylle avec Hollywood, qui donna entre autres le film *100 Men and a Girl* avec Deanna Durbin, la collaboration avec Walt Disney et Mickey Mouse dans *Fantasia* et une liaison romantique avec Greta Garbo à Rome, il dirigea l'orchestre du Hollywood Bowl, épousa Gloria Vanderbilt, fonda l'orchestre All-American Youth Orchestra, partagea le NBC Symphony avec Toscanini, et se révéla partout comme un infatigable défenseur de la nouvelle musique. En 1962, il créa l'American Symphony Orchestra et, trois ans plus tard, à 83 ans, le dirigea dans la première, qui fait date, de la *Quatrième Symphonie* de Charles Ives, furieusement compliquée et formidablement difficile. En 1971, on a calculé qu'il avait dirigé plus de deux mille premières sur environ sept mille concerts.

De retour à Londres, il continua à diriger avec la même magie, la même confiance inébranlable dans le pouvoir de la musique qui avait illuminé toute sa carrière.

Leopold Stokowski, late 1960s or early 1970s.

Leopold Stokowski, späte 60er/frühe 70er Jahre.

Leopold Stokowski, fin des années 60 ou début des années 70.

Stokowski, 14 June 1961.
Stokowski, 14. Juni 1961.
Stokowski, le 14 juin 1961.

1

2

(1, 2) Stokowski, late 1960s or early 70s. (3) Talking to Antal Dorati after a concert by the BBC Symphony Orchestra in New York at which Dorati conducted, April 1965.

(1, 2) Stokowski, späte 60er/frühe 70er Jahre. (3) Stokowski im Gespräch mit Antal Dorati nach einem Konzert des BBC Symphony Orchestra in New York unter dessen Leitung, April 1965.

(1, 2) Stokowski, fin des années 60 ou début des années 70. (3) Parlant avec Antal Dorati après un concert de l'Orchestre symphonique de la BBC à New York dirigé par Dorati, en avril 1965.

3

Rehearsing, 14 June 1961.
Beim Proben, 14. Juni 1961.
En répétition, le 14 juin 1961.

Evgeny Svetlanov in 1968. Full-blooded Russian conducting.

Jewgeni Swetlanow, 1968, ein russischer Vollblutdirigent.

Evgeny Svetlanov en 1968 : Tempérament russe en action.

EVGENY SVETLANOV   JEWGENI SWETLANOW   EVGENY SVETLANOV
*1928

Svetlanov's has been very much a Russian career. Its starting point was the theatre – quite literally, in fact, because his father had been a singer at the Bolshoy and his mother an actress in a company of mime players. He was born and studied in Moscow where, besides developing his talents as a pianist and a conductor, he was a composition pupil of the distinguished Soviet composer Yuri Shaporin, producing a piano concerto, a symphony and number of chamber and vocal works while he was in his 20s. His conducting career began when he was still a student at the Conservatory, but in 1955 he too felt the call of the theatre and took a job as assistant conductor at the Bolshoy, where he stayed for ten years, ending up as principal conductor for the last three.

At the Bolshoy he began to show the very Russian bent of his musical interests: he conducted most of the operas of Rimsky-Korsakov, and works by Borodin, Tchaikovsky and Dargomizhsky as well as new works by Soviet contemporaries. In 1964 he took the Bolshoy Company to La Scala, Milan, with a programme that included Musorgsky's *Boris Godunov*, Borodin's *Prince Igor*, Rimsky's *Sadko* and Prokofiev's *War and Peace*. After the Bolshoy, turning from opera to the concert hall, he became chief conductor of the USSR State Symphony Orchestra, with which he toured in Europe and the United States. He survived the orchestra's transformation into the Russian Federation State Symphony Orchestra and in the early 1990s went with it to Japan, where he recorded the whole cycle of the Tchaikovsky symphonies at live performances in Tokyo.

It was not his first Tchaikovsky cycle; that was back in 1967, and it was already beginning to earn high praise from knowing critics at the time when these photographs were taken. Stravinsky once said of Tchaikovsky that 'he never feared to let himself go', and the same might be said of Svetlanov. In spite of a relatively restrained platform manner, this is full-blooded, idiomatic conducting, very Russian in its rhythmic impetus and romantic colouring. It is not particularly subtle, or particularly elegant; the tempi can be rather unexpected, occasionally the excitement goes a bit over the top – some blatancy from the brass perhaps, or an overdone portamento from the strings. But there is drama, and passion vividly conveyed: the years at the Bolshoy are not forgotten. He may not have the aristocratic control of an older generation – Evgeny Mravinsky, for example – but he reaches out to the heart and guts of a repertory that covers the whole of Russian and Soviet music from Glinka to Shostakovich and from Glazunov to Shebalin, Myaskovsky and Eshpay, a repertory that few have championed as single-mindedly as Svetlanov.

Swetlanows Laufbahn ist eng mit der russischen Kunst verbunden. Sein Ausgangspunkt war das Theater: Sein Vater sang am Bolschoi Theater, und seine Mutter gehörte einer Schauspieltruppe an. Swetlanow ist gebürtiger Moskauer, und er studierte auch dort. Neben seiner Ausbildung zum Pianisten und Dirigenten studierte er Kompositionslehre bei dem berühmten sowjetischen Komponisten Juri Schaporin, woraufhin er bald ein Klavierkonzert, eine Symphonie, einige Kammermusikstücke und Vokalwerke schrieb. Seine Dirigentenlaufbahn begann bereits, als er noch Student am Konservatorium war. 1955 jedoch fühlte auch er sich zum Theater berufen und nahm eine Stelle als assistierender Dirigent am Bolschoi Theater an, wo er zehn Jahre lang blieb, davon die letzten drei Jahre als Chefdirigent.

Am Bolschoi Theater entwickelte sich die russische Musik allmählich zu seinem Schwerpunkt. Er dirigierte fast alle Opern von Rimski-Korsakow, Werke von Borodin, Tschaikowsky und Dargomischski und auch neue Werke zeitgenössischer sowjetischer Komponisten. 1964 brachte er das Bolschoi Ensemble in die Mailänder Scala. Zu seinem Programm gehörten auch Mussorgskis *Boris Godunow*, Borodins *Fürst Igor*, Rimski-Korsakows *Sadko* und Prokofjews *Krieg und Frieden*. Nach seiner Tätigkeit am Bolschoi Theater tauschte er die Opernbühne mit dem Konzertsaal und wurde Chefdirigent des Staatlichen Symphonieorchesters der UdSSR. Mit diesem Ensemble ging er auch in Europa und den USA auf Tournee. Er überstand die Umorganisation des Orchesters zum Staatlichen Symphonieorchester der Russischen Föderation, mit dem er in den frühen 90er Jahren nach Japan ging. Dort wurden sämtliche Symphonien von Tschaikowsky bei Live-Veranstaltungen mitgeschnitten.

Es handelte sich hierbei übrigens nicht um seinen ersten Tschaikowsky-Zyklus: Bereits 1967, als diese Fotos entstanden, hatten ihm kenntnisreiche Kritiker dafür ein hohes Lob ausgesprochen. Strawinsky sagte einmal über Tschaikowsky, daß „er nie Angst hatte, sich gehen zu lassen", und das gilt wohl auch für Swetlanow. Bei seinen Auftritten wirkt er zwar eher beherrscht, dirigiert aber durchaus leidenschaftlich und ausdrucksstark. Die rhythmische Kraft und die romantische Färbung beweisen das russische Temperament. Swetlanows Stil ist weder besonders subtil noch außergewöhnlich elegant. Die Tempi können recht unerwartet kommen, und gelegentlich schlägt die Erregung etwas zu hoch – tönen die Bläser vielleicht etwas zu durchdringend, oder das Portamento der Streicher wirkt übertrieben – aber das eben sind seine Fähigkeiten zu Dramatik und lebendiger Leidenschaft, die er vom Bolschoi Theater mitgebracht hatte. Swetlanow verfügt wohl nicht mehr über die aristokratische Manier der älteren Generation – wie z. B. Jewgeni Mrawinski –, aber er trifft ganz genau das Herz und die Gefühlswelt eines Repertoires, das die gesamte russische und sowjetische Musik von Glinka bis Schostakowitsch, Glazunow bis Schebalin und von Mjaskowski bis Eshpay umfaßt, ein Repertoire, das wenige so geradlinig gemeistert haben wie Swetlanow.

La carrière de Svetlanov fut très russe. Elle commença dans les salles de spectacles – son père était chanteur au Bolchoï et sa mère actrice dans une compagnie de mimes. Né à Moscou, il y étudia aussi. Il développa alors ses talents de pianiste et de chef d'orchestre. Il eut aussi des cours de composition enseignés par le remarquable compositeur soviétique Yuri Chaporine, et il produisit, alors qu'il n'avait pas encore vingt ans, un concerto pour piano, une symphonie, et des musiques de chambre et pour chants. Sa carrière de chef d'orchestre commença alors qu'il était encore au Conservatoire, mais il fut lui aussi attiré par les salles de ballets, et il accepta un poste de chef d'orchestre assistant au Bolchoï, où il resta dix ans dont les trois derniers comme premier chef d'orchestre.

Au Bolchoï, il commença à montrer le penchant bien russe de ses intérêts musicaux : il dirigea la plupart des opéras de Rimski-Korsakov, des œuvres de Borodine, Tchaïkovski, Dargomyjski ainsi que des nouvelles œuvres de ses contemporains soviétiques. En 1964, il emmena le Bolchoï jouer à la Scala, à Milan, un programme qui comprenait *Boris Godounov* de Moussorgsky, le *Prince Igor* de Borodine, le *Sadko* de Rimsky-Korsakov et *Guerre et Paix* de Prokofiev. Après le Bolchoï, quittant l'opéra pour la salle de concerts, il devint premier chef d'orchestre de l'Orchestre Symphonique de l'État Soviétique, avec lequel il fit des tournées en Europe et aux États-Unis. Il survécut à la transformation de l'orchestre devenu l'Orchestre symphonique de l'État Fédéral Russe, et au début des années 1990, il alla avec lui au Japon où il enregistra tout le cycle des symphonies de Tchaïkovski lors de représentations en direct de Tokyo.

Ce n'était pas là son premier cycle de Tchaïkovski ; il remontait à 1967, et commençait déjà à gagner l'estime des critiques bien informés quand ces photos furent prises. Stravinski dit un jour de Tchaïkovski qu' »il n'a jamais eu peur de se laisser aller, » on pourrait appliquer cette remarque à Svetlanov. Malgré son attitude très sobre sur l'estrade, c'est un chef d'orchestre robuste, très russe quant à ses élans rythmiques et ses tons romantiques. Il n'est pas particulièrement subtil ou particulièrement élégant ; les tempos peuvent parfois surprendre, et quelquefois l'excitation prend des proportions exagérées – les cuivres un peu trop criards peut-être, ou un portamento excessif des cordes. Mais le caractère dramatique et la passion sont transmis avec éclat : il n'avait pas oublié les années passées au Bolchoï. Il n'a peut-être pas le contrôle aristocratique d'une génération plus âgée – Evgeny Mravinski, par exemple, mais il alla au cœur du répertoire qui couvre toute la musique russe et soviétique de Glinka à Chostakovitch, et de Glazounov à Shebalin, Myaskovsky et Eshpay, un répertoire que peu ont défendu comme lui de façon aussi tenace.

GEORGE SZELL 1897-1970

Another Hungarian, but not this time originating in Budapest, Szell was brought up in Vienna, where he studied composition with Max Reger, and had made his début as composer, pianist and conductor by the time he was 17. A year later he was picked out by Richard Strauss for a staff position at the Staatsoper in Berlin, and after gaining experience in lesser musical centres returned there as a conductor in the late 1920s, during Erich Kleiber's regime, before himself taking up an appointment as music director at the German Theatre in Prague. Meanwhile he had toured in Europe, Russia and America and, after a couple of years with the Scottish Orchestra, he finally decided in 1939 to move to the United States.

During his first years in America he conducted widely and earned golden opinions with his Strauss and Wagner performances at the Metropolitan Opera in New York. But his real chance came in 1946 when he took over as principal conductor of the Cleveland Orchestra, and it was here that over a period of 24 years he built up the reputation for which he will always be remembered. Like Stokowski in Philadelphia, or Koussevitzky in Boston, Szell created out of the Cleveland players an orchestra in his own image – an instrument of amazing precision, efficiency and clarity of sound, drilled to a pitch of technical perfection that quickly put it among the finest ensembles in the world. He toured and recorded with it extensively (and was never known to sign a dud contract). He became a very successful conductor indeed.

And his musicianship was certainly stunning. A perfectionist with a phenomenal memory for musical detail and an acutely analytical ear, he could identify differences of pitch that none of his players could even hear and produce sounds out of his orchestra that they didn't know they could play. But they didn't love him for it. Like his idol, Toscanini, he believed in terrorizing his players, and he was a ruthless and frequently caustic disciplinarian: the problem was not that he didn't suffer fools gladly, but that he didn't suffer them at all. And the fact that he was virtually impossible to fault only made it worse. After he had walked out of the Metropolitan Opera following a row, somebody unwisely commented to Rudolf Bing, the manager, that Szell was his own worst enemy. 'Not while I'm alive,' said Bing.

His interpretations were not universally admired. 'Das ist nicht *La mer*, das ist Szell am See' said Klemperer after hearing a performance of Debussy's masterpiece; he acknowledged that Szell was 'a very good conductor, but ice-cold'. And yet it has to be said that this aloof, austere, unsmiling individual could produce performances with sensitivity and even tenderness, particularly in the late German romantic repertory and 'modern' (but never dangerously modern) music. All the same his view of the conductor's role was essentially undemonstrative and unsentimental, and in the more classical scores his insistence, like Toscanini, on fidelity to the composer's original intention could result in readings that lacked personal involvement. This applied to his Mozart, for example – though he didn't see it that way himself. As far as he was concerned 'you can't' he said, 'pour chocolate sauce on asparagus'.

George Szell conducting the Cleveland Orchestra in 1966, after honing it to perfection for 20 years.

George Szell dirigiert das Cleveland Orchestra, an dessen Perfektionierung er zwanzig Jahre lang gearbeitet hat, 1966.

George Szell dirigeant Orchestre de Cleveland en 1966, après avoir affûté jusqu'à la perfection pendant 20 ans.

George Szell, auch ein Ungar, jedoch nicht aus Budapest, wuchs in Wien auf. Dort studierte er bei Max Reger Kompositionslehre. Mit siebzehn Jahren hatte er bereits sein Debüt als Komponist, Pianist und Dirigent gegeben. Ein Jahr später nahm ihn Richard Strauss in das Ensemble der Staatsoper Berlin auf. Nachdem er dann in weniger exponierten musikalischen Zentren seine musikalischen Erfahrungen gesammelt hatte, kehrte er in den 20er Jahren als Dirigent an die Staatsoper zurück, die zu der Zeit von Kleiber geleitet wurde. Später nahm er selbst eine Stelle als Musikdirektor am Deutschen Theater in Prag an. In der Zwischenzeit war er durch Europa, Rußland und Amerika getourt, und nach einigen Jahren mit dem Scottish Orchestra entschloß er sich schließlich 1939, in die Staaten zu gehen.

In seinen ersten Jahren in Amerika trat er sehr häufig auf und erhielt glänzende Kritiken für seine Strauss und Wagner Aufführungen an der Metropolitan Opera in New York. 1946 bekam er seine wirkliche Chance. Er übernahm das Cleveland Orchestra als Chefdirigent und erarbeitete sich dort in über 24 Jahren eine unvergessene Reputation. Ebenso wie Stokowski in Philadelphia oder Kussewitzky in Boston schuf Szell aus dem Cleveland Ensemble ein Orchester nach seinen eigenen Vorstellungen – es wurde zu einem Instrument von erstaunlicher Präzision, Wirksamkeit und Klangreinheit auf einem so hohen technischen Niveau, daß es sich bald unter die besten Orchester der Welt einreihte. Szell ging mit ihm oft auf Tournee und machte auch unzählige Aufnahmen (dabei hat er nie einen schlechten Vertrag unterschrieben). Er wurde in der Tat ein sehr erfolgreicher Dirigent.

Als Musiker war er wirklich beeindruckend. Als Perfektionist mit einem phänomenalen Gedächtnis für musikalische Details und einem scharfen analytischen Ohr konnte er Unterschiede wahrnehmen, die keiner seiner Musiker hören konnte, und er entlockte seinem Orchester Klänge, die es selbst nicht für möglich gehalten hätte. Aber sie liebten ihn nicht dafür. Ganz wie sein Vorbild Toscanini neigte er dazu, seine Musiker zu tyrannisieren, und war ein gnadenloser und häufig sarkastischer Lehrmeister. Fehler ertrug er überhaupt nicht. Die Tatsache, daß er selbst praktisch keinen Fehler machte, verschlimmerte die Sache nur. Als er einmal nach einem Streit aus der Metropolitan Opera gerannt war, bemerkte jemand unvorsichtigerweise zu Rudolf Bing, dem Manager, Szell sei sich selbst sein größter Feind. „Nicht solange ich lebe", lautete Bings Antwort.

Szells Interpretationen wurden nicht durchgängig bewundert. „Das ist nicht *La mer*, daß ist Szell am See" stellte Klemperer fest, nachdem er die Aufführung von Debussys Meisterwerk gehört hatte. Er fand, Szell sei zwar „ein sehr guter Dirigent, aber eiskalt". Trotzdem konnte dieser distanzierte, melancholische, nie lächelnde Mensch äußerst sensible und sogar zartfühlende Aufführungen geben, insbesondere aus dem Repertoire der späten Romantik und der „modernen" (aber nicht allzu modernen) Musik. Er hatte im Grunde eine schlichte, unsentimentale Auffassung von der Aufgabe eines Dirigenten. Genau wie bei Toscanini konnte sein treues Beharren auf der ursprünglichen Intention des Komponisten, besonders bei den Klassikern, zu einem Mangel an eigener Beteiligung führen. Das gilt z. B. für seinen Mozart – obwohl er selbst es nicht so verstanden hat. Soweit es ihn betraf, „kann man über Spargel keine Schokoladensauce gießen", wie er sagte.

Encore un Hongrois, mais pas de Budapest cette fois-ci, puisque Szell a grandi à Vienne où il étudia ensuite la composition avec Max Reger avant d'y faire ses débuts comme compositeur, pianiste et chef d'orchestre à l'âge de 17 ans ! Un an plus tard, Richard Strauss lui proposait une place au sein du Staatsoper, à Berlin, où il reviendra à la fin des années 20, les années Erich Kleiber, après avoir complété son expérience dans des villes musicalement parlant moins prestigieuses. Il choisit ensuite l'Opéra allemand de Prague où il devient directeur de la musique et effectue des tournées dans toute l'Europe, pousse jusqu'à la Russie et aux États-Unis où il s'installe définitivement, en 1939, après quelques années aux commandes du Scottish Orchestra.

Ses premières années dans ce pays le conduisent un peu partout et lui valent des commentaires élogieux grâce à ses interprétations de Strauss et de Wagner au Metropolitan de New York. Cependant, il doit attendre 1946 pour que la chance lui sourisse pleinement, lorsqu'on lui demande de prendre la tête de l'Orchestre de Cleveland, avec lequel il allait, pendant près d'un quart de siècle, se forger une réputation admirable. Comme Stokowski à Philadelphie ou Koussevitzki à Boston, Szell a fait son orchestre à sa propre image. Il a créé un outil d'une précision, d'une efficacité et d'une clarté stupéfiantes, discipliné jusqu'à atteindre un idéal technique qui l'a rapidement classé parmi les meilleurs ensembles du monde. C'est avec ce merveilleux outil qu'il a parcouru la planète et s'est employé à enregistrer de nombreuses œuvres, sans qu'on eût jamais l'occasion de lui reprocher de ne pas honorer à la perfection ses contrats.

George Szell était à vrai dire un musicien hors pair, un perfectionniste dont la mémoire phénoménale retenait jusqu'au moindre détail d'orchestration et dont l'oreille musicale, incroyablement fine, identifiait des nuances de tonalité qu'aucun de ses interprètes ne pouvait même entendre. Ses qualités lui permettaient de tirer de ses orchestres des sons que les musiciens eux-mêmes ignoraient pouvoir produire. Mais, ses musiciens ne l'en aimaient pas plus pour autant. Comme son idole Toscanini, il les tenait dans la terreur. Il se montrait autoritaire, souvent caustique et toujours sans pitié. Ce n'était pas qu'il eût du mal à supporter la bêtise... Non ! Il ne la supportait pas, tout simplement ! Et, comme il ne commettait quasiment jamais d'erreur, il était d'autant plus intraitable sur celles des autres. Lorsqu'il claqua la porte du Metropolitan après une sérieuse algarade, quelqu'un eut le malheur d'aller s'épancher auprès de Rudolf Bing, alors directeur de l'opéra : « Szell est mon pire ennemi ! » « Pire ?! Pas tant que je serai vivant ! » répondit Bing.

Ses interprétations ne faisaient certes pas l'unanimité. Comme le fit remarquer Klemperer après l'avoir entendu diriger *La Mer* de Debussy : « Ce n'est pas *La Mer*, c'est Szell-sur-mer ! ». Pour Klemperer, Szell était un très bon chef d'orchestre, mais il était surtout glacial. Mais ce personnage si distant, si austère et avare de sourires, était toutefois capable de sensibilité et de douceur dans ses concerts, notamment lorsqu'il plongeait dans le répertoire du grand romantisme allemand et dans la musique « moderne » (mais pas trop !). Il considérait comme de son devoir de chef d'orchestre de ne pas exhiber ses sentiments. Lorsqu'il dirigeait les grands classiques, il insistait ainsi, à l'instar de Toscanini, pour que l'on respecte les intentions initiales du compositeur. Le résultat manquait alors inévitablement de personnalité, comme ce fut le cas dans ses interprétations de Mozart, par exemple. Bien entendu, George Szell ne l'entendait pas de cette oreille. Pour lui : « On ne sert pas les asperges avec une sauce au chocolat ! »

1

Conductors of the Younger Generation
Dirigenten der jüngeren Generation
Une nouvelle génération de chefs d'orchestres

Among the musical personalities whom Auerbach photographed towards the end of his career were a whole group of younger figures, many of whom have since made great reputations though they were only beginning on their careers in Auerbach's lifetime.

Unter den Musikerpersönlichkeiten, die Auerbach in seiner Spätphase portraitierte, waren auch etliche jüngere Künstler, die inzwischen berühmt geworden sind. Zu Auerbachs Zeiten standen sie jedoch erst am Anfang ihrer Laufbahn.

Parmi les personnalités musicales photographiées par Auerbach vers la fin de sa carrière, il y avait un groupe de personnages plus jeunes. Beaucoup ont depuis une grande réputation, alors qu'à l'époque d'Auerbach, ils ne faisaient que commencer leur carrière.

The Italian Claudio Abbado (1), though he was born as early as 1933, did not make his first public appearance in London until he conducted *Don Carlos* at Covent Garden in 1968 – the same year that he made his début at the Metropolitan Opera, New York, and was appointed principal conductor at La Scala, Milan. Here (2) he is discussing a point in one of the Chopin piano concertos with the young Argentinian pianist Martha Argerich (b. 1941) at a recording session for Deutsche Grammophon earlier the same year, 10 February 1968.

Der Italiener Claudio Abbado (1) kam zwar schon 1933 zur Welt, hatte seinen ersten öffentlichen Auftritt in London aber erst 1968 als er in Covent Garden den *Don Carlos* dirigierte – im gleichen Jahr gab er sein Debüt an der Metropolitan Opera in New York und wurde Chefdirigent an der Mailänder Scala. Hier (2) bespricht er bei einem Aufnahmetermin für die Deutsche Grammophon mit der argentinischen Pianistin Martha Argerich (geb. 1941) eine Stelle aus Chopins Klavierkonzerten, 10. Februar 1968.

L'Italien Claudio Abbado (1), bien que né en 1933, n' apparut en public pour la première fois que lorsqu'il dirigea *Don Carlos* à Covent Garden en 1968 – l'année de ses débuts au Metropolitan Opera de New York, et l'année aussi où on lui assigna le poste de premier chef d'orchestre à La Scala de Milan. Ici (2), il discute un passage de l'un des concertos de Chopin pour piano avec la jeune pianiste argentine Martha Argerich (née en 1941) lors d'une séance d'enregistrement pour le Deutsche Grammophon plus tôt cette année-là, le 10 février 1968.

2

3

4

5

6

(3, 4) Zubin Mehta (b. 1936) is one of the few Indian musicians to achieve distinction in Western music. By the time of these photographs (about May 1968) he had already been director of the Los Angeles Philharmonic Orchestra for six years (the youngest to hold such an appointment in any major American orchestra) and was touring in Europe with the Israel Philharmonic, with which he was to be closely associated throughout his career.
(5, 6) Riccardo Muti (b. 1941) read philosophy at university and only became a conductor by chance. But he rapidly made a name in his native Italy, and scored brilliant successes in Philadelphia, London and Vienna in the early 1970s. In London his début, with the New Philharmonia Orchestra, was followed by his appointment as its chief conductor in succession to Klemperer in 1973. These photographs, at rehearsal in the Royal Albert Hall, date from that period.

(3, 4) Zubin Mehta (geb. 1936) gehört zu den wenigen indischen Musikern, die im Westen Anerkennung fanden. Als diese Fotos entstanden (ca. Mai 1968), war er bereits seit sechs Jahren Direktor des Los Angeles Philharmonic Orchestra (und damit der jüngste Dirigent, der bei einem großen amerikanischen Orchester eine so renommierte Position bekleidete). Er befand sich gerade mit den Israelischen Philharmonikern auf Europatournee, einem Orchester, mit dem er seine ganze Laufbahn hindurch in enger Verbindung gestanden hat.
(5, 6) Riccardo Muti (geb. 1941) lehrte eigentlich Philosophie an der Universität und kam eher durch Zufall zum Dirigieren. In seiner Heimat Italien machte er sich jedoch schnell einen Namen und hatte in den frühen 70er Jahren auch in Philadelphia, London und Wien brillante Erfolge. Sein Londoner Debüt mit dem New Philharmonia Orchestra führte dazu, daß er Klemperer 1973 als Chefdirigenten ablöste. Aus der Zeit stammen auch diese Fotos von den Proben in der Royal Albert Hall.

(3, 4) Zubin Mehta (né en 1936) est l'un des rares musiciens indiens à se distinguer en Occident. A l'époque de ces photos (vers le mois de mai 1968), il avait déjà été directeur de l'Orchestre Philharmonique de Los Angeles pendant six ans (le plus jeune à occuper un tel poste dans un orchestre américain influent), et faisait des tournées en Europe avec l'Israel Philharmonic, qui restera lié à sa carrière tout au long de sa vie.
(5, 6) Riccardo Muti (né en 1941) étudia la philosophie à l'université et devint chef d'orchestre par hasard. Il fut rapidement connu dans son Italie natale, et connut de brillants succès à Philadelphie, Londres et Vienne, au début des années 1970. A Londres, ses débuts avec le New Philharmonia Orchestra, furent suivis de son poste de premier chef d'orchestre du New Philharmonia où il succéda à Klemperer en 1973. Ces photos prises durant une répétition au Royal Albert Hall, datent de cette période.

The Estonian Neeme Järvi (b. 1937) studied in Leningrad with the great Russian conductor Evgeny Mravinsky. But he subsequently returned to his native country and was from 1963 conductor of the Estonian Radio Orchestra and State Opera, so that his real impact on the West only really began in the late 1970s. The photograph dates from 1967.

Der Este Neeme Järvi (geb. 1937) studierte in Leningrad bei dem großen russischen Dirigenten Jewgeni Mrawinski. Danach kehrte er jedoch in seine Heimat zurück und leitete seit 1963 das Estische Rundfunkorchester und die Staatsoper. Erst in den späten 70er Jahren drang sein Ruf bis in den Westen vor. Diese Fotos entstanden 1967.

L'Estonien Neeme Järvi (né en 1937) étudia à Leningrad avec le grand chef d'orchestre russe Evgeny Mravinsky. Il retourna ensuite dans son pays d'origine, et à partir de 1963 fut chef d'orchestre de l'Orchestre de la Radio Estonienne et de l'Opéra de l'Etat. Il ne commença donc à s'imposer à l'Ouest qu'à la fin des années 1970. Cette photo date de 1967.

Seiji Ozawa, a Japanese born in China in 1935, studied in Tokyo but received his very Western polish from Karajan and Bernstein in the early 1960s. In June 1969, the date of these photographs, he was still director of the Toronto Symphony Orchestra, though in the following year he was to succeed Josef Krips at San Francisco, and only three years later was to take up his most celebrated appointment, with the Boston Symphony Orchestra.

Seji Ozawa, ein 1935 in China geborener Japaner, studierte zunächst in Tokio. Seinen sehr westlichen Schliff erhielt er aber in den frühen 60er Jahren von Bernstein und Karajan. Zur Zeit dieser Fotos, im Juni 1969, war er noch Direktor des Toronto Symphony Orchestra. Im folgenden Jahr sollte er bereits Josef Krips in San Francisco ablösen, und nur drei Jahre später nahm er seine größte Herausforderung an, die Leitung des Boston Symphony Orchestra.

Seiji Ozawa, un Japonais né en Chine en 1935, étudia à Tokyo, et s'occidentalisa grâce à Karajan et Bernstein au début des années 1960. En juin 1969, date de ces photos, il était encore directeur de l'Orchestre Symphonique de Toronto, bien que l'année suivante, il ait succédé à Joseph Krips à San Francisco. Trois ans plus tard seulement, il obtint le poste le plus célèbre de sa carrière à l'Orchestre Symphonique de Boston.

Conductors as Instrumentalists

Dirigenten als Solisten

Chefs d'orchestre-instrumentistes

A good many conductors have begun their careers as pianists; few (outside the British choral tradition, anyhow) have graduated from the organ. But Stokowski's first professional job was as organist at St James's, Piccadilly, in London, and at Auerbach's request he played again (1) on the organ of the Temple Church 60 years later, 15 July 1963. Like Toscanini, Barbirolli started his career as a cellist, but unlike Toscanini he went on playing chamber music in later life: (2) in a performance of the César Franck *Quintet* at King's Lynn, Norfolk, 1 June 1964, (3) 26 July 1962. The pianist in both cases was Ruth, Lady Fermoy, founder of the King's Lynn Festival and grandmother of the Princess of Wales. (4) Lorin Maazel was a virtuoso violinist before he was a virtuoso conductor. Here he holds his Giovanni Battista Guadagnini violin, in London in June 1970 on a visit to record the Mozart concertos with the English Chamber Orchestra. (5) The double bass is an unusual instrument to start on. Only Koussevitzky springs to mind among conductors (Toscanini, the cellist, used to refer to him scornfully as 'der bass player'), but Zubin Mehta made his start at the bottom of the orchestra and it has not affected his rise to the top.

Viele Dirigenten haben ihre Karriere als Pianisten begonnen, einige – entgegen der britischen Chortradition – auch als Organisten. Stokowskis erste Anstellung war die des Organisten der St. James Church, Piccadilly in London, und auf Bitten Auerbachs spielte er sechzig Jahre später noch einmal auf der Orgel der Temple Church (1), 15. Juli 1963. Barbirolli begann seine Laufbahn, ebenso wie Toscanini, als Cellist. Im Unterschied zu Toscanini spielte er aber auch später noch Kammermusik. Hier (2) zu sehen bei einer Aufführung von César Francks *Klavierquintett* in King's Lynn, Norfolk, 1. Juni 1964; und auch hier (3), 26. Juli 1962. Die Pianistin bei beiden Veranstaltungen war Lady Ruth Fermoy, Gründerin des King's Lynn Festival und Großmutter der Prinzessin von Wales. (4) Bevor Lorin Maazel sich zu einem virtuosen Dirigenten entwickelte, war er ein virtuoser Geiger. Hier hält er seine Giovanni Battista Guadagnini Geige. Er gastierte gerade in London, um mit dem English Chamber Orchestra Mozarts Konzerte aufzunehmen, Juni 1970. (5) Der Kontrabaß ist ein ungewöhnliches Ausgangsinstrument. Unter den Dirigenten fällt einem nur Koussevitzky dazu ein (der Cellist Toscanini nannte ihn immer spöttisch „den Bassisten"), aber auch Zubin Mehta fing in den hinteren Orchesterrängen an, ohne daß es seinen Aufstieg bis zur Spitze behindert hätte.

De nombreux chefs d'orchestre commencèrent leur carrière comme pianistes ; peu (à part la tradition chorale britannique, en tout cas), commencèrent comme organistes. Pourtant le premier poste de Stokowski fut celui d'organiste à St James's, Piccadilly à Londres. A la demande d'Auerbach, il rejoua de l'orgue (1) au Temple Church, 60 ans plus tard, le 15 juillet 1963. Comme Toscanini, Barbirolli débuta comme violoncelliste, mais contrairement à Toscanini, il continua à jouer de la musique de chambre : (2) lors d'une représentation du *Quintette* de César Franck à King's Lynn, dans le Norfolk, le 1er juin 1964 ; (3) le 26 juillet 1962. Dans les deux cas, la pianiste était Ruth, Lady Fermoy, fondatrice du Festival de King's Lynn et grand-mère de la Princesse du pays de Galles. (4) Lorin Maazel fut un virtuose du violon avant de devenir un virtuose de la baguette. Il a ici son violon Giovanni Battista Guadagnini, à Londres en juin 1970, venu pour enregistrer les concertos de Mozart avec l'English Chamber Orchestra. (5) Il est rare de commencer une carrière à la contrebasse. Seul Koussevitzky vient à l'esprit parmi les chefs d'orchestre (Toscanini, le violoncelliste, le traitait dédaigneusement de « joueur de basse ». Zubin Mehta commença au bas de l'échelle dans l'orchestre, mais cela n'affecta jamais sa réussite.

4

5

PERFORMERS
INTERPRETEN
INTERPRÈTES

Louis Kentner (1905-1987), pianist, May 1961.
Louis Kentner (1905-1987), Pianist, Mai 1961.
Louis Kentner (1905-1987), pianiste, mai 1961.

CLAUDIO ARRAU   1903-1991

By the 1960s, when these photographs were taken, Arrau had been a name in London for a long time. At his début in 1922 he had shared a concert with the redoubtable operatic veteran Dame Nellie Melba and the violinist Bronislaw Huberman who had played Brahms in the presence of Brahms – which sounds like a fairly daunting proposition for a 19-year-old from Chile. But Arrau was not one to be easily frightened: he had given his first piano recital in Santiago at the age of five, his first in Berlin at 11, toured Germany, Scandinavia and other parts of Europe by the time he was 15, played concertos under Arthur Nikisch, Willem Mengelberg and Wilhelm Furtwängler, and tucked under his belt six years of hard study in Berlin before landing up in London. One wonders if Melba and Huberman quite realized what they were up against.

During the 1920s and 30s he combined a career as soloist with a professorship of piano at the prestigious Stern Conservatory in Berlin, and it was in Berlin that he played the entire keyboard works of Bach in a series of 12 recitals in 1935. But Bach on the piano interested him less in later years, and his repertory remained firmly centred on the 19th century – Chopin, Liszt, Schumann, Brahms, above all Beethoven. Essentially a thoughtful pianist, he played with great depth of feeling and very little external demonstration of it. This was virtuoso playing of the old school combined with the authority of a powerful intellect – totally unostentatious, but compelling and often deeply moving. His complete performances of the Beethoven piano sonatas were acclaimed all over the world.

In 1940 he left Berlin and set up a piano school of his own in Santiago, but a year later moved on to the United States where he carried out a brilliantly successful recital tour and finally made a home with his wife and family in New York. By the time of these pictures he was received in London as a Grand Old Man, loved and respected by musicians, audiences and his many pupils. Another of music's ambassadors? Possibly – though more perhaps in appearance than in fact.

Because what made Arrau so special was not any specific national origin, but the combination of a Latin temperament with a classic German schooling and worldwide sympathies.

In den 60er Jahren, aus denen diese Fotografien stammen, war der Name Arrau in London bereits bestens bekannt. Als Debüt gab Arrau 1922 ein Konzert mit der großen alten Dame des Operngesanges Nellie Melba und dem Geiger Bronislaw Huberman, der bereits Brahms in Anwesenheit von Brahms gespielt hatte – ein recht gewagtes Unterfangen für einen 19jährigen Chilenen.

Doch Arrau ließ sich nicht so leicht einschüchtern: Mit fünf Jahren spielte er zum ersten Mal in Santiago, mit elf trat er in Berlin auf, bereiste Deutschland, Skandinavien und andere Teile Europas im Alter von 15 Jahren, spielte unter Arthur Nikisch, Willem Mengelberg und Wilhelm Furtwängler und verschrieb sich sechs Jahre lang einem intensiven Klavierstudium in Berlin, bevor er nach London ging. Es ist fraglich, ob Melba oder Huberman sich darüber im klaren waren, mit wem sie es zu tun hatten.

In den 20er und 30er Jahren verband Arrau seine Karriere als Solist mit einer Professur am renommierten Stern Konservatorium in Berlin. Ebenfalls in Berlin spielte er 1935 das gesamte Bach'sche Klavierwerk an zwölf Abenden. In späteren Jahren beschäftigte er sich nicht mehr mit Bach, sondern wandte sich ganz dem 19. Jahrhundert zu: Chopin, Liszt, Schumann, Brahms, vor allem aber Beethoven. Er war ein sehr vergeistigter Pianist, der mit tiefer innerer Bewegung spielte, ohne dies jedoch äußerlich zur Schau zu stellen. Sein virtuoses Spiel der alten Schule war gepaart mit intellektueller Größe, gänzlich ohne Allüren, doch außerordentlich fesselnd und häufig ergreifend. Seine Interpretation sämtlicher Beethoven-Sonaten ist weltberühmt geworden.

1940 verließ er Berlin und gründete eine eigene Schule in Santiago, ging jedoch schon ein Jahr später in die Vereinigten Staaten und ließ sich nach einer überaus erfolgreichen Konzerttournee mit seiner Frau und Familie in New York nieder. Zu der Zeit, aus der diese Fotografien stammen, wurde Arrau in London schon als Meister empfangen, der von Musikern, seinen Schülern und vom Publikum hoch verehrt wurde. Seine besondere Ausstrahlung, die ihn vielleicht sogar zu einem Botschafter der Musik machte, ist nicht an seiner Nationalität festzumachen, sondern sie rührte aus der Verbindung des südamerikanischen Temperaments mit einer klassischen deutschen Ausbildung und seiner internationalen Beliebtheit.

Dans les années 60, époque de ces photos, Arrau s'était fait un nom depuis longtemps à Londres. À ses débuts, en 1922, il avait donné un concert avec Dame Nellie Melba, redoutable figure emblématique de l'opéra, et le violoniste Bronislaw Huberman, qui avait joué Brahms en présence du compositeur lui-même, ce qui en soi aurait dû être plutôt intimidant pour ce musicien chilien de 19 ans. Mais on n'effrayait pas Arrau si facilement : il avait donné son premier récital de piano à Santiago à l'âge de 5 ans, à Berlin à 11 ans et, à 15 ans, avait fait des tournées en Allemagne, en Scandinavie et ailleurs en Europe. Il avait joué des concertos sous la direction d'Arthur Nikisch, de Willem Mengelberg et de Wilhelm Furtwängler, et s'était serré la ceinture pendant six ans d'études acharnées à Berlin avant d'atterrir à Londres. On se demande si Melba et Huberman ont bien réalisé ce à quoi ils se confrontaient…

Durant les années 20 et 30, il combina sa carrière de soliste avec celle de professeur de piano au prestigieux conservatoire Stern de Berlin, et ce fut à Berlin qu'il interpréta la totalité de l'œuvre pour clavier de Bach dans une série de douze récitals, en 1935. Mais son intérêt pour Bach diminua les années suivantes, et son répertoire resta fermement ancré dans le XIXe siècle – Chopin, Liszt, Schumann, Brahms, et par-dessus tout Beethoven. A la sobriété de son attitude au piano répondait la grande profondeur de sentiment de son jeu. C'était un jeu de virtuose de la vieille école, allié à l'autorité d'une puissante intelligence, absolument sans ostentation, mais irrésistible et souvent profondément émouvant. Ses interprétations parfaites des sonates pour piano de Beethoven ont été acclamées dans le monde entier.

En 1940, il quitta Berlin et ouvrit sa propre école de piano à Santiago, mais un an plus tard, il partit pour les États-Unis où il fit une tournée triomphale et, finalement, s'installa à New York avec sa famille. Quand ces photos ont été prises, il était considéré à Londres comme le patriarche de la musique, aimé et respecté par les musiciens, le public et ses nombreux élèves. Encore un autre ambassadeur de la musique ? Possible, mais davantage dans les apparences que dans les faits, car ce qui faisait la singularité d'Arrau n'était pas tant la spécificité de ses origines que l'union d'un tempérament latin avec une éducation classique allemande et des sympathies universelles.

Claudio Arrau, Chilean musical ambassador, 6 June 1966.

Claudio Arrau, musikalischer Botschafter aus Chile, 6. Juni 1966.

Claudio Arrau, ambassadeur musical chilien, le 6 juin 1966.

Arrau at a rehearsal of Chopin's *First Piano Concerto* and Beethoven's *Fourth* with the London Philharmonic Orchestra under Sir Adrian Boult, 7 June 1961.

Claudio Arrau bei einer Probe von Chopins *Erstem* und Beethovens *Viertem Klavierkonzert* mit dem London Philharmonic Orchestra unter Sir Adrian Boult am 7. Juni 1961.

Arrau lors d'une répétition du *Premier Concerto pour piano* de Chopin et du *Quatrième* de Beethoven, avec l'Orchestre philharmonique de Londres dirigé par Sir Adrian Boult, le 7 juin 1961.

ALFRED BRENDEL   *1931

A serious, rather professorial figure in horn-rimmed glasses, who might almost be going to give a lecture rather than play the piano, Brendel is the most thoughtful of pianists, perhaps today the most profoundly aware of the great issues lying at the heart of the masterpieces that he now almost exclusively plays. This thoughtfulness is a quality that brings to mind that other great thinking pianist, Artur Schnabel, though it was in fact from the master classes of Schnabel's contemporary Edwin Fischer that the young Brendel had his first, enduring lessons in the great German repertory from Bach to Brahms.

At the time of these pictures, however, he was still relatively little known in England. He had made recordings of Mozart, Schubert and Liszt and the complete piano works of Beethoven, and was known to be well regarded in Austria during the 1950s, but it was not until 1962 that he made his first impression on London – characteristically playing all 32 of the Beethoven piano sonatas in a series of recitals at the Wigmore Hall. But as a young man it was as much as anything his charismatic performances of Liszt that first attracted attention. It was very good Liszt, too: the *Second Piano Concerto* sounded a better work than you thought it was (or perhaps than it is) when Brendel played it. In spite of the brilliance and technical skill there was never anything flashy – and after all, there is plenty to think about in Liszt.

In those early days there was sometimes a certain tenseness about his performing manner which may have helped to produce sparks but did not always favour the more serious end of the repertory. But with maturity came a more relaxed approach, and with it a deeper understanding of the works that were gradually becoming his main preoccupation – the great Viennese classics, above all Mozart, Beethoven and Schubert. This is the world in which Brendel is most completely at home, where his analytical grasp, sensitivity of style and nuance, and extraordinary intellectual and emotional involvement can produce its most powerful results.

By the time of these photographs Brendel was still a young man, but the word for his Beethoven was already 'magisterial'.

Alfred Brendel, eher ein professoraler Typ mit Hornbrille, von dem man erwarten könnte, daß er eine Vorlesung hält, anstatt ein Konzert zu geben, ist ein höchst bedächtiger Pianist, der sich der großen Bedeutung der Meisterwerke, die er interpretiert, vollauf bewußt ist. Obwohl diese Bedachtsamkeit an den ebenfalls sehr tiefgründigen Pianisten Arthur Schnabel erinnert, war es dessen Zeitgenosse Edwin Fischer, der Brendel das deutsche Repertoire von Bach bis Brahms nahebrachte.

Zur Zeit der hier gezeigten Fotografien war Brendel in London noch relativ unbekannt. Er hatte Einspielungen von Mozart, Schubert, Liszt und von Beethovens gesamtem Klavierwerk gemacht und hatte sich schon in den 50er Jahren einen guten Ruf in Österreich erworben. In London wurde man erst 1962 auf ihn aufmerksam, als er – typisch für ihn – sämtliche 32 Beethovensonaten in suite in der Wigmore Hall spielte. Als junger Mann fiel er besonders durch eine sehr eigene Liszt-Interpretation auf, und tatsächlich erhielt das *Zweite Klavierkonzert* unter seiner Bearbeitung eine wesentlich höhere Qualität, als das Stück an sich vermuten läßt. Trotz aller Brillanz und technischer Versiertheit hat Brendels Spiel niemals etwas Kitschiges und macht deutlich, daß Liszt bei aller Virtuosität auch Tiefgründiges hat.

In dieser frühen Zeit wirkte Brendels Spielweise oft ein wenig angespannt, was sicherlich bestimmten Höhepunkten, nicht immer aber den getragenen Passagen zugute kam. Mit der Reife kam jedoch auch größere Gelassenheit und damit ein größeres Verständnis der Werke, die zu seinem Hauptanliegen wurden – der Wiener Klassik, vor allem Mozart, Beethoven und Schubert. In dieser Musik ist Brendel am stärksten verwurzelt, und hier bringt er mit seiner analytischen Interpretation, seinem Gespür für Nuancen sowie seinem außerordentlich intellektuellen und emotionalen Engagement die größten Leistungen hervor.

Als diese Bilder aufgenommen wurden, war Brendel noch ein junger Mann, doch seine Beethoven-Interpretation hatte bereits eine ungeheure Ausstrahlung.

Avec son air sérieux, professoral – il porte des lunettes à monture d'écaille –, pouvant faire croire qu'il va donner une conférence plutôt qu'un concert, Brendel est peut-être à ce jour le pianiste le plus profondément conscient des problématiques présentes au cœur des chefs-d'œuvre que, dorénavant, il interprète presque exclusivement. Ce pouvoir de réflexion est une qualité qui le rapproche d'Arthur Schnabel, cet autre grand pianiste. Par ailleurs, c'est d'Edwin Fischer, contemporain de Schnabel, que le jeune Brendel a reçu ses premières et durables leçons sur le grand répertoire allemand, de Bach à Brahms.

Quand ces photos ont été prises, il était encore relativement peu connu en Angleterre. Il avait réalisé des enregistrements de Mozart, Schubert, Liszt et de la totalité des pièces pour piano de Beethoven ; il avait acquis une certaine notoriété en Autriche, dans les années 50, mais ce ne fut qu'en 1962 qu'il fit sensation à Londres pour la première fois, avec une interprétation marquante des 32 sonates pour piano de Beethoven lors d'une série de récitals au Wigmore Hall. Mais, au début de sa carrière, ses interprétations de Liszt avaient d'emblée attiré l'attention sur lui. C'était du très bon Liszt : le *Second Concerto pour piano* paraissait meilleur qu'on le pensait (ou peut-être qu'il n'est) quand Brendel le jouait. En dépit de l'éclat de son jeu et de son aisance technique, rien n'était jamais superficiel – et, après tout, Liszt est suffisamment riche pour donner lieu à de multiples lectures.

Au début de sa carrière, sa manière de jouer recelait parfois une certaine tension qui a dû lui permettre de briller, mais qui ne servait pas toujours les œuvres les plus sérieuses du répertoire. Avec la maturité, son approche se fit plus détendue, abordant avec une compréhension plus profonde les œuvres de ses compositeurs de prédilection : les grands classiques viennois, surtout Mozart, Beethoven et Schubert. C'est le monde dans lequel Brendel est le plus à l'aise, où sa compréhension analytique, sa faculté de sentir le style et les nuances, et un fort engagement intellectuel et émotionnel peuvent produire leurs plus puissants résultats.

A l'époque de ces photographies, Brendel était encore un jeune homme, mais on qualifiait déjà son interprétation de Beethoven de magistrale.

Alfred Brendel in 1970 – intellectual concentration.

Alfred Brendel, in höchster Konzentration, 1970.

Alfred Brendel en pleine concentration, 1970.

PABLO CASALS 1876-1973

There are some musicians whose names have become household words – Toscanini, Caruso, Paderewski perhaps – and of these none is held in greater reverence in the musical world than the Catalan cellist Pablo Casals. The mere mention of his name evokes memories of a style of musicianship whose integrity, intellectual rigour and passionate pursuit of musical beauty were unequalled in his day and, as most later cellists would admit, have remained unequalled since. Again and again the word 'noble' has been used to describe the sound he produced, and there seems no possible reason for not using it now.

He made his début at 14 and supported himself by playing in the local cafés of Barcelona and later in a music hall in Paris. Helped by Albéniz to achieve a royal scholarship, he gave his first concerts in Paris and London in 1899 – playing to Queen Victoria at Osborne House in the same year. Yet the single most important musical event in his early life had nothing to do with royalty or studies or concert-giving. It was the discovery of Bach, and particularly of the *Six suites for solo cello*. He found the score in a second-hand shop when he was 13 years old: 'It was the great revelation of my life. I immediately felt that this was something of exceptional importance, and hugged my treasures all the way home. For 12 years I studied and worked at them every day, and I was nearly 25 before I had the courage to play one of them in public.'

It was characteristic of Casals that he should have dedicated so much time and effort to these neglected masterpieces. Though regarded at the time as unplayable, they were not 'showy' works of the kind that might have tempted many virtuoso players; instead he saw in them the embodiment of that ultimate musical truth for which he was to search whenever he made music. For though his supremacy as a soloist was unchallenged, he thought of himself as a musician first, cellist second: that is why he joined Jacques Thibaud and Cortot to form one of the greatest piano trios of all time, why he founded his own orchestra in Barcelona and rehearsed with it to all hours of the night, why he continued composing well into his 90s.

And then, in 1936, came the Spanish Civil War. Vowing that he would never return to Spain until Franco was defeated, Casals went into voluntary exile, refused offers of hospitality from Britain and America and settled eventually in Prades, a Catalan village just over the border on the French side of the Pyrenees. He was as good as his word – better, even, refusing to play in either Germany or Italy while Hitler and Mussolini remained in power, and later renouncing public performance altogether in protest at the refusal of world powers to move against the Spanish regime. He relented a little in 1950 for the bicentenary of Bach's death, when he invited a number of eminent musicians to join him in making music at Prades. The event turned into an annual festival, and he later directed festivals at nearby Perpignan and faraway Puerto Rico, where he finally settled in 1956. A great deal of his later life was given up to teaching, composition and conducting. And he still occasionally appeared as a soloist, often in response to rather grand invitations, such as one from the White House in 1961. No mean achievement to have played for President Kennedy and Queen Victoria at an interval of 62 years.

Es gibt nur wenige Musiker, deren Name ein Begriff geworden ist – Toscanini, Caruso, Paderewski vielleicht –, aber keinem wird größere Wertschätzung innerhalb der Musikwelt entgegengebracht als dem katalanischen Cellisten Casals. Allein die Nennung seines Namens ruft Erinnerungen an das Urbild einer Musikerpersönlichkeit wach, deren Integrität, rationale Präzision und leidenschaftliche Suche nach musikalischer Schönheit unübertroffen war zu jener Zeit und, wie die meisten Cellisten zugestehen würden, bis heute geblieben ist. Wieder und wieder hat man sein Spiel als „edel" bezeichnet, und es gibt keinen Grund, dies hier nicht zu wiederholen.

Sein Debüt gab er mit 14 Jahren, und er lebte zunächst von Auftritten in verschiedenen Cafés in Barcelona und später von einer zweitrangigen Cellistenstelle in Paris. Nachdem ihm Albéniz zu einem Stipendium in England verholfen hatte, gab er 1899 seine ersten Konzerte in Paris und London. Im selben Jahr spielte er auch vor Königin Viktoria im Osborne Haus. Dennoch hatte das wichtigste musikalische Erlebnis in seiner Jugend nichts mit königlichen Hoheiten, seiner Ausbildung oder dem Konzertspiel zu tun, sondern bestand in der Entdeckung von Bach, vor allem von dessen *Sechs Suiten für Violoncello solo*, die der gerade Dreizehnjährige in einem Antiquariat fand: „Es war die große Offenbarung meines Lebens. Ich wußte sofort, daß dies etwas von herausragender Bedeutung war, und ich hielt meinen Schatz auf dem ganzen Heimweg fest in den Armen. 12 Jahre lang studierte und arbeitete ich jeden Tag daran, und ich war beinahe 25, bevor ich den Mut hatte, eine der Suiten öffentlich aufzuführen."

Es war ein Charakteristikum Casals', so viel Zeit und Mühe diesen bis dahin von der Musikwelt vernachlässigten Meisterwerken zu widmen. Obwohl die Suiten als unspielbar galten, waren sie trotzdem nicht „publikumswirksam" genug, viele Virtuosen herauszufordern; Casals dagegen sah in ihnen den Inbegriff der musikalischen Wahrheit, die er zeitlebens in seiner Arbeit suchte. Obgleich seine Überlegenheit als Solist unangefochten war, empfand Casals sich selbst zuerst als Musiker, dann als Cellist: Aus diesem Grund fand er sich mit Jacques Thibaud und Cortot zu einem der bedeutendsten Klaviertrios zusammen, gründete weiterhin ein eigenes Orchester in Barcelona, mit dem er die Nächte hindurch probte, und komponierte bis über sein neunzigstes Lebensjahr hinaus.

Doch dann brach 1939 der Spanische Bürgerkrieg aus und Casals gelobte, solange nicht nach Spanien zurückzukehren, bis Franco entmachtet sei, und wählte, Angebote aus England und Amerika ausschlagend, sein freiwilliges Exil schließlich in Prades, einem katalanischen Dorf, das direkt hinter der spanischen Grenze auf der französischen Seite der Pyrenäen liegt. Er hielt sein Gelübde nicht nur ein, sondern verweigerte zudem alle Konzerte in Nazi-Deutschland oder Mussolinis Italien, später sogar sämtliche öffentliche Konzerte, um gegen die Nachsicht der Weltmächte gegenüber dem spanischen Regime zu protestieren. Erst 1950, zur Feier von Bachs 200jährigem Todestag, ließ er sich erweichen, einige der bedeutendsten Musiker nach Prades einzuladen, um gemeinsam mit ihnen zu musizieren. Aus diesem Treffen wurde ein jährliches Festival. Später organisierte er Festspiele im nahegelegenen Perpignan und im fernen Puerto Rico, wo er sich 1956 endgültig niederließ. Den Großteil seines Lebens widmete er von da an dem Unterrichten und Dirigieren sowie der Komposition. Gelegentlich trat Casals noch als Solist auf, oft als Dank für besondere Einladungen, wie etwa 1961 im Weißen Haus. (Nicht schlecht, im Abstand von 62 Jahren für Königin Viktoria und Präsident Kennedy gespielt zu haben ...)

Il est quelques musiciens dont les noms sont connus de tous – Toscanini, Caruso, Paderewski peut-être – mais aucun n'est tenu en plus grande estime, dans et hors du monde musical, que le violoncelliste catalan Pablo Casals. La simple mention de son nom évoque intégrité, rigueur intellectuelle et poursuite passionnée de la beauté musicale, en quoi il était sans égal à son époque et le reste de nos jours, comme la plupart des violoncellistes s'accordent à le reconnaître. Le mot « noble » n'a cessé d'être utilisé pour qualifier le son qu'il produisait ; pourquoi ne pas le faire encore une fois ?

Il fit ses débuts à 14 ans et gagna sa vie en jouant dans les cafés de Barcelone et, plus tard, dans un music-hall à Paris. Grâce à Albéniz, il obtient une bourse royale, donne ses premiers concerts à Paris et à Londres en 1899 et joue la même année, pour la reine Victoria au Osborne House. Cependant l'événement musical le plus marquant de ses jeunes années n'a rien à voir avec la royauté ou les concerts. Ce fut la découverte de Bach – à 13 ans – et particulièrement des *Six suites pour violoncelle seul* dont il trouva la partition dans une boutique d'occasion : « Ce fut la plus grande révélation de ma vie. J'ai immédiatement su que c'était d'une importance capitale, et j'ai serré mes trésors contre moi en rentrant à la maison. J'ai commencé à les jouer dans un état d'excitation indescriptible. Pendant douze ans, je les ai étudiées et travaillées chaque jour, et j'avais presque 25 ans quand j'ai eu le courage d'en jouer une en public. »

C'était caractéristique de Casals de dédier tant de temps et d'effort à ces chefs-d'œuvre méconnus à l'époque. Bien que considérées comme injouables, les suites n'avaient évidemment pas le clinquant qui aurait pu tenter nombre de virtuoses. Casals voyait en elles l'incarnation de cette vérité musicale suprême qu'il recherchait chaque fois qu'il faisait de la musique. Alors que sa suprématie en tant que soliste était incontestable et incontestée, il pensait qu'avant d'être violoncelliste il était d'abord un musicien : c'est pour cela qu'il rejoignit Jacques Thibaud et Alfred Cortot pour former l'un des plus prestigieux trios de tous les temps, puis qu'il fonda son propre orchestre à Barcelone, et qu'il continua à composer alors qu'il avait plus de 90 ans.

En 1936 éclate la Guerre civile espagnole : faisant le vœu de ne jamais retourner en Espagne tant que Franco ne serait pas vaincu, Casals s'exila volontairement, refusant les offres d'hospitalité venues d'Angleterre et d'Amérique, et s'installa finalement en France, dans le village catalan de Prades, dans les Pyrénées. Il a tenu parole – et même mieux, en refusant de jouer en Allemagne ou en Italie tant qu'Hitler et Mussolini seraient au pouvoir et, plus tard, en renonçant à donner des concerts en public pour protester contre le refus des grandes puissances d'agir contre le régime espagnol. Il fit une entorse à sa résolution en 1950 pour le bicentenaire de la mort de Bach, quand il invita un certain nombre d'éminents musiciens à le rejoindre pour jouer à Prades. Cet événement se transforma en un festival annuel et, plus tard, il dirigea des festivals dans la proche Perpignan et la lointaine Porto Rico, où il s'établit en 1956. Une grande partie de sa vie, dans les années suivantes, fut consacrée à l'enseignement, à la composition et à la direction d'orchestre. Il se produisait occasionnellement comme soliste, souvent en réponse à des invitations prestigieuses, comme celle de la Maison Blanche en 1961. Quel accomplissement d'avoir pu jouer pour le président Kennedy et la reine Victoria dans un intervalle de 62 ans.

Nobility in old age: Pablo Casals in his
89th year, 4 September 1965.

Vornehmes Spiel in hohem Alter:
Pablo Casals in seinem 89. Lebensjahr,
4. September 1965.

Le grand âge dans toute sa noblesse :
Pablo Casals dans sa 89ᵉ année,
le 4 septembre 1965.

Casals at the recording of the Dvořák *Cello Concerto* for His Master's Voice in Prague, April 1937. This was the first recording session that Auerbach photographed. The Czech Philharmonic Orchestra was conducted by George Szell, and Casals characteristically smoked his pipe throughout the proceedings.

Casals bei der Aufnahme von Dvořáks *Cellokonzert* für die Plattenfirma His Masters Voice in Prag, April 1937. Erstmals hielt Auerbach auf diesem Foto die im Vergleich zu Proben oder Konzerten gänzlich unterschiedliche Stimmung bei einer Plattenaufnahme fest. Dabei wurde das Tschechische Symphonie Orchester von George Szell dirigiert, und Casals rauchte während des gesamten Verlaufs der Aufnahme seine typische Pfeife.

Casals lors de l'enregistrement du *Concerto pour violoncelle* de Dvořák pour La Voix de son maître, à Prague, en avril 1937. C'était la première séance d'enregistrement photographiée par Auerbach. L'Orchestre philharmonique tchèque était dirigé par George Szell, et Casals, bien entendu, fuma sa pipe pendant toute la séance.

Casals rehearsing his oratorio *El Pesebre* ('The Manger'), written between 1943 and 1960 and conducted by the great cellist to launch a worldwide peace campaign in 1962. This rehearsal, at the Royal Festival Hall on 24 September 1963, was followed by a performance on the 29th – Casals's last public appearance in Britain.

Der große Cellist Casals hier als Dirigent bei Proben zu seinem Oratorium *El Pesebre* („Die Krippe"), das er zwischen 1943 und 1960 geschrieben hatte und dessen Uraufführung er 1962 anläßlich der Auftaktveranstaltung zu einer weltweiten Kampagne für den Frieden selbst dirigierte. Auf die hier dokumentierte Probe am 24. September 1963 in der Royal Festival Hall in London folgte das Konzert am 29. September 1963 – der letzte öffentliche Auftritt Casals' in Großbritannien.

Casals répétant son oratorio *El Pesebre* (« La Crèche »), écrit entre 1943 et 1960, et dirigé par lui-même pour lancer une campagne mondiale en faveur de la paix, en 1962. Cette répétition, au Royal Festival Hall le 24 septembre 1963, a été suivie par une représentation le 29 – la dernière apparition en public de Casals en Angleterre.

Walking in Zermatt with his second wife Marta, 60 years his junior, 4 September 1965.

Casals auf einem Spaziergang mit seiner 60 Jahre jüngeren Frau Marta in Zermatt am 4. September 1965.

Casals à Zermatt avec sa seconde épouse Marta, de soixante ans sa cadette, le 4 septembre 1965.

(1, 2, 3) Casals with a pupil at one of his master classes in Zermatt, September 1964. Casals was an inspiring teacher and had included Guilhermina Suggia and Gaspar Cassadó among his earlier pupils. (4, 5, 6) At Zermatt, 1965.

(1, 2, 3) Casals mit einem Schüler während eines seiner Meisterkurse in Zermatt im September 1964. Casals galt als inspirierender Lehrer und zählte Guilhermina Suggia und Gaspar Cassadó zu seinen frühen Schülern. (4, 5, 6) In Zermatt, 1965.

(1, 2, 3) Casals avec l'un de ses élèves à Zermatt, en septembre 1964. Casals, professeur qui suscitait l'inspiration, avait eu comme élèves Guilhermina Suggia et Gaspar Cassadó. (4, 5, 6) A Zermatt en 1965.

1

2

3

4

5

6

A small, gnome-like figure on the stage, Cherkassky approached the piano with a neatness and circumspection that could not quite conceal the bursting nervous energy within. He was a man who loved the big occasion, Carnegie Hall, the tumultuous applause. He was not a studio artist – all his best recordings were live, because he needed an audience, he needed someone to play to, someone to whom he could show all the miraculous new possibilities he had discovered in the works he had performed so many times. And the audiences loved it – you can hear the gasps and little ripples of laughter teased out of them by the unpredictability of his interpretations. A Cherkassky recital was a constant surprise, and no pianist had a greater genius for spontaneity and renewal.

Not everything was always right. That was part of the surprise. But on a good night the technique sparkled with improvisatory brilliance: nothing, absolutely nothing, was taken for granted, the great works of the romantic repertory – the Liszt *Sonata*, the Schumann *Études symphoniques*, the big Chopin pieces – were lovingly reconsidered between, one sometimes felt even *during*, every performance, and even war-horses like the Liszt *Hungarian Rhapsodies* were made to reveal something new. He was too idiosyncratic an artist to make an ideal interpreter of the classical masterpieces, but he was at home in the arrangements of Ferruccio Busoni or Leopold Godowsky. A Russian by birth, he had an instinctive feel for the music of his native country, and Tchaikovsky, Rachmaninov, Scriabin, Prokofiev were treated with rich imagination; even a salon piece like Rubinstein's *Melody in F* regained a tender freshness one thought it had lost for ever.

And of course he was the great pianist for encores. As a Cherkassky recital ended, the quicksilver quality which had informed his whole programme found a last outlet in a series of evocative last words, each just a little different from the last time you heard it ...

Auf der Bühne eine kleine, gnomartige Erscheinung, ging Cherkassky mit einer Akkuratheit und Aufmerksamkeit auf den Flügel zu, die die berstende Energie und Anspannung, die in ihm steckte, nicht ganz verbergen konnten. Er war ein Mann, der das große Ereignis liebte – Carnegie Hall, tosenden Applaus. Er war kein Künstler für das Tonstudio, und so sind seine besten Aufnahmen Livemitschnitte, denn er brauchte ein sichtbares Publikum, Menschen, denen er die wunderbaren Möglichkeiten vorführen konnte, die er in Werken, die er schon so oft gespielt hatte, neu entdeckt hatte. Und das Publikum liebte es – in den Aufzeichnungen hört man Seufzer und manchmal ein kurzes Lachen als unvermittelte Reaktion auf seine überraschende Interpretation. Ein Cherkassky-Abend war eine fortgesetzte Überraschung, und kein Pianist hatte eine vergleichbare Begabung für Spontaneität und Innovation.

Er spielte nicht immer alles richtig – das gehörte zur Überraschung. Doch an einem guten Abend wurde seine Technik von brillanter Improvisation gekrönt. Nichts, aber auch gar nichts wurde für selbstverständlich genommen. Die großen Werke der Romantik – die *Sonate* von Liszt, Schumanns *Études symphoniques*, die großen Chopinstücke – wurden zwischen, ja man hatte sogar den Eindruck *während* der Aufführung liebevoll neu überdacht. Auf diese Weise wurden selbst hochvirtuose Stücke wie Liszts *Ungarische Rhapsodien* zu einer Offenbarung. Er war ein allzu eigenständiger Künstler, um die klassischen Meisterwerke in einem idealen Sinn zu interpretieren; Werke von Ferruccio Busoni und Leopold Godowsky entsprachen ihm aber offenbar sehr. Als gebürtiger Russe hatte er einen Instinkt für die Musik seiner Heimat und interpretierte deshalb Tschaikowsky, Rachmaninow, Skrjabin oder Prokofjew ganz besonders phantasievoll. Aber auch ein Salonstück wie Rubinsteins *Melodie in F-Dur* gewann durch ihn eine Frische zurück, die längst verloren schien.

Darüber hinaus war er natürlich der Meister der Zugabe. Am Ende eines Cherkassky-Abends fand die immense Energie, die sein ganzes Spiel belebt hatte, ihr Ventil in der Aneinanderreihung glanzvoller Zugaben, eine jede eben ein wenig anders gespielt als normalerweise üblich ...

De petite taille, l'air d'un gnome sur scène, Cherkassky s'approchait du piano avec une élégance et une circonspection qui ne pouvaient complètement cacher l'énergie nerveuse qui l'habitait. Il adorait les soirées de gala, Carnegie Hall, le tumulte des applaudissements. Ce n'était pas un pianiste de studio – ses meilleurs enregistrements ont été réalisés en public, parce qu'il avait besoin d'un public, de quelqu'un pour qui jouer, de quelqu'un à qui il pouvait montrer toutes les merveilleuses nouvelles possibilités qu'il avait découvertes dans les œuvres tant de fois interprétées. Et le public adorait cela – ses interprétations imprévisibles lui arrachaient de petits cris de surprise et des vagues de rires. Un récital de Cherkassky était une surprise permanente et aucun pianiste ne fut plus doué pour la spontanéité et le renouvellement.

Tout n'était pas parfait. Cela faisait partie de la surprise. Mais, quand il était en veine, sa technique étincelait en éclatantes improvisations : rien, absolument rien n'était tenu pour acquis, les grandes œuvres du répertoire romantique – la *Sonate* de Liszt, les *Etudes symphoniques* de Schumann, les grands morceaux de Chopin – étant amoureusement reconsidérées entre chaque représentation, voire pendant. Il arrivait même à tirer du nouveau de «tubes» comme les *Rhapsodies hongroises* de Liszt. C'était un artiste trop original pour être un interprète idéal des chefs-d'œuvre classiques, mais il se sentait à l'aise avec les adaptations de Ferruccio Busoni ou Leopold Godowsky. Russe de naissance, il avait un sens instinctif de la musique de son pays d'origine, et Tchaïkovski, Rachmaninov, Scriabine, Prokofiev étaient traités avec beaucoup d'imagination ; même une œuvre de salon comme la *Mélodie en fa* de Rubinstein retrouvait sous ses doigts la tendre fraîcheur que l'on croyait à jamais perdue.

Et, bien entendu, il était le grand pianiste des rappels. Quand un récital de Cherkassky finissait, le vif-argent dans lequel avait baigné tout son programme était couronné d'un bouquet final juste un peu différent de celui de son précédent concert ...

Shura Cherkassky, 25 February 1960. A last link with the golden age of the romantic virtuoso.

Shura Cherkassky, 25. Februar 1960. Eine letzte Verbindung zum Goldenen Zeitalter dieses romantischen Virtuosen.

Shura Cherkassky, le 25 février 1960. Une dernière liaison avec l'âge d'or de ce virtuose romantique.

Before a recording session, making sure everything is just so. If you are as short as Cherkassky, the height of the piano stool is a matter of crucial importance... 25 February 1960.

Vor einer Aufnahme muß sichergestellt werden, daß alles seine Richtigkeit hat. Bei einer so geringen Körpergröße ist die Höhe des Pianohockers für Cherkassky eine Sache von entscheidender Wichtigkeit ..., 25. Februar 1960.

Avant une séance d'enregistrement, assurez-vous que tout est parfait. Quand vous êtes aussi petit que Cherkassky, la hauteur du tabouret est d'une importance capitale... 25 février 1960.

Cherkassky's hands, 25 February 1960.

Cherkasskys Hände, 25. Februar 1960.

Les mains de Cherkassky, le 25 février 1960.

Curzon on the platform was a very English figure, self-contained, almost retiring, certainly not demonstrative, and beside the more flamboyant visitors who flooded into London during the period following the war he presented a perhaps rather unromantic image to the concertgoing public. It was an impression that was encouraged by the comparative rarity of his appearances: a perfectionist, with a profound belief in the importance of constant practice and re-evaluation, he felt the necessity in his later years for long periods away from the public ear and eye. But, like that other very English artist Adrian Boult, he was dangerously easy to underrate. There was a great volcano of temperament under that civilized exterior, which could sometimes prove a painful trap for the unwary.

A student at the Royal Academy of Music at the age of 12, he made his first public appearance four years later as one of the soloists in a Bach triple concerto at the Queen's Hall. The performance was conducted by Sir Henry Wood, who remained a constant supporter of Curzon's until his death in 1945. But Curzon wasn't ready to take off yet. After a brief period as a junior professor at the Royal Academy he spent two years in Berlin with Arthur Schnabel, the greatest piano teacher of his generation and probably the greatest single influence in Curzon's artistic development, and followed them, by way of complete contrast, with a period in Paris working with Nadia Boulanger and the great harpsichordist Wanda Landowska.

Tours of Europe and America followed, with a repertory that in those days included most of the great virtuoso piano works of the romantic period, though in later years he tended to drop out of the more extrovert end of the market and concentrate his ever-intensifying attention on the classical composers, particularly Beethoven, Schubert and Mozart. But he was always interested in the music of his British contemporaries, giving first performances of works by Lennox Berkeley and Alan Rawsthorne; during the Second World War he became a close friend of Benjamin Britten, with whom he shared pacifist views, and gave a number of piano recitals which introduced Britten's own works for that medium to British audiences.

Curzon could sometimes appear tense in performance, and it often astonished people to see the ease with which, the minute a performance or a recording session was over, he would relax, and chat, and talk about books, or movies that he had seen. But the concentration while he was working, or preparing himself to work, was tremendous. On one occasion, when he was due to arrive in Vienna by train for a recording session, a group of colleagues from the recording studio went to the station to meet him, but he didn't emerge from the train and they walked up and down the platform calling his name. He was found an hour later, sitting practising at his dummy keyboard, in his special compartment, in a siding where his coach had been shunted, totally absorbed. He had noticed nothing.

Clifford Curzon with the English composer Sir Arthur Bliss at the first Leeds International Piano Competiton, at which they were judges, September 1963.

Clifford Curzon mit dem englischen Komponisten Sir Arthur Bliss beim 1. Internationalen Klavierwettbewerb in Leeds im September 1963, zu dem sie beide als Preisrichter bestellt waren.

Clifford Curzon en compagnie du compositeur anglais Sir Arthur Bliss lors du premier Concours international de piano de Leeds, où ils faisaient partie du jury, septembre 1963.

Sir Clifford Curzon bewahrte auf der Bühne stets eine sehr englische Haltung – selbstbeherrscht, fast zurückhaltend und ganz sicher nicht demonstrativ. Unter all den extravaganten Erscheinungen, die in der Nachkriegszeit nach London strömten, bot er dem Konzertpublikum ein eher schlichtes Bild. Seine verhältnismäßig seltenen Auftritte trugen das ihrige zu dieser Unauffälligkeit bei. Er war ein Perfektionist, der es für unerläßlich hielt, regelmäßig zu üben, zu lernen und sich zu verbessern. In späteren Jahren zog er sich deshalb oft aus der Öffentlichkeit zurück und war über längere Zeiträume weder zu sehen noch zu hören. Ebenso wie jener andere, sehr englische Künstler, Adrian Boult, wurde Curzon allzuleicht unterschätzt; unter der beherrschten Oberfläche verbarg sich jedoch ein heftiges Temperament, das den Ahnungslosen gelegentlich durchaus unangenehm überraschen konnte.

Bereits mit zwölf Jahren studierte er an der Royal Academy of Music. Vier Jahre später hatte er seinen ersten öffentlichen Auftritt als Solist in Bachs Tripelkonzert in der Queen's Hall unter der Leitung von Sir Henry Wood, der ihn zeit seines Lebens, bis 1945, weiter förderte. Curzon war jedoch noch nicht bereit für einen Karrierestart. Kurze Zeit unterrichtete er an der Royal Academy und ging dann für zwei Jahre nach Berlin zu Arthur Schnabel, dem größten Klavierlehrer seiner Generation. Schnabel übte wohl den deutlichsten Einfluß auf Curzons künstlerische Entwicklung aus. Danach verbrachte Curzon einige Zeit in Paris, um seinen Berliner Erfahrungen nun die Zusammenarbeit mit Nadia Boulanger und der großen Cembalistin Wanda Landowska entgegenzustellen.

Es folgten Tourneen in Europa und Amerika. Sein Repertoire umfaßte damals auch die großen, virtuosen Klavierstücke der Romantik. Später entfernte er sich zunehmend von dieser extremen Expressivität und wandte sich immer stärker den klassischen Komponisten zu, insbesondere Beethoven, Schubert und Mozart. Darüber verlor er jedoch nie das Interesse an zeitgenössischer englischer Musik. Werke von Lennox Berkeley und Alan Rawsthorne erlebten mit ihm ihre Uraufführungen, und während des Zweiten Weltkriegs entwickelte sich eine enge Freundschaft zu Benjamin Britten, der seine pazifistische Haltung teilte. Curzon führte das britische Publikum auch mit einigen Konzerten in Brittens Klavierstücke ein.

Curzon konnte während der Aufführungen sehr angespannt wirken. Seine entspannte Art direkt nach einem Konzert oder einer Studioaufnahme hat oft überrascht. Er lockerte sich, plauderte und unterhielt sich über Bücher oder über Filme, die er gesehen hatte. Während er spielte oder sich vorbereitete, war er jedoch äußerst konzentriert. Einmal fuhr er mit dem Zug zu einer Studioaufnahme nach Wien, und eine Gruppe von Kollegen war zum Bahnhof gekommen, um ihn abzuholen. Curzon erschien nicht, und sie liefen auf dem Bahnsteig auf und ab und riefen nach ihm. Eine Stunde später fand man ihn vor seiner Übungstastatur in seinem Sonderabteil auf einem Abstellgleis. Der Waggon war umrangiert worden, und Curzon war so in seine Arbeit vertieft gewesen, daß er es nicht bemerkt hatte.

Sur scène, Curzon était typiquement anglais, avec une retenue semblant presque friser la timidité. Il était certainement loin d'être expansif et, en comparaison à tous les hôtes qui éblouissaient Londres en cette période d'après-guerre, il offrait au public une image que certains ne trouvaient peut-être pas assez romantique à leur goût. Il entretenait d'ailleurs cette impression par la rareté de ses apparitions. En perfectionniste pour qui la constance du travail, les études et la remise en question étaient indispensables, il éprouvait souvent la nécessité de s'isoler du public et s'il était très facile de le sous-estimer comme c'était également le cas pour un autre artiste très « British », Adrian Boult, cela pouvait se révéler aussi dangereux. L'imprudent pris à ce piège n'avait souvent plus qu'à s'en mordre les doigts.

Curzon entra à la Royal Academy of Music à l'âge de 12 ans et effectua son premier concert seulement quatre ans après, comme soliste dans un triple concerto de Bach donné au Queen's Hall. Jusqu'à sa mort en 1945, Sir Henry Wood, qui dirigeait cette représentation, resterait un inconditionnel de Curzon qui, à l'époque, était pourtant encore loin de voler de ses propres ailes. Après un bref passage comme professeur à la Royal Academy, il décide de reprendre ses études auprès d'Arthur Schnabel, le plus grand professeur de piano de sa génération et celui qui le marquerait presque exclusivement de son influence. Il séjourne pour cela deux années à Berlin, qui contrastent singulièrement avec celles passées ensuite à Paris. Là, il travaillera avec Nadia Boulanger et la grande claveciniste Wanda Landowska.

Il enchaîne ensuite une série de tournées en Europe et en Amérique, distillant un répertoire qui comprenait à l'époque toutes les grandes œuvres romantiques pour piano. Plus tard, il ferait d'ailleurs le tri parmi celles-ci, excluant les plus exhibitionnistes, et par là-même, les plus commerciales pour ne plus se concentrer que sur les compositeurs classiques, dont Beethoven, Schubert et Mozart. Il garda cependant toujours un intérêt certain pour ses compatriotes contemporains et interpréta notamment pour la première fois les compositions de Lennox Berkeley et d'Alan Rawthorne. La Seconde Guerre mondiale le rapproche de Benjamin Britten qui exprime comme lui des opinions pacifistes et avec qui il se lie d'une profonde amitié. Il donnera de lui une série de récitals de piano qui feront connaître Britten auprès du public britannique comme un grand compositeur digne de cet instrument.

Curzon semblait parfois très tendu sur scène et il était étonnant de voir à quel point il pouvait être ensuite décontracté dès que le concert ou l'enregistrement était fini. C'était alors le moment pour lui de bavarder, de parler des livres qu'il venait de lire, des films qu'il avait vus. C'était le jour et la nuit. Lorsqu'il travaillait ou préparait un récital, son degré de concentration atteignait des sommets inouïs, à tel point que se rendant à Vienne pour un enregistrement, il causa une peur inattendue à ses collègues venus l'attendre à la gare. Alors que le train était arrêté depuis un long moment, il n'avait toujours pas donné signe de vie. Ses confrères avaient pourtant arpenté le quai en l'appelant à grands cris. Une heure plus tard, on le trouva enfin en train de répéter sur un clavier factice, dans son compartiment. Absorbé par le travail, il ne s'était même pas aperçu que son wagon avait été placé sur une voie de garage.

By all that is fair and just, Jacqueline Du Pré ought to be included in the section of this book reserved for the Younger Generation, but although she was born after Erich Auerbach arrived in London her career was over four years before he died, brought to an end at the age of only 28 by the ravages of multiple sclerosis.

She began young, taking her first lessons when she was five years old and making her London début at the Wigmore Hall only a few weeks after her sixteenth birthday. But this was no child prodigy: certainly there was a freshness, a natural quality about her playing and her personality that is not always found in more seasoned artists, but the breadth of understanding, the instinctive sense of style and the control of technique were already at a highly professional level, and the recital was a sensation. It was repeated a year later at the Festival Hall when she played the Elgar *Cello Concerto*, a work with which her name was always to be linked. Elgar's autumnal masterpiece brought out the best of her warm romantic temperament and the maturity that belied her years: she played it at her New York début, with Antal Dorati conducting, and many times with that great Elgarian, Sir John Barbirolli, with whom she made a recording which is still in a class by itself.

In 1967 she married the pianist and conductor Daniel Barenboim, with whom she shared much of her musical activity – as a chamber-music player in duet sonatas and in trios with Pinchas Zukerman, and as a soloist in concertos conducted by her husband. The freshness and spontaneity of her playing remained undimmed, and there seemed no limit to the artistic possibilities that opened up before her. Yet only four years later she had to take a year off from playing on medical advice. She made a brief return to the platform; it didn't last, but although she was compelled to give up her concert career in 1973, she was still able to give a series of master classes on television which were as remarkable for courage as for musical understanding.

Eigentlich müßte die Cellistin Jacqueline Du Pré in dem der jüngeren Generation vorbehaltenen Abschnitt dieses Buches behandelt werden, aber obwohl sie erst geboren wurde, nachdem Erich Auerbach nach London gekommen war, mußte sie ihre Karriere bereits vier Jahre vor dessen Tod wieder beenden, 28jährig, geschwächt von Multipler Sklerose.

Ihre ersten Unterrichtsstunden erhielt sie bereits mit fünf Jahren, ihr Londoner Debüt in der Wigmore Hall gab sie nur wenige Wochen nach ihrem sechzehnten Geburtstag. Aber sie war kein Wunderkind – sicher, die Frische und Ursprünglichkeit ihres Spiels und ihrer Persönlichkeit waren ungewöhnlich und fehlten selbst vielen renommierteren Künstlern; aber das Ausmaß ihres musikalischen Verständnisses, ihr instinktives Gefühl für die angemessene Ausdrucksweise und ihre technischen Fähigkeiten verrieten bereits höchste Professionalität, und das Konzert wurde zu einer Sensation. Dies wiederholte sich ein Jahr später in der Festival Hall, als sie Elgars *Cellokonzert* aufführte, das seither untrennbar mit ihrem Namen verbunden ist. In Elgars spätem Meisterwerk vermochte die Cellistin am besten ihr warmes, romantisches Temperament auszudrücken und die Reife, die ihr tatsächliches Alter längst übertraf. Sie spielte dieses Konzert unter dem Dirigenten Antal Dorati bei ihrem New Yorker Debüt, und später oftmals mit dem großen Elgarianer Sir John Barbirolli, mit dem sie auch eine Aufnahme einspielte, die nach wie vor ihresgleichen sucht.

1967 heiratete Jacqueline Du Pré den Pianisten und Dirigenten Daniel Barenboim, mit dem sie einen Großteil ihrer musikalischen Aktivitäten teilte – im Bereich der Kammermusik in Duosonaten oder, zusammen mit Pinchas Zukerman, in Klaviertrios, und als Solistin in Konzerten, die ihr Mann dirigierte. Die Frische und Spontaneität ihres Spiels blieb ungetrübt bestehen, und es schienen ihren künstlerischen Möglichkeiten keinerlei Grenzen gesetzt zu sein. Doch nur vier Jahre später mußte sie auf ärztliche Anordnung das Cellospielen für ein Jahr einstellen. Sie kehrte noch einmal kurz auf die Bühne zurück, mußte allerdings 1973 ihre Konzertkarriere endgültig aufgeben. Dennoch verblieb ihr die Möglichkeit, über das Fernsehen Meisterkurse zu erteilen, die ihren Lebensmut ebenso bemerkenswert vermittelten wie ihr musikalisches Verständnis.

En toute justice, Jacqueline Du Pré devrait apparaître dans la section de ce livre réservée à la jeune génération, mais, bien qu'elle soit née après l'arrivée d'Erich Auerbach à Londres, elle devait terminer sa carrière, à l'âge de 28 ans, quatre ans avant qu'il ne meure, en raison des ravages d'une sclérose en plaques.

Elle a commencé jeune, prenant ses premières leçons à 5 ans et faisant ses débuts à Londres, au Wigmore Hall, quelques semaines après son seizième anniversaire. Mais elle n'était pas une enfant prodige : il y avait sans aucun doute, dans son jeu et sa personnalité, une fraîcheur, une qualité naturelle que l'on ne trouve pas toujours chez des artistes plus confirmés, mais sa grande sensibilité, son sens instinctif du style et son contrôle de la technique avaient déjà atteint un niveau professionnel, et ce récital fit sensation. Sensation qui se renouvela un an plus tard, au Festival Hall, quand elle joua le *Concerto pour violoncelle* d'Elgar, une œuvre à laquelle son nom devait toujours resté lié. Le chef-d'œuvre automnal d'Elgar mettait en valeur son ardent tempérament romantique et sa maturité. Elle le joua pour ses débuts à New York, sous la direction d'Antal Dorati, et plusieurs fois avec le grand elgarien, Sir John Barbirolli, avec lequel elle en réalisa un enregistrement hors pair.

En 1967, elle épousa le pianiste et chef d'orchestre Daniel Barenboïm, avec qui elle a partagé une grande part de son activité musicale – comme membre de duos et trios avec Pinchas Zukerman et comme soliste dans des concertos dirigés par son mari. La fraîcheur et la spontanéité de son jeu étaient intactes, et il ne semblait pas y avoir de limites aux possibilités artistiques qui s'ouvraient devant elle. Cependant, quatre ans plus tard, elle dut, sur avis médical, s'arrêter pendant un an. Après un bref retour sur scène, elle fut obligée d'arrêter sa carrière de concertiste en 1973, ce qui ne l'empêcha pas de donner une série de cours à la télévision, qui furent remarquables autant pour son courage que pour sa compréhension de la musique.

Jacqueline Du Pré, 2 January 1962, three weeks before her 17th birthday.

Jacqueline Du Pré am 2. Januar 1962, drei Wochen vor ihrem 17. Geburtstag.

Jacqueline Du Pré, le 2 janvier 1962, trois semaines avant son 17ᵉ anniversaire.

Jacqueline Du Pré in a recital at the Queen Elizabeth Hall, London, with her husband, the pianist Daniel Barenboim, shortly after their marriage in 1967.

Jacqueline Du Pré bei einem Konzert in der Queen Elizabeth Hall in London, gemeinsam mit ihrem Mann, dem Pianisten Daniel Barenboim, kurz nach ihrer Heirat 1967.

Jacqueline Du Pré lors d'un récital au Queen Elizabeth Hall à Londres, avec son mari, le pianiste Daniel Barenboïm, peu après leur mariage en 1967.

Jacqueline Du Pré preparing a recital of Bach, Beethoven and Stravinsky with the pianist Stephen Bishop-Kovacevich at Goldsmiths' Hall, London, 15 October 1964.

Jacqueline Du Pré und der Pianist Stephen Bishop-Kovacevich, die in der Goldsmiths' Hall in London für ein Konzert mit Werken von Bach, Beethoven und Strawinsky proben. 15. Oktober 1964.

Jacqueline Du Pré préparant un récital de Bach, Beethoven et Stravinski avec le pianiste Stephen Bishop Kovacevitch au Goldsmiths' Hall à Londres, le 15 octobre 1964.

PIERRE FOURNIER   1906-1986

A man of great charm and distinction, elegant and very French, the cellist Pierre Fournier added to the impression of *grand seigneur* with the stick that he always used when walking – though in fact the limp which afflicted him all his life was very real and had its origin in an attack of polio suffered when he was a child. It was immediately clear from his platform manner that here was a civilized human being of intelligence and sensitivity, and it comes as no surprise to find that much of his artistic career was involved with chamber music rather than the more flamboyant virtuoso repertory.

Not that he wasn't a magnificent solo player – he gave highly personal, richly musical accounts of the great romantic concertos from Dvořák to Walton, a Don Quixote of great subtlety and pathos in Strauss's tone poems, and warm, infectiously enjoyable performances of the Bach solo sonatas. With contemporary music he could be robustly authoritative in works of which he was giving first performances, or which were written specifically for him like the concertos of Frank Martin and Bohuslav Martinů or the sonata by Poulenc.

But in the year of his début, at the age of 19, he had played the cello part in the first, private, performance of Fauré's string quartet, only a few months after the composer's death, and from then on chamber music played an important role in his life. In 1943, when Casals dropped out of the famous trio with Jacques Thibaud and Alfred Cortot, Fournier was the man who took his place, and four years later he joined almost equally illustrious forces with Joseph Szigeti, William Primrose and Artur Schnabel for chamber concerts, first in Europe and then in America. Later still he appeared in piano trios with Henryk Szeryng and Wilhelm Kempff, and gave with Kempff a memorable series of performances of the Beethoven cello sonatas which they also recorded.

Off the platform a warm, informal human being, with a sense of humour and keen enjoyment of the good things of life, Fournier was the finest kind of artist – not one to hog the limelight but to accept it with dignity as his due.

Der Cellist Pierre Fournier, ein sehr charmanter, distinguierter und eleganter Mann, ganz Franzose, wirkte um so mehr wie ein Grandseigneur, als er stets auf einen Spazierstock gestützt ging – keine Pose, sondern eine Notwendigkeit. Seit einer Kinderlähmung in jungen Jahren war er gehbehindert. Wenn man ihn auf der Bühne erlebte, erkannte man sofort, daß man es hier mit einem intelligenten, hochsensiblen Menschen zu tun hatte, und es überrascht nicht, daß er sich intensiver der Kammermusik widmete als einem pathetischen Repertoire.

Selbstverständlich war er ein ausgezeichneter Solist. Seine ausdrucksvollen Interpretationen der großen romantischen Tradition von Dvořák bis Walton zeugen von einem tiefen musikalischen Verständnis. Lieder von Strauss präsentierte er wie ein Don Quijote mit großer Subtilität und hohem Pathos, und die Solosonaten von Bach trug er mit Wärme und Kunstfertigkeit vor. Uraufführungen zeitgenössischer Musik gab er mit kompetenter Autorität, besonders wenn sie eigens für ihn geschrieben waren, wie z. B. die Konzerte von Frank Martin und Bohuslav Martinů oder die Sonate von Poulenc.

Im Jahr seines Debüts, im Alter von neunzehn Jahren, hatte er nur wenige Monate nach Faurés Tod den Cellopart in der ersten privaten Aufführung dessen Streichquartettes gespielt. Von da an spielte die Kammermusik eine wichtige Rolle in seinem Leben. Als Casals 1943 aus dem berühmten Trio mit Jacques Thibaud und Alfred Cortot austrat, übernahm Fournier seinen Platz. Vier Jahre später tat er sich mit ähnlich illustren Talenten – Joseph Szigeti, William Primrose und Artur Schnabel – zu einer Kammerkonzerttournee zusammen, die erst durch Europa und dann durch Amerika zog. Mit Henryk Szeryng und Wilhelm Kempff bildete er ein Klaviertrio, und mit Kempff gab er eine erinnerungswürdige Konzertreihe von Beethovens Cellosonaten, die auch aufgenommen wurde.

Außerhalb des Konzertsaals war Fournier ein warmherziger, unkomplizierter Mensch mit Sinn für Humor und einem Bewußtsein für die schönen Dinge des Lebens. Als Künstler gehörte er zu den Besten – er lief dem Erfolg nicht hinterher, sondern nahm ihn mit Würde als etwas Angemessenes entgegen.

D'un charme certain, d'une distinction et d'une élégance très françaises, le violoncelliste Pierre Fournier complétait sa silhouette de « grand seigneur » en ne se séparant jamais de sa canne, qui l'aidait à atténuer la boiterie qui l'affligea toute sa vie suite à une attaque de poliomyélite dans son enfance. On comprenait immédiatement en le voyant sur scène que l'on avait affaire à un artiste hautement humain, intelligent et sensible, et il n'est pas étonnant qu'il ait préféré développer son art en se consacrant à la musique de chambre plutôt qu'à un répertoire plus éclatant de grand concertiste.

Cela ne diminue en rien ses qualités de soliste et il sut effectivement donner une touche très personnelle, richement colorée, aux grands concertos romantiques, de Dvořák à Walton, ou prêter à Don Quichotte toute la subtilité et l'emphase qui sied à l'œuvre poétique de Strauss. Ses sonates de Bach en solo dégageaient également une chaleur et une impression de bonheur proprement contagieuses. Il se montrait en revanche d'une énergie très dictatoriale lorsqu'il créait une œuvre à la scène, surtout lorsqu'elle avait été écrite spécialement pour lui comme ces concertos de Frank Martin et Bohuslav Martinu ou la sonate de Poulenc.

Sa carrière est marquée lorsqu'il atteint 19 ans par la mort de Gabriel Fauré, dont il interprétera quelques mois plus tard le célèbre *Quatuor à cordes* pour une première se tenant en privé. A partir de ce jour, la musique de chambre allait prendre une place de choix dans sa vie et, en 1943, lorsque Casals délaisse le célèbre trio qu'il formait avec Jacques Thibaud et Alfred Cortot, Fournier est l'homme qu'il leur faut pour le remplacer. Quatre ans après, il rejoint d'autres talents illustres, Joseph Szigeti, William Primrose et Arthur Schnabel, pour présenter d'abord à l'Europe, puis à l'Amérique, une série de concerts de musique de chambre. Il apparut plus tard aussi dans des formations de trio pour piano avec Henryk Szeryng et Wilhelm Kempff, Kempff en compagnie de qui il enregistra et donna en concert ses mémorables sonates de Beethoven.

A la ville, Fournier était un être chaleureux, décontracté, doté d'un subtil sens de l'humour et d'une joie de vivre communicative. Il était de la veine des plus nobles artistes, de ceux qui, s'ils ne chérissent pas les feux de la rampe, acceptent avec retenue les honneurs qui leur sont dus.

Pierre Fournier, 29 September 1957. A profoundly civilized artist.

Pierre Fournier, 29. September 1957. Ein hochkultivierter Künstler.

Pierre Fournier, le 29 septembre 1957. Un artiste parfaitement accompli.

Pierre Fournier, 29 September 1957: thoughtful music-making, by an artist for whom the grandeur of the occasion was of no great importance. Once, when he was playing trios at the Central Hall, Westminster, with Szigeti and Schnabel, and Szigeti broke a string, the great pianist played on without noticing and to the delight of the audience Fournier brought him down to earth by tapping him on the shoulder with his bow. It was a small incident, but entirely characteristic.

Pierre Fournier am 29. September 1957: nachdenkliches Musizieren eines Künstlers, für den Konventionen wenig Bedeutung hatten. Einmal, während einer Darbietung eines Trios gemeinsam mit Szigeti und Schnabel in der Central Hall in Westminster, riß Szigeti eine Saite. Als der großartige Pianist jedoch unbeeindruckt weiterspielte, holte ihn Fournier dadurch auf den Boden der Tatsachen, indem er ihm – sehr zum Gefallen des Publikums – mit seinem Bogen auf die Schulter tippte. Eine kleine, jedoch typische Anekdote für diesen Künstler.

Pierre Fournier (29 septembre 1957) : une musique toute en profondeur, jouée par un artiste qui se moquait de la grandeur de l'instant. Lors d'un récital en trio avec Szigeti et Schnabel, au Central Hall de Westminster, Szigeti casse une corde ; Schnabel ne s'apercevant de rien continue à jouer et, au grand amusement du public, c'est Fournier qui le ramènera à la réalité en lui tapotant l'épaule de la pointe de l'archet. Anecdote dérisoire, certes, mais typique du personnage.

Rehearsing with the top accompanist of his day, the English pianist Gerald Moore, 29 September 1957.

Bei einer Probe mit dem führenden Klavierbegleiter seiner Zeit, dem englischen Pianisten Gerald Moore, 29. September 1957.

Répétition avec le meilleur accompagnateur de l'époque, l'Anglais Gerald Moore, le 29 septembre 1957.

EMIL GILELS 1916-1985

Of the two great pianists who emerged from the Soviet Union in the years following Stalin's death it was Gilels, 18 months the younger, who reached the Western capitals first, making his début in Paris in 1954 at a time when Sviatoslav Richter was still touring the Soviet Union and Eastern Europe (as he was to continue to do for another six years). The reasons for this were partly personal and inevitably political, but also lay in the nature of their early careers: where Richter was slow to commit himself wholly to the piano and didn't enter the Moscow Conservatoire until he was 22, Gilels, after a period of study in Odessa (where curiously enough Richter was working at the same time on his first job at the Opera), shot into the Soviet limelight by winning the first prize in the first USSR Music Competition at only 17 and subsequently beat Richter to the same Conservatoire – and the same teacher – by two years.

Gilels was a man of formidable power at the keyboard, a Russian bear beside the steely poetry and inner concentration of Richter, a pianist for the *Emperor Concerto*, or the Brahms *Second Piano Concerto*, or the Tchaikovsky *First*, for Liszt, Scriabin and Prokofiev. Certainly it was in this kind of repertory that he first presented himself in London, and he dispensed it with flawless virtuosity and the kind of authority that is the prerogative of the greatest pianists. But with all the physical exuberance of those early years there was always a strong controlling discipline that allowed him the greatest delicacy in gradations of tone and nuance, and this became a more and more essential component of his playing as he grew towards his 50s and took an increasing interest in chamber music (he played a lot with Mstislav Rostropovich and his brother-in-law Leonid Kogan) and in the more classical repertory: Haydn, Mozart, Schubert, and especially Beethoven.

The Beethoven sonatas were among the finest of all his performances: the words 'titanic' or 'Olympian' spring irresistibly to mind, though they have been used so many times before. Yet at the other end of the musical spectrum he rather endearingly recorded an entire CD of the Grieg *Lyric Pieces*, and brought to them the same commitment, the same integrity, the same complete musical conviction that he brought to the mighty challenges of Beethoven's *Hammerklavier*. His understanding of musical characterization and colouring was masterly, his pianistic grasp immense, his passionate involvement in the stuff of the music he was playing deeply Russian. Gilels was a true representative of the great Russian line of giants of the keyboard.

Von den zwei großen Pianisten, die in den Jahren nach Stalins Tod aus der UdSSR kamen, erreichte Emil Gilels die westlichen Metropolen als erster. Bereits 1954, als Swjatoslaw Richter noch die Sowjetunion und Osteuropa bereiste (was er weitere sechs Jahre lang tun sollte), gab der achtzehn Monate jüngere Gilels sein Pariser Debüt. Das hatte sowohl persönliche als auch politische Gründe, ist aber auch aus den unterschiedlichen Werdegängen zu verstehen. Richter hatte sich mit der endgültigen Entscheidung für das Klavier schwergetan und war erst mit 22 Jahren an das Moskauer Konservatorium gegangen. Gilels hatte in Odessa studiert (zur gleichen Zeit hatte Richter dort seine erste Stelle an der Oper) und trat bereits mit siebzehn Jahren ins sowjetische Rampenlicht, als er beim Allunionswettbewerb der Interpreten in Moskau den ersten Preis gewann. In der Folge war er Richter an demselben Konservatorium und auch bei demselben Lehrer um zwei Jahre voraus.

Gilels griff mit ungeheurer Kraft in die Tasten. Neben Richters strenger Poesie und Innerlichkeit wirkte Gilels wie ein russischer Bär. Er schien für den Vortrag des *Fünften Klavierkonzerts von Beethoven*, des *Zweiten* von Brahms oder des *Ersten* von Tschaikowsky, für Liszt, Skrjabin und Prokofjew wie geschaffen. Natürlich präsentierte er sich in London auch zuerst mit diesem Repertoire. Er absolvierte es mit makelloser Virtuosität und mit jener Souveränität, die ein Vorrecht der größten Pianisten bleibt. Neben all der physischen Kraft dieser frühen Jahre verfügte er jedoch stets über eine ausgeprägte, beherrschte Disziplin, die ihm eine sensibel abgestufte Differenzierung von Ton und Klangfarbe ermöglichte. Mit zunehmendem Alter trat diese Sensibilität in seinem Spiel immer stärker hervor, und er entwickelte ein immer größeres Interesse für die Kammermusik (er spielte oft mit Mstislaw Rostropowitsch und seinem Schwager Leonid Kogan) und das klassische Repertoire: Haydn, Mozart, Schubert und besonders Beethoven.

Zu seinen besten Aufführungen zählen die Sonaten von Beethoven. Unwillkürlich fallen einem Begriffe wie „titanisch" oder „olympisch" ein, obwohl sie schon so oft verwendet wurden. Aber man kennt auch die andere Seite seines musikalischen Spektrums: Es gibt von ihm eine bezaubernde CD-Einspielung mit den *Lyrischen Stücken* von Grieg, die er mit der gleichen Hingabe, Integrität und Überzeugungskraft intonierte, mit der er auch die gewaltige Herausforderung von Beethovens *Hammerklavier-Sonate* bewältigte. Er hatte ein meisterhaftes Gespür für die musikalische Charakterisierung und Färbung der unterschiedlichen Werke und verfügte über ein unglaublich weites Spektrum. Die leidenschaftliche Anteilnahme an der Musik, die er spielte, war kennzeichnend für sein russisches Temperament. Gilels zählt eindeutig zu den ganz großen russischen Pianisten.

Des deux pianistes qui émergèrent de l'Union Soviétique après la mort de Staline, Gilels, le cadet de 18 mois, fut le premier à atteindre les capitales occidentales, débutant à Paris en 1954, alors que Sviatoslav Richter poursuivait encore ses tournées en URSS et dans les pays de l'Est pendant six ans. Les raisons de cette différence sont bien entendu à la fois personnelles et, inévitablement, politiques. Cependant, un troisième élément entre en jeu : la nature de leur jeunesse musicale. Tandis que Richter fut un peu long à se consacrer entièrement au piano et à rejoindre le Conservatoire de Moscou, à 22 ans, Gilels se propulsa au contraire rapidement sur le devant de la scène russe en remportant le premier prix du premier Concours de musique d'URSS après une période d'étude initiale à Odessa, où la coïncidence voulut que Richter occupât alors son premier poste à l'Opéra. Il n'avait que 17 ans et battait ainsi son compatriote de deux ans pour son entrée au conservatoire, où ils se partagèrent les mêmes professeurs.

A son piano, Gilels se montrait d'une puissance effarante. A côté de la froideur poétique et de la concentration toute intériorisée de Richter, il incarnait l'ours russe ; il était le pianiste né pour le *Concerto de l'Empereur*, pour le *N°2* de Brahms, pour le *N°1* de Tchaïkovski, pour Liszt, Scriabine ou Prokofiev, et c'est d'ailleurs avec ce répertoire qu'il se présenta pour la première fois au public londonien. Il l'interprétait avec une virtuosité infaillible, une autorité qui n'appartient qu'aux plus grands et, malgré l'impétuosité et l'exubérance gestuelle de ses premières années, il faisait preuve d'une grande discipline et savait contrôler parfaitement son instrument pour en tirer avec délicatesse les nuances de tons et de couleurs les plus exquises. A mesure qu'il avançait dans ses années, cette maestria devint l'une des principales composantes de son jeu, et son intérêt pour la musique de chambre (il joua souvent avec Msitslav Rostropovitch et son beau-frère Leonid Kogan) et pour le répertoire classique (Haydn, Mozart, Schubert et, bien entendu, Beethoven) s'amplifia.

Ses sonates de Beethoven sont parmi les plus belles. « Grandiose », « divin » sont les adjectifs qui nous viennent immédiatement à l'esprit, même s'ils semblent parfois un peu galvaudés. Cela ne l'empêcha pas non plus de s'aventurer à l'autre bout de l'univers musical en enregistrant un CD absolument enchanteur des *Pièces lyriques* de Grieg, y apportant ce même dévouement, cette même intégrité et cette même conviction musicale dont il avait déjà fait preuve dans la *Sonate pour pianoforte* de Beethoven. Il comprenait et apprivoisait une à une, avec une indicible intelligence pianistique, les nuances et les colorations musicales de chaque œuvre et sa passion pour les pièces qu'il interprétait était typiquement russe. Il était en quelque sorte l'ambassadeur type de cette grande lignée de monstres sacrés du piano que l'Union Soviétique avait su engendrer.

Emil Gilels, about 1967 – magisterial pianism.
Emil Gilels, um 1967 – feierliches Klavierspiel.
Emil Gilels vers 1967, la maestria du piano.

Gilels practising in his London hotel bedroom, 3 November 1965.

Gilels beim Üben in seinem Londoner Hotelzimmer am
3. November 1965.

Gilels au piano dans sa chambre d'hôtel, à Londres,
le 3 novembre 1965.

GLENN GOULD   1932-1982

In his own way, no question about it, the Canadian Glenn Gould was a genius. But it was his own way. For many it was infuriating, for some it was simply unacceptable, but for most the unpredictability and the idiosyncrasy were justified in performances that were fresh, challenging and personal to a degree that no other pianist could match – or perhaps would want to.

Towards the end of his short life Gould had become a legend – a hypochondriac, almost Proustian figure, never appearing in public, turning out streams of brilliantly provocative recordings made mostly at night to the sometimes intrusive accompaniment of stifled groans and a not particularly melodious crooning voice. His concert career, studded with brilliant successes all over America, with Herbert von Karajan in Berlin, on tour in the Soviet Union, lasted a mere nine years from 1955, the date of his New York début (when he started as he meant to go on by breaking all conventions and serving up a complete performance of the Bach *Goldberg Variations* to a startled audience at Carnegie Hall). But to a reclusive character like Gould's the privacy of the recording studio was always a tempting alternative to the exposure of the concert platform, and in 1964 he gave up public performances altogether.

With no more audiences and concert managements to bother about, he was free to indulge and perfect his intensely personal approach to every branch of music, breaking down routine and thinking and re-thinking his interpretations so that he would often arrive for a recording session with two or three different versions of the same work meticulously prepared, still undecided which to commit to disc. His repertory was broad, stretching from 16th-century keyboard music to Schoenberg (whose complete piano works he recorded) and jazz. He hadn't much sympathy for Chopin, and his views on Beethoven were iconoclastic. He described that towering pillar of piano literature, the *Hammerklavier Sonata*, as 'hopelessly unpianistic... the longest, most inconsiderate and probably least rewarding piece that Beethoven wrote for the piano'. His performance of it was rugged, uncomfortable and uniquely compelling.

The composer with whom he had most in common was unquestionably Bach. There was a mathematical exactitude about Gould's mind which suited the musical structure; it was here above all that the quite extraordinary clarity of his fingerwork, and the wizardry with which he could draw together the intertwining lines in a sustained piece of polyphony, had their most crucial effect. Again, of course, everything was new, different, controversial. A fugue might start so slowly that you thought you could never bear it; there would be *staccatos* where everybody else plays *legato*, sudden unexpected accents, nonchalant freedom of phrasing – and, of course, a certain amount of vocal accompaniment... But the rhythmic subtlety, the glorious sense of spontaneous discovery, the absolute mastery of mood were all there. Maybe you had to get past the mannerisms – but when you did get past them, you heard the music for the first time all over again. He made you listen.

Auf seine Art, daran kann kein Zweifel bestehen, war der Kanadier Glenn Gould genial. Aber es war eben seine eigene Art, die viele in Rage brachte und für einige schlicht unakzeptabel war. Für die meisten wurden die Unvorhersehbarkeit und die Marotten des Künstlers gerechtfertigt durch Aufführungen, die so frisch, herausfordernd und persönlich waren, wie es kein anderer Pianist konnte oder wollte.

Gegen Ende seines kurzen Lebens war Gould bereits eine Legende – eine schwermütige, beinahe proustsche Figur, niemals in der Öffentlichkeit zu sehen, aber viele brillante und zugleich provozierende Aufnahmen produzierend, meist nachts aufgezeichnet, unter manchmal aufdringlicher Begleiterscheinung von ersticktem Stöhnen und einer nicht gerade melodischen, schmalzigen Stimme. Seine Konzertkarriere (mit überwältigenden Erfolgen in ganz Amerika, Konzerten unter Herbert von Karajan in Berlin und einer Tournee durch die Sowjetunion) dauerte gerade einmal neun Jahre: Sie begann 1955 mit seinem New Yorker Debüt – als er anfing, sämtliche Konventionen zu brechen, indem er dem fassungslosen Publikum in der Carnegie Hall den vollständigen Zyklus der *Goldberg Variationen* Bachs zu Gehör brachte. Aber einem so eigenbrötlerischen und zurückgezogenen Menschen wie Gould war die Privatheit eines Studios immer eine verlockende Alternative gegenüber der Exponiertheit auf der Bühne, so daß er schon ab 1964 keinerlei öffentliche Konzerte mehr gab.

Als er sich nicht mehr um Publikum oder Auftritte kümmern mußte, konnte er sich frei der Weiterentwicklung seines ganz persönlichen Zugangs zu allen Musikrichtungen widmen und seine Interpretationen wieder und wieder überdenken – mit dem Ergebnis, daß er häufig mit zwei oder drei verschiedenen, äußerst sorgfältig einstudierten Versionen ein und desselben Stücks ins Studio kam, ohne sicher zu sein, welche aufgenommen werden sollte. Sein zeitlich wie stilistisch weitgestreutes Repertoire umfaßte Klaviermusik vom 16. Jahrhundert bis zu Schönberg, aber auch Jazz. Chopin lag ihm nicht besonders, Beethoven versuchte er zu entglorifizieren. So äußerte er beispielsweise zu jenem überragenden Werk der Klavierliteratur, der *Hammerklavier-Sonate*, sie sei „hoffnungslos unspielbar ... das längste, völlig achtlos komponierte und wahrscheinlich am wenigsten lohnende Stück, das Beethoven für das Klavier geschrieben hat". Goulds Aufführung dieses Stückes war grob, unbequem und – unwiderstehlich.

Der Komponist, mit dem Gould zweifellos am meisten verband, war Bach. Die musikalische Struktur von Bachs Werken entsprach der mathematischen Exaktheit Goulds, der vor allem über eine schier unglaubliche Fingerfertigkeit verfügte. Und seine an Zauberei grenzende Fähigkeit, mit der er die verschlungenen Linien eines getragenen, polyphonen Stückes zu entschlüsseln vermochte, brachte erstaunlichste Wirkungen hervor. Auch hier war seine Interpretation völlig neu und selbstverständlich umstritten. Zum Beispiel konnte Gould eine Fuge so langsam beginnen, daß man glaubte, es nicht aushalten zu können. Er konnte staccato spielen, wo jeder andere legato wählte, konnte völlig unerwartet akzentuieren oder frei phrasieren – und all das natürlich unterstützt und begleitet von seiner Stimme ... Aber die rhythmische Feinheit, das sensible Gespür für spontane Entdeckungen, die absolute Beherrschung der Stimmungen, dies war immer da. Vielleicht muß man zunächst über seine Eigenarten hinwegkommen – hat man sie aber einmal in Kauf genommen, wird man die Musik jedesmal wieder wie zum ersten Mal entdecken. Denn Gould bringt einem das Hören bei.

Dans son genre, sans aucun doute, le Canadien Glenn Gould était un génie. Pour beaucoup il était exaspérant, pour quelques-uns ce qu'il faisait était tout bonnement inacceptable, mais pour la plupart, sa déroutante originalité se justifiait par des interprétations fraîches, stimulantes et singulières avec lesquelles aucun pianiste ne pouvait – ou peut-être ne voulait – rivaliser.

Vers la fin de sa courte vie, Gould était devenu une légende – hypocondriaque, figure quasi proustienne, n'apparaissant jamais en public, produisant des flots d'enregistrements brillamment provocateurs, réalisés principalement la nuit, parfois agrémentés de grognements réprimés et d'une voix fredonnant pas vraiment mélodieuse. Sa carrière de concertiste, émaillée de succès éclatants dans toute l'Amérique, à Berlin avec Herbert von Karajan, en tournée en Union soviétique, dura à peine neuf ans à partir de 1955, date de ses débuts à New York (où il commença, comme il ne cessera de le faire, en cassant toutes les conventions et en offrant au public médusé de Carnegie Hall un récital complet des *Variations Goldberg* de Bach). Mais, pour un solitaire comme Gould, l'intimité d'un studio d'enregistrement a toujours été une alternative tentante à l'exhibition sur une scène de concert et, en 1964, il abandonna totalement les concerts en public.

N'ayant plus à s'occuper du public ou d'organisation de concerts, il s'est senti libre d'exprimer et de perfectionner son approche profondément personnelle de chaque domaine de la musique, cassant l'habitude, pensant et repensant ses interprétations, de telle sorte qu'il arrivait souvent à une séance d'enregistrement avec deux ou trois versions différentes d'une même œuvre méticuleusement préparées, n'ayant toujours pas décidé laquelle serait retenue. Son répertoire était vaste, s'étendant de la musique pour clavier du XVIᵉ siècle à Schoenberg (dont il enregistra l'œuvre complète pour piano) et au jazz. Il n'aimait pas beaucoup Chopin et ses vues sur Beethoven étaient iconoclastes. Il décrivait la *Sonate pour pianoforte*, cet imposant pilier de la littérature pour piano, comme « désespérément injouable... le morceau le plus long, le plus inconsidéré et probablement le moins gratifiant que Beethoven ait écrit pour le piano. » Son interprétation en était rude, pénible et exceptionnellement irrésistible.

Le compositeur dont Gould se sentait le plus proche était indubitablement Bach dont la structure musicale convenait à l'exactitude mathématique de son esprit : c'était là que s'exprimait le mieux l'extraordinaire précision de son doigté ; sa façon de mener ensemble les lignes entrelacées d'une polyphonie particulièrement dense tenait de la magie. Tout, bien sûr, était toujours nouveau, différent, controversé. Une fugue pouvait démarrer si lentement que c'en était insupportable ; il y avait des staccatos là où tous les autres jouaient legato, des accents soudains et inattendus, une liberté nonchalante du phrasé – et, bien entendu, un accompagnement vocal... Mais la subtilité du rythme, le sens de la trouvaille magnifique, la maîtrise absolue du mode, tout était là. Il fallait parfois passer sur le maniérisme, mais quand vous l'aviez fait, vous entendiez alors la musique pour la première fois. Gould vous faisait écouter.

Wilhelm Kempff, Queen Elizabeth Hall, London, 5 June 1969.
Auerbach found that Kempff's intense enjoyment of music-making
happily made him forget the photographer.

Wilhelm Kempff in der Queen Elizabeth Hall in London am
5. Juni 1969. Auerbach wurde gewahr, daß Kempffs lebhafte
Freude am Musizieren ihn glücklicherweise den Fotografen vergessen ließ.

Wilhem Kempff, au Queen Elizabeth Hall, Londres,
le 5 juin 1969. Le bonheur qu'éprouvait Kempff lorsqu'il jouait
était si intense qu'il en oubliait la présence du photographe.

Kempff goes back almost as far as Rubinstein, and lived to very nearly as great an age, but no two careers could have been more different. Kempff came from a Prussian family of distinguished church musicians, went to the Berlin Hochschule für Musik when he was nine years old (where curiously enough he had the same teachers as Rubinstein), studied philosophy and music at university and in 1916 began his professional career by touring as pianist and organist with the Berlin Hedwig's Cathedral choir. It was a long, long way from the dazzling precocity of his Polish colleague, who had made débuts in Berlin and Paris and completed his first tour of the United States by the same age.

During the years between the wars Kempff's career was concentrated mainly in Germany, where he developed a lasting relationship with the Berlin Philharmonic Orchestra and achieved great distinction as a teacher. He undertook occasional tours in South America and Japan but it wasn't until after the Second World War, in 1951, that he made his first appearance in London, and not until 1964 that he reached New York.

By that time he was an artist of established mastery and commanding presence. His repertory was the classic piano repertory of the 19th century, and generally speaking the heavier end of it – his very first recital in Berlin in 1917 had included the Beethoven *Hammerklavier Sonata* as well as the whole of the Brahms *Paganini Variations*, and the two composers, especially Beethoven, were to remain at the centre of his artistic achievement throughout his life. But for all his mastery in the Beethoven concertos or late piano sonatas, his treatment of them was never heavy-handed: the authority was tempered with a spontaneity and an infectious sense of delight in the music that made you want to go on listening, the wisdom had sparkle. In Brahms and Schumann he found lightness and clarity (not always an easy thing to do) as well as warmth, in Chopin a lyrical poetry that could verge on the idiosyncratic. Nothing was ever stereotyped, nothing taken for granted.

Inevitably he was a magnificent partner in chamber music, where spontaneity and immediacy of contact and reaction are what create the music. Yehudi Menuhin, who played and recorded all the Beethoven violin sonatas with him in 1970, has said that they hardly ever rehearsed and would generally use the first 'take' of any movement on the final disc. 'Kempff', he wrote, 'was the noblest exponent of the German tradition, who remained true to the age when clock and metronome had not yet taken over the organic rhythm of the music, and who was at the same time true to our age in his self-discipline.' He had the flexibility of genius that allowed complete freedom of imagination within sovereign respect for the composer's intention. It is a rare combination.

Wilhelm Kempff gehörte beinahe der gleichen Zeit wie Rubinstein an und wurde fast ebenso alt, aber ihre Laufbahnen hätten nicht unterschiedlicher sein können. Kempff kam aus einer preußischen Familie namhafter Kirchenmusiker, besuchte im Alter von neun Jahren die Berliner Hochschule für Musik (er hatte dort erstaunlicherweise die gleichen Lehrer wie Rubinstein) und studierte Philosophie und Musik an der Universität. 1916 ging er mit dem Chor der Berliner Hedwigs-Kathedrale als Pianist und Organist auf Tournee. Damit begann seine professionelle Laufbahn. Der Unterschied zu der frühreifen Entwicklung seines polnischen Kollegen ist gewaltig. Rubinstein hatte in seinem Alter bereits seine Debüts in Berlin und Paris gegeben und seine erste Tournee durch die Staaten beendet.

Zwischen den Weltkriegen hielt sich Kempff vornehmlich in Deutschland auf. Er entwickelte eine dauerhafte Beziehung zu den Berliner Philharmonikern und fand große Anerkennung als Lehrer. Gelegentlich unternahm er auch Tourneen nach Südamerika oder Japan; seinen ersten Londoner Auftritt hatte er jedoch erst nach dem Zweiten Weltkrieg im Jahre 1951, und erst 1964 ging er nach New York.

Zu dieser Zeit war er bereits ein namhafter Künstler und ein anerkannter Meister seines Fachs. Sein Repertoire bestand aus den klassischen Klavierstücken des 19. Jahrhunderts mit einer Tendenz zu den ernsteren Stücken – bei seinem allererersten Auftritt in Berlin im Jahre 1917 hatte er Beethovens *Hammerklavier-Sonate* und sämtliche *Variationen über ein Thema von Paganini* von Brahms gespielt. Beide Komponisten, besonders aber Beethoven, bildeten zeit seines Leben das Zentrum seines künstlerischen Schaffens. Doch trotz aller Meisterschaft war seine Behandlung von Beethovens Konzerten und späten Klaviersonaten niemals schwer. Er milderte sie durch Spontaneität und ein ansteckendes Vergnügen an der Musik, so daß man Lust bekam, einfach immer weiter zuzuhören. In der Musik von Brahms und Schumann fand er Leichtigkeit und Klarheit (was nicht immer einfach ist) und auch Wärme, bei Chopin entfaltete er eine fast übertriebene lyrische Poesie. Es gab bei ihm keine Gleichförmigkeit und auch keine Gewißheit.

Das machte ihn unweigerlich zu einem guten Kammermusiker, denn in der Kammermusik entscheiden spontane Reaktionen und eine unmittelbare Verständigung unter den Musikern über die Qualität der Aufführung. Yehudi Menuhin, der 1970 alle Violinsonaten von Beethoven mit ihm einspielte, berichtete, daß sie fast nie geprobt hätten und sich bei der Endaufnahme eigentlich immer für die erste Version eines Satzes entschieden hätten. Er schrieb: „Kempff war der nobelste Vertreter der deutschen Tradition, der jener Zeit die Treue hielt, als Uhr und Metronom noch nicht die Herrschaft über die organische Rhythmik der Musik angetreten hatten, und der mit seiner Selbstdisziplin zugleich auch unserem Zeitalter treu war." Er besaß die Flexibilität des Genius, die, innerhalb des souveränen Respekts gegenüber den Intentionen des Komponisten, vollkommene Freiheit gestattete – eine wirklich seltene Gabe.

Kempff et Rubinstein sont presque nés à la même époque, et Kempff vécut presque aussi longtemps que cet autre grand pianiste. Pourtant, on ne peut guère trouver deux carrières plus opposées. Kempff est née d'une famille prussienne, de musiciens d'église. Il est entré à la Berliner Hochschule für Musik à l'âge de 9 ans, où il eut les mêmes professeurs que Rubinstein, a ensuite étudié la philosophie et la musique avant de commencer sa carrière en 1916 en tant que pianiste et organiste accompagnateur des Chœurs de la cathédrale de Berlin. On est loin, très loin du précoce et éblouissant génie de son confrère polonais qui, à ce même âge, avait déjà débuté à Berlin et Paris, et accompli sa première tournée aux États-Unis.

Durant l'entre-deux-guerres, Kempff se consacre presque exclusivement à l'Allemagne et tisse avec le Philharmonique de Berlin des liens qui dureront toute sa vie. Il effectua bien quelques tournées de temps à autre, en Amérique du Sud et au Japon, mais ce n'est pas avant la fin de la Seconde Guerre mondiale, en 1951, qu'il donne son premier récital à Londres. Il attendra ensuite jusqu'en 1964 pour s'aventurer jusqu'à New York.

Il est alors reconnu depuis longtemps comme un maître dans son art, sa présence en impose à tous et il s'est construit un répertoire subtil avec les œuvres classiques pour piano les plus puissantes, mais aussi les plus difficiles du XIXᵉ siècle. En 1917, son premier récital comporte, par exemple, la *Sonate pour pianoforte* de Beethoven, ainsi que l'ensemble des *Variations sur un thème de Paganini* écrites par Brahms. Tout au long de sa vie, ces deux compositeurs, et plus particulièrement Beethoven, constitueront la base de sa réussite. Il maîtrisait les concertos et les dernières sonates de Beethoven pour piano sans jamais manquer de légèreté, sa maestria étant naturellement nuancée par une spontanéité et un amour de la musique qui ne laissaient personne indifférent et vous donnaient au contraire envie de rester là, à l'écouter. Une sagesse étincelante de génie ! Dans ses interprétations de Brahms et de Schumann, il retrouvait légèreté, clarté (ce qui n'est pas toujours évident) et chaleur humaine. Dans Chopin, c'était le lyrisme de la poésie qu'il appréciait presque de manière exagérée. Il ne se répétait jamais, rien n'était standardisé, rien n'était pris à la légère.

Il fut bien évidemment un fantastique partenaire pour de nombreux interprètes de musique de chambre, une forme musicale qui demande beaucoup de spontanéité. Yehudi Menuhin, qui a joué et enregistré avec lui toutes les sonates pour violon de Beethoven en 1970, affirmait qu'ils n'avaient presque jamais répété ensemble et pouvaient malgré tout se contenter de ne faire qu'une seule prise lors des enregistrements. « Kempff, écrivit-il, était le plus noble représentant de la tradition allemande et restait fidèle à cette époque où chronomètres et métronomes n'étouffaient pas encore le rythme intrinsèque de la musique. Il était en même temps très fidèle à notre temps, par son autodiscipline. » Il avait la souplesse d'esprit des génies, celle qui permet à l'imagination de se libérer de tout carcan tout en servant respectueusement les intentions du compositeur, et l'union de ces deux qualités est assez rare pour qu'on la souligne ici.

Yehudi Menuhin, an idealist with a violin.
Yehudi Menuhin, ein Idealist mit einer Violine.
Yehudi Menuhin, un idéaliste avec un violon.

YEHUDI MENUHIN (LORD MENUHIN OF STOKE D'ABERNON)   *1916

Menuhin at 80, loaded with honours and universally respected and admired, has been a familiar figure on the British musical scene for so long that it is hard to remember that he started out as an American Jewish kid of Russian parentage, with Hebrew as his first language. The story of his first contact with British music is famous: his meeting, at the age of 16, with Elgar to record the *Violin Concerto*, and Elgar's fascination with the maturity and musical authority of the young soloist, who was able to discuss every point of the work on equal terms with its author and yet give a performance which has remained as fresh and spontaneous on disc as on the day it was made.

That Menuhin was a child prodigy goes without saying: he had his first lessons just after his fourth birthday, made his début in San Francisco at eight, in New York at ten, in Paris at 11 and made his first gramophone recordings at 12. In Paris he made a nuisance of himself by playing to Georges Enesco at six o'clock in the morning, while the celebrated Romanian violinist was packing his bags to leave his hotel; as a result he was taken on as a pupil, with lasting effect on his maturing musical wisdom. A period of study with Adolf Busch followed. Meanwhile Menuhin's international fame grew rapidly: his technical ability was accepted as being second to none, but always the qualities that struck listeners most were the energy and poetry of youthful spontaneity, combined with a profundity of musical understanding that seemed almost miraculous in one so young. As Bartók later said to him, 'I didn't believe a work could be played so beautifully until long after the composer was dead.'

His career as a violinist has been unceasingly active – and not always on the most orthodox of concert platforms. During the Second World War he gave something like 1,000 concerts for American and allied troops in every part of the globe. He played in Brussels during the battle of Arnhem, in Antwerp hours after it had been vacated by the Germans, and gave a recital with Benjamin Britten in Belsen a couple of weeks after its liberation – an experience that marked them both for life. He was the first artist to appear at the Paris Opéra after the occupation, the first Jewish artist to play with the Berlin Philharmonic Orchestra after the fall of the Nazis, the first Western soloist to get to Moscow after the war. He has played Indian music with Ravi Shankar and jazz with Stéphane Grappelli, as well as astonishing his 'classical' colleagues with bouts of yoga in the intervals of rehearsing Bach, Beethoven, Bartók...

In the 1950s he began to take up conducting, sometimes playing with the orchestra, later more frequently directing from the podium. He founded his own orchestra, and has appeared as a guest with many others. He has been director of the Gstaad Festival, the Bath Festival and the Windsor Festival, and founded the Menuhin School for musically talented children at Stoke d'Abernon near London. And he has been an untiring, dedicated worker for international understanding and world peace.

The extraordinary thing is that a man so unworldly, so 'gloriously vague' in normal life, should have achieved so much. But that gentle persistence can be quite relentless, and there is quiet obstinacy behind the desire for communication, the constant search for new ways of loving and giving. He has lived in London since 1959; he became a British citizen in 1985 and has been, after Britten, the only musician to receive a peerage from the Queen.

Der 80jährige Yehudi Menuhin, viel geehrt, weltweit respektiert und sehr bewundert, gehört schon so lange zu den vertrauten Figuren der britischen Musikszene, daß man sich kaum noch seiner Herkunft erinnert – ein amerikanischer Jude russischer Abstammung, dessen Muttersprache das Hebräische war. Die Geschichte seiner ersten Begegnung mit der englischen Musik ist berühmt: 16jährig traf er mit Elgar zusammen, um dessen *Violinkonzert* aufzunehmen; der Komponist staunte über die ungewöhnliche Reife und die musikalische Autorität des jungen Solisten, der das Werk in jedem Punkt mit dem Komponisten diskutieren konnte und überdies mit einer solchen Frische und Spontaneität spielte, daß es uns noch heute ebenso begeistert.

Menuhin war zweifellos ein Wunderkind. Kurz nach seinem vierten Geburtstag nahm er seine ersten Stunden, gab mit acht Jahren sein Debüt in San Francisco, mit zehn in New York und mit elf in Paris; mit zwölf machte er seine erste Aufnahme. In Paris spielte er dem berühmten rumänischen Geiger Georges Enesco um sechs Uhr morgens in dessen Hotelzimmer vor, während der seine Koffer packte, und wurde daraufhin sein Schüler. Anschließend studierte er eine Zeitlang bei Adolf Busch. Seine internationale Bekanntheit wuchs in dieser Zeit unaufhaltsam. Seine technischen Fähigkeiten galten als unvergleichlich; am meisten begeisterte jedoch sein profundes, an ein Wunder grenzendes Musikverständnis. Bartók sagte später einmal zu ihm: „Ich habe immer geglaubt, ein Werk könne erst dann so wunderbar gespielt werden, wenn der Komponist schon lange verstorben ist."

Unermüdlich trieb Menuhin seine Laufbahn als Geiger voran – und beschränkte seine Auftritte dabei durchaus nicht auf renommierte Bühnen und ordentliche Konzertsäle. Während des Zweiten Weltkriegs gab er in allen Teilen der Welt fast 1000 Konzerte für amerikanische und alliierte Truppen. Während der Schlacht von Arnheim spielte er in Brüssel. Wenige Stunden, nachdem die Deutschen abgezogen waren, trat er in Antwerpen auf, und ein paar Wochen nach der Befreiung gab er in Bergen-Belsen ein Konzert zusammen mit Benjamin Britten – eine Erfahrung, die sie beide fürs Leben geprägt hat. Menuhin war der erste Künstler, der nach der Besatzung in der Pariser Oper auftrat, der erste jüdische Künstler, der nach der Kapitulation mit den Berliner Philharmonikern spielte, und auch der erste westliche Solist, der nach dem Krieg nach Moskau ging. Mit Ravi Shankar spielte er indische Musik und Jazz mit Stéphane Grappelli. In den Pausen zwischen den Proben für Bach, Beethoven und Bartók erstaunte er seine „klassischen" Kollegen überdies mit Yogaübungen.

In den 50er Jahren begann er zu dirigieren – manchmal indem er zugleich das Solo spielte –, später stand er immer öfter am Dirigentenpult. Er gründete sein eigenes Orchester und gastierte bei vielen anderen, leitete das Gstaad Festival, die Festspiele in Bath und Windsor und gründete in Stoke d'Abernon in der Nähe von London die Menuhin Schule für musikalisch begabte Kinder. Unermüdlich und voller Hingabe bemüht er sich um internationale Verständigung und engagiert sich für den Weltfrieden.

Es überrascht dennoch, daß dieser Idealist, der im Alltag so „herrlich vage" sein kann, in seinem Leben so viel erreicht hat. Sanfte Beharrlichkeit kann jedoch sehr hartnäckig sein, und hinter dem Wunsch nach Austausch und der ständigen Suche nach neuen Wegen der Liebe und des Gebens verbirgt sich ein stiller Eigensinn. Seit 1959 lebt Menuhin in London. 1985 wurde er britischer Staatsbürger. Nach Britten ist er der einzige Musiker, den die Queen je in die Würde eines Pairs erhob.

A l'âge de 80 ans, Menuhin est couvert d'honneurs ; il est universellement respecté et admiré. Il joue un rôle important dans le monde musical britannique depuis si longtemps qu'il est difficile de se rappeler qu'il était d'abord juif américain d'origine russe avec, comme langue maternelle, l'hébreu. L'histoire de sa première prise de contact avec la musique britannique est célèbre : il rencontre à l'âge de 16 ans Elgar pendant l'enregistrement de son *Concerto pour Violon* et celui-ci est fasciné par la maturité incroyable de ce jeune joueur imposant qui était capable non seulement de discuter chaque point de l'œuvre d'égal à égal avec son compositeur, mais aussi de donner une représentation dont la fraîcheur et la spontanéité du jour de l'enregistrement restèrent gravées sur le disque.

Que Menuhin fût un enfant prodige, cela va sans dire : il eut ses premières leçons à l'âge de 4 ans, fit ses débuts à San Francisco à huit ans, à New York à dix ans, à Paris à onze ans, et fit son premier enregistrement lorsqu'il avait douze ans. A Paris il embêta tout le monde en jouant pour Georges Enesco à six heures du matin, pendant que celui-ci faisait ses bagages avant de quitter l'hôtel ; Enesco lui donna alors des cours, ce qui eut un effet durable sur sa sagesse musicale. Il étudia ensuite avec Adolf Busch. La réputation de Menuhin grandissait sur le plan international : on reconnaissait que pour ce qui était de la compétence technique il n'avait pas son pareil, mais les qualités qui frappèrent le plus son public étaient l'énergie et la poésie d'une spontanéité pleine de jeunesse mêlée à une compréhension profonde de la musique qui semblait presque un miracle chez quelqu'un d'aussi jeune. Bartók lui dira plus tard, « Je ne croyais pas qu'on puisse si bien jouer une œuvre avant que son compositeur soit mort depuis longtemps. »

Sa carrière de violoniste fut toujours extrêmement active – et les scènes sur lesquelles il joua ne furent pas toujours conventionnelles. Pendant la Deuxième Guerre mondiale, il donna quelque 1000 concerts pour les Américains et les troupes alliées dans tous les coins du monde. Il joua à Bruxelles pendant la bataille d'Arnhem, à Anvers quelques heures après le départ des Allemands. Il donna un récital avec Benjamin Britten à Bergen-Belsen deux semaines environ après sa libération – une expérience qui devait les marquer tous les deux à vie. Ce fut le premier artiste à paraître sur la scène de l'Opéra de Paris après l'occupation, le premier artiste juif à jouer à l'Orchestre philharmonique de Berlin après la chute des nazis, le premier soliste occidental à jouer à Moscou après la guerre. Il a également joué de la musique indienne avec Ravi Shankar et du jazz avec Stéphane Grappelli. Il a aussi étonné ses collègues « classiques » en faisant du yoga dans des pauses pendant des répétitions d'œuvres de Bach, Beethoven, Bartók.

Dans les années 1950, il commença à diriger des orchestres, quelquefois en jouant avec eux, plus tard de l'estrade, fonda son propre orchestre et en dirigea beaucoup d'autres comme invité spécial. Il fut directeur du Festival de Gstaad, de celui de Bath, et de celui de Windsor et fonda l'Ecole Menuhin pour des enfants doués pour la musique à Stoke d'Abernon, près de Londres. Totalement dévoué, il travailla ardemment pour l'entente internationale et la paix dans le monde.

Il est extraordinaire qu'un homme si détaché de ce monde, tellement « glorieusement vague » dans le quotidien, ait remporté autant de victoires. Cette douce persistance peut pourtant aussi être implacable, et une opiniâtreté sous-jacente se cache derrière son désir de communiquer, la recherche constante de nouvelles façons d'aimer er de donner. Il vit à Londres depuis 1959 : il obtint la nationalité britannique en 1985 et fut après Britten, le second musicien à être anobli par la Reine.

A study in concentration. Menuhin, music on his lap, practises amid the confusion of festival organization in a small Bath church, 4 June 1959. This was Menuhin's first year as artistic director of the Bath Festival.

Eine Konzentrationsstudie. Menuhin, die Noten in seinem Schoß, probt inmitten des Durcheinanders, das die Festivalorganisation mit sich bringt, in einer kleinen Kirche in Bath am 4. Juni 1959, in seinem ersten Jahr als künstlerischer Direktor des dortigen Festivals.

Une étude de la concentration. Menuhin, une partition sur les genoux, s'exerce au milieu du chaos qui accompagne le festival dans une petite église de Bath, le 4 juin 1959. Cette année-là, Menuhin est pour la première fois directeur artistique du Festival de Bath.

1

2

(1) Menuhin with his son Jeremy, 6 October 1964. (2) With the 13-year-old Jeremy, and Menuhin's sisters, the pianists Hephzibah and Yaltah, 22 May 1966. (3) Indian music, cross-legged, with Alla Rahka and Ravi Shankar, 21 October 1969.

(1) Menuhin mit seinem Sohn Jeremy am 6. Oktober 1964.
(2) Mit dem 13jährigen Jeremy und mit Menuhins Schwestern, den Pianistinnen Hephzibah und Yaltah am 22. Mai 1966.
(3) Indische Musik, im Schneidersitz, mit Alla Rahka und Ravi Shankar am 21. Oktober 1969.

(1) Menuhin avec son fils Jeremy, le 6 octobre 1964.
(2) Avec Jeremy, 13 ans, et les sœurs de Menuhin, les pianistes Hephzibah et Yaltah, le 22 mai 1966. (3) Musique indienne, assis en tailleur, avec Alla Rahka et Ravi Shankar, le 21 octobre 1969.

3

1

2

3

(1) David Oistrakh, Yehudi Menuhin and Igor Oistrakh (David's son) rehearse at the Royal Albert Hall, 28 September 1963. (2) Taking it in turns at the Royal Albert Hall, 28 September 1963. Menuhin conducts, while the Oistrakhs father and son play the solos. (3) Rehearsing the Beethoven *Violin Concerto* with David Oistrakh in the previous year, 22 September 1962.

(1) David Oistrach, Yehudi Menuhin und Igor Oistrach (Davids Sohn) proben gemeinsam in der Royal Albert Hall am 28. September 1963. (2) Aufgabenteilung in der Royal Albert Hall am 28. September 1963. Menuhin dirigiert (1), während Vater und Sohn Oistrach die Soli spielen. (3) Probe des *Violinkonzertes* von Beethoven mit David Oistrach im vorangegangenen Jahr, am 22. September 1962.

(1) David Oïstrakh, Yehudi Menuhin et Igor Oïstrakh (fils de David) en répétition au Royal Albert Hall, le 28 septembre 1963. (2) Jouant à tour de rôle au Royal Albert Hall, le 28 septembre 1963. Menuhin dirige (1), pendant que Oïstrakh père et fils jouent les solos. (3) En répétition du *Concerto pour violon* avec David Oïstrakh, le 22 septembre 1962.

David Oistrakh accompanies with evident affection while Menuhin takes the solo role, 28 September 1963.

David Oistrach begleitet mit offensichtlicher Hingabe Menuhin, als dieser das Solo übernimmt, 28. September 1963.

David Oïstrakh accompagnant Menuhin avec une émotion manifeste quand celui-ci interprète le solo, le 28 septembre 1963.

Menuhin tutoring the seven-year-old Nigel Kennedy in a master-class for BBC 2 television at the Riverside Studios, London, 6 October 1964.

Menuhin unterrichtet den siebenjährigen Nigel Kennedy während eines Fernseh-Meisterkurses für BBC 2 in den Riverside Studios in London, 6. Oktober 1964.

Menuhin donnant des cours particuliers à Nigel Kennedy, sept ans, dans un cours télévisé de maîtrise pour la BBC 2 aux Riverside Studios de Londres, le 6 octobre 1964.

ARTURO BENEDETTI MICHELANGELI   1920-1995

For translucent clarity of texture, absolute technical control and an unerringly sensitive combination of classical poise with romantic ardour, Michelangeli had no equal among the pianists of his day. It was a pity therefore that one could hear him so seldom, for he must have cancelled at least as many performances as he gave. Partly this was due to long-standing ill health, partly to a difficult and often volatile temperament, but mostly perhaps to an innate perfectionism that prevented him from committing himself in public until he was certain that the circumstances, and his own state of preparation, were as close as possible to an ideal that only he could envisage. When the conditions were right, the result was unforgettable – but that was not always an acceptable consolation to disappointed audiences and impresarios.

His wartime experiences, as a pilot in the Italian Air Force and later in the anti-fascist resistance movement, may have helped to develop the ascetic, very private person that he later became: he gave little of himself away off the concert platform (or, it has sometimes been suggested, on it either), and his repertory remained very limited, but the intense dedication produced interpretations that could have been no one else's – passionate intellectual control in Beethoven, an almost Mozartian precision in Debussy, an unexpected but wonderfully revealing Latin clarity in the Brahms *Paganini Variations*, a classical elegance in the Ravel *Piano Concerto*.

As a teacher he inspired the most intense devotion, and the typical black roll-neck pullover became something of a uniform among his pupils. It was a pupil so attired, listening to a recording of Vladimir Horowitz, who commented, 'Marvellous, but this is momentum pianism' – that is, piano playing that relies on the sheer onward rush of technical excitement to produce its effect. Nothing could better express what Michelangeli's pianism was not.

Keiner seiner Zeitgenossen konnte es mit Michelangeli in Hinsicht auf strukturelle Klarheit, technische Perfektion und das Gefühl für die Verbindung von klassischer Getragenheit und romantischer Verve aufnehmen. Um so bedauerlicher war es, daß er nur so selten zu hören war, denn er muß wohl ebensoviele Konzerte abgesagt haben, wie er gegeben hat. Dies hing einerseits mit seiner fortwährend angeschlagenen Gesundheit zusammen, andererseits mit seinem wechselhaften Temperament; zum größten Teil lag es aber wohl an seinem ausgeprägten Perfektionismus, der ihn davon abhielt, öffentlich zu spielen, bevor er nicht vollkommen sicher war, daß alle äußeren Umstände wie auch seine eigenen Vorbereitungen seinem persönlichen Ideal so nahe wie möglich kamen. Wenn dann allerdings die Bedingungen stimmten, so war das Ergebnis unvergeßlich – ein geringer Trost freilich für all die enttäuschten Zuhörer und Agenten.

Seine Kriegserfahrungen als Flieger bei der italienischen Luftwaffe und danach als Mitglied der Resistenza mögen dazu beigetragen haben, daß er sich zu einem äußerst asketischen und zurückgezogenen Menschen entwickelte. Von sich selbst teilte er außerhalb der Konzerthalle wenig mit (ebensowenig auf dem Podium selbst, wie auch behauptet wurde), und sein Repertoire blieb sehr begrenzt. Doch brachte die absolute Konzentration, mit der er sich der Musik widmete, unverwechselbare Interpretationen hervor: Mit leidenschaftlich intellektueller Kontrolle gab er Beethoven; Debussy war bei ihm geprägt von geradezu mozartscher Präzision; in unerwarteter, aber wunderbar neuer Weise durchflutete südländische Klarheit Brahms' *Variationen über ein Thema von Paganini*; und dem *Klavierkonzert* von Ravel verlieh er klassische Eleganz.

Seine Schüler hielt Michelangeli zu intensiver Hingabe an, und sein charakteristischer schwarzer Rollkragenpullover wurde so etwas wie eine Uniform unter ihnen. Einer von ihnen kommentierte eine Horowitz-Einspielung mit den Worten: „Wunderbar, aber das ist vergängliche Klavierkunst", was heißen sollte: Klavierspiel, das auf dem Vorwärtsdrängen atemberaubender Virtuosität beruht. Dies war die wohl treffendste Beschreibung dessen, was Michelangelis Kunst gerade nicht darstellte.

Michelangeli n'avait pas d'égal parmi les pianistes de son époque pour la clarté translucide de la structure, le contrôle absolu de la technique et l'association toujours infaillible d'équilibre classique et d'ardeur romantique. Il est donc dommage qu'on on l'ait si peu entendu, car il a annulé au moins autant de concerts qu'il en a donnés. État de fait en partie dû à sa mauvaise santé, en partie à son tempérament difficile et souvent versatile, mais surtout, peut-être, à son perfectionnisme qui l'empêchait de se produire en public avant qu'il soit certain que les circonstances et son propre degré de préparation étaient aussi proches que possible de l'idéal qu'il s'était fixé. Quand les conditions étaient bonnes, le résultat était inoubliable – mais ce n'était pas toujours une consolation pour le public et les impresarios.

Pendant la guerre, son expérience de pilote dans l'aviation italienne et, plus tard, dans la résistance antifasciste a sans doute façonné ce personnage ascétique et très secret qu'il devint plus tard : il livrait peu de lui-même hors de la scène (et même sur scène, comme on a pu le dire), et son répertoire est resté très limité, mais ses interprétations n'appartenaient qu'à lui – contrôle intellectuel fervent dans Beethoven, précision presque mozartienne dans Debussy, clarté latine inattendue mais merveilleusement révélatrice dans les *Variations sur un thème de Paganini* de Brahms, élégance classique dans le *Concerto pour piano* de Ravel.

Comme professeur il a inspiré la plus intense des dévotions, et son éternel pull-over noir à col roulé devint presque un uniforme chez ses élèves. C'est un élève vêtu ainsi qui, écoutant un enregistrement de Vladimir Horowitz, commenta : « Merveilleux, mais il joue sur son élan », c'est-à-dire d'une manière reposant sur le simple élan de l'ivresse technique. Rien ne pouvait mieux exprimer ce que la technique du piano de Michelangeli n'était pas.

The demonic intensity of Arturo Benedetti Michelangeli.

Die dämonische Intensität von Arturo Benedetti Michelangeli.

La puissance démoniaque d'Arturo Benedetti Michelangeli.

Michelangeli before a recital, checking the final adjustments to his instrument (and his fingernails) with his 'tuner', the distinguished Italian piano-maker Ettore Tallone, 26 June 1959.

Michelangeli vor einem Konzert. Er prüft die abschließenden Stimmarbeiten an seinem Instrument (und seine Fingernägel) zusammen mit seinem „Stimmer", dem herausragenden italienischen Klavierbauer Ettore Tallone, 26. Juni 1959.

Michelangeli avant un récital, vérifiant son instrument (et ses ongles) avec son « accordeur », le célèbre fabricant de piano italien Ettore Tallone, le 26 juin 1959.

JOHN OGDON   1937-1989

A burly, rather bear-like figure at the keyboard, John Ogdon's appearance suggested power rather than agility – though in performance there was never any doubt that he possessed immense reserves of both. His intellectual background was well known: after studying in Manchester he had joined the Manchester New Music Group, whose other members included Peter Maxwell Davies, Harrison Birtwistle and Alexander Goehr, and his own compositions tended in similar directions. But the piano was always his main interest, and his first performances of early works by these stalwarts of the British avant-garde were a recurring source of disquiet to the musical establishment in Manchester.

His London début was very much to his own scale, with a performance of Busoni's vast and intimidating *Piano Concerto*, at that time a comparatively little-known work, with which he achieved a spectacular success. From then he moved from strength to strength, winning the Moscow Tchaikovsky Competition jointly with Vladimir Ashkenazy in 1962, and launching into a brilliant career with a vigour and an all-embracing musical enthusiasm that took in everything from the Viennese classics through the great romantic repertory to the most arcane works of the 20th century. Rarities of all kinds featured in his programmes, and were always given the same commitment as the acknowledged masterpieces of the piano. Imagination he had in plenty, technical brilliance and unlimited power – though not always subtlety and sometimes not ideal clarity. But the grandiose sweep and sheer inspiration of a good Ogdon performance left little inclination to carp about details.

Sadly, this triumphant career became clouded during the later 1970s by mental illness, and for a time Ogdon disappeared entirely from the concert platform. It was not an easy period for his wife and duet partner Brenda Lucas, though his periodic reappearances from hospital revealed a musicianship and technical command undimmed by ill health. The recordings from this period tend to be of works out of the mainstream of the piano repertory, but that doesn't mean they were any less challenging. During the last years of his life he made recordings of Busoni's formidable and rarely played *Fantasia contrappuntistica* and Sorabji's legendary *Opus Clavicembalisticum* – at nearly three hours the longest non-repetitive piano piece ever published. It was a suitably intrepid final gesture from a pianist whose intentions were always on the grandest scale.

Am Flügel eine stämmige, bärenhafte Erscheinung, erwartete man von John Ogdon eher Kraft als Flexibilität und Leichtigkeit, doch ließ sein Spiel niemals Zweifel daran, daß er beide Eigenschaften in höchstem Maß besaß. Er hatte einen renommierten, intellektuellen Hintergrund: Nach seinem Studium in Manchester trat er der Manchester New Music Group bei, deren übrige Mitglieder Maxwell Davies, Harrison Birtwistle und Alexander Goehr waren, an deren Stil sich auch Ogdons eigene Kompositionen orientierten. Doch galt sein Hauptinteresse immer dem Klavierspiel, und seine ersten Aufführungen der frühen Werke dieser Protagonisten der britischen Avantgarde boten dem Musik-Establishment in Manchester immer wieder Anlaß zu vehementer Kritik.

Sein Debüt in London bestritt er – ganz seinem Stil entsprechend – mit Busonis umfangreichem und beeindruckendem *Klavierkonzert*, einem zu jener Zeit noch relativ unbekannten Stück, mit dem er herausragenden Erfolg erzielte. Von nun an bewegte sich seine Karriere von einem Höhepunkt zum nächsten: 1962 gewann er zusammen mit Wladimir Ashkenazy den Tschaikowsky-Wettbewerb in Moskau und gab sich dann mit aller Energie und großem Enthusiasmus seiner Kunst hin, die alles von der Wiener Klassik über die Romantiker bis hin zu schwer zugänglichen Werken des 20. Jahrhunderts umspannte. In seinen Konzerten stellte er Raritäten aller Art vor, die stets mit dem gleichen Maß an Aufmerksamkeit gespielt wurden, wie geläufigere Klavierstücke. Er verfügte über außerordentlichen Einfallsreichtum, technische Brillanz und unbegrenzte Energie, auch wenn seinem Spiel nicht immer ideale Differenziertheit und Klarheit zu eigen war. Aber der große Schwung und die absolute Originalität eines Konzertes von Ogdon ließen kaum noch Raum für solcherlei Kritik am Detail.

Bedauerlicherweise wurde seine Laufbahn gegen Ende der 70er Jahre von einer psychischen Krankheit überschattet, die zur Folge hatte, daß Ogdon eine Zeitlang ganz der Bühne fernbleiben mußte. Für seine Frau und Duopartnerin Brenda Lucas war dies keine leichte Zeit, wenn auch die wenigen Konzerte, die er geben konnte, in ihrer musikalischen Gestaltung und technischen Perfektion von der Krankheit nicht beeinträchtigt wurden. Die Aufnahmen aus dieser Zeit sind nicht im üblichen Kanon der Klaviermusik angesiedelt, stellen deshalb jedoch keine geringere Herausforderung dar. In seinen letzten Lebensjahren spielte er Busonis herausragende und selten zu hörende *Fantasia contrappuntistica* sowie Sorabjis legendäres *Opus Clavicembalisticum* ein – mit drei Stunden Spieldauer eines der längsten Werke ohne Wiederholungen, das je veröffentlicht wurde. Dies war die angemessene letzte große Leistung eines Pianisten, dessen Arbeit stets auf das allerhöchste Niveau ausgerichtet war.

Une forte carrure, l'air d'un ours au clavier, John Ogdon suggérait davantage la puissance que l'agilité, bien qu'il ne fasse aucun doute qu'il possédait d'immenses réserves de l'une et de l'autre. Après avoir étudié à Manchester, il rejoignit le Manchester New Music Group, dont les autres membres étaient, entre autres, Peter Maxwell Davies, Harrison Birtwistle et Alexandre Goehr, et ses propres compositions suivirent des directions similaires à celles de ces derniers. Mais le piano fut toujours son centre d'intérêt principal, et ses premières interprétations des œuvres de jeunesse de ces vaillants représentants de l'avant-garde britanniques étaient une source permanente d'inquiétude pour les caciques de la musique à Manchester.

Ses débuts à Londres furent dignes de lui, avec une interprétation du *Concerto pour piano* de Ferruccio Busoni, pièce énorme et intimidante, à cette époque relativement peu connue, qui fut un succès spectaculaire. De là il vola de victoire en victoire, remportant le concours Tchaïkovski de Moscou avec Vladimir Ashkenazy en 1962, et se lançant dans une brillante carrière avec une vigueur et un enthousiasme total pour la musique, qui incluait tout, des classiques viennois jusqu'aux morceaux les plus hermétiques du XXe siècle, en passant par le grand répertoire romantique. Toutes sortes de raretés figuraient dans ses programmes, qu'il traitait toujours avec le même soin que les chefs-d'œuvre reconnus. De l'imagination il en avait, ainsi qu'une technique éclatante et une puissance illimitée, bien qu'il manquât parfois de subtilité et de clarté. Mais la grandiose envergure et la belle inspiration d'une bonne interprétation d'Ogdon décourageaient les critiques de détail.

Malheureusement, cette triomphale carrière fut assombrie par la maladie mentale à la fin des années 1970, et Ogdon disparut de la scène pour un temps. Ce ne fut pas une période facile pour Brenda Lucas, sa femme et partenaire dans les duos, même si ses réapparitions périodiques révélaient une maestria et une maîtrise de la technique que la maladie n'avaient pas entamées. Les enregistrements de cette époque sont surtout des œuvres tirées du grand répertoire pour piano, mais ils n'en sont pas moins stimulants. Dans les dernières années de sa vie, il fit des enregistrements du morceau redoutable et rarement joué de Busoni, *Fantasia contrappuntistica*, et du légendaire *Opus Clavicembalisticum* de Sorabji, de presque trois heures, la plus longue pièce pour piano non répétitive jamais écrite. Intrépide geste final bien propre à un pianiste dont les intentions se sont toujours situées tout en haut de l'échelle.

John Ogdon getting inside the music, 2 October 1962.

John Ogdon verliert sich in der Musik, 2. Oktober 1962.

John Ogdon se perd dans la musique, le 2 octobre 1962.

DAVID OISTRAKH   DAVID OISTRACH   DAVID OÏSTRAKH
1908-1974

By the standard of world-class virtuosi, Oistrakh's early career was not particularly meteoric. While still a student in his home town, Odessa, he appeared as soloist with the local symphony orchestra and even gave a performance of the Glazunov *Violin concerto* under the baton of the composer; he made his début in Leningrad at the age of 19, in Moscow at 20, and six years later joined the staff of the Moscow Conservatoire, where he was to teach, advise and guide a whole generation of pupils including his own son Igor. He won golden opinions within the Soviet Union, but it was not until 1937 that he at last broke out of his Soviet background to win the Queen's Prize in the first Concours Eugène-Ysaÿe in Brussels.

This should have been the beginning of a brilliant international career, but the Soviet authorities demurred, the war intervened, and he found himself playing in factories and hospitals, in Leningrad under bombardment, and to the troops at the front. When it was all over the authorities were still intractable and foreign tours in the West seemed as far away as ever. There were tentative links with Western artists: Yehudi Menuhin visited Moscow in 1945 and began a lasting friendship – but thanks to official obstruction had to leave without hearing Oistrakh play. Two years later the two violinists met again in Prague for a performance of the Bach *Double Concerto* (the first of many that they were to give together), but it was not until Stalin died in 1953 that controls were finally relaxed and Oistrakh became the first, as well as the oldest, of the group of Soviet artists who burst upon Europe and America in the later 1950s. He played in Paris that year, in London a year later, and in New York in 1955.

But Oistrakh, like his close friend Shostakovich, was never much attracted by the glamour of the West, and in spite of its obvious drawbacks certainly never considered moving out of the Soviet Union. 'I owe the state everything', he said to Menuhin. 'They are responsible for my upbringing and have seen to it that I have had the best musical education and training. My family are there. It would be disloyal of me to live elsewhere.' He saw himself as an apologist for Soviet music wherever he played. At his début in New York he offered the Americans their first chance of hearing Shostakovich's tormented first *Violin Concerto*, which like its successor was written for him, and he missed no opportunity of presenting the works of Prokofiev, Khachaturian and Myaskovsky alongside the ravishingly lyrical, heartfelt warmth of his Mozart, Beethoven and Brahms.

Although he came across on early recordings as a lush, rich toned player, his performances in the West revealed him as an artist of nobility, refinement and a profoundly balanced musical intelligence. His visits to England, often accompanied by his son and sometimes featuring joint performances with Menuhin or recitals with his compatriot Sviatoslav Richter, were as welcome for his supreme artistry as for his personal qualities. A pity that the regime to which he was so loyal should have worked him so hard in the last years of his life: he travelled, taught and played relentlessly to the very end, and was still travelling when he died in Amsterdam at the age of 66.

Verglichen mit anderen Weltklasse-Virtuosen war Oistrach zunächst kein kometenhafter Karrierestart beschieden. Zu Studienzeiten in seiner Heimatstadt Odessa sammelte er erste solistische Erfahrungen mit dem städtischen Symphonieorchester und führte Glasunows *Violinkonzert* auf, unter dem Dirigat des Komponisten; 19jährig debütierte er in Leningrad, mit 20 in Moskau, wo er sechs Jahre später als Lehrkraft ins Konservatorium aufgenommen wurde, um eine ganze Generation von Schülern (darunter auch seinen Sohn Igor) zu unterrichten, zu beraten und zu begleiten. Er sammelte glänzende Kritiken innerhalb der Sowjetunion, doch erst 1937 überwand er die Grenzen, und gewann den ersten Preis beim Eugène-Ysaÿe-Wettbewerb in Brüssel.

Dies hätte der Beginn einer brillanten internationalen Karriere sein können, aber die sowjetischen Machthaber verhinderten dies, der Krieg kam dazwischen, und Oistrach fand sich in Fabriken, Krankenhäusern und an der Front spielend wieder – in Leningrad sogar während der Bombardierung. Aber auch nach dem Krieg waren Tourneen in den Westen für ihn so unmöglich wie eh und je. Allerdings gab es vorsichtige Fühlungnahme mit dem Westen: Yehudi Menuhin besuchte 1945 Moskau und knüpfte eine dauerhafte Freundschaft zu diesem erstaunlichen russischen Geiger – aber infolge offizieller Restriktionen mußte er das Land wieder verlassen, ohne Oistrach spielen gehört zu haben. Zwei Jahre später trafen sich die beiden Geiger in Prag wieder, um Bachs *Doppelkonzert* aufzuführen (es sollte das erste vieler gemeinsamer Konzerte sein), aber erst nach Stalins Tod 1953 wurden die Kontrollen eingestellt, und Oistrach war der erste – und älteste – sowjetische Künstler, der Europa und Amerika in den späten fünfziger Jahren im Sturm eroberte. 1953 spielte er in Paris, ein Jahr später in London, 1955 in New York.

Oistrach ließ sich, ebenso wie Schostakowitsch, nicht allzu sehr von westlichem Glamour beeindrucken und erwog trotz aller Nachteile nie, sein Heimatland zu verlassen. „Ich verdanke diesem Staat alles", sagte er zu Menuhin. „Er ist verantwortlich für meine Ausbildung und hat darauf geachtet, daß ich den besten Musikunterricht und die beste Fortbildung bekam. Meine ganze Familie ist dort. Ich würde treulos handeln, lebte ich irgendwo anders." Er betrachtete sich, wo auch immer er spielte, als Repräsentant russischer Musik. Als er in New York debütierte, bekamen die Amerikaner durch ihn erstmalig Schostakowitschs beunruhigendes *Erstes Violinkonzert* zu hören, ein Werk, das der Komponist (ebenso wie sein nächstes) für Oistrach geschrieben hatte. Oistrach nutzte jede Gelegenheit, neben seinen lyrischen und herzenswarmen Mozart-, Beethoven- und Brahms- Interpretationen auch Prokofjew, Khatschaturian und Mjaskowski aufzuführen.

Oistrachs frühe Aufnahmen konservieren die üppig-reiche Klangfarbe seines Spiels; die späteren Konzerte im Westen offenbarten ihn jedoch als Künstler, der musikalische Eleganz ebenso wie ein reifes und ausgewogenes Klangbild zu erzeugen vermochte. Seine Reisen nach England – auf die ihn häufig sein Sohn begleitete und wo er sich manchmal für gemeinsame Auftritte mit Menuhin oder mit seinem Landsmann Swjatoslaw Richter traf – waren dem herausragenden Künstler in zweifacher Hinsicht wichtig: aus musikalischen, aber auch persönlichen Gründen. Es ist wirklich bedauerlich, daß der Staat, dem gegenüber er sich derart loyal verhielt, ihm in seinen letzten Lebensjahren so viel abverlangte: Oistrach reiste, unterrichtete und spielte bis zuletzt pausenlos – auch als er mit 66 Jahren starb, war er nicht in seiner Heimat, sondern auf einer Tournee in Amsterdam.

Si l'on se réfère à la carrière des virtuoses de classe internationale, le début de celle d'Oïstrakh ne fut pas particulièrement fulgurant. Quand il était encore étudiant à Odessa, sa ville natale, il joua en soliste avec l'orchestre symphonique local et interpréta même le *Concerto pour violon* de Glazounov sous la direction du compositeur ; il fit ses débuts à Léningrad à 19 ans, à 20 ans il était à Moscou et, six ans plus tard, il rejoignait le personnel du conservatoire de cette ville, où il enseigna, donna des conseils et guida toute une génération d'élèves, y compris son fils Igor. Son jeu lui valut prix sur prix et les meilleures appréciations dans son pays, mais ce n'est qu'en 1937 qu'il sortit enfin de l'environnement soviétique pour gagner le prix de la Reine au premier concours Eugène-Ysaÿe à Bruxelles.

Cela aurait dû être le début d'une brillante carrière internationale, mais les autorités soviétiques s'y opposèrent ; la guerre éclata et il se retrouva sous les bombardements, jouant à Léningrad dans les usines et les hôpitaux, et sur le front pour les troupes. Quand tout cela fut fini, les autorités restèrent intraitables et les tournées à l'extérieur de l'URSS semblaient toujours aussi lointaines. Néanmoins, des liens hésitants commençaient à se tisser avec des artistes de l'Ouest : Yehudi Menuhin, venu à Moscou en 1945, entama une amitié de longue durée avec cet étonnant violoniste russe mais, grâce aux bons soins des officiels, il partit sans avoir entendu Oïstrakh jouer. Deux ans plus tard, les deux violonistes se rencontrèrent de nouveau à Prague, pour une représentation (la première d'une longue liste) du *Concerto pour deux violons* de Bach, mais ce n'est qu'à la mort de Staline, en 1953, que les contrôles se relâchèrent et qu'Oïstrakh devint le premier, et le plus âgé, du groupe d'artistes soviétiques qui firent irruption en Europe et en Amérique à la fin des années 50. Il joua à Paris cette année-là, à Londres un an plus tard et à New York en 1955.

Mais Oïstrakh, comme son ami Chostakovitch, n'a jamais succombé aux charmes de l'Ouest et ne pensa certainement jamais à quitter son pays en dépit des inconvénients évidents que présentait la vie en Union soviétique. « Je dois tout à l'État, dit-il à Menuhin. Ils se sont chargés de mon instruction et ont veillé à ce que je reçoive la meilleure formation musicale. Ma famille est là-bas. Ce serait déloyal de ma part de vivre ailleurs.» Partout où il jouait, il se considérait comme un défenseur de la musique soviétique. À ses débuts à New York, il offrit aux Américains l'occasion de découvrir le tourmenté *Premier concerto pour violon* de Chostakovitch qui, comme le suivant, avait été écrit pour lui, et il ne manquait jamais de présenter les œuvres de Prokofiev, Khatchatourian et Miaskovski en même temps que la chaleur lyrique ravissante de ses Mozart, Beethoven et Brahms.

Bien que dans ses premiers enregistrements il apparaisse comme un interprète aux tonalités riches, voire luxuriantes, ses interprétations à l'Ouest révélèrent un artiste à l'intelligence musicale noble, raffinée et profondément équilibrée. Ses visites en Angleterre, souvent en compagnie de son fils et parfois en concert avec Menuhin, ou en récitals avec son compatriote Sviatoslav Richter, étaient appréciées pour son talent souverain et ses qualités humaines. Il est dommage que le régime auquel il était si loyal ait tant exigé de lui les dernières années de sa vie : il a travaillé, enseigné et joué sans arrêt jusqu'à la fin, et voyageait encore quand il mourut à Amsterdam, à l'âge de 66 ans.

David Oistrakh, about 1965 – authority with persuasive warmth.

David Oistrach, um 1965: Autorität mit verbindlicher Wärme.

David Oïstrakh, vers 1965 - autorité avec chaleur persuasive.

1

2

3

4

(1, 3) David Oistrakh and his son Igor in rehearsal with Colin Davis, 18 February 1961. (2) Exchanging the violin for the viola, 28 September 1963. (4) Rehearsing the Brahms *Double Concerto* with Mstislav Rostropovitch for a concert with the Moscow Philharmonic Orchestra conducted by Kirill Kondrashin, Royal Albert Hall, London, 9 October 1965.

(1, 3) David Oistrach und sein Sohn Igor proben mit Colin Davis, 18. Februar 1961. (2) Die Bratsche im Austausch für die Violine, 28. September 1963. (4) Probe von Brahms' *Doppelkonzert* mit Mstislaw Rostropowitsch für ein Konzert mit dem Philharmonischen Orchester Moskau unter Kirill Kondrashin, Royal Albert Hall, London, 9. Oktober 1965.

(1, 3) David Oïstrakh et son fils Igor répétant avec Colin Davis, le 18 février 1961. (2) Échange du violon pour l'alto, le 28 septembre 1963. (4) Répétition du *Double Concerto* de Brahms avec Mstislav Rostropovitch pour un concert avec l'Orchestre philharmonique de Moscou dirigé par Kirill Kondrachine, au Royal Albert Hall à Londres, le 9 octobre 1965.

Oistrakh being presented with a gold disc by Jean Roire of
Le Chant du Monde in celebration of his 60th birthday,
12 September 1968.

Oistrach wird am 12. September 1968 anläßlich seines
60. Geburtstages in der Sendung *Le Chant du Monde* von Jean
Roire mit einer goldenen Schallplatte geehrt.

Oïstrakh recevant un disque d'or des mains de Jean Roire, du
Chant du Monde, pour son 60e anniversaire, le 12 septembre 1968.

Oistrakh in about 1972.

Oistrach, um 1972

Oïstrakh, vers 1972.

(1) The Oistrakh Trio – Lev Oborin (piano), David Oistrakh and Svyatoslav Knushevitsky (cello) – with the producer Walter Legge (left), in the playback room at the Abbey Road studios, London, 16 May 1958. This was their first visit to Britain as a trio and they recorded the Beethoven *Triple Concerto* and various chamber works for EMI. (2) In the recording studio again, playing the Bach *Double Concerto* with his son Igor, about 1965.

(1) Das Oistrach-Trio – bestehend aus Lev Oborin (Klavier), David Oistrach und Swjatoslaw Knuschewitzkij (Cello) – zusammen mit dem Produzenten Walter Legge (links), im Aufnahmeraum der Abbey Road Studios in London, 16. Mai 1958. Es war der erste Besuch des Trios in Großbritannien, und man zeichnete für die Plattenfirma EMI Beethovens *Tripelkonzert* sowie verschiedene Kammermusikwerke auf. (2) David und Igor Oistrach bei einer Studioaufzeichnung von Bachs *Doppelkonzert*, um 1965.

Le Oïstrakh Trio – Lev Oborin (piano), David Oïstrakh et Svyatoslav Knushevitsky (violoncelle) – avec le producteur Walter Legge (à gauche) dans la salle d'enregistrement des studios Abbey Road, Londres, le 16 mai 1958. C'était leur première visite en Grande-Bretagne en tant que trio et ils enregistrèrent le Triple Concerto de Schubert et divers morceaux de musique de chambre pour EMI. (2) Toujours dans le studio d'enregistrement, jouant le Double Concerto de Bach avec son fils Igor, vers 1965.

1

2

SVIATOSLAV RICHTER   SWJATOSLAW RICHTER   SVIATOSLAV RICHTER
*1915

Richter came late to the West, performing in Chicago and New York in 1960 but not appearing in the major European centres until 1961. During the early 1950s his reputation had reached London fitfully through a few rather inadequate Soviet recordings and the reports of people who had heard him play in Russia or the Soviet bloc, but from the mid-50s onwards a series of stunning recorded performances – Schumann, Schubert, Rachmaninov, Prokofiev – made it clear that a formidable talent was being nurtured in the East.

Richter was a child prodigy but, unusually, entirely self-taught. He got a job as répétiteur at the opera in Odessa at the age of 15 and a year later made his public début as a pianist. But it was not until he was 22 that he began to study the piano systematically, entering the Moscow Conservatoire where he was hailed by his teacher as 'a musical genius, possessed of great intellectual powers'. While he was still a student he gave the first performance of Prokofiev's *Sixth Piano Sonata*, thus launching himself on a lifelong championship of Prokofiev's piano works – he was to give the first performances of the *Seventh* and *Ninth Sonatas* as well (the *Ninth* was dedicated to him) and make his only appearance as a conductor accompanying Rostropovich in the first performance of the *Sinfonia Concertante for cello and orchestra* in 1952.

His first recitals in London, when they came, were predictably sold out from day one. But in other respects Richter has never been a predictable artist. For absolute technical control and total mastery of his instrument he had hardly an equal in the post-war years, and at its best the combination of virtuosity with a deeply introspective Russian temperament can produce extraordinary results – particularly in composers like Schubert and Schumann, where muscular articulation and poetic refinement provide a perfect equilibrium that keeps romantic emotionalism at bay. But the intense self-searching could sometimes go too far, and it could be the audience who felt they were being kept at bay. More than most pianists, Richter was sensitive to atmosphere and easily put off by adverse circumstances, and when that happened there might be times when one found oneself wondering whether the equilibrium had become an end in itself.

He was a wonderful partner in chamber music, or as an accompanist to artists with whom he was in sympathy like Dietrich Fischer-Dieskau or Elisabeth Schwarzkopf, and could be at his best in the sudden, spontaneous gesture. The occasion when he gave an unscheduled Schubert recital in the parish church at the 1964 Aldeburgh Festival will not be forgotten by those who were lucky enough to hear it. He had been introduced to Britten by Rostropovich in London in 1961 and became a frequent visitor to Aldeburgh thereafter: the intimate surroundings suited his needs, adverse circumstances were reduced to a minimum, and the duet recitals which they gave together, whether four hands on one piano or in works like the Mozart *Sonata for two pianos*, provided a rare opportunity to hear the interplay of musical intelligence at its purest. Britten was no mean pianist himself, but in his view Richter was quite simply 'the best pianist ever'.

Richter kam erst spät in den Westen. Zwar gab er 1960 in Chicago und New York Konzerte, aber die europäischen Hauptstädte besuchte er nicht vor 1961. Sein Name war bereits in den frühen fünfziger Jahren in London bekannt geworden aufgrund einiger, nicht besonders hochwertiger sowjetischer Aufnahmen und vor allem nach Berichten von Leuten, die ihn in der Sowjetunion oder Ländern des Warschauer Paktes spielen gehört hatten. Aber Mitte der fünfziger Jahre stellte sich auf Grund einer Reihe verblüffender Aufnahmen – von Schumann, Schubert, Rachmaninow, Prokofjew – schnell heraus, daß sich dort hinter dem Eisernen Vorhang ein unglaubliches Talent entwickelt hatte.

Das Wunderkind Richter hatte sich das Klavierspielen vollständig selbst beigebracht. Bereits mit 15 Jahren bekam er an der Oper von Odessa eine Anstellung als Korrepetitor, ein Jahr später debütierte er als Pianist. Doch erst im Alter von 22 Jahren begann er systematischen Unterricht am Moskauer Konservatorium zu nehmen, wo ihn sein Lehrer als „musikalisches Genie, ausgestattet mit großer geistiger Potenz" pries. Noch während seines Studiums gab er die Uraufführung der *Sechsten Sonate* von Prokofjew, womit er seine lebenslange Meisterschaft im Klavierwerk Prokofjews begründete – auch die Uraufführungen der *Siebenten* und *Neunten Sonate* oblagen ihm (wobei der Komponist die *Neunte* sogar ihm gewidmet hatte); und seinen einzigen Auftritt als Dirigent hatte Richter, als er 1952 mit Rostropowitsch die *Sinfonia Concertante für Violoncello und Orchester* uraufführte.

Seine ersten Konzerte in London waren – wie vorherzusehen – sofort restlos ausverkauft. In künstlerischer Hinsicht allerdings konnte man bei Richter nie etwas vorhersehen. Seine absolute technische Perfektion und Beherrschung des Instrumentes suchte in den Nachkriegsjahren ihresgleichen; und die Kombination von Virtuosität und tiefer Innerlichkeit des russischen Temperaments konnte die allerbesten Resultate zeitigen – vor allem bei Werken von Schubert oder Schumann, in denen kräftige Artikulation und poetische Feinheit ganz und gar ausgewogen sind und den romantischen Überschwang in seine Schranken verweisen. Aber eine derart intensive Innenschau konnte auch manchmal zu weit gehen, so daß sich letztlich das Publikum als in die Schranken verwiesen vorkommen mußte. Richter war mehr als andere Pianisten von der Konzertatmosphäre abhängig und ließ sich leicht von ungünstigen Stimmungen verunsichern. Dann erlebte der Zuhörer, wie diese Ausgewogenheit plötzlich an sich selbst zerbrach.

In verschiedenen kammermusikalischen Besetzungen, aber auch als Begleiter von Künstlern, die er mochte, wie Dietrich Fischer-Dieskau oder Elisabeth Schwarzkopf, spielte Richter wundervoll, und mit seiner spontanen Gestik und Mimik begeisterte er das Publikum. Sein unangekündigtes Konzert in der Gemeindekirche während des Aldeburgh Festivals 1964 wird denjenigen, die das Glück hatten, es mitzuerleben, unvergeßlich bleiben. 1961 machte Rostropowitsch ihn in London mit Britten bekannt, woraufhin er ein regelmäßiger Gast in Aldeburgh wurde. Die intime Atmosphäre dort entsprach seinen Bedürfnissen, Störungen wurden weitestgehend vermieden, und die gemeinsamen Konzerte, ob vierhändig oder wie in Mozarts *Sonate für zwei Klaviere*, boten den Zuhörenden die seltene Gelegenheit, einem Wechsel- und Zusammenspiel brillantester musikalischer Auffassungsgabe in Reinstform zu lauschen. Britten war selbst sicher kein schlechter Pianist, aber in seinen Augen war Richter ganz einfach „der beste Pianist überhaupt".

Richter vint tardivement à l'Ouest, jouant à Chicago et New York en 1960, mais ne se produisant dans les centres européens majeurs qu'en 1961. Dès le début des années 50, sa réputation avait atteint Londres par à-coups, à travers quelques enregistrements soviétiques plutôt médiocres et ce qu'en disaient ceux qui l'avaient entendu jouer en Russie ou dans le bloc soviétique. Mais, au milieu des années 50, une série d'enregistrements stupéfiants – Schumann, Schubert, Rachmaninov, Prokofiev – révéla qu'un talent formidable existait à l'Est.

Richter était un enfant prodige mais, étrangement, complètement autodidacte. Il trouva un emploi de répétiteur à l'opéra d'Odessa à l'âge de 15 ans et, un an après, fit ses débuts de pianiste. Mais ce n'est qu'à 22 ans qu'il commença à prendre vraiment des cours de piano, entrant au conservatoire de Moscou, où son professeur le salua comme « un génie musical, d'une grande intelligence. » Il était encore étudiant quand il donna la première exécution de la *Sixième Sonate* pour piano de Prokofiev dont il se fera désormais le champion des pièces pour piano – il devait également donner les premières interprétations des *Septième* et *Neuvième sonates* (la *Neuvième* lui était dédiée). Il est apparu une seul fois comme chef d'orchestre, avec Rostropovitch, pour la première exécution de la *Sinfonia Concertante pour violoncelle et orchestre* en 1952.

Ses premiers récitals à Londres se firent à guichets fermés, comme on pouvait s'y attendre. Qquant à Richter lui-même il n'a jamais été un artiste prévisible. Pour le contrôle technique et la maîtrise de son instrument, il n'avait pratiquement pas d'égal dans les années d'après-guerre. L'alliance de sa virtuosité et de son tempérament russe profondément introspectif peut produire des résultats extraordinaires – particulièrement avec des compositeurs comme Schubert et Schumann, où la puissance du doigté et le raffinement poétique donnent un équilibre parfait qui tient à distance la sensiblerie romantique. Mais l'introspection intense peut parfois aller trop loin, et c'est le public qui sentait qu'il était tenu à distance. Richter était, plus que la plupart des pianistes, sensible à l'ambiance et facilement troublé par des circonstances défavorables et, quand cela se produisait, on pouvait parfois se demander si l'équilibre n'était pas devenu une fin en soi.

Il était un partenaire merveilleux pour la musique de chambre, ou pour accompagner des artistes avec lesquels il s'entendait bien, comme Dietrich Fischer-Dieskau ou Elisabeth Schwarzkopf, et pouvait donner le meilleur de lui-même dans un mouvement soudain et spontané. Ceux qui ont eu la chance d'assister au récital imprévu qu'il donna de Schubert, lors du festival d'Aldeburgh en 1964, ne sont pas près de l'oublier. Il avait été présenté à Britten par Rostropovitch en 1961 à Londres et était devenu par la suite un habitué d'Aldeburgh : l'environnement intimiste lui convenait, les circonstances défavorables étaient réduites au minimum, et les récitals en duo qu'il donnait avec Britten, soit à quatre mains sur un seul piano, soit dans des œuvres comme la *Sonate pour deux pianos* de Mozart, donnaient l'occasion rare d'entendre l'interaction de l'intelligence musicale dans ce qu'elle a de plus pur. Britten lui-même était loin d'être un pianiste médiocre, mais, à son avis, Richter était simplement « le meilleur pianiste de tous les temps ».

Sviatoslav Richter after recording a Prokofiev piano sonata, on his first visit to London, July 1961. Though Auerbach was not permitted to take photographs during the actual recording, he did stay in the studio to turn the pages for the pianist, and was rewarded afterwards with a series of informal studies in the playback room.

Swjatoslaw Richter nach der Aufnahme einer Klaviersonate von Prokofjew im Juli 1961, während seines ersten Londonaufenthaltes. Obwohl es Auerbach nicht gestattet war, während der Aufnahmen zu fotografieren, blieb er im Studio, um dem Pianisten die Noten umzublättern, und wurde nachher damit belohnt, daß er eine Reihe ungezwungener Bilder im Aufnahmeraum machen durfte.

Sviatoslav Richter après l'enregistrement d'une sonate pour piano de Prokofiev, en juillet 1961, pendant sa première visite à Londres. Auerbach, qui n'avait pas eu l'autorisation de photographier pendant l'enregistrement, resta dans le studio pour tourner les pages de la partition et en fut récompensé par une série d'études informelles prises dans la salle d'écoute.

◀ Sviatoslav Richter at the Royal Festival Hall on his first visit to London, 10 July 1961.

Swjatoslaw Richter bei seinem ersten Konzert in London in der Royal Festival Hall, 10. Juli 1961.

Sviatoslav Richter au Royal Festival Hall lors de sa première visite à Londres, le 10 juillet 1961.

Richter and the cellist Mstislav Rostropovitch are friends and colleagues who have often played together in chamber music. But the ways of Soviet officialdom, even in the years of the thaw after Stalin's death, were unpredictable, and Rostropovitch, though 12 years younger than Richter, achieved his London début five years before him. This was therefore the first occasion on which they were able to play together in a London studio, and the performances that they recorded in July 1961 of the whole series of the Beethoven cello sonatas are classics that have remained unsurpassed to this day. Not that the mood at the session on 24 July appears to have been entirely without its lighter side.

Richter und der Cellist Mstislaw Rostropowitsch sind private wie musikalische Freunde, die häufig gemeinsam Kammermusik gespielt haben. Aber die Ratschlüsse der sowjetischen Obrigkeit waren auch in den Jahren des Tauwetters nach Stalins Tod nicht vorhersagbar, so daß Rostropowitsch, obwohl er 12 Jahre jünger als Richter ist, bereits fünf Jahre vor ihm in London debütieren konnte. Die erste Möglichkeit zu gemeinsamen Aufnahmen in einem Londoner Studio bot sich für sie im Juli 1961, als sie sämtliche Cellosonaten Beethovens einspielten. Diese Aufnahmen werden nicht zu Unrecht als klassisch bezeichnet und bleiben bis heute unübertroffen. Die Fotos vom 24. Juli zeigen, daß auch derart hochrangige Leistungen ihre fröhlichen Seiten haben.

Amis et collègues, Richter et le violoncelliste Mstislav Rostropovitch ont souvent joué ensemble de la musique de chambre. Mais les voies de la bureaucratie soviétique, même dans les années de dégel après la mort de Staline, étaient imprévisibles, et Rostropovitch, bien que plus jeune de douze ans que Richter, fit ses débuts à Londres cinq ans avant lui. C'était donc leur première occasion de jouer ensemble dans un studio londonien et leur interprétation de toutes les sonates pour violoncelle de Beethoven, enregistrées en juillet 1961, est un classique inégalé à ce jour. L'ambiance de la séance du 24 juillet ne semble pas totalement dépourvue de légèreté.

The hands of Sviatoslav Richter, 24 July 1961.

Die Hände von Swjatoslaw Richter, 24. Juli 1961.

Les mains de Sviatoslav Richter, le 24 juillet 1961.

The hands of Mstislav Rostropovitch, 24 July 1961.

Die Hände von Mstislav Rostropowitsch, 24. Juli 1961.

Les mains de Mstislav Rostropovitch, le 24 juillet 1961.

The jutting chin, the beaming smile, the instant warmth, the overflowing fountain of energy – first impressions of Rostropovich are more than anything of a man who loves life. It is above all life that he carries with him on to the concert platform, whether as cellist, pianist or conductor, for he is a musician of multiple talents and absolute commitment in all of them. And not only a musician either. 'He knows everything and he can do anything,' said Shostakovich. 'Anything at all. I'm not even talking about music here, I mean that Rostropovich can do almost any manual or physical work and he understands technology.'

Nevertheless, it was as a cellist that he first burst upon the West in the mid-1950s, and the impact he made was immediate. Effortless technical accomplishment and an astonishing range of tone were combined with passionate lyricism, rugged power and an instinctive understanding of widely differing musical styles that left no doubt that this was one of the great artists of his generation. If sheer excess of enthusiasm sometimes raised critical doubts, these were soon swept away by the breadth of vision that it fuelled, and the eagerness with which he tackled new and unknown repertory. Among the many composers who wrote works for him were Prokofiev, Khachaturian and his friend and mentor Shostakovich, as well as Britten, with whom he formed a close friendship in 1960 and whom he visited at many subsequent Aldeburgh Festivals.

He was an accomplished pianist too, and after his marriage in 1955 to the soprano Galina Vishnevskaya he often appeared as accompanist at her recitals. And he loved chamber music. But, as with Casals in a previous generation, the desire for a more comprehensive means of musical expression became irresistible: by the early 1960s he was already experimenting with orchestral direction as a soloist and in 1968 he made his full début as a conductor in Tchaikovsky's *Yevgeny Onegin* at the Bolshoy Theatre in Moscow.

But already the sands were running out for Rostropovich in his home country. A couple of years later his public defence of the dissident Russian author Alexander Solzhenitsyn earned him the displeasure of the Soviet authorities: he found his foreign trips dramatically restricted, so that in 1974, when he was finally granted permission for a two-year visit to Britain, he took his wife and family with him and did not return. A year after his appointment as music director of the National Symphony Orchestra in Washington DC he was stripped of his Soviet citizenship, but received it back in 1990 when he was invited to take the orchestra to Russia.

As a conductor, however, he has sometimes been found to indulge emotional expression at the expense of precision, and it is as a cellist that he is still most highly regarded. It was in this capacity that he was presented in 1970 with the treasured gold medal of the Royal Philharmonic Society in London. Reading from a small piece of paper he said to the audience: 'Four years ago, when I received the gold medal of the Society on behalf of my friend Dmitry Shostakovich, who was not able to come to London, I kept it under my pillow and did not sleep until I had handed it to him in Moscow. Now that I have one of my own' – pause, turn of the page, beaming smile – 'I shall never sleep again.'

Das hervorstehende Kinn, das strahlende Lächeln, die unmittelbare Wärme, die überquellende Energie – die ersten Eindrücke von Rostropowitsch sind die eines Mannes, der das Leben liebt. Es ist vor allem diese Lebendigkeit, die er mit sich auf die Bühne bringt, sei es als Cellist, als Pianist oder als Dirigent, denn er ist ein Multitalent und in vielen musikalischen und auch anderen Bereichen zuhause. „Er weiß alles und er kann alles", so Schostakowitsch. „Alles nur mögliche. Und ich spreche hier nicht allein von der Musik, ich meine, daß Rostropowitsch so gut wie jede Hand- oder geistige Arbeit selbst machen kann und die Technologie versteht."

Mitte der 50er Jahre kam er in den Westen – und wurde dort schlagartig berühmt. Mühelose technische Perfektion und eine erstaunliche Klangfülle in Kombination mit leidenschaftlichem Gefühlsüberschwang, unbändiger Kraft und einem intuitiven Einfühlungsvermögen in selbst weit auseinanderliegende musikalische Stile ließen keinerlei Zweifel daran aufkommen, daß Rostropowitsch einer der größten Musiker seiner Generation war. Wenn wahre Exzesse seiner Leidenschaft auch manchmal Zweifel bei den Kritikern aufkommen ließen, wurden diese doch gleich wieder ausgeräumt von der visionären Kraft, die aus ihm strömte, und von der Begeisterung, mit der er sich alter wie neuer und unbekannter Werke annahm. Viele Komponisten schrieben für ihn, darunter Prokofjew, Khatschaturian und sein Freund und Mentor Schostakowitsch, ebenso wie Britten, mit dem ihn ab 1960 eine enge Freundschaft verband und den er immer wieder beim Aldeburgh Festival besuchte.

Er war auch ein guter Klavierbegleiter: Nachdem er 1955 die Sopranistin Galina Wischnewskaja geheiratet hatte, begleitete er sie am Klavier. Er liebte die Kammermusik, aber (darin Pablo Casals ähnlich) nach und nach wuchs in ihm der immer dringlichere Wunsch, mit umfassenderen Mitteln den musikalischen Ausdruck weiter zu vertiefen: In den frühen 60er Jahren machte er noch als Solist erste Erfahrungen mit dem Dirigieren, und 1968 debütierte er am Moskauer Bolschoi Theater mit Tschaikowskys *Eugen Onegin* als Dirigent.

Aber schon damals lief in seinem Heimatland die Zeit gegen ihn. Als er einige Jahre später den russischen Schriftsteller und Dissidenten Alexander Solschenizyn öffentlich verteidigte, erregte er den Unwillen der sowjetischen Machthaber: Er sah seine Auslandsreisen derart einschneidenden Restriktionen unterworfen, daß er 1974, als ihm dann doch ein Zweijahresvisum für England ausgestellt wurde, mit seiner Frau und seiner Familie endgültig die Heimat verließ. Ein Jahr nach seiner Ernennung zum musikalischen Direktor des National Symphony Orchestra von Washington wurde ihm die sowjetische Staatsbürgerschaft entzogen, die er erst 1990 zurückerhielt, als man ihn mit seinem Orchester nach Rußland einlud.

Dem Dirigenten Rostropowitsch hat man manchmal vorgeworfen, sich derart dem emotionalen Ausdruck der Musik verschrieben zu haben, daß die Präzision darunter leide, und so ist es auch der Cellist, dem nach wie vor die größte Achtung gezollt wird. Als eben diesem wurde ihm 1970 die begehrte Goldmedaille der Royal Philharmonic Society verliehen. In seiner Dankesrede, die er von einem kleinen Blatt Papier ablas, formulierte er: „Vor vier Jahren, als ich für meinen Freund Dmitri Schostakowitsch, der nicht nach London kommen konnte, dessen Goldmedaille entgegennahm, habe ich sie unter meinem Kopfkissen verborgen und konnte solange nicht schlafen, bis ich sie ihm wohlbehalten in Moskau übergeben hatte. Nun habe ich meine eigene" – Pause, er dreht das Blatt um und lächelt entwaffnend – „und werde niemals mehr schlafen."

Le menton saillant, le sourire épanoui, tout de suite chaleureux, une source débordante d'énergie – les premières impressions données par Rostropovitch sont celles d'un homme qui aime la vie. C'est par-dessus tout la vie qu'il apporte avec lui sur scène, tant comme violoncelliste que comme pianiste ou chef d'orchestre, car c'est un musicien complet, aux talents multiples, et qui s'investit totalement en chacun d'eux. Pas uniquement un musicien d'ailleurs. « Il connaît tout et il peut tout faire, absolument tout, disait Chostakovich. Je ne parle même pas de musique ici, je veux dire que Rostropovitch peut faire presque tous les travaux manuels et il comprend la technologie. »

Il apparut à l'Ouest au milieu des années 50, et l'impact qu'il produisit fut immédiat. Une technique fluide et un registre de tonalités étonnant étaient alliés à un lyrisme passionné, une rude puissance, et à une compréhension instinctive de styles musicaux très différents qui ne laissait aucun doute sur le fait qu'il était l'un des plus grands artistes de sa génération. Si de purs excès d'enthousiasme soulevaient parfois des doutes critiques, ils étaient rapidement balayés par l'ampleur de la vision que ces excès sous-tendaient et par l'ardeur avec laquelle Rostropovitch s'attaquait au répertoire récent et inconnu. Parmi les nombreux musiciens qui composèrent pour lui, on trouve Prokofiev, Khatchatourian et Chostakovich, ainsi que Britten, avec lequel il devint très ami en 1960 et à qui il rendit visite lors de nombreuses éditions postérieures du festival d'Aldeburgh.

Pianiste accompli, après son mariage en 1955 avec la soprano Galina Vichnievskaia, il fut souvent l'accompagnateur de ses récitals. Il adorait aussi la musique de chambre. Mais, comme pour Casals à la génération précédente, son désir d'un moyen d'expression musicale plus complet devint incontournable : au début des années 60, il avait déjà fait l'expérience de la direction d'orchestre tout en étant soliste et, en 1968, il fit ses débuts de chef d'orchestre dans *Eugène Onéguine* de Tchaïkovski, au théâtre du Bolchoï de Moscou.

Mais les sables se faisaient déjà mouvants pour Rostropovitch dans son pays natal. Deux ans plus tard, sa défense publique de l'auteur russe dissident Alexandre Soljenitsyne lui valut le mécontentement des autorités soviétiques : ses voyages à l'étranger furent considérablement limités, ce qui fit qu'en 1974, quand on lui accorda finalement l'autorisation de partir deux ans en Grande-Bretagne, il emmena sa famille avec lui et ne revint pas. Un an après sa nomination comme directeur musical de l'Orchestre symphonique national à Washington, il fut déchu de sa citoyenneté soviétique, mais elle lui fut rendue en 1990 quand il fut invité avec l'orchestre en Russie.

Cependant, en tant que chef d'orchestre, on a parfois trouvé qu'il privilégiait par trop l'émotion aux dépens de la précision, et c'est en tant que violoncelliste qu'il est toujours le plus hautement considéré. C'est à ce titre qu'on lui remit, en 1970, la précieuse médaille d'or de la Royal Philharmonic Society de Londres. Lisant un petit bout de papier, il dit au public : « Il y a quatre ans, quand j'ai reçu la médaille d'or de la Société au nom de mon ami Dimitri Chostakovich, qui n'avait pas pu venir à Londres, je l'ai gardée sous mon oreiller et je n'ai pas dormi tant que je ne la lui ai pas remise, à Moscou. Maintenant que j'en ai une à moi – une pause, il retourne le bout de papier, un sourire épanoui –, je ne dormirai plus jamais. »

▸ In a programme that included three concertos by Vivaldi, Tartini, and Boccherini. Rostropovitch, soloist and conductor, pitching into a rehearsal with the London Symphony Orchestra, 26 June 1965.

Rostropowitsch, Solist und Dirigent zugleich, feuert das London Symphony Orchestra bei einer Probe für eine Aufführung von drei Konzerten von Vivaldi, Tartini und Boccherini an, 26. Juni 1965.

Rostropovitch, soliste et chef d'orchestre, commençant une répétition avec l'Orchestre symphonique de Londres dans un programme incluant trois concertos – de Vivaldi, Tartini et Boccherini, le 26 juin 1965.

Mstislav Rostropovitch at the cello – ebullient, expressive, pugnacious, but always with the richness and variety of tone, the Russian depth of feeling, the conviction of the total musician.

Mstislav Rostropowitsch am Cello – überschwenglich, ausdrucksstark, kämpferisch, aber immer mit dem ihm eigenen üppigen und variationsreichen Ton, der russischen Gefühlstiefe, der Überzeugungkraft einer verkörperten Musikalität.

Mstislav Rostropovitch au violoncelle, exubérant, expressif, pugnace, mais toujours avec la richesse et la variété de tons, la profondeur de la sensibilité russe, la conviction d'un musicien complet.

Rostropovitch rehearsing, probably in 1968, at the Snape Maltings near Aldeburgh.

Rostropowitsch bei einer Probe in den Snape Maltings in der Nähe von Aldeburgh, wahrscheinlich 1968.

Rostropovitch en répétition, probablement en 1968, au Snape Maltings près d'Aldeburgh.

Cellist, conductor – and now pianist, rehearsing for a recital with his wife, the soprano Galina Vishnevskaya, 26 February 1959. Curiously enough, the score lying beside him on the piano, a Tchaikovsky piano trio, completes the circle of his musical activities.

Cellist, Dirigent – und nun auch noch Pianist. Bei einer Probe mit seiner Frau, der Sopranistin Galina Wischnewskaja, am 26. Februar 1959. Interessanterweise liegt zudem die Partitur eines Klaviertrios von Tschaikowsky neben ihm auf dem Klavier, die den Kreis all seiner musikalischen Aktivitäten schließt.

Violoncelliste, chef d'orchestre – et maintenant pianiste, répétant avec son épouse, la soprano Galina Vishnevskaya, le 26 février 1959. Chose curieuse, la partition se trouvant à côté de lui sur le piano, un trio pour piano de Tchaïkovski, complète le champ de ses activités musicales.

Probably no pianist has given so much pleasure to so many people as Artur Rubinstein – or indeed, one often felt, to himself. There was an amazingly relaxed, almost improvisatory, feel about his performances, a sense of innate musicianship backed by immense reserves of energy, and a timeless lyricism that went directly from the heart of the music to the heart of the listener. He hated practising, and as a matter of principle never practised any piece that he was going to play in public in the near future. So it was hardly surprising that the technical control was not always flawless – but virtuosity of another kind was never lacking, the virtuosity of an absolutely sovereign performer, honed and sharpened by a lifetime of platform experience. By the time of these photographs he was nearing 80 years old: the authority was absolute, but the old fire still burned, the old romantic ardour still suffused his playing.

He had been a child prodigy, giving his first recital at the age of five, playing a Mozart concerto at 13 (with Brahms's friend Joachim as the conductor) and splashing out into a career of dazzling potential during those heady years before the First World War. The same precocious exuberance welled over into his social life. He was a wild, socially voracious young man, and though there could be no question about his genius there was reasonable doubt about the artistic discipline that might have been expected to go with it.

But in 1932 he married. It would perhaps be an overstatement to say that he settled down – no man who exerted the magnetic attraction over women that Rubinstein continued to radiate until the end of his life could really be expected to do that. He did, however, take honest stock of his professional situation, and he did withdraw from public appearance and give his musical and technical equipment the intensive study that it needed and deserved. As a result, he emerged into his fifties a serious artist: the old brilliance and panache were now tempered with a new, more balanced discipline, and Rubinstein took his place as one of the great pianists of the 20th century.

In his early days he had been deeply involved with contemporary music, French, Spanish and Russian particularly, and could be aggressive in its defence: booed by an audience for playing Ravel's *Valses nobles et sentimentales* at a recital, he simply repeated the entire work as an encore. As his repertory broadened he gave more time to the great classical and romantic masterpieces, and in later life was not unknown to give both Brahms concertos or three by Beethoven in a single concert (probably following it with a convivial dinner party at which the ladies could be seen swooning round the table while the men looked politely bored). But, curiously, it took time for Chopin to replace Brahms as the composer with whom he most readily identified, and with whom he is now most intimately associated.

Until the very end of his career as a pianist, which lasted for the best part of 80 years, he never lost the sense of spontaneity and freshness in each new performance. 'A concert is like a bullfight,' he said, 'the moment of truth.' Perhaps after all it did have something to do with love.

Wahrscheinlich hat kein anderer Pianist so vielen Menschen Freude bereitet wie Rubinstein, wenn man auch häufig meinen konnte, er spiele hauptsächlich für sich selbst. Er vermochte es, eine so gelöste Stimmung zu verbreiten, daß man das Gefühl hatte, einer verkörperten Musikalität von unerschöpflicher Energie zu lauschen. Die Emotionalität seines Spiels übertrug seine Musik direkt in die Herzen der Zuhörer. Er haßte das Üben und studierte die Stücke, die er in Kürze aufführen wollte, prinzipiell nicht ein. So kann es kaum erstaunen, daß ihm technische Perfektion selten gelang – dagegen fehlte eine andere Art von Virtuosität nie, nämlich die des souveränen Künstlers, der zeit seines Lebens Bühnenerfahrung gesammelt hat. Als diese Fotografien entstanden, war Rubinstein beinahe 80 Jahre alt und ein Inbegriff absoluter Autorität; aber sein Spiel wurde getragen von der in seinem Herzen immer noch brennenden Flamme romantischer Leidenschaft.

Und dies mit gutem Grund. Rubinstein verhehlte nie, daß der Musik mit gleicher Wichtigkeit die Frauen in seinem Leben gegenüberstanden, und in seiner Autobiographie häufen sich Affären und Intrigen. Das Wunderkind Artur gab schon im Alter von fünf Jahren sein erstes Konzert, mit 13 führte er ein Mozart-Klavierkonzert auf (das Brahms' Freund Joachim dirigierte), und bis zum Ersten Weltkrieg entfaltete sich das erstaunliche musikalische Potential Rubinsteins in einer furiosen Karriere, die mit beinahe demselben Überschwang auch in sein Privatleben Einzug hielt. Er war ein unersättlicher Lebemann, und wenn auch sein Genie nie in Frage stand, so bestanden doch Zweifel an der künstlerischen Disziplin.

Dennoch heiratete er im Jahr 1932. Es wäre wahrscheinlich eine Übertreibung zu behaupten, er sei damit auch unter die Haube gekommen – niemand, der die magnetische Anziehungskraft auf Frauen, die Rubinstein bis zu seinem Lebensende ausstrahlte, je kennengelernt hat, hätte dies von ihm erwartet. Jedoch unterzog er seine künstlerische Situation einer kritischen Bestandsaufnahme, zog sich daraufhin von der Bühne zurück und begann intensiv, an seiner technischen und musikalischen Ausdruckskraft zu arbeiten. Als ernsthafter Künstler kehrte er zurück, nun schon über 50 Jahre alt. Seine frühere Brillanz und Selbstdarstellungssucht waren jetzt gebändigt durch eine neue, zu mehr Ausgewogenheit verhelfende Disziplin, und Rubinstein konnte von nun an ohne Zweifel als einer der größten Pianisten des 20. Jahrhunderts gelten.

In seiner Jugend setzte Rubinstein sich intensiv mit zeitgenössischer Musik auseinander, vor allem mit französischer, spanischer und russischer, und er verteidigte sie mit fast aggressiver Vehemenz: Als ihn einmal das Publikum nach der Aufführung von Ravels *Valses nobles et sentimentales* ausbuhte, spielte er das Stück kurzerhand als Zugabe noch einmal. Nachdem sein zeitgenössisches Repertoire nahezu umfassend war, begann er sich klassischen und romantischen Werken zu widmen, so daß es für ihn später nicht ungewöhnlich war, beide Brahms-Klavierkonzerte oder auch drei von Beethoven in einem Konzert aufzuführen (und sich wahrscheinlich im Anschluß daran auf einer Dinnerparty von Frauen umschwärmen zu lassen). Erstaunlicherweise brauchte es dennoch geraume Zeit, bis Chopin Brahms als denjenigen Komponisten ablösen konnte, mit dem sich Rubinstein ganz und gar identifizierte, und mit dessen Werk er heute am meisten verbunden wird.

Rubinsteins Konzerte behielten bis zum Ende seiner Karriere, die bis weit in seine Achtziger hineinreichte, immer die Spontaneität und Frische seiner Jugend bei. „Ein Konzert ist wie ein Stierkampf", sagte er, „der Moment der Wahrheit." Vielleicht hatte es doch mit Liebe zu tun ...

Artur Rubinstein peut sans doute être considéré comme le pianiste du plaisir, plaisir qu'il se donnait à lui-même autant qu'aux autres. Ses représentations dégageaient une confondante impression de décontraction, presque d'improvisation ; sa maestria était soutenue par d'immenses réserves d'énergie, et son perpétuel lyrisme allait directement du cœur de la musique au cœur de celui qui écoutait. Il détestait répéter et, par principe, ne travaillait jamais un morceau qu'il allait prochainement jouer en public. Rien d'étonnant donc à ce que sa technique de virtuose ne fût pas toujours impeccable – mais une virtuosité d'un autre ordre ne lui faisait jamais défaut, celle d'un interprète absolument souverain, poli et affiné par une vie entière de concertiste habitué à la scène. À l'époque de ces photographies, il approchait de ses 80 ans : son autorité était absolue, le même feu brûlait toujours, la même ferveur romantique baignait toujours son jeu.

Enfant prodige, il donna son premier récital à 5 ans, joua un concerto de Mozart à 13 ans (sous la direction de Joachim, l'ami de Brahms) et se lança dans une carrière aux perspectives éblouissantes durant les années exaltantes d'avant la Première Guerre mondiale. Il se jeta avec la même précocité exubérante dans sa vie sociale, qu'il croquait à belles dents, ce dont pâtissait la discipline artistique qui était censée accompagner son indubitable génie.

Mais il se maria en 1932. Il serait peut-être exagéré de dire qu'il s'assagit – on ne peut attendre cela d'un homme qui exerçait sur les femmes l'attraction magnétique que Rubinstein continua à dégager jusqu'à la fin de sa vie. Cependant, il fit honnêtement le point sur sa situation professionnelle, n'apparut plus en public et entreprit un travail intensif pour compléter, enfin, son bagage musical et technique. Ainsi devint-il, aux abords de la cinquantaine, un artiste sérieux ; l'éclat et le panache d'antan étaient maintenant tempérés par une discipline nouvelle, plus équilibrée, et Rubinstein prit rang parmi les plus grands pianistes du XXᵉ siècle.

Au début de sa carrière, il s'était profondément engagé dans la musique contemporaine, en particulier française, espagnole et russe, et pouvait la défendre de façon agressive : hué par le public parce qu'il avait joué les *Valses nobles et sentimentales* de Ravel, il les avaient redonnées en entier lors du rappel. Mais lorsque son répertoire s'élargit et mûrit, il se consacra davantage aux grands chefs-d'œuvre classiques et romantiques et, sur le tard, il lui arriva de jouer les deux concertos de Brahms ou les trois de Beethoven dans le même concert (probablement suivi d'un dîner où les dames se pâmaient autour de la table tandis que les messieurs s'ennuyaient poliment). Brahms fut d'abord son compositeur d'élection, puis Chopin remplaça Brahms, ce qui, curieusement, prit un certain temps. Il semble que son extraordinaire affinité pour Chopin, qui le rendit célèbre plus tard, n'avait pas grand-chose à voir avec leur origine polonaise commune.

Jusqu'à la fin de sa carrière de pianiste, qui dura quatre-vingts ans, il ne perdit jamais sa spontanéité et sa fraîcheur à chaque nouvelle représentation. « Un concert est comme une corrida – disait-il –, un moment de vérité. » Après tout, cela avait peut-être un rapport avec l'amour...

In the artists' room at the Royal Festival Hall, London, 3 October 1963, Artur Rubinstein prepares for a recital. It was an experience, said Auerbach, that he likened to an execution – though there is little to suggest it in his manner as he hands over his hat and silk scarf to his wife, Aniela. The hands receive special attention – first the fingernails, then loosening the joints, then a few exercises at the keyboard. And finally a brush on the collar to ensure the unfailing Rubinstein elegance as he appears on the platform.

Artur Rubinstein bereitet sich für ein Konzert vor. Das Foto entstand in der Künstlergarderobe der Royal Festival Hall in London am 3. Oktober 1963. Auerbach verglich diese Erfahrung mit einer Exekution – auch wenn nichts in der Art und Weise, wie Rubinstein seinen Hut und seinen Schal seiner Frau Aniela überreicht, darauf schließen läßt. Den Händen wird besondere Aufmerksamkeit geschenkt – zuerst den Fingernägeln, dann durch das Lockern der Handgelenke, danach ein paar kleine Übungen auf der Tastatur. Und schließlich ein kurzes Bürsten des Kragens, um das vollendete Erscheinungsbild des Künstlers sicherzustellen, wenn er die Bühne betritt.

Dans le foyer des artistes du Royal Festival Hall à Londres, le 3 octobre 1963, Arthur Rubinstein se prépare pour un récital. D'après Auerbach, c'était une expérience qu'il comparait à une exécution – bien que rien ne le laisse supposer dans la manière dont il tend son chapeau et son écharpe de soie à son épouse Aniela. Ses mains recevaient une attention particulière, d'abord les ongles, puis assouplissement des jointures, ensuite quelques exercices au clavier ; enfin, un coup de brosse sur le col, dernière touche à la parfaite élégance de Rubinstein en scène.

◀ Artur Rubinstein, debonair as ever at 74, receives the Gold Medal of the Royal Philharmonic Society after a concert at the Royal Festival Hall, London, 19 April 1961.

Artur Rubinstein, der hier – bereits 74jährig – genauso aufgeräumt wie immer erscheint, erhält die Goldmedaille der Royal Philharmonic Society nach einem Konzert in der Royal Albert Hall in London, 19. April 1961.

Arthur Rubinstein reçoit, à 74 ans, la médaille d'or de la Royal Philharmonic Society, après un concert au Royal Festival Hall, à Londres, le 19 avril 1961.

Rubinstein with the BBC Symphony Orchestra at the Royal
Festival Hall, London, 26 November 1957.

Rubinstein mit dem BBC Symphony Orchestra in der Royal
Festival Hall in London, 26. November 1957.

Rubinstein avec le BBC Symphony Orchestra au Royal Festival
Hall, à Londres, le 26 novembre 1957.

Unflagging vitality in his 80s – rehearsing with Zubin Mehta for a concert with the Israel Philharmonic Orchestra, Royal Festival Hall, London, about 1969.

Uneingeschränkte Vitalität auch in seinen 80ern – bei einer Probe gemeinsam mit Zubin Mehta für ein Konzert mit dem Israel Philharmonic Orchestra in der Royal Festival Hall, London, um 1969.

Une vitalité incroyable à 80 ans – en répétition avec Zubin Mehta en vue d'un concert avec le Israel Philharmonic Orchestra, Royal Festival Hall, Londres, vers 1969.

ANDRÉS SEGOVIA
1893-1987

JULIAN BREAM
***1933**

JOHN WILLIAMS
***1942**

When Segovia was a young man the guitar was not regarded, outside Spain at any rate, as an instrument to be taken seriously. But Segovia, who was self-taught and therefore perhaps less bound by a traditional view of the instrument than other Spanish guitarists of his day, was passionately determined to bring it back into the world of serious music. Transcribing, performing and recording works by Bach, Handel, Mozart and Chopin, and reviving the music of the Renaissance *vihuela* and the old Spanish lutenists, he created a reputation for himself and a new image for the guitar which entirely altered the perception of the instrument by musicians and public alike. New works were written for him by 'serious' composers like Falla, Villa-Lobos, Castelnuovo-Tedesco and many others, and even those guitar pieces which were not created specifically for his performance (such as the most famous of all, Rodrigo's *Concierto de Aranjuez*) would have been unthinkable without his example. More than anyone else, Segovia was responsible for the revival of the classical guitar in the 20th century, and for the great enrichment of the musical repertory that went with it.

Segovia was of course an abiding inspiration to young guitarists the world over. In England, Julian Bream heard his records as a boy when he was evacuated from London during the war, and in 1947 was 'absolutely spellbound' by Segovia's first post-war London recital. He had a job persuading the authorities at the Royal College of Music to accept the instrument – in fact he didn't persuade them: they obviously thought the guitar (even playing Bach) was a subversive influence, and Bream was kept firmly to his studies on the piano and cello. But like Segovia he persevered: his innate artistry would not be denied, and like Segovia he ended up with a string of compositions written specially for him – by Britten, Berkeley, Walton, Henze, Tippett and many more.

For about a decade Bream was the unchallenged star of the British guitar world. But towards the end of the 1950s a young Australian, who had attracted the attention of Segovia and actually had some teaching from the great man, appeared on the London scene. This was John Williams, and at first the situation was a little delicate. The idea of anyone who was not Spanish making a success of the guitar had been difficult enough to establish with the British public: by this time it had become accepted that one English-speaking guitarist did actually exist – but two? Happily, there was room for both, and in fact some of the greatest triumphs of the two artists have been achieved together. Isn't it Chopin who is reputed to have said, 'The only thing more beautiful than one guitar is two'?

Als Segovia ein junger Mann war, wurde die Gitarre – zumindest außerhalb Spaniens – nicht als ein ernstzunehmendes Instrument angesehen. Doch setzte Segovia, der als Autodidakt vielleicht weniger mit dem traditionellen Bild der Gitarre verband als seine Zeitgenossen, alles daran, seinem Instrument wieder Bedeutung in der ernsthaften Musik zu verschaffen. Indem er Werke von Bach, Händel, Mozart und Chopin transskribierte und die Musik der Vihuela aus der Renaissance sowie die der spanischen Lautenspieler wieder zum Leben erweckte, wurde er selbst bekannt und verhalf der Gitarre sowohl bei Musikern als auch beim Publikum zu einem neuen Image. „Ernsthafte" Komponisten wie de Falla, Villa-Lobos, Castelnuovo-Tedesco und viele andere schrieben für ihn; doch selbst Werke, die nicht speziell für sein Spiel gedacht waren (wie das wohl bekannteste Stück, Rodrigos *Concierto de Aranjuez*), wären ohne ihn unbekannt geblieben. Segovia allein kommt das Verdienst zu, die klassische Gitarre für das 20. Jahrhundert wiederentdeckt zu haben, und es ist ebenfalls ihm zuzuschreiben, daß das Repertoire für dieses Instrument erheblich erweitert wurde.

Natürlich war Segovia eine Offenbarung für die Gitarristen weltweit. In England hörte Julian Bream seine Plattenaufnahmen, als er als kleiner Junge während des Krieges aus London evakuiert war, und 1947 war er von Segovias erstem Nachkriegskonzert „vollkommen gebannt". Es kostete ihn große Mühe, die Autoritäten des Royal College of Music dazu zu bringen, dieses Instrument zu akzeptieren – und tatsächlich scheint er sie nicht wirklich überzeugt zu haben: Offensichtlich betrachteten sie die Gitarre als subversives Instrument (selbst wenn Bach darauf gespielt wurde) und fesselten Bream an seine Klavier- und Celloausbildung. Doch ebenso wie Segovia konnte er sich durchsetzen: Sein Talent sollte nicht verkannt bleiben, und gleich Segovia wurden ihm eine ganze Reihe von Konzerten gewidmet, unter anderem von Britten, Berkeley, Walton, Henze und Tippett.

Etwa fünfzehn Jahre lang war Bream der unangefochtene Star der britischen Gitarrenmusik-Szene. Doch Ende der 50er Jahre tauchte plötzlich ein junger Australier in London auf, der bereits Segovias Aufmerksamkeit erweckt und sogar Unterricht bei ihm genommen hatte. Es war John Williams, durch dessen Erscheinen zunächst eine etwas heikle Situation entstand. Das britische Publikum hatte schon Schwierigkeiten, einen erfolgreichen Gitarristen nicht-spanischer Herkunft zu akzeptieren. Nun aber zwei? Glücklicherweise war Platz genug für beide, und in der Tat kam es zu den größten musikalischen Höhepunkten, wenn sie gemeinsam spielten. Und sagte nicht schon Chopin: „Das einzige, was schöner ist als eine Gitarre, sind zwei Gitarren."

Quand Segovia était jeune, la guitare n'était pas considérée comme un instrument sérieux, du moins hors d'Espagne. Mais Segovia, qui était autodidacte et donc peut-être moins tributaire de la tradition que les autres guitaristes espagnols de son époque, était bien décidé à ramener la guitare dans le monde de la musique sérieuse. Transcrivant, jouant et enregistrant des œuvres de Bach, Haendel, Mozart et Chopin, et faisant revivre la musique de la vihuela de la Renaissance et des vieux joueurs de luth espagnols, il se forgea une réputation et donna une nouvelle image de la guitare, qui transforma complètement la perception qu'avaient les musiciens et le public de cet instrument. Des compositeurs « sérieux » comme Falla, Villa-Lobos, Castelnuovo-Tedesco et beaucoup d'autres lui écrivirent de nouveaux morceaux, et des pièces pour guitare qui n'avaient pas été écrites spécialement pour lui (comme la plus fameuse de toutes, le *Concierto de Aranjuez* de Rodrigo) n'auraient pas été concevables sans son exemple. Plus qu'à tout autre, on doit à Segovia le renouveau de la guitare classique au XXᵉ siècle, ainsi que le vaste enrichissement du répertoire musical qui alla de pair.

Segovia devint bien entendu une source d'inspiration constante pour les jeunes guitaristes du monde entier. En Angleterre, Julian Bream entendit ses enregistrements quand il était enfant et fut « absolument ensorcelé » par le premier récital londonien d'après-guerre de Segovia, en 1947. Il eut du mal à persuader ses maîtres du Royal College of Music d'accepter son instrument – en fait, il ne les persuada pas : ils pensaient évidemment que la guitare (même pour jouer Bach) avait une influence subversive et Bream fut fermement maintenu dans ses études de piano et de violoncelle. Mais, comme Segovia, il persévéra. Bien lui en prit : son talent fut reconnu et comme Segovia, il fut le dédicataire d'une série d'œuvres composées par Britten, Berkeley, Walton, Henze, Tippett et d'autres.

Pendant environ dix ans, Bream fut la vedette incontestée de la guitare britannique. Mais vers la fin des années 50, un jeune Australien, qui avait attiré l'attention de Segovia – il lui avait d'ailleurs donné quelques leçons – apparut sur la scène londonienne. C'était John Williams et, au début, la situation fut un peu délicate. Il avait déjà été très difficile de convaincre le public britannique que quiconque n'étant pas espagnol puisse réussir à la guitare. Alors, qu'il existe un vrai guitariste de langue anglaise, passe encore, mais deux ? Fort heureusement, il s'avéra qu'il y avait de la place pour deux et, en fait, c'est ensemble qu'ils obtinrent quelques-uns de leurs plus grands triomphes. N'est-ce pas Chopin qui est censé avoir dit : « La seule chose qui est plus belle qu'une guitare, c'est deux guitares ? »

Doyen of guitarists – Andrés Segovia, with the familiar footstool, 7 May 1963.

Der Doyen der Gitarristen – Andrés Segovia mit seinem üblichen Fußschemel, 7. Mai 1963.

Le doyen des guitaristes, Andrés Segovia, avec son fameux repose-pied, le 7 mai 1963.

Julian Bream, 4 April 1968. First on the guitar scene in England.

Julian Bream, 4. April 1968. Vorreiter in der Gitarrenszene Englands.

Julian Bream, le 4 avril 1968. Précurseur dans le monde de la guitarre en Anleterre.

John Williams, 28 September 1965. Room for two at the top.

John Williams, 28. September 1965. Platz für zwei an der Spitze.

John Williams, le 28 septembre 1965. De la place pour deux au sommet.

Segovia with John Williams, evidently enjoying a cup of coffee and an abundance of young female company after a recital at the Camden School for Girls in London, 19 May 1966.

Segovia und John Williams genießen zusammen offensichtlich sowohl ihren Kaffee als auch die Menge junger weiblicher Fans nach einem Konzert in der Mädchenschule Camden in London, 19. Mai 1966.

Segovia avec John Williams, savourant apparemment une tasse de café et la nombreuse compagnie féminine, après un récital à Camden School for Girls à Londres, le 19 mai 1966.

A Serkin recital was always a serious affair. This was a man whose reputation for intellectual profundity went before him and was justified anew at every performance. It was founded on a long history of involvement with deeply serious music-making. His student days in Vienna, where he had been a composition pupil of Schoenberg and made his début with the Vienna Symphony Orchestra at the age of 12, were hardly over when a chance concert engagement led to his meeting with the great German violinist Adolf Busch, founder of the Busch Quartet and the Busch Chamber Orchestra, with whom he formed a partnership that was to last until Busch's death over 30 years later.

Whether it was Busch who was responsible for the direction that Serkin's taste and ideals now took, or whether the older man was naturally drawn towards an artist who already placed intelligence, clarity and absolute integrity above easy sentiment and superficial display, the relationship led Serkin's repertory in the direction of Bach and the chamber works of Beethoven, Schubert and Brahms, and set a standard of excellence in this field that has never been surpassed. In 1935 Serkin married Busch's daughter, and four years later the whole family escaped from Germany to the United States where, after the war, the two men set up the Marlboro Music Festival in Vermont to promote the ideals of chamber music as they understood them.

In his solo recitals and concert appearances Serkin never strayed far from the musical world he inhabited with Busch. His Beethoven was grand, his Schubert finely controlled, his Mozart pellucid, his Brahms magisterial. He was not always an easy pianist to listen to: there was no light relief in his repertory, and in his performances the deliberate rejection of anything suggesting charm or sentimentality (perish the thought) could endanger the element of human warmth. His absolute commitment to the composer's intention drove him to struggle afresh with the problems and complexities of the great masterpieces each time he tackled them, and he made no concessions to his audience in the process. Indeed, so oblivious was he of the audience that the most extraordinary extramusical noises would escape from the platform – singing, groaning, the grinding of heels under the piano, the clattering of feet on the pedals.

It all assorted oddly with the shy walk to the instrument which opened the recital and the gentle, reserved bow which ended it. No pianist was ever less concerned about publicity or popularity, and perhaps for that reason few pianists have been so widely held in affection, admiration and respect.

Ein Konzert von Rudolf Serkin war eine ernste Angelegenheit. Sein Ruf für intellektuelle Durchdringung der Musik eilte ihm stets voraus, und er bestätigte ihn bei jedem Auftritt aufs neue. Dieser Ruf basierte auf der langen Geschichte seines Engagements für eine außerordentlich ernsthafte Interpretation von Musik. Sein Studium in Wien, währenddessen er an Schönbergs Kompositionskursen teilnahm und mit den Wiener Symphonikern debütierte, war kaum beendet, als er durch eine zufällige Konzertverpflichtung mit dem großen Geiger Adolf Busch zusammentraf, dem Begründer des Busch Quartetts und des Busch Kammerorchesters. Mit Busch sollte ihn fortan eine Freundschaft verbinden, die bis zum Tode Buschs 30 Jahre später währte.

Ob es nun die Persönlichkeit Buschs war oder aber sein Intellekt, seine Klarheit und vollkommene Integrität, die sich über jede Sentimentalität und oberflächliche Zurschaustellung erhob und den Ausschlag für Serkins musikalische Orientierung gab. In jedem Fall war es diese Verbindung zu dem älteren Künstler, die eine Konzentration seines Repertoires auf Bach und das kammermusikalische Werk Beethovens, Schuberts und Brahms' mit sich brachte. Hierdurch setzte er in diesem Gebiet einen Maßstab, der bis heute unübertroffen geblieben ist. 1935 heiratete Serkin Buschs Tochter, und vier Jahre später floh die gesamte Familie in die Vereinigten Staaten, wo die beiden Musiker das Marlboro Music Festival in Vermont ins Leben riefen, mit dem sie ihre Vorstellung von Kammermusik einer breiteren Öffentlichkeit zugänglich machen wollten.

In seinen Konzerten – ob als Solist oder mit einem Orchester – entfernte sich Serkin nie weit von dem Kanon, der für ihn und Busch galt. Seine Beethoven-Interpretation war erhaben, Schubert höchst differenziert, Mozart kristallklar und Brahms meisterhaft. Es war nicht immer einfach, seinem Spiel zuzuhören: Er lockerte sein Repertoire nie durch leichtere, erholsame Stücke auf, und der fehlende Charme oder Gefühlsausdruck seines Vortrags konnte leicht die menschliche Wärme verdecken, die der Künstler persönlich ausstrahlte. Zugunsten der großen Gewissenhaftigkeit, mit der er stets die Intention des Komponisten herauszuarbeiten suchte, war er bereit, die Schwierigkeiten und die Komplexität eines Meisterwerks jedesmal aufs neue zu erkunden, ohne Zugeständnisse an das Publikum zu machen. In der Tat konnte er die Anwesenheit von Zuhörern gänzlich aus seinem Bewußtsein streichen, so daß sehr befremdliche Nebengeräusche wie Summen, Stöhnen, das Knirschen der Schuhsohlen oder besonders vehementer Pedaleinsatz nicht zu überhören waren.

All das schien wenig zusammenzupassen mit dem Bild eines Mannes, der sich seinem Instrument außerordentlich schüchtern näherte und der den Applaus mit einer höflichen und reservierten Verbeugung quittierte. Es gab keinen Pianisten, der sich derart wenig für „Publicity" oder seine Beliebtheit interessierte, und dies ist vielleicht auch der Grund, weshalb ihm wie kaum einem anderen Sympathie, Bewunderung und Respekt entgegengebracht wurden.

Un récital de Serkin était toujours empreint de gravité. Il était précédé par sa réputation – que chaque nouvelle représentation confirmait – de profonde intellectualité, réputation fondée sur un engagement de longue date dans la vie musicale. Il avait été élève de Schoenberg en composition et avait fait ses débuts avec l'Orchestre symphonique de Vienne à 12 ans. À peine avait-il terminé ses études qu'il fut, par hasard, engagé pour un concert où il rencontra le grand violoniste allemand Adolf Busch – fondateur du Quattuor Busch et de l'Orchestre de chambre Busch – dont il fut le partenaire jusqu'à la mort de Busch, plus de trente ans plus tard.

Que ce soit Busch qui ait été responsable de la direction que prirent alors les goûts et les idéaux de Serkin, ou que le vieil homme ait été attiré vers un artiste qui plaçait déjà l'intelligence, la clarté et l'intégrité au-dessus de la sentimentalité facile et de l'étalage superficiel, leur relation conduisit le répertoire de Serkin vers Bach et les œuvres de musique de chambre de Beethoven, Schubert et Brahms, établissant un pôle d'excellence dans ce domaine qui n'a jamais été dépassé. En 1935, Serkin épousa la fille de Busch et, quatre ans plus tard, toute la famille quitta l'Allemagne pour les États-Unis où, après la guerre, les deux hommes lancèrent le Marlboro Music Festival à Vermont, pour promouvoir les idéaux de la musique de chambre, comme ils les entendaient.

Dans ses récitals en solo et ses concerts, Serkin ne s'éloignait jamais du monde musical qu'il habitait avec Busch. Son interprétation de Beethoven était magnifique, celle de Schubert admirablement contrôlée, celle de Mozart limpide, celle de Brahms magistrale. Ce n'était pas un pianiste toujours facile à écouter : son répertoire ne cédait pas à la facilité et il éliminait délibérément de ses interprétations tout ce qui pouvait suggérer le charme ou la sentimentalité, au risque d'en chasser aussi toute chaleur humaine. Son respect total des intentions du compositeur l'amenait à se débattre encore et encore avec les problèmes et les complexités des grands chefs-d'œuvre chaque fois qu'il les abordait et, là encore, il ne faisait aucune concession à son public. De fait, il oubliait tellement ledit public qu'il s'échappaient parfois de la scène des sons extramusicaux des plus curieux : chansons, grognements, frottements des talons sous le piano, cliquetis des pieds sur les pédales.

Ces manifestations s'accordaient étrangement avec les pas timides vers l'instrument, qui ouvraient le récital, et le salut réservé qui le concluait. Aucun pianiste ne s'est senti moins concerné par la publicité ou par la popularité et, pour cette raison peut-être, peu de pianistes ont autant été l'objet d'affection, d'admiration et de respect.

Rudolf Serkin, 24 October 1963. Bracing himself for the struggle.
Rudolf Serkin, 24. Oktober 1963. Konzentration vor dem Einsatz.
Rudolf Serkin, le 24 octobre 1963. Se concentrant avant l'ataque.

Though from the age of one his childhood, student days and the formative years of his youth were all spent in San Francisco, Isaac Stern was born in Russia of Russian parents, and his roots are in his Russian inheritance. There is no artist whose commitment to the communication of his art is more personal, more human or more all-embracing – 'a process of intellectual and personal involvement with music as an idea and a way of life, not as a profession or career, but a rapport with people who think and feel and care about something'. And, 'If you don't speak with the violin, and just play it, you might as well get a machine to do it better.'

He is above all things a communicator – almost, some have felt, to excess. A BBC interviewer, accustomed to fishing around for suitable subjects to tempt distinguished artists into speech, asked Stern an opening question – and didn't get a chance to open his mouth again for 25 minutes. (Characteristically, Stern rang up the following day to apologize.) On the platform, what matters is the audience not the performer, the music not the technique. Of course the technique is superb, but it is a vehicle for the warmth and exuberance of the man, never – but never – an end in itself. And with it go an instinctive sense of style and a natural feeling for harmonic structure which stand him in good stead as he moves from Bach, Mozart and Beethoven to Bartók, Webern, Maxwell Davies or the first performance of a concerto by Bernstein or William Schuman. He has not wasted much time (or disc space) on the usual trivia of the violin repertory – but he can turn out an impeccable encore when the occasion demands.

He has always been proud of his American citizenship and vigorously involved in the musical life of his adopted country. His generosity and practical help to young artists is legendary, and in 1960, hearing that the Carnegie Hall in New York was in danger of demolition by an aggressive property developer, Stern mobilized support including a galaxy of star performers from Casals to Bernstein, accused the Mayor of New York of 'an act of irresponsibility damaging to the United States and our prestige in the entire civilized world', got two bills pushed through the State Legislature to help with funds and in a matter of months saved the hall for posterity.

His travels abroad have been continuous. He has played with practically all the great orchestras of the world, conducted some of them, and been accepted everywhere as the elder statesman of violinists. But perhaps the most typical and most moving testimony of his work is the film which was made of the master classes he gave to groups of young violinists in China. Personal communication, human warmth; isn't this where we came in?

Obwohl Isaac Stern bereits mit einem Jahr nach San Francisco kam, dort seine Kindheit, die prägenden Jahre der Jugend und des Studiums verbrachte, ist er, als Kind russischer Eltern in Rußland geboren, ganz mit der russischen Tradition verwurzelt. Kein Künstler hat sich in solch persönlicher, menschlicher und allumfassender Weise der Botschaft seiner Kunst verschrieben: ein „Prozeß intellektuellen und persönlichen Engagements für die Musik als Idee und Lebensform, nicht als Beruf und Karriere, sondern als eine Beziehung zu nachdenkenden, empfindsamen und engagierten Menschen". Und: „Wenn man mit der Geige nicht spricht, kann man ebensogut eine Maschine spielen lassen."

Vor allen Dingen will er mitteilen und dies, so scheint es, bisweilen bis zum Exzess. Ein Moderator der BBC, daran gewöhnt, selbst nach Themen zu suchen, mit denen er erlesene Künstler ins Gespräch verwickeln kann, stellte Stern eine Frage und kam in den folgenden 25 Minuten nicht mehr zu Wort. (Charakteristischerweise entschuldigte sich Stern am nächsten Tag dafür.) Was für Stern zählt, sobald er die Bühne betritt, ist das Publikum und nicht der Interpret. Nicht die Technik, sondern die Musik selbst steht im Vordergrund. Selbstverständlich ist auch seine Technik überragend, doch dient sie als Mittel, die Wärme und Ausstrahlung dieses Menschen in das Auditorium zu transportieren. Nie, aber auch wirklich niemals ist sie Selbstzweck. Sein Instinkt für Stil und ein natürliches Gespür für harmonische Gefüge leisten ihm gute Dienste, wenn er zwischen Bach, Mozart oder Beethoven und Bartók, Webern, Maxwell Davies oder der Uraufführung eines Konzertes von Bernstein oder William Schuman wechselt. Er hat nie viel Zeit – auch keine Spielzeit von Tonträgern – auf gängiges Repertoire verwendet, doch kann er im geeigneten Moment auch eine perfekte Zugabe spielen.

Er war stets stolz auf seine amerikanische Staatsangehörigkeit und immer lebhaft ins musikalische Geschehen seiner angenommenen Heimat involviert. Seine Großzügigkeit und sein Einsatz für junge Künstler sind sprichwörtlich, und als 1960 das Bestehen der Carnegie Hall durch einen aggressiven Spekulanten bedroht war, organisierte Stern eine Kampagne für ihren Erhalt. Er bat unendlich viele Künstler von Casals bis zu Bernstein um ihre Unterstützung, empörte sich öffentlich über die „Unverantwortlichkeit" des New Yorker Bürgermeisters, mit welcher der „das Ansehen der Vereinigten Staaten in der ganzen zivilisierten Welt ruiniere", setzte zwei Eingaben beim Obersten Gerichtshof zur finanziellen Unterstützung durch und konnte so innerhalb weniger Monate den berühmten Konzertsaal für die Nachwelt erhalten.

Stern hat schon immer viele Auslandsreisen unternommen. Er hat mit nahezu allen bekannten Orchestern der Welt gespielt, einige davon auch dirigiert und wurde überall als großer Meister aufgenommen. Doch das vielleicht typischste und bewegendste Zeugnis seiner Arbeit ist ein Film, der bei seinen Meisterkursen für junge Geiger in China gemacht wurde: persönliche Mitteilung, menschliche Wärme – ist nicht das der Ursprung aller Dinge?

Bien qu'à partir de 1 an il ait passé son enfance, ses années d'études et de formation à San Francisco, Isaac Stern est né russe de parents russes, et ses racines résident dans cet héritage. Il n'y a pas d'artiste qui s'engage de façon plus personnelle, plus humaine, plus complète pour communiquer son art. C'est « un processus d'engagement intellectuel et personnel dans la musique, une idée et une manière de vivre, pas une profession ou une carrière, mais un rapport avec les gens qui pensent, et ressentent, et s'intéressent à quelque chose. » Et, « si vous ne parlez pas avec le violon, mais en jouez seulement, vous pouvez aussi bien prendre une machine qui le fera mieux que vous. »

Il est, par-dessus tout, quelqu'un qui communique – presque à l'excès, d'après certains. Un animateur de la BBC, maître dans l'art de faire parler les artistes, avait tout juste eu le temps de poser une question introductive à Stern puis n'avait pu placer un mot pendant 25 minutes. (Stern téléphona le lendemain pour s'excuser). Sur scène, ce qui compte c'est le public et non pas l'interprète, la musique et non pas la technique. Celle de Stern est, bien entendu, excellente, mais elle n'est qu'un moyen de faire passer la chaleur et la jovialité de l'homme, elle n'est jamais – absolument jamais – une fin en soi. Avec elle, un sens instinctif du style et une compréhension naturelle de la structure harmonique lui permettent de passer de Bach, Mozart et Beethoven à Bartók, Webern, Maxwell Davies ou à la première interprétation publique d'un concerto de Bernstein ou de William Schuman. Il n'a pas perdu beaucoup de temps (ou de plages de disques) avec les habituelles bagatelles du répertoire pour violon, mais il peut produire un rappel impeccable quand l'occasion l'exige.

Il a toujours été fier d'être citoyen américain et il s'est beaucoup impliqué dans la vie musicale de son pays d'adoption. Sa générosité et l'aide concrète qu'il apporte aux jeunes artistes sont légendaires. En 1960, ayant appris que Carnegie Hall, à New York, risquait d'être démoli par un promoteur entreprenant, Stern lança une action de soutien, mobilisant une myriade de musiciens prestigieux, de Casals à Bernstein, accusa le maire de New York d'avoir commis « un acte irresponsable dommageable pour les États-Unis et pour notre prestige dans tout le monde civilisé », réussit à faire voter deux lois au parlement de l'État pour recueillir des fonds et, en quelques mois, sauva la salle pour la postérité.

Voyageant constamment à l'étranger, il a joué avec presque tous les grands orchestres du monde, en a dirigé quelques-uns, et a été reçu partout comme le vétéran des violonistes. Cependant, le témoignage le plus caractéristique et le plus émouvant de son travail est le film des cours qu'il donna en Chine à de jeunes violonistes. Échanges personnels, chaleur humaine ; tout Isaac Stern est là.

Isaac Stern in rehearsal with the London Symphony Orchestra, 13 June 1966.

Isaac Stern bei einer Probe mit dem London Symphony Orchestra 13. Juni 1966.

Isaac Stern en répétition avec le London Symphony Orchestra, le 13 juin 1966.

As well as a soloist, Stern has always been a dedicated chamber-music player. Here he is (2 November 1961) in a London sitting room, rehearsing a Beethoven trio with the pianist Eugene Istomin and the cellist Leonard Rose – a group formed in the previous year which achieved immediate success.

Stern war nicht nur Solist, sondern immer auch ein begnadeter Kammermusiker. Hier sieht man ihn (am 2. November 1961) in einem Londoner Wohnzimmer zusammen mit dem Pianisten Eugene Istomin und dem Cellisten Leonard Rose bei der Probe eines Beethoven-Trios. Diese drei Musiker hatten sich im Jahr zuvor zusammengefunden und waren sofort sehr erfolgreich.

Stern n'était pas seulement un soliste, mais aussi l'interprète très doué de musique de chambre. On le voit ici dans un salon à Londres, le 2 novembre 1961, répétant un trio de Beethoven avec le pianiste Eugene Istomin et le violoncelliste Leonard Rose – le groupe s'était formé l'année précédente et avait connu un succès immédiat.

A poet among cellists, Tortelier looked the part with his fine-drawn, sensitive features and mass of unruly hair. But there was muscular strength in those large hands, and depth of passion behind the cultivated manner. It is perhaps not surprising to find that he was also a composer, and that he saw composition as a source for the re-creation which lies at the heart of every truly spontaneous performance. There was always something of the composer's understanding in his performances, something which controlled and united the sensuous tenderness of expression on the one hand and the dedicated but extrovert enthusiasm on the other.

His international reputation did not really take off until after the war, and more particularly after his London début in Strauss's *Don Quixote* with Beecham in 1947. He played and recorded most of the great cello repertory from Bach to Dvořák, Tchaikovsky and Brahms. But he was a Parisian by birth and temperament and spent much of his career teaching in his native city, as well as indulging an addiction to family chamber music: his wife was a former cello pupil, his daughter a pianist, and his son Yan Pascal a violinist (though more recently known as a conductor), and the experience of these intimate family sessions did much to mould the supple phrasing and sensitive colours of the public performances.

Tortelier's interest in teaching soon spread to the field of the master class, and in the 1960s he found a new outlet for his talent in a BBC television series, where his romantic appearance and infectious enthusiasm inevitably made him a star. But the Gallic temperament sometimes found itself sadly at odds with British habits of mind: groping desperately for a simile to describe the reserve he found so inexplicable, 'twin beds, so boring', he said to one astonished young lady. It was the cry of an artist for whom the poetry of expression and the communication of passion had been the very centre of his musical life.

Mit seinen feinlinigen, sensiblen Gesichtszügen und dem ungebändigten Haarschopf sieht Paul Tortelier in der Tat wie der Poet unter den Cellisten aus. Aber seine großen Hände verfügten über eine ungeheure Kraft, und hinter der kultivierten Erscheinung verbarg sich eine tiefe Leidenschaft. So erstaunt es wohl kaum, daß er auch komponiert hat und das Komponieren als Quelle für die Wieder-Erschaffung ansah, die jeder wirklich originären Aufführung innewohnte. Seine Konzerte vermittelten immer etwas von dem Musikverständnis, das er als Komponist gewonnen hatte, etwas, das Kontrollfunktion und verbindendes Element zugleich war für die sinnliche Zärtlichkeit seines Ausdrucks und für seinen hingebungsvollen, aber nach außen gerichteten Enthusiasmus.

Sein internationaler Ruf begann sich erst nach dem Krieg zu festigen, besonders nach seinem Londoner Debüt 1947 in Strauss' *Don Quixote* mit Beecham als Dirigenten. Die meisten großen Werke der Celloliteratur von Bach bis Tschaikowsky, Dvořák und Brahms führte er auf und spielte Aufnahmen davon ein. Aber da ihm als gebürtiger Pariser auch der französische Charakter innewohnte, brachte er einen Großteil seiner Zeit in seiner Heimatstadt zu, um zu unterrichten und seiner Leidenschaft für die Hausmusik nachzugeben: Seine Frau ist ebenfalls Cellistin, seine Tochter Pianistin und sein Sohn Yan Pascal Geiger (obwohl er inzwischen größere Bekanntheit als Dirigent erlangt hat), und die musikalischen Erfahrungen aus dieser familiären Intimität trugen viel dazu bei, die einfühlsamen Phrasierungen und die gefühlvollen Klangfarben in Torteliers Konzerten zu vervollkommnen.

Torteliers Freude am Unterrichten erstreckte sich bald auch auf Meisterkurse, und 1960 fand er bei der BBC ein neues Betätigungsfeld in Fernsehkursen, wo seine romantische Erscheinung und seine ansteckende Begeisterungsfähigkeit ihn unausweichlich zu einem Star werden ließen. Doch manchmal konnte dieser wundervoll französische Charakter auch tieftraurig werden, vor allem wenn er auf britische Gewohnheiten stieß: Verzweifelt nach einem sinnfälligen Bild suchend, um die britische Reserviertheit zu beschreiben, sagte er zu einer sehr verwunderten jungen Dame: „Zwei einzelne Betten, wie langweilig". Dies war der Aufschrei eines Künstlers, in dessen Leben die Poetik des Ausdrucks und das Mitteilen von Leidenschaften im absoluten Mittelpunkt standen.

Poète parmi les violoncellistes, Tortelier en avait l'air, avec ses traits fins et délicats et sa masse de cheveux indisciplinés. Mais il y avait de la force dans ses grandes mains et de la passion derrière ses manières distinguées. Il était aussi compositeur, et ça n'était pas sans conséquence sur sa pratique du violoncelle, car il considérait la composition comme la source de la re-création qui est au cœur de chaque interprétation vraiment spontanée. Il y avait toujours un peu du compositeur dans ses concerts, quelque chose qui contrôlait et unifiait la tendresse sensuelle de l'expression, d'une part, et le caractère réfléchi de son bel enthousiasme, d'autre part.

Sa réputation internationale ne se fit vraiment qu'après la guerre et plus particulièrement après ses débuts à Londres avec Beecham, en 1947, dans le *Don Quichotte* de Strauss. Il joua et enregistra la majeure partie du grand répertoire pour violoncelle, de Bach à Dvořák, Tchaïkovski et Brahms. Mais il était parisien de naissance et de tempérament, et passa le plus clair de sa carrière à enseigner dans sa ville natale ainsi qu'à s'adonner à son goût pour la musique de chambre en famille : sa femme avait appris le violoncelle, sa fille était pianiste et son fils Yan Pascal violoniste (bien qu'il soit maintenant plus connu comme chef d'orchestre). L'expérience de ces concerts en famille fit beaucoup pour façonner le phrasé souple et les couleurs délicates de ses interprétations.

L'intérêt de Tortelier pour l'enseignement se développa dans le cadre des master class et, dans les années 60, il put en outre exercer son talent dans une série télévisée de la BBC, où son air romantique et son enthousiasme contagieux en firent inévitablement une vedette. Mais son tempérament français se trouvait parfois en opposition avec l'état d'esprit britannique : un jour, cherchant désespérément une comparaison pour décrire la réserve typiquement anglaise qu'il trouvait si inexplicable, il dit à une jeune femme médusée : « Des lits jumeaux, c'est si ennuyeux ». C'était le cri d'un artiste pour qui la poésie de l'expression et la communication de la passion avaient été le centre même de sa vie musicale.

Paul Tortelier – serious music making.
Paul Tortelier in tiefer Konzentration.
Paul Tortelier jouant avec concentration.

Can intensity go further? Tortelier, poet of the cello, draws from his instrument the passion so clearly visible in his face. This picture was taken by Auerbach at his first meeting with Tortelier in 1948; many others followed, but 'never again', said Auerbach, 'was I able to capture quite such an ecstatic mood'.

Kann Innigkeit noch weiter gehen? Tortelier, der Poet unter den Cellisten, vermag seinem Instrument jene Leidenschaft zu entlocken, die seine Gesichtszüge so sehr zeigen. Dieses Bild machte Auerbach 1948, als er erstmals mit Tortelier zusammentraf; viele weitere entstanden, aber, so erinnerte Auerbach, „es ist mir nie wieder gelungen, eine derart ekstatische Bewegtheit einzufangen".

L'intensité peut-elle être plus grande ? Tortelier, poète du violoncelle, tire de son instrument la passion si clairement visible sur son visage. La photographie a été prise par Auerbach, lors de sa première rencontre avec Tortelier en 1948 ; beaucoup d'autres ont suivi, mais « jamais plus, dit Auerbach, je ne pus saisir une atmosphère si proche de l'extase ».

1

2

(1, 2, 3) Tortelier, 25 May 1961. (4) Conducting the English
Chamber Orchestra from the cello in a Haydn concerto, Royal
Festival Hall, London, 23 January 1964. (5) The Tortelier family
in rehearsal, left to right: Yan Pascal, Maria de la Pau (at the
piano), Paul, and his wife and former cello pupil Maude Martin,
10 October 1965.

(1, 2, 3) Tortelier, 25. Mai 1961. (4) Vom Cello aus dirigiert er das
English Chamber Orchestra bei einem Haydn-Konzert, Royal
Festival Hall, London, 23. Januar 1964. (5) Die Familie Tortelier
bei einer Probe, von links nach rechts: Yan Pascal, Maria de la Pau
(am Klavier), Paul und am Cello seine Frau Maude Martin, die
früher seine Schülerin gewesen war, 10. Oktober 1965.

(1, 2, 3) Tortelier, le 25 mai 1961. (4) Dirigeant l'English Chamber
Orchestra depuis le violoncelle dans un concerto de Haydn, au
Royal Festival Hall à Londres, le 23 janvier 1964. (5) La famille
Tortelier en répétition, de gauche à droite : Yan-Pascal, Maria de la
Pau au piano, Paul et son épouse et ancienne élève, Maude Martin,
le 10 octobre 1965.

4

3

5

Musicians Relaxing

Die Entspannung der Musiker

Des musiciens se détendent

Making music, whether composing it or performing it, is an exhausting business, and the need for relaxation is very real in any musician's life. Among composers Mozart's passion for billiards is well known, Richard Strauss spent most of the time when he wasn't writing music playing skat, Elgar went to the races, Schoenberg and Gershwin played tennis together, Britten and Shostakovich played Happy Families, Rossini just ate. Paganini was a great chess player (he had a special travelling chess set for use on his journeys between performances), and these photographs indicate that the interest has continued among Russian violinists at least – even if the smile on Rostropovich's face suggests that in one case it is a cellist who is winning. The same combination of relaxation with intellectual stimulus makes the card table another obvious attraction, at all levels of seriousness: the game here shown in progress looks a sober enough affair, but many musicians' card sessions are less solemn – Michael Tippett is reputed to be a devil at Racing Demon (something to do with counterpoint, perhaps?), and John Cage was addicted to poker, cribbage and Scrabble. At the other end of the scale, there are those who are more concerned with their bodily and spiritual well-being, like cooking or yoga, or – well, just sitting and relaxing over the proofs of photographs like these.

Die Arbeit eines Musikers – sei es als Komponist oder als Interpret – ist aufreibend, so daß das Bedürfnis nach Entspannung sehr präsent ist. Unter den Komponisten ist Mozarts Vorliebe für Entspannung beim Billard bekannt, Richard Strauss verbrachte die meiste Freizeit beim Skat, Elgar zog es zum Pferderennen, Schönberg und Gershwin spielten miteinander Tennis, und Britten und Schostakowitsch spielten Quartett während Rossini vor allem tafelte. Paganini war ein begabter Schachspieler (er führte sogar ein Reiseschach bei sich, um zwischen den Auftritten spielen zu können), und wie diese Fotos belegen, hat sich das Interesse am Schach wohl unter russischen Geigern vererbt – auch wenn Rostropowitschs Lächeln erkennen läßt, daß in diesem Fall einmal ein Cellist die Partie gewinnt. Offenbar ist es dieselbe Mischung aus Entspannung und geistiger Herausforderung, die das Kartenspiel so attraktiv macht, und zwar unanbhängig vom Ernst des Spiels. Die hier abgebildete Partie war scheinbar relativ entspannt – aber Michael Tippet ist für seine ungehemmte Spielleidenschaft bekannt und John Cage war geradezu versessen auf Poker, Kribbage und Scrabble. Andererseits gibt es natürlich die eher auf Körper und Seele gerichteten Entspannungen, wie etwa Kochen und Yoga – oder aber auch die einfache Kontemplation über Fotos wie diesen.

Faire de la musique, que ce soit en la composant ou en la jouant, est un travail exténuant, et les moments de détente sont indispensables dans la vie de tout musicien. Parmi les compositeurs, on connaît la passion de Mozart pour le billard, Richard Strauss passait beaucoup de temps à jouer au skat, Elgar allait aux courses, Schoenberg et Gershwin jouaient ensemble au tennis, Britten et Chostakovitch jouaient aux jeu des Sept Familles ; quant à Rossini, il mangeait. Paganini était un grand joueur d'échecs (il avait un jeu spécial qu'il emportait dans ses voyages, pour passer le temps entre les concerts) et ces photographies montrent que le goût pour ce jeu est toujours présent chez les violonistes russes – même si le sourire de Rostropovitch suggère que, dans ce cas, c'est un violoncelliste qui gagne. Le même mélange de détente et de stimulus intellectuel fait des cartes une autre agréable distraction : le jeu que l'on voit ici semble relativement sage, mais beaucoup de parties entre musiciens sont moins solennelles : John Cage était un fanatique du poker, du cribbage et du Scrabble. Par ailleurs, il y a ceux qu'intéresse davantage leur bien-être physique et spirituel, qui aiment faire la cuisine ou du yoga, ou juste s'asseoir et se détendre en regardant des photographies comme celles-ci.

1

2

(1) Antal Dorati sketching in St James's Park, 26 September 1963.
(2) Sir John Barbirolli at the stove in his Manchester flat. Even in
1949, in austerity Britain, this must surely be a tin of pomodori
pelati for the pasta sauce? (3) Emil Gilels watches Mstislav
Rostropovitch and Leonid Kogan playing chess in their Kensington
Hotel, 18 February 1959. (4) The Oistrakhs, father and son,
locked in battle, 17 February 1961. (5) In 1955 the British pianist
Solomon suffered a paraplegic stroke and was forced to give up
playing in public, but he could still enjoy a game of cards with his
old friend, the pianist Benno Moiseiwitsch (right), at his home in
St John's Wood, London, 23 December 1958.

(1) Antal Dorati zeichnet im St. James's Park, 26. September 1963.
(2) Sir John Barbirolli in seiner Wohnung in Manchester am
Herd. Selbst im genügsamen England des Jahres 1949 wird dies
doch sicherlich eine Dose geschälter Tomaten für die Pasta-Sauce
sein? (3) Emil Gilels beobachtet Mstislaw Rostropowitsch und
Leonid Kogan bei einer Schachpartie im Kensington Hotel,
18. Februar 1959. (4) Vater und Sohn Oistrach, ins Spiel vertieft,
17. Februar 1961. (5) 1955 erlitt der britische Pianist Solomon
einen Schlaganfall und war von da an gezwungen, alle öffentlichen
Auftritte einzustellen, aber er konnte noch ein Kartenspiel mit seinem alten Freund, dem Pianisten Benno Moiseiwitsch (rechts),
genießen; in seinem Haus in St. John's Wood, London, 23.
Dezember 1958.

(1) Antal Dorati dessinant à St James's Park, le 26 septembre 1963.
(2) Sir John Barbirolli au fourneau dans son appartement de
Manchester. Malgré l'austérité de l'après-guerre – nous sommes en
1949 –, n'est-ce pas une boîte de pomodori pelati pour la sauce des
pâtes ? (3) Emil Gilels regarde Mstislav Rostropovitch et Leonid
Kogan jouer aux échecs dans leur hôtel de Kensington le 18 février
1959. (4) Les Oïstrakh, père et fils, au cours d'une partie serrée le
17 février 1961. (5) En 1955, le pianiste britannique Solomon
devint paraplégique et dut abandonner les concerts en public, mais
il pouvait toujours apprécier une partie de cartes avec son vieil ami,
le pianiste Benno Moiseivitch (à droite), chez lui à St John's Wood,
à Londres, le 23 décembre 1958.

3

4

5

(1) John Ogdon at billiards, 9 August 1965. (2) Daniel Barenboim playing table tennis, 6 April 1966. (3) Yehudi Menuhin's yoga sessions were of the greatest importance to him, and would often take place in the intervals of rehearsals – to the surprise of colleagues who weren't used to the habit, July 1976.

(1) John Ogdon beim Billardspiel, 9. August 1965. (2) Daniel Barenboim beim Tischtennisspiel, 6. April 1966. (3) Seine Yogaübungen waren für Yehudi Menuhin von allergrößter Wichtigkeit. Er machte sie häufig auch in Probenpausen – sehr zum Erstaunen der anderen Musiker, für die der Anblick sehr ungewöhnlich war, Juli 1976.

(1) John Ogdon au billard, le 9 août 1965. (2) Daniel Barenboïm jouant au ping-pong, le 6 avril 1966. (3) Yehudi Menuhin tenait beaucoup à ses séances de yoga, qu'il pratiquait souvent pendant la pause aux répétitions – à la surprise de ses collègues qui n'étaient pas au courant de cette habitude, juillet 1976.

1

2

3

Isaac Stern, in his hotel room at Claridge's, going through the
contact sheets of photographs of himself by Erich Auerbach,
2 October 1970.

In seinem Hotelzimmer im Claridge's sieht sich Isaac Stern die
Kontaktabzüge der Fotografien an, die Erich Auerbach von
ihm gemacht hat, 2. Oktober 1970.

Isaac Stern, dans sa chambre d'hôtel au Claridge's, regardant les
planches contacts de photographies de lui-même prises par Eric
Auerbach, le 2 octobre 1970.

1

2

Performers of the Younger Generation
Musiker der jüngeren Generation
Interprètes de la jeune génération

As with conductors, there were a number of young instrumentalists who arrived on the London scene during Auerbach's life, who still had the greater part of their careers before them when he died. A few of these he caught at their earlier appearances during the 1960s or early 70s, though not all the photographs can be precisely dated.

Ebenso wie die Dirigenten kam auch eine große Anzahl junger Musiker nach London, um die blühende musikalische Szene, die Auerbachs Fotografien zeigt, mitzugestalten. Sie hatten, als der Fotograf starb, noch den größten Teil ihrer Karrieren vor sich. Einige von ihnen konnte er dennoch bei ihren ersten Auftritten in den 60er oder frühen 70er Jahren festhalten, wenngleich die Datierungen dieser Bilder teilweise fraglich sind.

Comme pour les chefs d'orchestre, nombre de jeunes instrumentistes arrivèrent sur la scène londonienne du vivant de Auerbach, et étaient encore en début de carrière quand il mourut. Il saisit quelques-unes de leurs premières apparitions, dans les années 60 ou au début des années 70 (on ne peux pas dater précisément toutes les photographies).

(1) Itzhak Perlman (b. 1945), another Israeli violinist, was deprived of the use of his legs by an attack of polio at the age of four and plays sitting down. This has not prevented a brilliant international career, and he is here seen rehearsing the Sibelius concerto at the Royal Festival Hall, London, 23 February 1975. (2) The German pianist Christoph Eschenbach (b. 1940) came to the fore in the second half of the 1960s, making his first London appearance in 1966. A scrupulously careful and sensitive performer, he is clearly not afraid of keeping the orchestra waiting while he checks a point in the score, April 1970.

(1) Der 1945 geborene Geiger Itzhak Perlman, ebenfalls aus Israel stammend, wurde durch eine Erkrankung an Kinderlähmung im Alter von vier Jahren der Funktionsfähigkeit seiner Beine beraubt und spielt seitdem sitzend, eine Tatsache, die einer glänzenden internationalen Karriere jedoch nicht im Weg stand. Auf diesem Foto sieht man ihn bei Proben zu Sibelius' Violinkonzert in der Royal Festival Hall in London, 23. Februar 1975. (2) Der deutsche Pianist Christoph Eschenbach (geboren 1940) wurde in der zweiten Hälfte der 60er Jahre bekannt, denn 1966 trat er erstmals in London auf. Als unerbittlich genauer und sensibler Solist scheut er sich nicht, das ganze Orchester warten zu lassen, um ein Detail in der Partitur zu überprüfen, April 1970.

(1) Itzhak Perlman (né en 1945), violoniste israélien, privé de l'usage de ses jambes par la poliomyélite à 4 ans, joue assis. Cela ne l'a pas empêché de faire une brillante carrière internationale. On le voit ici répétant le concerto de Sibelius au Royal Festival Hall à Londres, le 23 février 1975. (2) Le pianiste allemand Christoph Eschenbach (né en 1940) se fit remarquer dans la seconde moitié des années 60, apparaissant pour la première fois à Londres en 1966. Interprète scrupuleux et sensible, il n'hésite pas à faire attendre l'orchestre pendant qu'il vérifie un point sur la partition, en avril 1970.

(3) Vladimir Ashkenazy (b. 1937) has now, like Barenboim, become almost better known as a conductor than as a pianist. But it was not until the mid-1970s that the conducting really took off; his London début on the piano came as early as 1963, and at the time of this picture he was still the latest phenomenon from Russia at the beginning of a fabled pianistic career. (4) Most sensitive of pianists, the American Murray Perahia has surely never made an un-beautiful sound. He was born in 1947, studied with the 76-year-old Mieczyslaw Horszowski (Casals's accompanist), and made his first appearance in London in 1973, when this photograph was taken (Royal Festival Hall, 18 January). (5) The youngest practising musician in this book, the French pianist Michel Béroff was born in 1950. A protégé of Messiaen, he devoted much of his early attention to 20th-century music, though he has broadened his repertory since. He made his first appearance at the age of 18, and cannot have been very much older at the time of this photograph.

(3) Vladimir Askkenazy (geboren 1937) ist – wie Barenboim – inzwischen ein bekannterer Dirigent als Pianist. Dabei begann er erst Mitte der 70er Jahre richtig als Dirigent zu arbeiten. Auf dem Klavier debütierte er bereits 1963 in London, und als diese Fotografie entstand, sah man in ihm vor allem das jüngste russische Genie, das am Beginn einer sagenhaften Pianistenkarriere stand. (4) Der feinfühligste unter den Pianisten, der Amerikaner Murray Perahia, hat mit Sicherheit nie einen unschönen Klang hervorgebracht. Geboren 1947, erhielt er seine Ausbildung von dem 76jährigen Mieczyslaw Horszowki (dem Begleiter von Casals). Sein erstes Konzert in London gab er 1973, als diese Fotografie entstand (Royal Festival Hall, 18. Januar). (5) Der jüngste Musiker, der in diesem Buch Aufnahme fand, ist der 1950 geborene französische Pianist Michel Béroff. Der Schüler von Messiaen widmete sich zunächst der zeitgenössischen Musik, erweiterte dann aber sein Repertoire. Sein erstes Konzert gab er im Alter von 18 Jahren, und er wird auf diesem Foto wohl auch nicht viel älter sein.

(3) Vladimir Ashkenazy (né en 1937) est maintenant, comme Barenboïm, presque plus connu comme chef d'orchestre que comme pianiste. Mais ce n'est qu'au milieu des années 70 qu'il commença vraiment la direction d'orchestre. Ses débuts au piano datent de 1963 et, au moment de cette photographie, il était toujours le dernier phénomène venu de Russie débutant une fabuleuse carrière de pianiste. (4) Pianiste des plus sensibles, l'Américain Murray Perahia n'a sûrement jamais produit un seul son sans beauté. Né en 1947, il fit ses études avec Mieczyslaw Horszowski (l'accompagnateur de Casals), qui était alors âgé de 76 ans, et fit sa première apparition à Londres en 1973, date de cette photographie (Royal Festival Hall, le 18 janvier). (5) Né en 1950, le pianiste français Michel Béroff est le plus jeune musicien en exercice mentionné dans ce livre. Protégé de Messiaen, il commença sa carrière en privilégiant la musique du XXᵉ siècle ; depuis, son répertoire s'est élargi. Il donna son premier concert à 18 ans et ne doit pas être beaucoup plus âgé sur cette photographie.

3

4

5

(1) The pianist Stephen Bishop-Kovacevich (b. 1940), an American of Yugoslav parentage, studied in London with Myra Hess before making his Wigmore Hall début in 1961. Known in those days simply as Stephen Bishop, he has more recently used only the second half of his surname. (2) Maurizio Pollini (b. 1942), a Milanese pianist who made his first public appearance at the age of nine, won golden opinions in Italy and then all over Europe, making his New York début in 1968. His amazingly wide repertory stretches from Bach to Boulez and, like Kovacevich, he later took to orchestral conducting. (3) Victoria Postnikova (b. 1944), the wife of the conductor Gennady Rozhdestvensky, is a pianist of great sensitivity. She made her London début at a Promenade Concert in 1967 and has reappeared, often with her husband, on many occasions since.

(1) Der Pianist Stephen Bishop-Kovacevich (geboren 1940), ein Amerikaner jugoslawischer Abstammung, studierte in London bei Myra Hess, bevor er 1961 in der Wigmore Hall debütierte. Damals nannte er sich einfach Stephen Bishop, während er heute die zweite Hälfte seines Nachnamens bevorzugt. (2) Der Mailänder Pianist Maurizio Pollini (geboren 1942) trat bereits im Alter von neun Jahren erstmals öffentlich auf, erhielt zunächst in Italien, später in ganz Europa glänzende Kritiken und debütierte im Jahr 1968 in New York. Sein erstaunlich weitgefächertes Repertoire reicht von Bachs Klavierwerk bis Boulez. Nach einiger Zeit begann er, wie vor ihm schon Kovacevich, auch zu dirigieren. (3) Das Klavierspiel der mit dem Dirigenten Gennadi Roschdestwenski verheirateten Victoria Postnikova (geboren 1944) zeichnet sich vor allem durch großes Feingefühl aus. Ihr Londoner Debüt gab sie bei einem Promenadenkonzert im Jahr 1967 und trat seitdem bei vielerlei Gelegenheiten auf, oft zusammen mit ihrem Ehemann.

(1) Le pianiste Stephen Bishop Kovacevitch (né en 1940), Américain d'origine yougoslave, étudia à Londres avec Myra Hess avant de faire ses débuts au Wigmore Hall en 1961. Connu à cette époque sous le nom de Stephen Bishop, il n'utilise maintenant que la seconde partie de son nom. (2) Maurizio Pollini (né en 1942), pianiste originaire de Milan, a donné son premier concert à 9 ans, reçut les meilleures critiques en Italie puis partout en Europe, et fit ses débuts à New York en 1968. Son répertoire, étonnamment vaste, va de Bach à Boulez. Comme Kovacevitch, il est ensuite passé à la direction d'orchestre. (3) Victoria Postnikova (née en 1944), épouse du chef d'orchestre Gennadi Rojdestvenski, est une pianiste d'une grande sensibilité. Elle fit ses débuts à Londres lors d'un Promenade Concert en 1967 et, depuis, est revenue fréquemment, souvent avec son mari.

4

5

6

(4) Daniel Barenboim's career has been so meteoric that it is difficult to remember he was born as recently as 1942. He was about 27 when this picture was taken: already widely acclaimed as one of the world's most talented pianists, he had also begun conducting – though his greatest successes in that capacity still lay before him. (5) Radu Lupu (b. 1945), a Romanian, studied in Moscow with Heinrich Neuhaus, the teacher of Richter and Gilels. He won the Leeds International Piano Competition in 1969 and made his London début in the same year, when this photograph was taken. (6) Pinchas Zukerman (b. 1948) is an Israeli of Polish descent who studied in New York under the legal guardianship of Isaac Stern. His first appearance in Britain, at Brighton in 1969, was quickly followed by his London début – with the exception of Nigel Kennedy (see pages 260-261) he is probably the youngest violinist to have been caught on camera by Auerbach.

(4) Daniel Barenboims unglaublich schnelle und steile Karriere läßt vergessen, daß er erst 1942 geboren wurde. Als diese Aufnahme entstand, war er ungefähr 27 Jahre alt und schon überall als einer der besten Pianisten der Welt bejubelt. Außerdem hatte er begonnen zu dirigieren. (5) Der Rumäne Radu Lupu (geboren 1948) studierte in Moskau bei Heinrich Neuhaus, der auch Richter und Gilels Unterricht gab. Er gewann 1969 den Internationalen Klavierwettbewerb in Leeds und debütierte im gleichen Jahr in London, wobei diese Fotografie entstand. (6) Pinchas Zukerman (geboren 1948) ist ein Israeli polnischer Herkunft, der in New York bei seinem Vormund Isaac Stern studierte. Seinem ersten Auftritt in England – in Brighton 1969 – folgte schnell sein Londoner Debüt. Abgesehen von Nigel Kennedy (vgl. S. 260-261) ist Zukerman höchstwahrscheinlich der jüngste Geiger, den Auerbach auf einer Fotografie festhielt.

(4) La carrière de Daniel Barenboïm est déjà si bien remplie que l'on est toujours étonné lorsqu'on se souvient qu'il n'est né qu'en 1942. Il avait environ 27 ans sur cette photographie : déjà largement reconnu comme l'un des pianistes les plus talentueux au monde, il a également commencé à diriger ; à cette époque, ses plus grands succès en tant que chef sont encore à venir. (5) Le Roumain Radu Lupu (né en 1945) étudia à Moscou avec Heinrich Neuhaus, professeur de Richter et de Gilels, et remporta le Leeds International Piano Competition en 1969. Il fit ses débuts à Londres la même année, quand cette photographie fut prise. (6) Pinchas Zukerman (né en 1948), Israélien d'origine polonaise, étudia à New York sous la tutelle légale d'Isaac Stern. Sa première apparition en Grande-Bretagne, à Brighton en 1969, fut rapidement suivie par ses débuts à Londres. A l'exception de Nigel Kennedy (voir pages 260-261), il est probablement le plus jeune violoniste photographié par Auerbach.